SOTHIS PRESS

Sothis Press aims to completely reimagine the public domain book with an emphasis on universal access to captivatingly designed print editions. We believe that technology will enable every single book ever published to be perpetually accessible in beautiful print form. Sothis is beauty in ubiquity.

www.sothis.press
1 Waterhouse Square, London, ECIN 2ST

Household Manufactures in the United States 1640 1860

A Study in Industrial History

Rolla Milton Tryon

SOTHIS PRESS

ISBN 978-1-0365-2696-2

This edition is published by Sothis Press © 2023. The company is registered in England and Wales. The Company Number is 14900389.

HOUSEHOLD MANUFACTURES

1640–1860

THE UNIVERSITY OF CHICAGO PRESS
CHICAGO, ILLINOIS

Agents

THE BAKER & TAYLOR COMPANY
NEW YORK

THE CUNNINGHAM, CURTISS & WELCH COMPANY
LOS ANGELES

THE CAMBRIDGE UNIVERSITY PRESS
LONDON AND EDINBURGH

THE MARUZEN-KABUSHIKI-KAISHA
TOKYO, OSAKA, KYOTO, FUKUOKA, SENDAI

THE MISSION BOOK COMPANY
SHANGHAI

Household Manufactures in the United States 1640–1860

A Study in Industrial History

By

ROLLA MILTON TRYON

Assistant Professor of the Teaching of History

University of Chicago

THE UNIVERSITY OF CHICAGO PRESS

CHICAGO, ILLINOIS

Published May 1917

Composed and Printed By
The University of Chicago Press
Chicago, Illinois, U.S.A.

PREFACE

In any historical study the closer one gets to the everyday life of the common people the better basis one has for understanding that people's history. Few historical subjects offer better opportunities to get very near the actual life of the common people than the one treated in the following pages. In order to determine the extent to which household manufacturing was carried on in the United States prior to 1860, the phases and processes relative to the industry, and the products resulting therefrom, it was necessary for the writer to go right into the homes of the people engaged in such manufacturing. Such, of course, was historically but not actually possible. Historically speaking, the writer was able to see the system of family manufacturing in operation through the accounts of those persons who both actually saw and were a part of it and were for this reason in a position to record facts, describe conditions, and estimate amounts relative to the system.

Because of the author's desire to get as near to the daily life of the people as possible, much use has been made of contemporary accounts, personal recollections, local histories, and census returns. All these have been used with a full realization of their character and of the danger involved in using them solely as a basis for final historical conclusions. Nevertheless, when a census official went into the home and secured data from first-hand sources, when the traveler did likewise and described what he saw, and when a responsible individual in his later years wrote in considerable detail of his early life, it does not seem that any better sources could be found for a subject like the one herein discussed, even though one admits that they are subject to all sorts of human frailties. It is certainly true that no adequate history of household manufactures in the United States prior to 1860 could be written without a large use of such materials.

It is the writer's belief that a history of any special phase of the life of a people, treating that phase in more or less isolation from the various other phases of that people's life, would be of no great value. Because of this belief an attempt has been made throughout the discussion to relate household manufactures to the people's social, political, and general industrial life. While the reader will not get many details relative to England's commercial policy toward the colonies, the handicraft and factory systems, transportation, commerce, and the like, yet at the same time he will throughout the book be conscious of the existence of these factors and their relation to the family system of manufacturing. Such a treatment has occasionally forced the discussion somewhat away from the main topic, but in the end it has added facts and impressions essential to the paramount issue.

Since this special care has been taken to portray the system of household manufacturing as it existed up to 1860 in its relation to the industrial life and prosperity of the nation as a whole, the book may prove a valuable adjunct to history courses in elementary, high, and normal schools and colleges, and to certain courses in the department of home economics and household arts wherever they are given. The book contains material to satisfy, partially at least, the present-day demand for industrial-history material in history courses. It also furnishes the domestic-science and household-arts teachers a historical background for their courses by giving an account of certain phases of their work as it was done in the home before the school ever thought of doing it.

It is with deep gratitude that the writer acknowledges his indebtedness to Professors A. C. McLaughlin, W. E. Dodd, and M. W. Jernegan, all of the University of Chicago, for their valuable assistance throughout the writing of this account. To Professor Jernegan he is especially indebted for his suggestions as to form and content of the discussion, for his careful reading and keen criticisms of the manuscript, and for his helpful guidance in seeking and evaluating sources. It was upon Professor Dodd's suggestion that the work was begun; his counsel and advice were always cheerfully given whenever sought; he also read the manuscript and made valuable suggestions. Professor McLaughlin gave serviceable aid in the general plan and organization of the field and in securing access to valuable source material.

R. M. T.

CHICAGO, ILL.
December, 1916

TABLE OF CONTENTS

LIST OF TABLES

CHAPTER I

INTRODUCTORY

The nature of the subject treated in the following pages makes it necessary to state rather specifically at the outset what it does and does not include. Stated positively, the term "household manufactures" as used in this discussion comprises all those articles now made almost wholly in shop or factory which were formerly made in the home and on the plantation by members of the family or plantation household from raw material produced largely on the farm where the manufacturing was done. Negatively expressed, the subject does not include: (1) goods wrought for sale, the manufacture of which was the only or principal occupation of those concerned and employed in making them; (2) things made in the home as a supplement to factory operations; (3) products of the home factory from materials furnished from sources other than the shop or the factory; (4) articles made on the plantation primarily for sale; (5) commodities such as bread, butter, jellies, etc., which are yet common productions of farm homes, even though they are made in large quantities in factories. Some concrete examples will clarify these eliminations.

Goods wrought for sale by those whose chief or only business was their manufacture embrace the products of the handicraft system. While the home occasionally made wares for sale, yet at the same time the business of making them was but an adjunct to the ordinary routine of farm life, such goods being exchanged for those that the home produced with considerable difficulty, or not at all. To draw a hard-and-fast line of demarkation between the handicraft and household systems of manufacture has not been possible at all times. In many cases some of the processes connected with the manufacture of certain articles were performed in the home and others in the shop or mill. In the manufacture of woolen cloth the carding, fulling, dyeing, shearing, and pressing were often performed in an establishment and only the spinning and weaving were done in the home, either by members of the family or by itinerant spinners and weavers. In all cases where the manufactured articles resulted from the combined efforts of the family and the foregoing agencies they have been denominated household manufactures. Strictly shop-made goods have been eliminated when at all possible, because the handicraft system of manufacturing as it once existed in this country is worthy of a treatment apart from other systems.

Articles made in the home merely as a supplement to factory or shop operations have been excluded in order to eliminate all the so-called sweatshop-made goods. Such an elimination includes all sorts of manufacturing in the home where the material was furnished by the factory or shop, and where the worker had nothing but his labor invested. For example, as early as 1784, after the invention of a machine for cutting wire teeth for wool cards and one for piercing leather backs, the women and children found a new employment at home, setting teeth in the backs, an operation in the manufacture of wool cards that was not done in the factory until fifteen years later.[1] Another case in point is the garment-making industry as it existed before the sewing-machine came into common use. A few decades prior to 1850 large quantities of garments were cut out by the dealers in New York, Boston, and Philadelphia and sent to the country towns, where the daughters and wives of the farmers and sailors made them in their own homes.[2] When possible, all such home operations have been eliminated, because the subject under consideration is not at all concerned with goods produced by sweatshop labor.

Another limitation excludes articles made in the homes from materials other than those furnished by shop or factory and at the same time not produced upon the farm or plantation where they were manufactured. Chief among such exclusions are the poplar and palm-leaf hats, made in large quantities in many New England homes for some years after 1800. The material for making these hats was kept largely by traders or storekeepers, the women and girls securing it from them and receiving a certain sum for each hat made.[3] This home industry might be considered an important step in the transition from home- to factory-made goods in New England, since the women could buy the latter with the income from their hat-making, thus

[1] Earle, *Home Life in Colonial Days*, p. 205.

[2] Abbott, *Women in Industry*, p. 220.

[3] Chase, *Hist. of Old Chester, N.H.*, p. 434; Norton, *Hist. of Fitzwilliam, N.H.*, p. 414.

relieving them of the arduous labor connected with carding, spinning, bleaching, weaving, and dyeing.[1]

Plantation manufacturing has not been included when it was chiefly carried on for profit rather than to supply the plantation needs. For example, Colonel Scarburgh, of Northampton County, Virginia, as early as 1652 had a small malt-house and a shoe factory in which nine shoemakers were employed, both of which were run for profit.[2] While Washington did weaving for the neighbors in his establishment, yet he did not maintain it primarily for this purpose. Plantation manufacturing means, throughout the discussion, that done mainly to supply the plantation necessities and not that done for sale.

Since the discussion is concerned solely with those articles once made in the home or on the plantation, but now universally made in factories, it has been thought best to eliminate all articles quite generally made at the present time by the wives and daughters of the farmers. Such articles are included in the last elimination mentioned above. While the making of these articles may in time pass to the factory, just as many others once made in the home have done, yet such is not the case at present, hence a reason for their exclusion.

The importance of household manufactures in the history of this country to about 1830 can hardly be realized by one who has not given the subject special consideration.

[1] Nail-making has not been eliminated. While the farmer secured the rods from the nearest store, yet at the same time he consumed much of the product. For this reason it has been included.

[2] Wise, *The Eastern Shore of Va. in the 17th Cent.*, p. 302.

The almost economic independence of many homes and communities was a great asset to the people of the Revolutionary days in their struggle for political liberty. War and blockade only drove them back to more primitive conditions and established an industrial independence of both foreign and domestic markets. After seven years of costly warfare, England finally realized the difficulty of conquering colonists who could within their homes manufacture the necessities that her blockade aimed to keep out. The service rendered by this family industry during the Revolutionary War is the more significant when contrasted with what the South attempted through it during the Civil War. In spite of its reversion to the primitive ways of supplying necessities, the Confederacy was unable to escape what the federal blockade finally brought.

Aside from the part played by the system of household manufactures during the Revolutionary days in securing and maintaining an industrial independence, it was of very great moment to the nation at large in its early history as a supplement to agriculture—of necessity a prevailing industry in a new country. Without a European market, or in fact any market at all, agricultural profits were always very small. This was especially true on the frontier and in all sections devoid of transportation facilities, because there were so many farmers, hence a small number depending on others for their agricultural products. The fertility of the soil also gave a liberal return for the work involved. Now, since there was no market for the labor of the field, the farmer had to exchange his leisure hours for a supply of clothing and other necessities which he could have purchased if he had had a market for his staples. Until this market came his dependence upon the household factory was almost absolute. It is certainly no exaggeration to say that civilization could not have been maintained in sections of the New England and middle states during the colonial period, and on the frontier everywhere for several years after the appearance of the first settlement, without the system of household manufactures.

The social life of many communities also centered in the system of family manufactures. It was in the social gatherings connected with spinning, carding, and fulling that the people, young and old, found wholesome enjoyment. The spinning, carding, and fulling bees, the spinning societies and contests, all gave the people opportunities to satisfy their social instincts and desires. Furthermore, the socializing effect, upon both the individual and the community, of the give-and-take necessary to support the system was also very great. Everyone had to do his part in the support of the family or neighborhood. Since most of the work was done in the home or on the farm, the system produced a home-bred, home-living, and a home-loving people—a people who found both their employment and their pleasure in their own or their near neighbor's home.

While the discussion deals primarily with the history of household manufactures in the United States prior to 1860, and makes no special attempt to point out the physical, educational, and moral influences of the system on the people engaged in it, yet these influences should not be wholly overlooked, in spite of the fact that their intangibleness makes it almost impossible to evaluate and treat them historically. After realizing the diligence, industry, perseverance, economy, skill, and a number of other virtues that were required to maintain the system, one is in a position to approximate its physical, educational, and moral effects. As an aid in such an approximation, we have the testimony of certain individuals who really knew the system first-hand. In speaking of the general influence of domestic chores on the growing boy, Drake remarked: "When I look back upon the useful arts which mother and I were accustomed to practice, I am almost surprised at their number, and although I did not then regard them as anything but incidents of poverty and ignorance, I now view them as knowledge, as elements of mental growth."[1] G. Stanley Hall on one occasion spoke as follows concerning the effects of the old New England life: "Despite certain evils this life [old New England] at its best appears to me to have constituted the best educational environment for boys at a certain stage of their development ever realized in history, combining physical, industrial, technical, with civil and religious elements in a wise proportion and pedagogic objectivity."[2] On the moral influence, Niles, in 1821, commented as follows:

> Household industry cannot be broken down even by the ever-watchful influence of Great Britain, nor be bribed to prostration by her conspired manufactures, if once more fully established in the United States; for we have learned wisdom too dearly through

[1] *Pioneer Life in Ky.*, p. 99. For a longer quotation on the same subject see *ibid.*, p. 109.

[2] "Boy Life in a Massachusetts Town," *Proc. Am. Ant. Soc.*, N.S., VII, 107 f.

suffering, to be led astray again. It is based on virtue—cheerfulness is its companion, happiness is its fruit, and independence is its result. Women thus reared will not give suck to a breed of slaves: but teach their offsprings a knowledge of their own powers, having furnished them strength to maintain their rights.[1]

Similar testimony is on record as to the effects of the system on the health, constitution, and habits of the women. In commenting, in 1848, on the domestic habits of New England women, an elderly lady of Montpelier, Vermont, said that she was firmly convinced that among the changes and revolutions in domestic habits and customs in modern times, so far as the welfare of her own sex was concerned, the change most to be regretted was the one which led to the disuse of the old-fashioned family spinning-wheel. It was her opinion that the movement necessary in drawing out and running up the thread which required a constant march backward and forward, while the arms were alternately lifted in the operation, and also that of turning, brought all the muscles into play, and made just the exercise necessary for the development of the human system.[2]

It is through the foregoing phases that the historical treatment of household manufactures in the United States is connected with present-day conditions. The manual-training, domestic-science, and household-arts courses in our current educational programs for both the elementary and the secondary schools are attempting to do what was

[1] *Register*, XXI, 35.

[2] Cited by Thompson, *Hist. of Montpelier, Vt.*, p. 76. Thompson, who wrote in 1860, felt that it would be much better for the health, constitution, and habits of the females if they were compelled to resort to the old way of clothing themselves and their families (*ibid.*, p. 75).

done in the eighteenth and part of the nineteenth century in the homes. The social pressure that operated in placing these subjects in the schools during the last quarter of the nineteenth century was largely an expression of the feeling that much valuable training had been lost through the decay of the household system of manufacturing—a system that taught the girl by the time she was twenty to spin, weave, sew, embroider, knit, darn, crochet, patch, do laundry work well, prepare wholesome meals, make butter, cheese, and candles, and perform other duties connected with good housekeeping; a system that taught the boy to employ the spare moments of his farm life in the manufacture from wood of such farm implements as plows, harrows, sleds, wagons, carts, shovels, flails, swingling knives, handles for spades, axes, hoes, and pitchforks, as well as various aids to domestic comfort, such as brooms, baskets, wooden bowls and bread troughs, butter-paddles, cheese-hoops, and other kitchen and table utensils; and, finally, a system that engendered such virtues as cheerfulness, happiness, frugality, independence, diligence, perseverance, skill, and self-reliance. It was largely the training that this system gave that the advocates of manual training, domestic science, and household arts called upon the school to give as soon as it was discovered what had been lost in the decay of the system of household manufacturing. School authorities began to heed this call during the last quarter of the nineteenth century, and had by the end of the first decade of the twentieth quite generally introduced such subjects into the school. Their mere introduction by no means solved the problem. Their content, value, and administration remain a problem with many people. It is the hope of the writer that the following historical discussion of the family factory, in which such subjects were formerly so well taught, will furnish a background for a better understanding of present-day conditions and tendencies along these important educational lines.

A few words regarding the general plan of treating the subject seem desirable before this brief introduction is closed. A combination of the chronological and topical methods has been employed. The colonial period has been covered four times, twice rather intensively and chronologically and twice less intensively and with little regard to chronology. Each of the four times the field has been covered with a very definite aim in view: the first, to determine and elucidate the various factors affecting household manufactures; the second, to connect these factors with real situations; the third, to consider the multifarious products of the family factory; and the fourth, to find evidences of the transfer from family- to shop- and factory-made goods. The period from 1783 to 1810 has been treated chronologically with a view to showing influencing factors and amounts made, and topically for the purposes mentioned in three and four above. After 1810 the discussion has largely to do with the transition from home- to factory-made goods, and adapts itself admirably to a straightforward chronological treatment. Continually to connect the subject with the general economic and political history of the nation, and to portray it as one of the dominant elements in the industrial life of this country for nearly two centuries, and for a time the one great factor in securing and sustaining an almost economic independence from foreign nations, and to place before the reader, in as concrete a form as the data at hand warrant, the territorial extent, amount, and products of such manufactures, have been the controlling aims throughout the discussion.

Because the system of household manufactures so thoroughly dovetailed itself into the contemporaneous handicraft, shop, and small-factory systems, and because in one section of the country one system predominated, while in another section a different system was in force, generalizations for any large section of the country at a specific time have been practically impossible. While the older towns and communities were in the shop stage, the new ones on the frontier were still making almost everything in the home. It should be said, however, that the stages in the evolution from home- to shop-, to small-factory-, to large-factory-made goods became briefer and briefer on the arrival of the steamboat, the canal, and the railroad. In time the first stage dropped out altogether. As soon as manufactured goods could be supplied from the sale or barter of the products of the farm, the home gave up its system of manufacturing, which had been largely carried on more through necessity than desire. Generally speaking, by 1860 the factory, through the aid of improved means of transportation, was able to supply the needs of the people for manufactured commodities. For this reason the discussion closes with this date. While it is true that the South during the Civil War reverted to some extent to the primitive system, and that it existed in certain out-of-the-way places throughout the nineteenth century and even into the twentieth, yet it is also true that by 1860 it had passed out of the life of the nation at large as a factor in its economic development and industrial prosperity.[1]

[1] On near present-day conditions in certain sections of the country, see Kephart, *Our Southern Highlanders;* Earle, *op. cit.*, pp. 249 ff.; Williams, "A Fragment of the Passing Frontier," *Hist. Teacher's Mag.*, VI, 33; MacClintock, "The Kentucky Mountaineers and Their Feuds," *Am. Jour. Soc.*, VII, 1 ff., 171 ff.; Vincent, "A Retarded Frontier," *ibid.*, IV, 1 ff.; and Fox, "The Southern Mountaineer," *Scribner's Mag.*, XXIX, 387, 556.

CHAPTER II

FACTORS AFFECTING HOUSEHOLD MANUFACTURES IN THE COLONIES

During the colonial period there were certain general factors which tended to increase or diminish, encourage or discourage, the making of many of the necessities of life in the household or on the plantation. Stated generally, these factors were: (1) the policy of England toward the commerce and manufactures of her dependencies; (2) the general and special encouragement given household manufactures by the various colonial legislative assemblies; and (3) certain economic conditions and political notions prevalent in the colonies prior to the close of the Revolution. To show the effects of these three general factors on household manufactures during the colonial period is the purpose of this chapter. No minute consideration of the complicated phases of each of the large divisions is attempted. They are considered only in so far as they affected, directly or indirectly, the making within the home or on the plantation of such articles as were made.

ENGLAND'S COLONIAL POLICY AND HOUSEHOLD MANUFACTURES

The mercantile colonial system which England attempted to administer throughout the century, beginning with the Restoration, was based on a political and economic theory generally current during the seventeenth century. According to this theory, colonies were merely possessions, subject to economic exploitation by the people at home. Fundamentally, the doctrine which England attempted to apply was that colonial dependencies should be subordinated, as far as their economic life was concerned, to the welfare of the mother-country. The application of this doctrine found expression in a series of laws, which included measures respecting navigation and enumerated articles, encouragements to colonial industry, and restrictions on colonial manufactures and the exportation of men with a knowledge of, and implements used in, the manufacture of cotton, linen, and silk cloth. All these measures worked co-operatively during the colonial period, both directly and indirectly, toward encouraging and sustaining household manufactures, or toward discouraging and preventing them, just how and to what extent the following discussion attempts to portray.[1]

Prior to the Navigation Act of 1651 the colonies enjoyed a relative freedom of commerce. In truth, under the operations of this act they felt little or no restraint. It

[1] The writer's sole interest in the English colonial system is its relation to but one of the phases of the industrial life of the colonies, namely, household manufactures. For brief discussions of the commercial phases of the system see the following: Ashley, "The Commercial Legislation of England and the American Colonies, 1660–1760," *Surveys, Historic and Economic*, pp. 309 ff.; Howard, *Preliminaries of the Revolution*, chap. iii; Channing, "The Navigation Laws," *Proc. Am. Ant. Soc.*, VI, 160 ff.; Rabbeno, *American Commercial Policy*, chaps. i–iii; and Callender, *Econ. Hist. of U.S.*, chap. iii. A more extended discussion is found in Beer's *The Commercial Policy of England toward the American Colonies*.

was not until its virtual renewal in 1660[1] that restrictions began to affect them. As renewed, the act said that no produce could be imported into, or exported from, England, or from her colonies, except in ships belonging to, and built by, the people of England, Ireland, Wales, Berwick on the Tweed, or any of the plantations; that colonial produce should be imported into England only in English or colonial ships; that foreign carriers should be absolutely excluded from the colonial market, whether shipping their own goods or not; and that certain products should be known as "enumerated articles" which could not be carried from the colonies to other places even in English ships. These articles were "sugars, tobacco, cotton-wool, indigoes, ginger, fustic, or other dyeing woods."[2] Closely following this measure were those enacted in 1663 and 1672. The former intended to cut off entirely the import trade of the colonies in European goods, except salt for the New England fisheries, wines from the Western Islands or Azores, servants, horses, and victuals from Ireland and Scotland;[3] and the latter subjected the whole traffic in "enumerated goods" between one colony and another to a penalty, compelling the trader who wished to carry a cargo of tobacco from Virginia to New York either to pay a tribute at the place of shipment or to give bond to unload his cargo in

[1] 12 Charles II, c. 18. (All citations to the English laws are to Pickering's *Statutes at Large*.)

[2] This list was enlarged from time to time. Rice and molasses were added to it in 1705; and copper, beaver skins, and other furs in 1722 (3 and 4 Anne, c. 5, sec. 12; 8 Geo. I, c. 15, sec. 24, and c. 18, sec. 22). For a history of these enumerated commodities see Beer, *op. cit.*, chap. iii.

[3] 15 Charles II, c. 7, secs. 5 and 6.

an English port.[1] Since these two laws, together with the one of 1660, formed the basis of the complex and multifarious restrictions and regulations on trade and commerce during most of the colonial period, it will add nothing to the discussion to go into the variations of, and additions to, them. Enough has been said to call attention to their existence and the general nature of their provisions. The discussion will now turn to their probable effects upon household manufactures during the period of their existence.

While the navigation laws were loosely administered and generally evaded, yet they seem to have had certain observable effects on the amount of manufacturing done by the people, both in and out of their homes, or the opposite effect of discouraging them in their attempts to manufacture, by making other employments more profitable, whereby means could be secured to buy foreign goods. Prior to 1660 the colonists, when possible, obtained most of their textile supplies directly from Holland or from Great Britain, paying for them with tar, boards, tobacco, hides, and farm products. The laws of 1660, 1663, and 1672, by stimulating shipbuilding in New England, by subjecting the traffic in enumerated goods between one colony and another to a penalty, and by forbidding trade with the Dutch, from whom goods could be procured cheaper than from the English, tended to stimulate the manufacture of sailcloth for the New England ships, as well as articles that had previously been secured in a free and open market. Such manufacturing was carried on chiefly in the homes or on the plantations, since the handicraft system and manu-

[1] 25 Charles II, c. 7, sec. 2.

facturing establishments had but a vague existence in any of the colonies[1] so early in their history.

Home manufacturing was also augmented, especially in New England, the middle colonies, and the back-country region of the southern colonies, by certain regulations and restrictions in favor of the English proprietors. These included the prohibiting of the importation into England from the colonies of agricultural products, such as rye, barley, peas, beans, oats, and wheat; and of salt provisions, including beef, pork, bacon, and butter.[2] The cutting off of these staple commodities from the localities mentioned above forced the people to seek markets elsewhere. Since these markets were largely found in countries doing little or no manufacturing, their ships could not bring back manufactured commodities, hence had to make a roundabout trip and load in England, where cash had to be exchanged for ready-made articles. Thus, as Howard remarks, "the economic policy of Parliament had partially deprived the colonists of the means of importing the manufactures which they needed."[3] Hence it followed that "New England, and later the Middle Colonies, not being allowed to exchange their normal products for England's

[1] It should be said, however, that these laws also stimulated manufacturing outside of the homes. Commenting on this point, Rabbeno remarks: "It was therefore precisely that monopoly, by means of which the mother-country sought to bind the colonial trade, to the advantage of her own merchants, which compelled the work and the capital of the colonists to be dedicated to the neglected field of domestic manufactures" (*The American Colonial Policy*, p. 57).

[2] Beer, *op. cit.*, p. 74.

[3] *Preliminaries of the Revolution*, p. 61.

manufactures, were forced to begin manufacturing for themselves."[1]

Certain contemporary reports attest the truth of these statements. In 1705 Lord Cornbury gave as a cause of the beginning of manufactures in New York "the want wherewithal to make returns for England."[2] It was said of Massachusetts in 1721 that necessity and not choice forced the people to manufacturing, because they did not have sufficient commodities of their own to give in exchange for those they received from Great Britain.[3] A report of the Board of Trade to the House of Commons, in February 1731/32, referring to the section north of Maryland, said: "They have no staple commodities of their own growth to exchange for our manufactures, which puts them under great necessity, as well as under greater temptation, of providing them for themselves."[4]

The restrictions on certain enumerated articles had the effect in the southern colonies of inducing them to raise their staple products and exchange these in England for all sorts of manufactured articles. Virginia and Maryland and the northern part of North Carolina exchanged tobacco for such commodities; South Carolina and Georgia, rice and indigo; and North Carolina, naval stores. A monopoly of the English market was given these colonies on all such staples, with a bounty on naval stores extra. To make the monopoly complete, the production of tobacco

[1] Beer, *op. cit.*, p. 75.

[2] *Docs. Rel. Col. Hist. of N.Y.*, IV, 1151.

[3] *Ibid.*, V, 598.

[4] Macpherson, *Annals of Commerce*, etc., III, 190.

was prohibited in England, and Spanish tobacco was excluded by very high duties.[1] To help South Carolina and Georgia monopolize the rice trade it was provided in George II's reign that, after September, 1730, they could send their rice directly to any country south of Cape Finisterre.[2] Bounties on naval stores, offered both in England and in North Carolina, were the inducements to their production and exportation.[3]

Besides the monopolized English market which the southern colonies had for their tobacco, special arrangements existed in Maryland and Virginia whereby it could be conveniently exchanged for English merchandise. On the navigable rivers and bays in these two colonies were tobacco warehouses, at a distance of about twelve or fourteen miles from each other, to which all the tobacco in the provinces could be brought and inspected according to law.[4] The inspectors gave the planters notes of receipt and the merchants took these notes for their goods. Warehouses in which were kept all sorts of British commodities and manufactures were also established by the merchants all over the provinces. To these the planters would resort and supply themselves with what they wanted, paying for it in inspection receipts or taking credit.[5] On the whole, therefore, the most profitable employment of the people

[1] Beer, *op. cit.*, pp. 46 f.

[2] 3 Geo. II, c. 28, sec. 2. This act was to continue for five years. It was renewed from time to time. See 8 Geo. II, c. 19; 15 Geo. II, c. 33; 20 Geo. II, c. 47; and 27 Geo. II, c. 18.

[3] These bounties are discussed in the following section.

[4] Hening, *Statutes at Large of Va.* (Richmond, 1820), IV, 251.

[5] *Am. Husbandry* (1775), I, 225 f.

of the southern colonies along the navigable rivers was agriculture, since their staple products found such a ready and monopolized market in Europe. Except when the tobacco and rice markets became dull, the crops failed, or transportation was obstructed, they gave little attention to manufacturing on the plantations prior to 1765.

Brief mention should be made of another phase of the restrictions upon imports and exports, namely, the system of duties and drawbacks which was intended to encourage the colonies to trade with England, and at the same time keep them satisfied in doing so, thus preventing their engaging in any kind of manufacturing. As early as 1642/43 Parliament passed an act which tended to decrease the small amount of manufacturing that was being done at this date in the homes. This act provided that all merchandise intended for the use of the colonies should be exempted from duties, subsidies, and taxation, as well as colonial produce exported to England. It was expected that such a law would make the colonists producers of raw materials, since they could be furnished with a cheap supply of manufactured goods from England.[1] From this feeble beginning the drawback system later developed into a very complicated affair. As a general rule the colonial products sent to England paid the same duties as products from foreign countries, and commodities exported to the colonies were charged the same duties as those sent to foreign states. To both these rules, however, there were many exceptions in favor of the colonies. Their tobacco paid less duty than Spanish; their pig and bar iron, hemp

[1] Bishop, *Hist. of Am. Manufactures*, I, 303.

and lumber, indigo and raw silk, pot and pearl ashes, were all exempt from duties by 1751.[1] The drawbacks were equally favorable to them. These often amounted to almost the entire duty, and in some cases the whole duty was actually repaid on re-exportation from England. This was true of tobacco under the reigns of James II, William III, Anne, George I, and George II.[2]

One very important effect of the system of drawbacks was the making possible of the enormous consumption of foreign linens in the region south of Pennsylvania. Beer states that the inhabitants of England often complained of the system because the colonies were thereby able to get certain foreign commodities more cheaply than they themselves could purchase them.[3] Nearly all the linens imported from Germany and Holland were re-exported thither, since they could not compete with similar Irish and English goods on account of the heavy import duties. The whole system was intended to encourage the colonists in their production of raw materials as well as their consumption of manufactured goods from England, thus making it more convenient and profitable for them to get on without applying themselves to manufacturing of any kind.

The measures relating to the encouragement of colonial industries took the form of bounties on the growth and production of a number of articles which were either not

[1] For iron, see Saxby, *British Customs*, p. 32; indigo, *ibid.*, p. 177; raw silk, 23 Geo. II, c. 20; ashes, 24 Geo. II, c. 51; lumber, 8 Geo. I, c. 12; tobacco, 12 Chas. II, c. 4; hemp, 8 Geo. I, c. 12.

[2] For the various subsidies, see 9 and 10 William III, c. 23; 2 and 3 Anne, c. 9; and 21 Geo. II, c. 2.

[3] *Op. cit.*, p. 106.

produced in England at all, or, if produced, not in sufficient quantities to supply the demand for them. These encouragements were given especially for the benefit of the colonies north of Maryland. The bounties were expected to give this region staples to send to England to exchange for manufactured goods—for the lack of such staples some manufacturing had already been done.

The bounty system, as worked out after 1705, included premiums on indigo, tar, pitch, hemp, turpentine, masts, and allied products. During Queen Anne's reign the following bounties were offered: good merchantable tar and pitch, £4 a ton of eight barrels; turpentine or rosin, £3 a ton; hemp, water-rotted, bright and clear, £6 a ton; and all masts, yards, bowsprits, £1 a ton, allowing 40 feet to each ton. The law was to be in force for nine years.[1] On expiring it was renewed for eleven years,[2] and was continued with more or less uniformity until the Revolution.[3]

Meager results were obtained from hemp and masts by the foregoing act,[4] but those from pitch and tar were more encouraging. The products of New England under the first year of the act amounted to 6,191 barrels of tar, 647 of pitch, 1,145 of turpentine, and 90 of rosin. While these were of an inferior quality, yet the bounty was allowed on

[1] 3 and 4 Anne, c. 10.

[2] For renewals, see 12 Anne, c. 9, and 2 Geo. II, c. 35.

[3] Beer, *op. cit.*, 95. Indigo was included in the foregoing list by the act of 1748, which offered a bounty of six pence a pound for all indigo imported into England from the colonies (21 Geo. II, c. 30, sec. 1).

[4] Beer, *op. cit.*, pp. 96, 99.

them, because it was felt that, if disallowed, the New Englanders would be discouraged in their attempts at further production and return to their spinning-wheels and looms.[1]

Between 1706 and 1729 bounties were paid on naval stores to the amount of £430,178, and between 1729 and 1774, £1,028,584.[2] About the year 1717 the tar, pitch, and turpentine sent to England annually was worth £47,072.[3] But in spite of these figures the bounty system failed to give the people north of Maryland a staple. The pine forests were in the South, and it was from here that most of the goods on which bounties were paid came. Governor Johnson, of North Carolina, writing to the Board of Trade in 1734, said: "There is more pitch and tar in the two Carolinas than in all the other Provinces on the Continent and rather more in this than in South Carolina."[4] The same thing was true of indigo. In 1734 South Carolina exported 216,924 pounds, and shortly before the Revolution the amount reached 1,107,660 pounds.[5]

But how did the bounty system affect home manufactures? The Board of Trade felt that it lessened them. In 1728, when the law was up for renewal, this body reported to a committee of the Privy Council as follows: "Upon further Inquiry into the Matter, we don't find that

[1] Lord, *Indust. Experiments in the British Colonies*, p. 66.

[2] Channing, *Hist. of U.S.*, III, 35, note.

[3] *Docs. Rel. Col. Hist. of N.Y.*, V, 617.

[4] *Col. Rec. N.C.*, IV, 5.

[5] Ramsay, *Hist. of S.C.*, II, 212.

these People had the same Temptation to go on with these Manufactures [meaning those in the home] during that Time the Bounty upon Naval Stores subsisted, having then Encouragement to employ their leisure Time in another way, & more profitable to themselves and this Kingdom."[1] The same idea was expressed in a report which the Board of Trade made to the House of Lords in 1733, with the additional information that even though household manufacturing had been diminished, yet the quantity of goods then made in New England was sufficient to lessen the amount of Great Britain's exports thither.[2] This was a mild way of admitting that the bounty system as it worked out failed to give the northern people a staple to send to England to exchange for manufactured goods. It should be said, however, that it did add to those the South already had, thus making this section more able to purchase imported goods and relieving the people of the laborious and unprofitable task of manufacturing them in their homes. The diminishing effect in the northern colonies was probably very slight.

The restrictions on manufactures were of two kinds, namely, those forbidding the setting up of certain manufactures in the colonies, and those prohibiting the exportation of men with a knowledge of, and implements used in, fabricating cotton, woolen, linen, and silk cloth. It was not until the close of the seventeenth century that the colonial manufactures became of sufficient importance to arouse the effective opposition of the English manufacturers

[1] *N.J. Archives*, 1st ser., V, 209.

[2] *Conn. Hist. Soc. Colls.*, V, App., 461.

and merchants. The laws of 1699, 1732, and 1750, restraining and restricting such operations, sought to crush whatever forms had already sprung up; and those of 1718, 1750, 1774, 1781, and 1782, relating to the machinery used in, and men with a knowledge of, the manufacture of textile fabrics, sought to keep within the kingdom the knowledge of all the novel processes and improvements along these lines.

On account of what was called at the time the daily increase of woolen manufactures in the English plantations in America, the following law was enacted in 1699:

> That from and after the first day of December, in the year of our Lord one thousand six hundred ninety-nine, no wool, woolfells, shortlings, mortlings, woolflocks, worsted, bay, or woollen yarn, cloth serge, bays, says, frizes, druggets, cloth-serges, shalloons, or any other drapery stuffs or woollen manufactures whatsoever, made or mixed with wool or woolflocks, being a product or manufacture of any of the English plantations in America, shall be loaden on board any ship or vessel, in any place or parts within any of the said English plantations, upon any pretence whatsoever.[1]

This law also provided that none of the foregoing manufactures could be loaded upon any horse, cart, or carriage to be exported to any of the other English plantations. However, it did not interfere with the making of woolen articles within the family for domestic needs. But fearing that the German Palatines, who came to New York in 1709, would set up woolen manufactures in opposition to this law, the Board of Trade provided that a clause could be placed in the patent making it void if they should apply

[1] 10 and 11 William III, c. 10.

themselves in this direction. Such a clause was actually inserted when the patent was issued.[1]

A somewhat similar policy found expression in the laws of 1732 and 1750. The former aimed to localize the hat-making industry by providing that no hats could be exported to any other colony, and that only those who had served an apprenticeship could engage in making hats.[2] In order to create a greater demand for woolen and other manufactures of Great Britain by encouraging the colonies to send bar and pig iron thither, it was enacted in 1750 that bar iron be duty-free to the port of London, and pig iron to any port of England; and that no mill or other engine for rolling or slitting iron, no plating forge to work with a tilt hammer, nor any furnace for making steel be erected in the colonies.[3]

In 1718 the mother-country began her policy of protecting her own manufacturing interests by a series of acts forbidding the exportation of men with a knowledge of, and implements used in, the fabrication of cotton, woolen, linen, and silk cloth. It was enacted in this year that anyone convicted of enticing from England any artificer or manufacturer should be fined £100 and imprisoned for three months.[4] This act was renewed in 1750, with an extra provision making it unlawful to export from Great Britain or Ireland any utensils made use of in the woolen and silk manufacture. The fine for enticing away artificers or manufacturers was increased to £500 and twelve

[1] *Docs. Rel. Col. Hist. of N.Y.*, V, 88, 118.

[2] 5 Geo. II, c. 22.

[3] 23 Geo. II, c. 29.

[4] 5 Geo. I, c. 27.

months' imprisonment, and for exporting utensils £200 and forfeiture of the tools.[1] In 1774 this law was extended to include utensils used in the manufacture of cotton and linen cloth.[2] In 1781 the law of 1774 was extended by an elaborated act, which imposed a penalty of £200 and twelve months' imprisonment for the attempt to export any machine, engine, tool, press, paper, utensil, or implement used for preparing, working, completing, or finishing woolen, cotton, linen, or silk manufactures.[3] The next year (1782) the acts of 1718 and 1750 were renewed and elaborated so as to make it a penalty to entice out of Great Britain a workman acquainted with novel processes in the manufacture of cotton and linen goods.[4]

Taken as a whole, all the foregoing measures regarding colonial manufactures tended to increase the amount of manufacturing in the homes. Under such restrictions no general shop or factory system of manufacturing textile commodities could grow up; hence it was necessary to make within the homes or on the plantations textile and other supplies which could not be furnished by obstructed importations and shop manufacturing. Commenting on this point, Rabbeno says: "The high price of imported textile fabrics caused by the monopoly, compelled the colonists to make use of skins as clothes, and at the same time was a stimulus to the domestic industry of weaving, which, however, could only be carried on almost secretly within

[1] 23 Geo. II, c. 13.

[2] 14 Geo. III, c. 71. Wool cards were not included.

[3] 21 Geo. III, c. 37.

[4] 22 Geo. III, c. 60.

the walls of private houses and with primitive implements."[1] Bolles, discussing the same points, remarks: "The law could not reach these private factories. Parliament could club down the ripening fruit which hung in plain sight on the branches; but the million buds forming in secret under the bark, which a favoring time would eventually bring out into bloom, were beyond its reach."[2]

THE COLONIES' POLICY OF ENCOURAGEMENT

During all the time that Parliament was busy legislating to bring about the success of England's antiquated commercial policy toward the colonies the corresponding bodies in the various provinces were equally as busy legislating to bring about in their communities conditions which would free them, partially at least, from the burdens of such a policy. The colonial legislation affecting household manufactures pertained mainly to the encouragement of the raising of wool, hemp, and flax, and the manufacturing of these into clothing and household textile supplies. All this legislation is of special importance to the subject under discussion, as a supply of clothing was one of life's necessities. Since the acquisition of an abundant supply from the outside world was hampered by so many factors, the lawmakers, early in the history of many of the colonies, took upon themselves the solution of the problem through legislative enactments. In order to show the trend of this legislation, the laws enacted in Massachusetts and Virginia have been considered at some length. Only brief

[1] *Op. cit.*, p. 69.

[2] *Indust. Hist. of U.S.*, p. 371.

footnote mention of, and reference to, similar measures in the remaining colonies have been deemed necessary, since they were largely duplications of those passed by the assemblies of Massachusetts and Virginia.

In 1640[1] the General Court of Massachusetts passed two laws to encourage the manufacture of linen, woolen, and cotton cloth. In May of this year it was ordered that the magistrates and deputies of the towns inquire what seed there was in every town; what men and women were skilful in breaking, spinning, and weaving; what means there were for providing wheels; and see that the boys and girls were taught to spin.[2] The other law provided for a bounty on linen, woolen, and cotton cloth made in the province. It was passed in October and read as follows:

> For incouragement of the manufacture of linnen, woollen, and cotton clothe, it is ordered, that whosoever shall make any sort of the said cloathes fit for use & shall shewe the same to the next magistrate, or to 2 of the deputies of this Court, upon certificate thereof to this Court, or the Court of Assistants, the party shall have allowance of 3 *d* in the shilling of the worth of such cloth, according to the valewation wch shalbee certified wth it. And the said magistrate, or deputies shall set such marke upon the same cloth as it may bee found to have bene alowed for; pvided, this order shall extend onely

[1] The Plymouth Colony had done some legislating even before this date. On July 1, 1633, the General Court ordered "that no sheep be sold out of the colony, under penalty of forfeiting their due value" (*Rec. Plymouth Col.*, I, 13). If anyone owning sheep moved out of the colony, he must first offer them for sale. If no buyers appeared, he was then permitted to take his sheep along with him (*ibid.*, II, 17). On June 4, 1639, it was ordered that every householder sow one "rodd of ground square at least with hemp or flax yearly" (*ibid.*, XI, Part I, 32).

[2] *Rec. Co. Mass. Bay*, I, 294.

to such cloth as shall bee made wth in this iurisdiction, & the yarne heare spun also, & of such materials as shalbee raised also wth in the same, or else of cotton. This order to continue 3 years next following.[1]

The enthusiasm of the deputies exemplified in this October law proved to be greater than the financial condition of the colony could sustain. It was repealed in less than a year, because the people felt that it was "burthensome to their wants."[2]

On the same day that the bounty law was repealed one was passed relating to the growing and gathering of wild hemp to take the place of cotton, which was then very scarce. This law provided that the deputies of the General Court should see that in their several towns speedy notice be given to masters of families of the wild hemp, with direction when to gather and how to use it. Should anyone harvest more than was needed for home consumption, there was a ready market for it. The deputies were to aid in marketing the surplus. Clothing at this time seems to have been rather scarce, for the court made mention of the want of clothing which was likely to come upon them the next winter. It was also desired that all mothers should see that their children and servants were industriously employed in spinning so that the mornings and evenings might not be lost as they had formerly been.[3] Another law was passed in 1642, which purposed to increase

[1] *Rec. Co. Mass. Bay*, I, 303.

[2] *Ibid.*, I, 321. The following is found in the records of June 1, 1641: "Henry Kemball & John Witheredge alowance for 83½ yrd. of cloth, valewed at 12 *d* p yrd" (*ibid.*, p. 316).

[3] *Ibid.*, I, 322.

household manufacturing through the fostering of a knowledge of spinning and weaving. By this law the selectmen were given power to apprentice the children of parents unable to bring them up in accordance with its provisions. Such children were to be set to weaving and spinning. A sufficient supply of hemp, flax, tools, and implements was to be provided by the selectmen.[1]

These first laws related more to linen than to woolen manufactures. But beginning with the order of May, 1645, there followed during the next twenty years several measures relating to sheep and wool. Conditions at this date are vividly set forth in the preamble of the 1645 law, which read as follows:

> Forasmuch as wollen cloth is so useful a comodity wthout wch wee cannot so comfortably subsist in these pts by reason of could winters, it being also at p sent very scare & deare amongs^{t} us, & is likely shortly so to be, in all those pts fro^{m} whenc we can expect it, by reason of ye warrs in Europe destroying, in a great measure, ye flocks of sheepe amongst y^{m}, & also ye trade & meanes it selfe of making woollen cloath & stuffs, by ye killing & oth^{r}wise hind^{r}ing of such p sons whose skill & labo^{r}s tended to y^{t} end; & whereas, through ye want of woollen cloaths & stuffs, many pore people have suffered much could and hardship, to ye impairing of some of y^{ir} healths, & ye hazarding of some of y^{ir} lives, & such who have bene able to p

[1] *Ibid.*, II, 7. While Massachusetts Bay was busy legislating to encourage the manufacture of linen and cotton goods, the lawmakers of Connecticut were not idle. As early as February, 1640, the General Court ordered each family to sow hemp and flax so that in time it might have a supply of linen clothing (*Pub. Rec. Col. Conn.*, I, 61). At the same session of the court it was enacted that the governor should order a supply of cotton, and that each town should take its share of the same (*ibid.*, p. 59). When the cotton arrived in September, 1642, Winsor took 90 pounds worth; Wethersfield, 110; and Hartford, 200 (Bishop, *op. cit.*, I, 300).

vide for y^{ir} child^{r}n cloathing of cotton cloth (not being able to get oth^{r}) have, by y^{t} meanes, had some of y^{ir} child^{r}n much scorched wth fire, yea, divers burt to death, this Co^{r}t y^{r} fore doth hereby desire all ye townes seriously to weigh ye p mises, & accordingly y^{t} yo^{u} will carefully endeavo^{r} ye p servation & increase of such sheepe as they have already, as also to p cure more, wth all convenient speede, nto y^{ir} sev^{r}all townes, by all such lawfull wayes and meanes as God shall put into their hands.[1]

Further encouragement was given in 1648 by provisions made for the pasturing of sheep upon the Common[2] and offering bounties for the killing of wolves, which were very destructive of all sorts of small live stock.[3] In 1654 the exportation of sheep and the killing of any under two years of age, save for the use of the owner's family, was prohibited.[4] The exportation of wool to any foreign country was forbidden in 1675.[5]

One of the most important early laws looking to the supply of clothing was the one passed in May, 1656. To remedy the inconvenience and suffering arising from the

[1] *Rec. Co. Mass. Bay*, I, 105.

[2] *Ibid.*, I, 251 f.

[3] It was a fixed policy to pay bounties for killing wolves. As early as 1630 a bounty was offered for killing them. This was repealed in 1632, but renewed in 1640. The bounty was increased in 1644, 1645, 1648, 1661, and 1662. For these laws in the order named, see *ibid.*, 81, 102; II, 85, 103, 252; IV, 2. This was a fixed policy, not only in Massachusetts, but in all the other colonies as well. Since wolves were a general danger, and destroyed other stock as well as sheep, no attempt has been made to trace this legislation in the various colonies.

[4] *Ibid.*, III, 355 f.

[5] *Ibid.*, III, 28. Such legislation was very common in many of the northern colonies and in some of the southern. Since it related but indirectly to household manufactures, no detailed consideration has been given it.

inadequate supply of wearing apparel, the General Court ordered

> that all hands not necessarily employd on other occasions, as woemen, girles, & boyes, shall, & hereby are, enjoyned to spin according to their skill & abilitie; & that the selectmen in euery towne doe consider the condition & capacitie of euery familie, & accordingly to assess them, as one or more spinners. . . . . 2ly. & that euery one thus assessed for a whole spinner doe, after this psent year, 1656, spin, for 30 weekes euery yeare. 3 pound p weeke of lining, cotton, or wooling . . . . under the poenalty of 12 *d* for euery pound short.

If families were employed otherwise the greater part of their time, they were to be assessed a half or a quarter of a spinner.[1]

Weeden thinks that from 1660 to the end of the century there was a decline in the interest in promoting manufactures.[2] This decline was caused by the activity in fishing and shipbuilding, growing out of the events accompanying the Restoration. The navigation acts tended to stimulate shipbuilding and trade in New England. Fishing to load ships and building ships to carry cured fish absorbed much of the energy of the people in the coast towns during these years. On their return for more fish the vessels would bring cargoes of textiles and other manufactured goods. But on the opening of the new century and as a result of the shipbuilding craze the lawmakers again took up the problem of increasing hemp-growing and its manufacture into clothing, as well as into duck, canvas, and cordage to equip the ships.

[1] *Ibid.*, III, 396 f. [2] *Econ. and Soc. Hist. of N. Eng.*, I, 303.

During the first forty years of the eighteenth century there was considerable legislating to stimulate the raising of hemp and flax. In June, 1701, the General Court granted a bounty of 1 farthing a pound to anyone who would purchase all the hemp grown in the colony at 4 farthings a pound.[1] Another act bearing on the same subject was passed in 1715. It provided for a premium of 9*s*. 4*d*. on every 112 pounds of water-rotted, well-cured, and cleanly dressed hemp, and so in proportion for a greater quantity.[2] This bounty was doubled in 1718,[3] and in 1725 the act was re-enacted with the additional provision that if anyone brought 224 pounds, all of which he had grown in one year, he should have 4*s*. 18*d*. a hundred additional to the usual recompense. In 1728 this act was renewed; and in 1731 the reward was raised to 29*s*. on each 112 pounds, and the bonus was increased to 7*s*. a hundred. Another advance was made in 1735. The gratuity at this time was fixed at 58*s*. for 112 pounds of well-dressed hemp, and 37*s*. 4*d*. for 112 pounds of well-dressed flax. To anyone bringing over 112 pounds of hemp, an additional 14*s*. a hundred was given. For flax the bonus was 9*s*. a hundred.[4] The climax of this legislation came in 1742, when, by order of the General Court, flax certificates were received by the province treasurer for tax.[5]

Along with and following the foregoing acts were those intended to foster the manufacture of articles made from

[1] *Acts and Resolves, Public and Private, of the Prov. Mass. Bay*, I, 473.

[2] *Ibid.*, II, 28.

[3] *Ibid.*, p. 102.

[4] *Ibid.*, pp. 362, 498, 588, 737 f.

[5] *Ibid.*, XIII, App., VIII, 188.

hemp and flax. One of the first of these was a law to promote the linen manufacture, especially the making of canvas or duck for ships' sails, passed in 1722. This measure provided that the justices of each county or someone appointed by them should once a year pass on all pieces of linen twenty yards long and one yard wide made of flax of the growth and manufacture of the province. Three of the best pieces were to be selected and the owners were to be paid double their value, said value to be determined by a "just and equal appraisement." The treasurer of the colony was to select three of the best pieces presented to him and pay a premium of 40*s*. in bills of credit. The act was to continue for five years.[1] The reward was renewed on canvas and duck in 1726.[2] The records show that bounties were claimed in 1724 and allowed in 1727 and 1728.[3]

The next important act was the one to encourage the making of linen cloth, passed in 1753. Its intent and purpose was to provide instruction in spinning, weaving,

[1] *Ibid.*, II, 241 f.

[2] *Ibid.*, XI, App., VI, 52.

[3] In 1724 Nathan Thomas petitioned for the premiums on two pieces of linen cloth which he had presented to the county of Plymouth as the best made therein. The court refused to give him a certificate signifying that his pieces were the best, because no others had been presented (*ibid.*, X, App., V, 541). In 1727 the province treasurer was ordered to pay to the county treasurer of Bristol County £19 for premiums on three pieces of linen (*ibid.*, XI, App., VI, 290). The treasurer of Hampshire County was voted, in 1728, £13 1*s*. 8*d*. to reimburse the county for money paid for the three best pieces of linen (*ibid.*, XI, App., VI, 322).

In 1734 Connecticut passed a measure similar to the one summarized above. In May of this year the General Court offered a premium of 4*d*. a

and other phases of the linen manufacture. For this purpose the sum of £1,500 was voted by the General Court in the form of a tax on every coach, chariot, chaise, calash, and chair within the province. The money thus raised was to be spent in providing in Boston a house in which at least one person from every town was to be instructed free of charge in spinning, weaving, and the other requisite operations connected with the manufacture of linen cloth. The idea was to furnish work for the destitute women and children in many of the towns. The tax was to continue for five years. It was supposed that at the end of this time the £1,500 would be raised.[1] The law expired by limitation, and the house provided from the tax which it imposed was ordered sold in 1780 to secure money for the army.[2] During the remainder of the colonial period the people of Massachusetts were left to their own initiative to employ themselves in raising wool, hemp, and flax, and in manu-

pound for every pound of good hemp, well-dressed, water-rotted, grown in the colony; one of 20*s*. for every bolt or piece of well-wrought canvas or duck, fit for use, and thirty-six yards in length and thirty inches wide, weighing not less than forty-five pounds, and made in the colony; also one of 2*s*. a yard for fine linen cloth, well-spun, woven, and whitened, a yard wide, and made of yarn that was eight runs to the pound, and pro rata for cloth wider or narrower, provided that none was to be narrower than three-fourths of a yard (*Pub. Rec. Col. Conn.* [1726–35], p. 512). This act expired by limitation in five years, at which time it was renewed for another period of equal length because of the profit and advantage that had accrued to the people from it during the past five years (*ibid.* [1735–43], p. 318).

[1] *Acts and Resolves, Public and Private, of the Prov. Mass. Bay*, III, 680.

[2] *Acts and Laws of the Commonwealth of Mass.* (1780–81), pp. 210, 220.

facturing them into wearing apparel and household textile supplies.[1]

During the seventeenth century Virginia consistently followed the policy of encouraging weaving, spinning, and the raising of sheep, hemp, and flax. As early as 1646 it was provided that two children from each county should be sent to James City to be employed in carding, knitting, and spinning. Two houses in which they were to be taught these trades were to be built in the city. By the same law it was provided that certain children could be bound out to tradesmen and husbandmen to be brought up in some

[1] The remaining New England colonies were not entirely indifferent to encouraging the manufacture of linen and woolen cloth. At the 1750–51 session of the General Assembly in Rhode Island an act was passed for promoting the raising of flax and wool and for manufacturing them into cloth. The bounty on cloth manufactured of wool or flax, of a certain texture and length, was one-third its appraised value; that on every pound of cured and dressed flax, one penny a pound (*Rec. Col. R.I. and Providence Plantations*, V, 318). This law was repealed in June, 1751, before it went into effect, for fear the part referring to wool would be unwelcome in England (*ibid.*, p. 340). New Hampshire as early as 1719 offered a bounty of 12 pence a pound for a period of three years on all merchantable hemp grown in the province (*Laws of N.H.*, edited by Batchellor, II, 330). This same year sheep were exempted from taxation for seven years, and to kill any ewe lamb during the next two years was a crime (*ibid.*, p. 335).

The middle colonies did not pursue the consistent policy of encouraging the production of hemp and wool and manufacture of cloth that was pursued in New England. Nothing of any consequence was done in Delaware and New York. Pennsylvania and New Jersey offered limited bounties, the former beginning quite early. The following is a record of part of the proceedings of the Council held in Philadelphia on the twenty-sixth of the first month, 1684: "A Bill read for hemp & flax, Linnen & Wool'n Cloth. Linnen & Woollen Cloth to have a price set upon it by ye County Court, ye hemp at 5*d*. the pound and ye flax at 8*d* p pound; Quest: put; past in ye Affirma" (*Minutes of the Council of Pa.*, I, 98). In 1701 it was ordered

useful calling.[1] This measure was followed by others of more or less importance to household and plantation manufacturing. In 1656 authority was given Northampton County to govern and promote her own manufactures, among which the woolen industry was of considerable importance.[2] Following this came a number of laws relating to wool. A fine of 50 pounds of tobacco was imposed in 1658 for every pound of wool exported. This law was repealed the next year, but was re-enacted in 1662. In 1671 it was again repealed, only to be re-enacted eleven years later. Such a law was in reality intended more for the encouragement of the handicraftsmen than family manufactures. These tradesmen, however, did not seem to take advantage of it, since their failure in this respect was given as the reason for its repeal in 1671.[3]

Beginning in 1662 a series of laws to stimulate the spinning and weaving of cloth was enacted. On account of the low price of tobacco and the abundance of the crop, the Assembly in this year passed a measure which was intended to turn the attention of the planters to things other than

that everyone that owned 40 acres of cleared land should keep at least ten sheep (*ibid.*, II, 27). In 1722 the bounty was 1*d.* a pound on hemp (*Pa. Statutes at Large*, III, 314); and from March 5, 1729, to January 26, 1730, it was paid on 35,251 pounds of hemp, and from March 3, 1730, to July 2, 1731, upon 17,266 pounds (Giesecke, *Am. Commercial Legislation before 1789*, p. 63). New Jersey granted a bounty on hemp and flax in 1765 and renewed it in 1768 (*N.J. Archives*, 1st ser., XVII, 414, 498).

[1] Hening, *Statutes at Large* (New York, 1823), I, 336.

[2] *Ibid.*, p. 396; also Wise, *op. cit.*, p. 303.

[3] For these laws in the order mentioned, see Hening, *op. cit.*, I, 488, 525; II, 124, 287, 493.

the raising of this single staple. A premium of 3 pounds of tobacco was offered to "whoever will spin the fflax and cause the yarne to be weaved into cloath of a yard wide," and 5 pounds for "every yard of woollen cloath made of yarne here spun in the country."[1] This law was repealed four years later (1666), because it was then felt that the people could see how beneficial it was to make linen and woolen cloth, and hence would continue it of their own accord.[2] However, in order to provide for the more difficult operation of weaving, an ordinance was passed the same year requiring each county to maintain a weaver and loom at its own expense. The obstructions to trade and the nakedness of the country at the time required that some steps be taken for promoting manufactures. The idea in the law was to secure weavers and looms to weave the yarn spun by the women and children. It was estimated that five women or the same number of children of twelve or thirteen years of age could annually spin enough yarn to supply sufficient clothing for thirty persons. A thousand pounds of tobacco was the penalty for non-compliance with the law. No county was excused, even if private looms had been set up.[3] The scope of this law was enlarged in September, 1668, when the commissioners of each county court, by the assistance of the vestries of the parishes of the county, were empowered to build houses in which poor children were to be educated and instructed in the arts of spinning, weaving, and other useful occupations and trades.[4]

[1] *Ibid.*, II, 120.

[2] *Ibid.*, p. 241.

[3] *Ibid.*, p. 238.

[4] *Ibid.*, p. 267.

In 1682[1] the law for the encouragement of the manufacture of linen and woolen cloth, enacted in 1662, was re-enacted and enlarged. Premiums were offered for dressed flax and hemp, linen and woolen cloth, linsey-woolsey, hats, and woolen or worsted hose. Every tithable was also compelled to make one pound of dressed hemp and flax or two pounds of either. The law was to continue for three years.[2] It was disallowed, however, by the Commissioners of the Customs on the ground that it diminished correspondence between the mother-country and the colony; weakened the dependence of the colonial population upon England; curtailed the freight which was furnished to English shipping; narrowed the market for English woolens and other manufactures; advanced the cost of tobacco to the English consumer by raising the charges on navigation; and, finally, reduced the volume of the customs.[3] Because of this disallowance the law was

[1] This same year Maryland passed an act to encourage the making of linen and woolen cloth within the province. For every yard of linen cloth three-quarters of a yard wide a premium of 6 pounds of tobacco was offered, and for every yard of woolen cloth the same width one of 10 pounds of tobacco (*Archives of Md.*, VII, 324). A reward was also offered this same year of one pound of tobacco for every pound of good merchantable flax or hemp raised in the province (*ibid.*, pp. 325 f.). Both these laws were to run three years. The latter was renewed in 1688 with the bounty doubled. This act was to continue for seven years (*ibid.*, XIII, 222). At the same session an act forbidding the exportation of wool out of the province was passed (*ibid.*, p. 223). In 1695 a hundred pounds of tobacco were given to each person who converted a hundred pounds of flax or hemp into cordage (*ibid.*, XIX, 173).

[2] Hening, *op. cit.*, II, 503.

[3] "Report of the Commissioners of Customs, 1683," *British State Papers*, "Colonial," sec. 82; cited by Bruce, *Econ. Hist. of Va.*, etc., II, 464.

repealed in 1684, but re-enacted in 1686 to continue till the end of the 1690 session of the Assembly,[1] at which time, April, 1691, it was revived for a period of three years.[2] In 1693 the part referring to linen was continued for six years longer.[3]

After the law limiting the fabrication and exportation of woolen manufactures, enacted by Parliament in 1699,[4] Virginia seems to have given up her general policy of encouraging such industries. Since this law was in direct conformity to the one passed by her Assembly in 1682, there was probably little opposition to it in this colony. Whatever clothing the planter made was largely for use on the plantation and not for exportation. There was little indication at this time that woolen manufactures would ever pass beyond the point of supplying the plantation needs; hence, why should there be any objection to a law forbidding the exportation of such goods? At any rate, whatever manufacturing was done after 1700 was largely on the initiative of the manufacturer, for the general policy of public encouragement was abandoned after this date.[5]

[1] Hening, *op. cit.*, III (Philadelphia, 1823), 16, 30.

[2] *Ibid.*, p. 50.

[3] *Ibid.*, pp. 121 f.

[4] See above, p. 25.

[5] The southern colonies as a whole took little interest in encouraging the production and manufacture of hemp, flax, and wool between 1700 and 1765. While South Carolina periodically offered during these years bounties on the production of hemp, yet such bounties were intended to encourage its production for exportation more than for manufacture in the colony For these bounty laws, see Cooper, *Statutes at Large of S.C.*, III, 184, 436, 616; and IV, 29, 49, 166, and 428. During the decade next following 1765

The definite effect of the policy of encouraging both the production of raw material and its manufacture into clothing and household textile supplies, by the system of premiums, is somewhat difficult to determine. The records show that bounties were actually paid.[1] Commenting on this point in connection with the production of hemp and flax, Giesecke says: "Furthermore, the importance of the domestic manufactures coupled with the fact that the spinning-wheel, the loom, and the hand card were found in most of the homes of the northern colonies gives us good evidence of the production of hemp and flax." Con-

some legislative encouragements were given to manufacturing in the home and elsewhere. Maryland, in 1765, provided that each county court should pay out 8,000 pounds of tobacco anually in prize money for the best manufactured pieces of linen (*Laws of Md.*, 1787, c. 6, Session of 1765; cited by Giesecke, *op. cit.*, p. 65). South Carolina, in 1770, provided, for a five-year term, a bounty of £30 for every hundred pounds' value of "good merchantable linens and thread made in the province" (Cooper, *op. cit.*, IV, 316).

In 1775 the Provincial Council of North Carolina offered a bounty of £100 to the person who within twelve months produced to the Council 6 pieces of woolen cloth of twenty yards each, not less than three-quarters of a yard wide (*Col. Rec. N.C.*, X, 218). In the same year the Council also offered a premium of £50 to the person who should first make 50 pairs of cotton cards of wire as good as the cards imported from England; also a like reward to the first person to make 100 pairs of wool cards of equal quality (*ibid.*, p. 217). Chowan County also provided for premiums this same year. Her Committee of Safety offered a reward of £10 to any person who within twelve months first produced 100 yards of well-fulled woolen cloth to the committee; also a bonus of £10 for 100 yards of well-bleached linen of a quality that usually cost 2*s.* sterling in Great Britain, and £5 for 100 yards of a quality that usually cost 1*s.* in Great Britain. All of the foregoing had to be made in the county (*ibid.*, IX, 1142). Four persons claimed the bounty on linen, which was divided equally among them (*ibid.*, X, 829).

[1] See pp. 30, 35; also Giesecke, *op. cit.*, p. 63.

cerning the bounties on the cloth made from these products, the same author remarks: "In the northern colonies we find a greater degree and variety of household manufactures than in the southern colonies, and this in part accounts for the comparatively numerous bounties in the former colonies for the manufacture of linen and sailcloth."[1] So, whether household manufactures were a cause or a result of the bounties and premiums granted in the various colonies, it seems quite evident that there was a close connection between them.

ECONOMIC AND POLITICAL CONDITIONS

Whatever manufacturing was done in the homes and on the plantations before 1765 was done chiefly from necessity rather than desire. It was not until Parliament entered upon the policy of taxing the colonies that they began to plan quite deliberately and uniformly to supply themselves with the articles that they had formerly been glad to get from the mother-country. While England's restrictive policy was an important factor in bringing about this inclination, and the laws, made by the colonial assemblies in attempting to encourage it, added legal sanction, yet, at the same time, certain economic conditions and, after 1765, political notions probably did more to promote family and plantation manufacturing than both the policy of England and that of the colonial assemblies. The chief economic conditions were: (1) a general decline in prices and the uncertainty of supplies just after 1640; (2) adequate or inadequate transportation facilities; (3) occupation of the

[1] *Op. cit.*, pp. 63, 60.

people; (4) staple crops; (5) fluctuations in the supply and price of tobacco; and (6) favorable or unfavorable balance of trade. After 1765 the political conditions were: the opposition to the Stamp Act and other taxing measures, and, above all, the Revolution itself, which forced upon the colonies as a whole the problem of supplying themselves very largely with what had before been coming from the outside world. The homes were in a large measure responsible for the clothing during these trying times. It is with these economic and political factors and their influence on household manufactures that this section deals.

The results in New England of the great decline in immigration after 1640 caused those who had come up to this date to look elsewhere for the necessities of life that the English ships had been bringing them. This decline in immigration had two important effects: first, it cut off a regular supply of commodities that had been coming along with the settlers; and, secondly, it caused such a reduction in the quantity of commodities produced in New England that the people no longer had the means wherewith to supply themselves with clothing and other necessities. Winthrop, writing of conditions about 1641, said:

> This [reform begun by Parliament in 1641] caused men to stay in England in expectation of a new world, so as few coming to us, all foreign commodities grew scarce, and our own of no price. Corn would buy nothing: A cow which cost last year £20 might now be bought for 4 or £5, etc. . . . . These straits set our people on work to provide fish, clapboards, planks, etc., and to sow hemp and flax (which prospered very well), and to look out to the West Indies for a trade in cotton.[1]

[1] *Hist. of N. Eng.* ("Orig. Nar. of Early Am. Hist." ed.), p. 31.

The effect of the decline in immigration on the price of cattle greatly inconvenienced the people who had been getting their supplies from the surplus of cattle which they sold to the newcomers at fancy prices. These conditions and inconveniences were admirably set forth by Hubbard,[1] when he wrote of the New England colony, about 1640, as follows:

Hitherto divine Providence did, with Arms of abundant Goodness, as a nursing father, uphold this infant Province of New England, as was said of Ephriam, when God learned him to go, taking him by the hand. But for the future they were left more to stand upon their own legs, and shift for themselves; for now there was a great change in the state of the country, the inhabitants being put to great straits by reason of the fall of the price of cattle, the breeding and increase of which had been the principal means of upholding the county next under divine favor, shining out upon them, by many unexpected advantages; for whereas before, all sorts of great cattle were usually sold for 25 £ the head, by reason of the continual coming over of new families every year to plant the wilderness, now that the fountain began to be dried, and the stream turned another way, and many that intended to have followed their neighbors and friends into a land not sown, hoping by the turn of the times and the great changes that were then afoot, to enjoy that at their own doors, which the others had travelled so far to seek abroad, there happened a total cessation of any passengers coming over; yea, rather as the turn of the tide, many came back with the help of the same stream that carried them thither; insomuch that now the County of New England was to seek a way to provide themselves of clothing, which they could not attain by selling their cattle as before; which now were fallen from the huge price fore-mentioned, first to 14 £, and 10 £ an

[1] Hubbard was born in 1621. He was a member of the first class of graduates of Harvard College, in 1642, and was for a long time the minister at Ipswich. His history was not published until 1815, when it was printed in the *Mass. Hist. Soc. Colls.* It was reprinted in 1848 by the same society.

head, and presently after (at least, within a year) to 5£ a piece; nor was their at that rate ready vent for them neither. Thus the flood that brought in much wealth to many persons, the contrary ebb carried all away, out of their reach. To help in this their exigent, besides the industry that the present necessity put particular persons upon, for the necessary supply of their families, the General Court made several orders for the manufacture of woollen and linen cloth; which, with God's blessing upon man's endeavor, in a little time stopped this gap in part, and soon after another door was opened by Special Providence. For when one hand was shut by way of supply from England, another was opened by way of traffic, first to the West Indies and Wine Islands, whereby among other goods much cotton-wool was brought into the country from the Indies; which the inhabitants learned to spin, and breeding of sheep, and by sowing of hemp and flax, they soon found out a way to supply themselves with many necessaries of linen and woollen cloth.[1]

So, whether the New Englanders desired it or not, the foregoing conditions, so well pictured by Hubbard, forced upon them the necessity of supplying themselves with many of the commodities which, prior to 1640, had come from the outside world. Since no textile manufacturing establishments were in existence at this early date, it was necessary to turn the homes into factories and to set the women and children to making clothing and household textile supplies, while the men made farming implements, household utensils, and other necessities.[2]

[1] *Gen. Hist. of N. Eng.*, in *Mass. Hist. Soc. Colls.*, 2d ser., V, 238 ff.

[2] According to Johnson, economic conditions had become somewhat more favorable to the colonists by 1652. Concerning the state of affairs at this date he said: "For rayment, our cloth hath not been cut short, as but of late years the traders that way have increased to such a number, that their shops have continued full all the year long, all one England; besides the Lord hath been pleased to increase sheep extraordinarily of

As the colonies advanced both in population and in material prosperity, certain economic conditions developed which tended to keep them at the business of supplying themselves with the ordinary necessities of life. South of Pennsylvania, except Somerset County, Maryland, and the whole back-country, these conditions were the fluctuations in the price of their chief staples as well as the commodities they received from England. North of Maryland and the back-country in the South the conditions were more complex. They included an abundant supply of accessible raw material, lack of a staple to exchange for English goods, and inadequate transportation facilities. In 1728 William Keith in a letter to the Secretary of the Lords of Trade summarized the reasons for the people in this region making their own clothing as follows: (1) The principal products of the farm being stock and grain, it was profitable for every farmer to have a few sheep to run on the pasture, the wool from which was made into clothing during the winter season when there was nothing else to do. (2) Flax was easily raised and the coarse cloth made from it would do twice the service as the cloth of the same fineness from Europe. Hemp was also raised which was made into bags, plow traces, and halters which were better than those bought in shops. (3) The old women and children who

late, hemp and flax here is great plenty, hides here are more for the number of persons than in England; and for cloth, here is and would be materials enough to make it; but the Farmers deem it better for their profit to put away their cattle and corn for cloathing, than to set upon making cloth; if the Merchants trade be not kept on foot, they fear greatly their corne and cattle will lye in their hands" (*Wonder-Working Providence* ["Orig. Nar. of Early Am. Hist." ed.], p. 211).

could not work out of doors were given profitable employment in carrying on family manufactures. (4) Grain being the chief product enabling them to buy European goods, the settlements in the back-country had no market for their grain, hence raised only enough for their own use, the remainder of their time being spent in making clothing and other supplies.[1]

The people in the back-country and on the frontier, both in the northern and in the southern colonies, were greatly handicapped in the exchange of their commodities for supplies from the outside world by inadequate transportation facilities. The plantations along the southern rivers, and the coast towns of the North, had the facilities to dispose of their products for English or other manufactures; but not so with the back-country and frontier peoples, who might drive a few cattle and hogs to market, send by pack-trains a few hides, beeswax, and whisky, but could not dispose of their grain and other bulky products of the farm. Conditions in western Virginia and Pennsylvania between 1763 and 1783 furnish an excellent example of home manufacturing being forced upon a people because of their economic isolation. Since these communities had no market for their produce, it became necessary for each family to become self-supporting in almost every particular. Hominy blocks and mills were in use in almost every household. The clothing was practically all of household manufacture.

[1] *N.J. Archives*, 1st ser., V, 205. The Lords of Trade also gave similar reason in a report they made in 1728 to a committee of the Privy Council (*ibid.*, p. 208). These reasons were repeated in 1733 in a report the Board of Trade made to the House of Lords ("Representation of the Board of Trade to the House of Lords," etc., *Conn. Hist. Soc. Colls.*, V., App., 461).

Plows, harrows, sleds, cooper-ware, cedar-ware, and looms were likewise homemade. In fact, almost everything needed in eking out the good or bad living had to be made in the household, for there were at this time few persons who devoted all their time to any one of the mechanic arts.[1]

The overstocking of the slave market led in turn to an overproduction of tobacco in Virginia and Maryland. When the price became so low that the planters could no longer exchange their crop for the necessary supplies, they were forced to make many of these on the plantation. In writing to the British Council of Trade in March, 1710–11, Governor Alexander Spotswood of Virginia called attention to the fact that the recent increase in the production of tobacco disproportionate to the consumption had forced the people to diversify their industry. He said:

> This [the increase in production of tobacco] was felt in those parts of the Country where Tobacco is reputed mean, and the people being disappointed of the necessary supplies of Cloathing for their familys in return for their tobacco, found themselves under necessity of attempting to Cloath themselves with their own Manufactures. And the Market for Tobacco still declining and few stores of goods brought in, other parts of the Country, through the like necessity,

[1] Doddridge, *Notes on the Settlements and Indian Wars of the Western Parts of Va. and Pa.*, from a reprint in Kercheval's *Hist. of the Valley of Va.* (2d ed., 1850), p. 235. The conditions in North Carolina were much the same as those in Virginia and Pennsylvania. In speaking of them Saunders, in his prefatory notes to Vol. III of *Col. Rec. N.C.*, says: "British Commodities, as they were called, were brought from Virginia by land or in canoes in small quantities at unreasonable rates, but the bulk of the cloth used in the country, whether cotton, linen, or woolen, was made at home, each plantation, or at least each neighborhood, supplying its own needs from its own products and its own labor, the housewives of the country being very proficient in such matters" (Introd., p. xv).

have been forced into the same humour of planting Cotton and Sowing Flax, and by mixing the first with their wool to supply the wants of course Cloathing and Linen, not only for their Negros, but for many of the poorer sort of housekeepers. This is now become so universal that even in one of the best Countys for Tobacco, I'm credibly informed there has been made this last year above 40,000 yards of divers sorts of Woolen, Cotton and Linnen Cloth, and other Countys where tobacco is less valuable have no doubt advanced their manufactures proportionately. Tho' this be at present the General humor of the Country, it is introduced more by necessity than inclination, and the people are so little skilled in this kind of Manufacture that they will with difficulty attain any tolerable perfection in it, and own that what they make now costs dearer than they usually had from England when their tobacco bore but a moderate price.[1]

The people north of Maryland were considerably handicapped during the entire colonial period because the balance of trade with Great Britain was continually against them.[2] This situation was caused by the similarity of staple products of this section and those of England. Because of this similarity, as has already been shown,[3] the mother-country had shut out the staples of this region

[1] "Letters of Governor Spotswood," *Va. Hist. Colls.*, N.S., I, 72.

[2] From 1697 to 1773, inclusive, there was not a single year in which New England did not have a large balance against her. In 1771 this balance was £1,269,737. During the same time New York and Pennsylvania had a balance against them every year but one, 1697. This balance at times reached over half a million pounds annually in each of these colonies. On the other hand, Virginia and Maryland, most of the time, had the balance in their favor. This was the case in all but sixteen of the seventy-two years after 1696. The same is true of the Carolinas. From 1732 to 1773 the balance was against Georgia all the time except ten years, nine of these after 1754 (Whitworth, *State of the Trade of Great Britain, 1697–1773*, pp. 53, 54, 63–70, 78).

[3] See above, p. 17.

by high duties. To mitigate this condition of affairs the New England and middle colonies were forced to transfer their products to Barbados and Jamaica, to South of Europe and to Africa, in order to secure a medium of exchange for clothing, furniture, utensils, tools, implements, and other manufactured commodities from England.[1] This was not true of the southern colonies. Virginia's and Maryland's tobacco, North Carolina's naval stores, and South Carolina's and Georgia's rice and indigo, which could all go directly to England, succeeded in keeping the balance of trade between them and the mother-country in their favor. This situation made it easier for the South (back-country excepted) to live on agriculture alone, while the North finally saw that before agriculture and commerce could exert their best economic force, they must have manufacturing combined with them. With the large balance of trade against them, the people north of Maryland

[1] The following table gives an idea of the amount of this trade:

TOTAL EXPORTS OF THE COLONIES FOR THE YEAR 1769

Colonies	To Great Britain	To South of Europe	To West Indies	To Africa
	£	£	£	£
New England	142,755	81,173	208,426	17,711
New York and New Jersey	113,382	50,885	68,855	1,313
Pennsylvania	28,112	203,752	178,331	560
Maryland and Virginia	759,961	140,190	91,249	....
North Carolina and South Carolina	405,014	76,119	87,758	690
Georgia	82,270	614	13,285	....

Of the total exports (£450,065) from New England, but £142,755 went to Great Britain; and of a total of £410,755 from Pennsylvania, but £28,112. In the South the opposite was true. Of a total of £991,400 from Virginia and Maryland, £759,961 went to Great Britain. This clarifies the point made in the foregoing paragraph (Macpherson, *op. cit.*, III, 572).

were forced to turn upon themselves and seek an industry to combine with their agriculture and commerce. This industry was manufacturing, which was carried on both in and out of the homes.

Up to about 1763 the household manufacturing that had been going on in the colonies was more or less local, induced and sustained by the factors considered above. From this date to and including the Revolution itself events occurred in rapid succession which tended both to generalize the custom and to increase the quantity that had heretofore been made. These events were the taxing measures enacted by Parliament and the retaliatory means used by the various colonies and the Continental Congress. The act providing for the strict enforcement of the navigation and customs laws in America, the renewal of the Sugar Act of 1733, with the addition of coffee, Spanish and Portuguese wines, and other less important articles, and the Stamp and the Townshend acts, were the unexpected stimuli of a general movement toward household manufactures. This movement was popularized and sustained by the non-importation, non-consumption, and non-exportation agreements and associations formed in the separate colonies and adopted by the First Continental Congress. How all of these worked themselves out in generalizing the custom and increasing the amount of goods made in the homes and on the plantations is the theme of the next few paragraphs.

Until the attempted enforcement of the Grenville policy the colonies had offered little resistance to the right of England to regulate their commerce. But beginning with the announcement of this policy stubborn opposition developed, first by amicable means, later by bellicose. In 1765 the merchants of New York, Rhode Island, Massachusetts, and Pennsylvania entered into what they called non-importation agreements. They agreed among themselves not to import any goods from Great Britain, to countermand orders already given, and to refuse to sell goods sent on commission until the Stamp Act was repealed. These resolutions began in New York and were soon adopted in the other colonies named. The people also in large numbers agreed to wear nothing but goods of domestic manufacture. In November, 1764, a society for the promotion of arts, agriculture, and economy was formed in New York. Rewards for the production of both raw materials and finished goods were offered by this society. In 1765 prizes ranging from £30 to £10 were announced for the five largest quantities of linen yarn spun under the direction of one person; for linen cloth, in like manner, five premiums, ranging from £25 to £5; for woven stockings, £16 to £12; and smaller amounts for shoes, dressed deerskins for breeches, and beaver skins for gloves; for the greatest quantity of flax raised by one farmer from £30 to £10; and from £15 to £5 for the greatest quantity on one acre. Gratuities were also offered in 1766 similar to the foregoing.[1] To lessen the inconveniences caused by the non-importation resolutions, a fair was opened in New York City in 1765 for the sale of home manufactures. To wear silks and broadcloths was accounted a disgrace, and the wealthiest and most fashionable appeared clad

[1] Bishop, *op. cit.*, I, 368 f.

in homespun linsey-woolsey.[1] The people then for the first time began to appreciate the internal resources of their country—a lesson they did not soon forget.

The king signed the bill that repealed the Stamp Act in March, 1766. This exultant victory of the colonies, however, was of short duration, for the very next year came the Townshend acts, which called forth non-importation agreements similar to those of 1765. That these agreements really existed even among the consumers is shown by a letter from a gentleman who was returning to Philadelphia from a visit in Virginia. The letter was written to a gentleman in this city and printed in the *Pennsylvania Journal*, April 20, 1769. In speaking of the revenue act, dissolving the assemblies, etc., the writer said:

> These things have blown up the minds of the people into a high flame for industry all over the counties, so that several townships as I came along were resolving speedily to meet and enter into strict agreements against buying any more English goods, especially their woolen, silk and callico fineries, but each family vigorously to set about to manufacturing their own cloathing, and every other necessary article. . . . . At another gentleman's house where I was, his lady was spinning fast, and had five clever girls spinning along with her ever since they heard that the Boston Parliament was dissolved; it's expected that they will soon have a good deal of cloth to sell.[2]

The making and wearing of homemade clothes at this date became a social as well as an industrial custom. In 1769 the president and the first graduating class of Brown

[1] Booth, *Hist. of the City of N.Y.*, p. 424.

[2] "Newspaper Extracts," VII, 1768–69, p. 420, in *N.J. Archives*, 1st ser., XXVI.

University appeared at the Commencement exercises in garments made of wool grown in Rhode Island. The Harvard graduates followed their example the next year.[1] Women in all the colonies became members of societies resolving to forego luxuries and to spin, card, and wear clothing of their own make. A suit of homespun became a mark of popular distinction.[2] Rhode Island was a leader in both the social and the industrial phases of this movement. The "Daughters of Liberty" held an all-day session in Providence. Commenting on what was done in Newport, the *New York Journal* of May 30, 1768, said:

> What a glorious example Newport has set us. Rouse, O, my Countrymen! We are well informed that one married lady and her daughter of about sixteen, have spun full sixty yards of good fine linen cloth, nearly a yard wide, since the first of March, besides taking care of a large family. The linen manufacture is promoted and carried on, with so much spirit and assiduity, among all ranks, that we are assured there is scarcely enough flax to be had in town, to supply the continued Consumption of that Article.[3]

That the people of New England, New York, and Pennsylvania really meant what they said in the non-importation agreements is shown by a glance at the amount of imports for the years 1768 and 1769 (Table I). The figures also bring out the fact that the "boycott" was not very effective in the southern colonies.

A falling off in the imports into the northern colonies of more than £900,000 is certainly evidence that the people

[1] North, "The New England Wool Manufactures," *The N. Eng. States*, I, 194.

[2] Simms, *Hist. of Schoharie Co., N.Y.*, p. 175.

[3] Quoted by Paterson, *Hist. of R.I.*, p. 111.

were much in earnest. The uniform increase in the importations into the South during the same time shows that this section was not at this time willing to make the leap into economic darkness. Their sources of home supply were not at this time so adequate as were those of their northern neighbors.

TABLE I

VALUE OF IMPORTS FROM GREAT BRITAIN*

Colonies	Christmas, 1767, to Christmas, 1768	Christmas, 1768, to Christmas, 1769	Difference
	£	£	£
New England	419,797	207,993	−211,804
New York	482,930	74,918	−408,012
Pennsylvania	432,107	199,909	−232,198
Maryland and Virginia	475,954	488,362	+ 12,408
North Carolina and South Carolina	289,868	306,600	+ 16,732
Georgia	56,562	58,340	+ 1,778

* Whitworth, *State of Trade of Great Britain*, pp. 72, 73. Shillings and pence omitted in all cases.

To make the non-importation and non-exportation agreements generally effective required but the action of the Continental Congress. One of the most important acts of this body was the adoption of the "Association," which included an agreement to import no English products after December 1, 1774, and to export nothing to any British port, European or colonial, after September 10, 1775.[1] This "Association" was readily ratified in all the colonies except New York and Georgia. In the former, however, there were enough Whigs to secure its general observance through the work of their local committees. Tables II and

[1] *Jour. Cont. Cong.* (L.C. ed.), I, 75 ff.

III show the effectiveness of the "Association" as enforced by the local committees in all the colonies except Georgia, the first revealing the effect on woolen goods imported into the colonies from England and the second exhibiting the total imports from and exports to Great Britain a few years before the outbreak of the Revolution.

TABLE II

VALUE OF WOOLEN GOODS OF ALL SORTS EXPORTED FROM ENGLAND TO THE COLONIES*

Colonies	1772	1773	1774	1775
	£	£	£	£
New England	284,553	147,717	168,815	8,382
New York	128,879	76,498	129,547	345
Pennsylvania	216,055	135,119	217,205	10
Maryland and Virginia	185,437	99,308	133,912	5
North Carolina and South Carolina	84,226	73,403	91,361	1,106
Georgia	26,492	16,982	14,627	39,719

* Macpherson, *op. cit.*, III, 602. Shillings and pence omitted in all cases.

These tables (II and III) reveal the fact that the colonies "boycotted" not only woolen goods from England but all others as well. They also show the general effectiveness of the non-importation and non-exportation agreements, the former assisting to make the imports in all the colonies except Georgia practically negligible before the end of the year 1775, the latter affecting exports similarly the next year. Conditions remained thus, especially in the northern section, except New York, to the end of the Revolution.[1] Supplies of all sorts had either to be made in the country, captured on the high seas, or acquired from countries

[1] See Table IV.

other than England at the risk of capture. All these methods were used—just to what extent it is difficult to determine.

The Revolutionary War was the climax of all the forces tending to throw the colonists upon their own resources to acquire the necessities of life. What had been going on in the back-country of the South and in most of the northern

TABLE III

OFFICIAL VALUE OF THE EXPORTS AND IMPORTS OF THE COLONIES TO AND FROM GREAT BRITAIN, CHRISTMAS, 1773, TO CHRISTMAS, 1776*

Colonies	Christmas, 1773, to Christmas, 1774		Christmas, 1774, to Christmas, 1775		Christmas, 1775, to Christmas, 1776	
	Exports	Imports	Exports	Imports	Exports	Imports
	£	£	£	£	£	£
New England	172,248	562,476	116,588	71,625	762	55,050
New York	80,008	437,937	187,018	1,228	2,318	....
Pennsylvania	69,611	625,652	175,966	1,366	1,421	365
Maryland and Virginia	612,030	528,738	758,356	1,921	73,226	....
North Carolina and South Carolina	432,302	378,116	579,549	6,245	13,688	....
Georgia	67,647	57,518	103,477	113,777	12,569	....

* Macpherson, *op. cit.*, III, 564, 585, 599. Shillings and pence omitted in every case.

section was now forced upon the towns on the coast and the plantations along the rivers. No longer could the English ships come to the plantations laden with all sorts of luxuries and necessities to exchange for their tobacco, rice, and indigo. The table of imports from Great Britain during the years of the Revolution shows how completely the supply from this section was cut off from most of the colonies (Table IV).

Four significant facts are revealed by Table IV. They are: first, the complete cutting off of the trade between Great Britain and New England, Pennsylvania, Maryland, and Virginia during the war; second, the success of the New York towns in securing supplies during all of the seven years; third, the renewal of the trade relations with

TABLE IV

IMPORTS FROM GREAT BRITAIN*

Colonies	Christmas, 1776, to Christmas, 1777	Christmas, 1777, to Christmas, 1778	Christmas, 1778, to Christmas, 1779	Christmas, 1779, to Christmas, 1780	Christmas, 1780, to Christmas, 1781	Christmas, 1781, to Christmas, 1782	Christmas, 1782, to Christmas, 1783
	£	£	£	£	£	£	£
New England..	....	....	....	....	....	....	199,558
New York....	57,294	26,449	349,917	496,602	502,977	186,242	547,132
Pennsylvania..	....	7,537	....	....	....	....	239,462
Maryland and Virginia.....	....	....	....	....	....	....	199,657
North Carolina and South Carolina....	....	....	....	236,940	330,847	69,742	226,736
Georgia.......	....	....	85	91,888	14,058	339	22,682

* Macpherson, *op. cit.*, III, 614, 632, 651, 673, 706, 727; IV, 40. Shillings and pence omitted in all cases.

the Carolinas and Georgia during the years that this section was occupied by the British armies; and, finally, the anxiety of the whole country to return to English goods after the war was practically over, this anxiety being evidenced by the heavy importations in 1782–83.

The clothing for the family and the general supplies for the household, like bedding, table linen, etc., during these years was made mainly by the women in the homes. Macy's picture of conditions on Nantucket Island, and

Jefferson's statement of what was done in Virginia, are typical of what was going on throughout the North and South as a whole during the war. Of Nantucket Island, the former said:

> The suffering for clothing was inconsiderable throughout the war. For immediately, on being cut off from the use of English manufactures, the women engaged within their own families in manufacturing of various kinds of cloth for domestic use. They thus kept their household decently clad, and the surplus of their labors they sold to such as chose to buy rather than make for themselves. In this way the female part of families, by their industry and strict economy, frequently supported the whole domestic circle; evincing the strength of their attachment and the value of their service to those on whom they themselves were wont to depend for protection and support. There being from twelve to sixteen thousand sheep owned on the island, it was easy to procure as much wool as was needed. A considerable quantity of flax was raised yearly and some was imported from the continent; so that means were furnished for all that were inclined to labor, to clothe their families.[1]

Jefferson pictured the conditions in Virginia as follows:

> We never had an interior trade of any importance. Our exterior commerce has suffered very much from the beginning of the present conflict. During this time we have manufactured within our families the most necessary articles of cloathing. Those of Cotton will bear some comparison with the same kinds of manufactures in Europe; but those of wool, flax, and hemp are very coarse, unsightly, and unpleasant.[2]

The discussion in the succeeding chapter will show that these statements were not overdrawn and that all the foregoing factors materially affected the amount of manufacturing done in the homes and on the plantations.

[1] *Hist. of Nantucket*, p. 110.

[2] *Notes on Va.*, p. 273.

CHAPTER III

THE STATUS OF HOUSEHOLD MANUFACTURES IN THE COLONIES

The rather extended discussion of the factors affecting the rise and progress of household manufactures during the colonial era presented in the preceding chapter has demonstrated the fact that influences tending to increase the output of the home factory in one part of the country had the opposite effect in another—just how much and how little it is difficult to determine because definite statistics on this phase of colonial life seem never to have been collected. To determine in statistical form the extent and amount of all kinds of articles manufactured in the homes and on the plantations prior to 1783 is not possible from the meager records that have come down to us from this period. But with the scant and scattering accounts that are now accessible one can formulate in a somewhat general fashion a statement of the status of such manufactures during the settlement and progress of the colonies until their complete separation from the mother-country. It is the purpose of this chapter to formulate such a statement.

SEVENTEENTH-CENTURY BEGINNINGS

Little attention was given to any sort of manufacturing in New England prior to 1640. During these years of beginnings the people were content to engage principally in farming, lumbering, fishing, and cattle-raising. So long as the ships came from, and returned to, England with considerable regularity, as they did between 1630 and 1640, necessary articles of clothing and other supplies could be secured from the mother-country. But on the assembling of the Long Parliament, as has been pointed out in the preceding chapter,[1] there occurred a great falling off in the immigration to this section, and at the same time a discontinuance of the regular supply of necessities that had been coming along with the ships that brought the settlers. Out of these conditions arose the serious problem of furnishing some twenty-four thousand people,[2] then in New England, with suitable clothing and other supplies needed in a region of long and severe winters. The decline in immigration mentioned above further complicated the situation by causing a corresponding diminution in the price of what those who had come over had to sell, thus making it very difficult for them to acquire the means of exchange for the few goods that were imported.[3]

The graveness of the economic situation in which these northern colonists found themselves in 1640 was soon realized by the lawmakers, who attempted to mitigate the conditions then confronting the people by legislative enactment, the Massachusetts and Connecticut laws[4] of 1640 and 1642 being direct products of the foregoing uncontrol-

[1] See p. 44.

[2] Based on Dexter's estimates, *Proc. Am. Ant. Soc.*, N.S., V, 23, 25, 29, 31.

[3] See chapter ii for a full treatment of these factors.

[4] See pp. 29 f. for a full discussion of both of the laws.

lable circumstances. The effect of these laws is difficult to determine definitely. It is known from the records that people did apply for the premiums, and that the bounty law was repealed because it proved to be too much of a burden on the people, a fact affording some evidence of the effectiveness of such legislation.[1]

Some spinning and weaving had been done in New England even before the lawmakers took up the problem of encouraging these industries. According to Palfrey, thread and yarn were spun by women in their homes prior to 1640.[2] The author of *New England's First Fruits*, commenting on the prosperity of the colony at about the same date, said, in enumerating the ways in which God had prospered them:

> In prospering hempe and flaxe so well, that its frequently sowen, spun and woven into linnen cloth; (and in a short time may serve for cordate) and so with cotton-wooll which we may have at very reasonable rates from the (islands) and our linnen Yarne, we can make dimittees and fustians for our summer clothing. And having a matter of 1,000 sheep, which prosper well, to begin withall, in a competent time we hope to have woollen cloath there made. And great and small cattel, being now very frequently killed for food; their skins will afford us leather for boots and shoes, and other uses: So that God is leading us by the hand into a way of clothing.[3]

This statement of a contemporary writer indicates that in reality little had been done before 1640 in the way of spinning yarn and weaving cloth. There is also an intimation in the latter part of the quotation that the skins of

[1] See p. 30.

[2] *Hist. of N. Eng.* (Boston, 1892), II, 53.

[3] Reprint in *Mass. Hist. Soc. Colls.*, 1st ser., I, 247 (first published in London in 1643).

the cattle had been little utilized in the making of boots and shoes prior to this date.

One might properly ask here, Whence came the knowledge of the arts of spinning and weaving required to make even the small amount of cloth that was probably made at such an early date? To answer this query one has but to recall the fact that the settlers were from a country that had but recently passed out of the family stage of manufacturing. In truth, during much of the seventeenth century the practice of spinning and weaving in the homes was quite common over all of rural England. Commenting on this point, Rogers remarked:

> It must not be forgotten, however, that in many places spinning and weaving were a bye-product in English industry, and that they were generally and assiduously practiced. The spinning wheel and the weaver's frame were I am certain common all over rural England not only in the seventeenth century, but during a considerable part of the eighteenth also. Home-spun was the clothing of many peasants and workmen, and in the interpretation of the manner in which wages were exchanged for laborer's needs, we must take into account that not a little of his clothing was the work of himself and his family after his agricultural or other labors were ended.[1]

With such conditions existing in rural England at the time of the great migration to New England between 1630 and 1640, it is quite possible that among the immigrants there were many of both sexes well skilled in the arts of spinning and weaving. In fact, among those who came over in the "Mayflower" were a wool-carder, a silk-maker, and a fustian-maker. Another wool-carder came in 1621 in the "Fortune"; and a silk-maker and a wool-carder

[1] *Hist. of Agr. and Prices in Eng.*, V, 587.

were among those who came in 1623 in the "Ann" and the "Little James."[1] Furthermore, among these early settlers were some Yorkshire weavers, who settled about six miles from Ipswich, Massachusetts, calling the place Rowley. In a very short time they were busy at their former trade, weaving; and in 1642 one John Pearson from Lynn set up among them the first fulling-mill in this country.[2] It was these people who, according to Winthrop, exceeded all others as early as 1643 in the spinning and weaving operations.

The legislation concerning spinning and weaving discussed in the previous chapter makes it clear that the lawmakers did not intend that the knowledge of these arts should pass away with the first generation. While all these laws affected directly or indirectly the amount of manufacturing done in the home, the one of 1656 seems to have touched the subject more closely than any other single one. By assessing each family with one spinner, and requiring this spinner to spin for thirty weeks each year at the rate of three pounds of cotton, linen, or woolen yarn a week, under penalty of 12*d.* for every pound short,[3] the responsibility of supplying yarn for the looms was placed upon the individual homes. Just how generally this responsibility was assumed by the homes during the seventeenth century in New England is quite difficult to determine. One writer states that there was not at the beginning of the eighteenth century one family in forty in Essex

[1] *The Hist. Mag.*, 1st ser., III, 262.

[2] Brown (editor), *Textile Industries in the U.S.*, I, 127.

[3] See p. 33 for the law.

County, Massachusetts, that did not spin and weave the cloth for its own clothing.[1] It is quite true that the seventeenth century in New England was in reality the age of homespun industries. The spinning-wheel, the loom, and the dyepot were in practically every farmer's kitchen.[2] Most of the tailoring and the dressmaking and much of the hatmaking and shoemaking were done by members of the household. Linsey-woolsey was the commonest fabric. Tow cloth was made into towels and other coarse goods. Cotton came into use quite early and was spun on the large wheel. Checked and striped goods were manufactured, and when in excess of the household needs were exchanged for calico and silk. The goods bartered by the industrious women were bunting, serges, druggets, brooms, hats, and cotton and linen goods.[3]

[1] Philbrick, "Spinning in the Olden Time," *Essex Antiquarian*, I, 88.

[2] Weeden, *Econ. and Soc. Hist. of N. Eng.*, I, 305.

[3] An example of this bartering is the following itemized statement of the articles credited to Mrs. Mary Avery during the years 1685–89, by a Boston storekeeper (from an old account-book of a Boston shopkeeper now in the MSS collection of the Boston Public Library; cited by Abbott, *Women in Industry*, p. 24):

By 2 yard ½ of buntin att	?	?	?
By yard ½ ditto att 14*d*	£0	3*s*.	3*d*.
By 3 yard ¼ of half thick Kersey att 3*s*. 3*d*	0	10	6
A coverlid	1	0	0
By 16 yards of drugget att—and a broom 3*d*	1	17	7
By 20 yards black searge at 4*s*. 6*d*	4	10	0
By 20 yards searge at 3*s*. 6*d*	3	3	4
By 3 yds. buntin at 3*d*	0	3	3
By 18½ yds. searge at 3/8	3	7	10
By a hatt 5–6	0	5	6
By 53 yds. of cotton and linnin at 2–9	7	5	9
By ½ doz. ? a carpett 30	2	14	0
By 7 hatts att 5-*sd*	1	16	9
By 4 yds. searge att ?	2	4	0
By ditto at ?	1	10	0
By 4 yds. black searge	0	18	0
By searge	8	19	4½
By 34 yds. Searge at 3*s*. 6*d*	6	7	6
By 24 yds. searge at ?	6	0	0

The status of household manufactures during the seventeenth century was much the same in the middle colonies as it was in New England. In fact, in all the territory north of Maryland conditions were very similar in respect to this important industry, because this region produced practically the same staples, thus making the trade relations with the mother-country very similar. This similarity was more striking after all the territory came under the control of the English. A few references to actual conditions will substantiate this general statement.

Holland and England assumed a similar attitude toward their colonies in regard to textile manufactures. Rule XXIX of the *Freedom and Exemption* granted by the West Indian Company to all patrons, masters, or private persons who should plant colonies in New Netherlands read as follows: "The colonists shall not be permitted to make any woolen, linen, or cotton cloth, nor weave there, on pain of being banished, and being arbitrarily punished as perjurers."[1] This rule, on its face, was more inclusive and arbitrary than any law ever passed by the English on the same subject. But, in spite of its arbitrary nature, the Dutch seem to have regarded it rather lightly, for spinning-wheels and looms were very common among them during the early history of New Netherlands. On these the women and girls expended their leisure moments, producing piles and piles of homespun cloth and snow-white linen.[2]

[1] O'Callaghan, *Laws and Ordinances of New Netherlands*, p. 10.

[2] Booth, *op. cit.*, p. 186; Clute, *Annals of Staten Island*, pp. 77 f.

The passing of New Netherlands from Dutch to English control seems to have had no diminishing effect on the output of the family factory. Of the people of New York six years after the territory passed under the control of the English, Denton said: "For the manner how they get a livelihood, it is principally by Corn and Cattel, which will there fetch them any Commodities; likewise they sowe store of Flax, which they make every one Cloth of for their own wearing, as also woollen Cloth, and Linsey-woolsey, and had they more Tradesmen among them, they would in a little time live without the help of any other Countrey for their Clothing."[1] The historian of Rye, Westchester County, asserts that the wearing apparel about 1684 was mostly of family manufacture. Leather garments were very common, the skins of the deer, raccoon, fox, wolf, and beaver being much used. "Every house possessed a loom; a shop for weaving, frequently built of stone, would be found on nearly every farm."[2] While such statements portray conditions in general, yet it should be said that by the end of the century, especially in the older settlements, "each well-to-do man owned a suit of clothes, and perhaps a trooper's coat, made of imported cloth."[3] These suits often lasted for years, and were handed down from father to son, from generation to generation. However, the fact remains that most of the common wearing apparel and the

[1] *A Brief Description of New York, Formerly Called New Netherlands*, p. 58 (reprint from the original edition of 1670).

[2] Baird, *Hist. of Rye, Westchester Co., N.Y.*, p. 129; see Weise, *The Hist. of Albany, N.Y.*, pp. 186 f., for a similar statement of conditions in Albany in 1685.

[3] Cravens, *Hist. of Mattituck, L.I.*, p. 76.

necessary household fabrics were homemade and remained so for nearly another century.[1]

Conditions similar to those in New York during the early stages of its history existed in the other middle colonies. In 1663 there were eighty sheep in New Sweden. The people made enough linen and woolen cloth to supplement their furs and give them bed and table linen. They also tanned their own leather and made their own boots and shoes—when they wore any. All well-to-do families had a good store of linen for bedclothes, and other textile household necessities. The washing was not done often, hence it was necessary to have the chests of drawers well filled with homespun. The ox-yokes had bows made of bent hickory wood; for horses' traces the people used twisted deerskin; plaited corn husks served for collars; and the rest of the harness was homemade of the same or similar serviceable materials.[2] In New Jersey conditions were similar to those in Delaware. A contemporary writer, speaking of the products of this colony in 1681, concluded as follows: "The Country also produces Flax and Hemp, which they already Spin and Manufacture into Linnen: They make severaly Stuffs and Cloath of Wool for Apparel:

[1] At the end of the seventeenth century the trades in the interior were seldom sufficiently differentiated for one to live by one of them wholly. To eke out a living in these early days one had to have a farm. In 1700 Mattituck, Long Island, had 100 residents; among them were blacksmiths, carpenters, masons, joiners, coopers, wheelwrights, cordwainers, shoemakers, saddlers, fullers, tailors, tanners, and millers. These men carried on their trades as an adjunct to their farming activities (*ibid.*, p. 80).

[2] Scharf and Westcott, *Hist. of Phila.*, I, 136, 140, 151.

They Tan Leather Make Shoes and Hats."[1] These manufactures were introduced by Quakers from Yorkshire and London, who settled Salem and Burlington in 1678. They made serges, druggets, crapes, good plushes, and several varieties of linen goods. Some Scotch immigrants also came to West Jersey before 1684, among whom during these early days were always found the cultivation and home manufacture of hemp and flax.[2]

As has been pointed out in the previous chapter,[3] the colonies south of Pennsylvania had much less occasion for reverting to the primitive modes of supplying the necessities of life than did their northern neighbors. Generally speaking, these southern colonies, except Virginia and a part of Maryland at times, never gave the mother-country much concern in the working out of her commercial policy. The production of tobacco, rice, and indigo chiefly engaged the energy and capital of the settlers from the Chesapeake southward. They were satisfied to exchange these staples for British goods rather than manufacture such commodities in their homes. The exceptions in Virginia and Maryland

[1] "The Present State of the Colony of West Jersey, in America, September, Anno. Dom. 1681," *Pa. Mag. of Hist.*, XVIII, 158 f.

[2] Raum, *The Hist. of N.J.*, II, 351. What one man was thinking concerning spinning is reflected in Thomas Budd's *Good Order Established in Pennsylvania and New Jersey*, printed in 1685. This writer proposed the establishment of spinning schools, similar to those then existing in Germany, for these two colonies. He wished to have such schools in the principal cities and towns and oblige the parents by law to put their children in these schools. He felt that by such an arrangement these two colonies could soon be making enough linen for their own use, with some to export to other colonies.

[3] See p. 51.

were largely confined to communities where dependence was almost entirely upon tobacco, which they exported to England and in exchange received English manufactures equal to their demands, except in certain years when the supply was meager, or the price low, or some disturbance of trade prevented their getting it to market. As early as 1689 traders to Virginia and Maryland asserted that these provinces depended on them wholly for clothing and other necessaries from England.[1] Lists of the goods sent from the mother-country to these two colonies show that, not only necessities, but all sorts of luxuries were handled by these traders. For example, from Christmas, 1698, to the same date in 1699, they imported from England 189 articles of English manufacture and 215 of foreign.[2] These lists included practically every product, both raw and manufactured, then known to the civilized world. Inventories of the possessions of both rich and poor show that there was much variation in both the character and the extent of these English and foreign manufactures. They ranged all the way from expensive luxuries to the commonest necessities, and were widely distributed throughout the provinces.[3]

While Virginia and Maryland depended almost wholly upon England for their manufactured goods, yet there were times when the supply was not equal to the demand. This often inadequate supply was due to the fact that the amount of tobacco they exported to England varied greatly from year to year. On this account the English merchants

[1] Morriss, *Col. Trade of Md.*, p. 58.

[2] *Ibid.*, App., II, 139 ff.

[3] *Ibid.*, pp. 60 ff.

hesitated to send large quantities of domestic and foreign goods to them, which in the event of a bad crop or a low price might be left on their hands. Morriss asserts that in average years the supply seemed inadequate to meet the needs of the inhabitants, and that in bad years it fell far below the average requisite amount.[1] This uncertain and insufficient supply of needful articles forced the planters of both of these colonies to manufacture on their plantations a sufficient quantity of the necessities to make up the shortage from England. Thus, during the years when imports were extremely scarce, there developed on the individual plantations considerable activity in the fabrication of cotton, linen, and woolen cloth for clothing, as well as household linens and general supplies. This form of activity was purely of a household and plantation nature, as it was not carried on in any center.

There is evidence that as early as 1649 plantation manufacturing was carried on in the Virginia colony. It was said at this time of Captain Mathews, who resided on Blunt Point on the Lower James, that he had a fine house and all things answerable to it; that he sowed yearly a store of hemp and flax and caused it to be spun; that he kept weavers, and had a tan-house; caused leather to be dressed and made into shoes; and that he had eight shoemakers employed in their trade and forty negro servants whom he brought up to the trades in his home.[2] Of the

[1] Morriss, *Col. Trade of Md.*, p. 64.

[2] "A Perfect Description of Virginia," Force, *Tracts*, II, No. 8, p. 15. Mathews' custom of bringing up his negroes to the trades was not an exceptional case. This seems to have been rather common before 1700.

people as a whole it was asserted that they had three thousand sheep, six public brew-houses, but most people brewed their own beer; and that they produced much hemp and flax, in spite of the fact that ships at this time were bringing in linen and woolen cloth of all sorts, as well as stockings and shoes.[1]

From these two statements one infers that on some plantations manufacturing was carried on regardless of the quantity of supplies from England. And such was the case, especially in counties farthest removed from the British sources of supply; and such continued to be the case during the remainder of the seventeenth century. Some evidence of this is found in the inventories of the period. Wise, who examined many of these in the counties of the Eastern Shore, found frequent mention of woolen wheels, wool cards, and looms. That of William Taylor, who died about 1690, included thirty-five yards of Virginia cloth, which had been manufactured on his plantation.[2] After examining many inventories covering the same period in other counties, Bruce remarks: "So numerous are references to linen-wheels in this interval, that it would be impossible to give a full list of them. . . . . In one

Commenting on this point, Bruce says: "The wills of the seventeenth century on record in the county courts indicate that there were many negroes, more especially of the female sex, who had been carefully educated to take part in domestic manufactures. After the cloth had been made, it was converted into suits either by the slaves or by the servants." Bruce also refers to a letter of William Byrd, March 8, 1685, to his correspondent in England, in which mention is made of the rivalry among his dependents as to who spin the most cotton (*Econ. Hist. of Va. in the 17th Cent.*, II, 460, 471).

[1] "A Perfect Description of Virginia," Force, *op. cit.*, pp. 3, 5.

[2] *Eastern Shore of Va.*, p. 303.

inventory, the Osborne, eighteen will be found included among the items of property belonging to the estate."[1]

The legislation in Virginia and Maryland during the seventeenth century and the response to it are indicative of the straits to which these colonies were put at times for necessary supplies. The effects of this legislation are partly revealed by the county records, which show that premiums were actually awarded under the acts encouraging the manufacture of clothing and household fabrics. Ralph Wormeley, Christopher Wormeley, Captain Henry Creyk, John Farrell, and Richard Parrott, all of Middlesex County, Virginia, claimed rewards in 1684. The claim of each individual in the order named was for 14, 95, 61, 35, and 34 yards of cloth.[2] In 1694 the York County Court ordered bounties paid to Thomas Chrisman and Thomas Fowler for cloth made in their homes by members of their families. Similar gratuities were awarded John Smith, of Middlesex County, and Thomas Cocke, of Henrico, the following year. Tobias Hall, of Lancaster County, was awarded premiums in 1697 and 1698.[3] Thus it becomes clear that the legislation was really a factor in promoting, encouraging, and sustaining a certain type of manufacturing in the homes and on the plantations. After the Wool Act of 1699,[4] the influence of this factor ceased, and the maintaining of whatever beginnings that had been made up to this date was left to the operators of the household factory.[5]

[1] *Op. cit.*, p. 458, note.

[2] *Ibid.*, II, 463.

[3] *Ibid.*, p. 459.

[4] Cf. p. 25.

[5] The Carolinas were settled so late in the century that it seems best to omit them in this connection.

PROGRESS AFTER 1700

From 1700 to about 1766 is a well-marked period in the history of household manufactures in the colonies. During all these years, on the basis of the interest in, and the amount of, manufacturing done in the homes, two well-defined geographic divisions existed. These were the territory north of Maryland and that south of Pennsylvania, except the back-country in the South, which, during most of the period, was simply a projection of Pennsylvania; and Somerset County, Maryland, which was inhabited largely by Scotch-Irish. Conditions in each of these large divisions, thus designated, were so similar to about 1766 that one scarcely needs to specify the exact locality when speaking of household manufactures in either of them. The northern district, including the foregoing exceptions in the South, was often characterized as a region where the people were in the habit of manufacturing in their homes clothing and household fabrics for their own families,[1] while the southern section never gave the mother-country much concern as an industrial competitor. As hinted above, manufacturing in the homes and on the plantations in this region was practiced mainly when the exigencies of the times forced it upon the people.[2]

Of that division composed of the territory north of Maryland and the exceptions noted, New England was

[1] "Reports of the Lords of Trade and Plantation on the Condition of the Colonies in February, 1731/32," quoted by Macpherson, *Annals of Commerce*, III, 187.

[2] The effects of England's mercantile system and the economic conditions in these sections have been considered in chapter i, and should be recalled in this connection.

certainly the acknowledged leader in household manufacturing. Before 1766 this domestic industry had become so incorporated into the habits of the people of this region that its industrial importance escaped much special notice. Weeden thinks that written testimony does not indicate the large amount of homemade goods really produced by this diffused industry during the greater part of the eighteenth century.[1] The town histories, inventories, and reports on conditions at various times give some idea of the amount; but at best only rough estimates can be made from sources of such a general nature. Yet, in the absence of more explicit data, one is obliged to rely upon such material for a statement of the extent and amount of the articles manufactured in the family way in the various sections of the country at different times throughout much of the colonial period.

The effects of England's restrictive legislation began to be seen and felt in New England soon after the Wool Act of 1699. These effects were noted in the occasional reports of the king's officers in the colonies to the Board of Trade. In 1704 Brenton, the surveyor of customs in New England, reported that in a recent journey he made it his business to inform himself on the subject of sheep-raising, and found that in some towns where formerly there were not one hundred sheep kept, there would shortly be a thousand. He also found that Nantucket, Martha's Vineyard, and other adjacent islands which once supplied neighboring towns with wool were working up their own supply for wearing apparel in much greater quantities than

[1] *Op. cit.*, II, 679.

formerly, instead of selling it and purchasing a finer sort of woolen manufactures from England.[1] Two years later J. Bridger, who had charge of the king's masts in Maine, wrote to the Board of Trade that from December 3, 1705, to March 5, 1706, 155 dozens of wool cards had entered New England as well as a great quantity of wool combs.[2] In 1708 E. Bridger addressed a letter from Boston to the same body, in which he said: "The country people or planters are entered so far into the making of their own woollens, that not one in forty but wears his own carding, spinning, etc. If the growing trade of woollens be no way prevented in its growth, England must loose the woollen export to all this part of America."[3] Governor Dudley, of Massachusetts, reported the next year that the trade with England had greatly fallen off and that the people were clothing themselves with their own wool.[4] Ten years later J. Bridger wrote as follows, in answering a query of the Board of Trade:

I cannot omit giving your Honr an account of the Growth & Progress of the Woolen Manufacture in this Province. In a great many sorts, as Clothes, Serges, Shaloons, Kerseys, all sorts of Stuffs allmost and some Linnen and there is scarce a Country man comes to town or wooman but are clothed with their own Spinning. Every

[1] Cited by Lord, *op. cit.*, p. 129. It should be kept in mind that the reports of the governors and other officers to the Board of Trade were not always consistent. While one governor or officer exaggerated the amount of manufacturing done in the homes, another, through his sympathy with the colonists, minimized the extent of this sort of manufacturing. One must keep this fact constantly in mind when reading such reports and statements based on them.

[2] Felt, *Annals of Salem*, II, 160.

[3] *Ibid.*, p. 160.

[4] Cited by Lord, *op. cit.*, p. 131.

one Incourages the Growth and Manufacture of this Country and not one person but discourages the Trade from home, and says tis pitty any goods should be brought from England, they can live without them.[1]

It was also stated that much cotton was at this date imported from the Indies. The validity of this statement is attested by a report the next year (1720) by Armstrong, collector of customs for the district of New Hampshire. Speaking of his own district, he said that the woolen industry did not thrive so well as elsewhere, but that within three years about five hundred Irish families had settled in the province and had stimulated the inhabitants along the line of the linen-cloth industry. He asserted that the making of woolen fabrics in the other New England colonies had been brought to such perfection that thousands of pounds worth of stuffs and druggets were sold in the Boston shops.[2] Furthermore, in a report of the Lords Commissioners of Trade and Plantation, in 1721, on the state of the colonies, it was said of Massachusetts Bay: "In this Province there are all sorts of Common manufactures. The inhabitants have always worked up their own wool into coars Clothes, druggets and serges; but these, as well as their homespun linen, which is generally half cotton, serve only for the use of the meanest sort of people."[3]

In spite of the complicated bounty system that Parliament inaugurated in 1705 and attempted to administer during the next seventy years, the foregoing indicated increase of household manufactures in New England seems

[1] Baxter (editor), *Doc. Hist. of the State of Me.*, X, 122.

[2] Lord, *op. cit.*, p. 136.

[3] *Docs. Rel. Col. Hist. N.Y.*, V, 598.

to have been steadily maintained during the second quarter of the century.[1] This augmentation was not so much due, except in special instances, to the inclination of the people as to sheer necessity. Governor Dudley, of Massachusetts, testified to this fact when he said, in speaking of his people in 1709, that they were proud enough to wear the best cloths from England, if chopping, sawing, and building ships would pay for them.[2] Since they could not pay for the foreign goods by these or other methods, such commodities rapidly became, as the century increased, a luxury, enjoyed only by the well-to-do in the towns.

The considerable legislation relating to textile manufactures which was enacted, especially in Massachusetts, between 1700 and 1766 shows that the problem of supplying these necessities was continually a perplexing one.[3] It is also indicative of the increasing interest in the production of these fabrics. This increase was repeatedly called to the attention of the Board of Trade, and in February, 1731/32, through the pressure brought upon the House of Commons by the London merchants, led to an elaborate account of the trade carried on and the manufactures set up in the colonies detrimental to the trade and manufactures of Great Britain. This report was made by the Board of Trade to Parliament and resulted in the act forbidding the manufacture of hats in the colonies. Concerning household manufactures the report said:

[1] See pp. 21 ff. for a discussion of the bounty system and its relation to household manufactures.

[2] Lord, *op. cit.*, p. 132.

[3] See pp. 34 ff. for a discussion of this legislation.

In New England, New York, Connecticut, Rhode-island, Pennsylvania, and in the county of Somerset, in Maryland, they have fallen into the manufacture of woolen cloth and linen cloth, for the use of their own families only.

For the products of those colonies being chiefly cattle and grain, the estates of the inhabitants depends wholely on farming, which could not be managed without a certain quantity of sheep; and their wool would be entirely lost were not their servants employed during winter in manufacturing it for the use of their families.

Flax and hemp being likewise easily raised, the inhabitants manufactured them into a coarse sort of cloth, bags, traces, and halters, for their horses, which they found did more service than those they had from any part of Europe. However, the high price of labour in general in America rendered it impracticable for people there to manufacture their own linen cloth at less than 20 per cent more than the rate in England, or woolen cloth at less than 50 per cent dearer than that which is exported from hence for sale.[1]

The foregoing statement was based on communications from the governors, who described conditions in their several colonies. Governor Belcher said that the inhabitants of Massachusetts worked up their wool and flax into cloth for their own use, but did not export any. In New Hampshire the manufacture of flax into linen was daily increasing because of the recent resort thither of people from Ireland. In general, the governor felt that the people did not make over one-third of their clothing.[2]

[1] Quoted by Macpherson, *op. cit.*, III, 187. It should be noted that the high price of labor spoken of above helped to keep the manufacturing in the homes. No one could afford to compete with the English goods when labor had to be purchased to manufacture articles. But as long as the women and children could do most of the work and the men could assist them when they could do little else, there was some gain in the end. The household factory furnished a market for labor which otherwise would have been lost.

[2] *Ibid.*, pp. 189 f.

A little closer approach than that attained by means of the preceding general evidence is gained through the inventories of any given period. The presence of raw materials and implements used in connection with home manufacturing and the finished products of the home factory indicates that such an industry existed, even though its extent cannot be definitely determined from such a source. As an example of what some of the inventories covering a decade beginning with 1716 contain, a tabulation of typical ones from the records of Providence, Rhode Island, is given in Table V.

TABLE V

HOUSEHOLD MANUFACTURES IN PROVIDENCE, RHODE ISLAND, AS EXHIBITED BY RAW MATERIALS, IMPLEMENTS, AND FINISHED PRODUCTS LISTED IN INVENTORIES*

	Value of Articles Listed		
1. Obadiah Browne, 1716:			
Flax in sheaf	£ 1	0*s.*	0*d.*
Two linen wheels and an old woolen wheel	0	8	0
Hemp on stalk	0	18	0
Six pounds of dressed hemp	0	5	0
Six yards of linen cloth	0	12	0
Seventeen pounds of dressed flax	0	14	2
Thirteen yards of linen cloth	1	6	0
Nine yards of "Casy" cloth	2	5	0
One hatchel, some tow yarn, and a bunch of field hemp	0	9	6
Fourteen yards of linen cloth	1	6	0
White leather skin and calfskin	0	3	0
2. Jonathan Knight, 1717:			
Two spinning-wheels and chairs	0	11	0
Sheep's wool and new cloth	4	5	0
Two calfskins and shoe leather	0	7	0
Yarn, taglocks, and tow	0	17	4

* *Early Records of the Town of Providence, R.I.*, XVI, 1, 26, 88, 109, 137, 189, 217, 236, 323, 385, 463. Out of a total of ninety-one itemized inventories, seventy contained either materials, implements, or products relating to goods made in families.

TABLE V—*Continued*

	Value of Articles Listed		
3. John Paine, 1718:			
Leather	1	3	0
Ten pounds of woolen yarn, two pounds of cotton yarn	1	15	10
Sheep's wool	2	0	0
Worsted, twelve yards	1	12	0
One weaver's loom and five slays	2	0	0
Small bull's hide and four sheepskins	0	8	0
4. Ensign R. Waterman, 1719:			
Fifteen and one-half yards new linen cloth, and six yards new cotton and linen cloth	3	17	0
Table linen and new woolen cloth	4	15	6
Two spinning-wheels and one pair cards	0	19	0
Cider, beer, and apple-mill and cider-press	3	9	0
Two dressed deerskins	1	11	0
5. Stephen Arnold, 1720:			
Two woolen cards and one basket	0	11	0
Thirty-three yards woolen cloth	9	1	6
Ten yards tow cloth	1	0	0
Six yards woolen cloth and some linen cloth	2	7	0
Eleven yards worsted cloth	2	9	6
Fifteen yards osnaburg	2	10	0
6. Jonathan Whipple, 1721:			
Yarn and wool	1	0	0
One linen wheel	0	3	0
One woolen wheel	0	4	0
Leather	0	10	0
Flax	0	10	0
One hatchel, one and one-half calfskins	0	4	0
One cider-mill and press	1	0	0
7. Aleizer Arnold, 1722:			
Three "bits" of new cloth	1	17	4
Spinning-wheel and warming-pan	1	4	0
Twenty-seven and one-half pounds wool	2	0	0
One blanket, eight pounds of wool, and a bedcord†	0	15	0

† Such items as sheets, pillowcases, towels, tablecloths, napkins, coverlids, blankets, etc., were very numerous in the inventories. They have not been generally included in this list because they were not designated as homemade. In all probability most of them were.

TABLE V—*Continued*

	Value of Articles Listed		
8. Joanna Inman, 1723:			
A loom, quill wheel, and warping tackle	3	0	0
One and one-half yards woolen cloth and a bit of flannel	0	11	6
Six and one-half yards cotton and linen cloth	0	16	0
Seventeen yards worsted cloth	4	5	7
Two pairs of cards	0	8	0
Flax	0	4	0
Cotton wool	1	3	0
Sheep's wool	0	7	6
Linen wheel	0	6	0
One and one-half pair of worsted combs	1	5	0
9. Richard Borden, 1724:			
Four pounds woolen yarn and one pound linen yarn	0	14	0
Four yards cotton and linen cloth	0	14	0
Two yards tackling and three wheels, three pounds of combed wool	0	9	0
Ninety-two and three-fourths pounds sheep's wool	6	3	8
Flax and tow	0	4	0
Tanned leather	2	0	7
Three pairs of old cards	0	6	0
Cider-mill and cider-press	1	5	0
Nine barrels cider	5	1	4
Eight barrels apple beer	0	16	0
Fourteen and one-half pounds linen yarn	2	15	7
Five and one-fourth yards napkin cloth	0	13	0
10. Arthur Fenner, 1725:			
Thirty-eight yards new cloth	10	9	10
Two yards cloth and four and one-half pounds yarn	0	15	0
Flax	1	2	0
One pair worsted cards, and three pairs of cards	2	14	0
Fifteen pounds hemp	0	10	0
Sixteen yards new cloth	6	8	0
Four spinning-wheels and a clock reel	1	8	0
Eighteen pounds cotton wool	2	2	0
Sixty-six pounds sheep's wool	4	2	6
Two looms, with harness, slays, and warping bars	3	0	0
Tanned leather	3	8	0

TABLE V—*Continued*

	Value of Articles Listed		
11. Josiah Thornton, 1726:			
Woolen yarn	3	4	6
Thirteen pounds wool and thirty-four pounds flax	2	13	2
New cloth	5	16	0
Two spinning-wheels and two brooms	0	11	0
One barrel of cider and three empty barrels	0	16	3
Linen cloth and some table linen	0	15	0

Space will not permit a continuation of these interesting inventories. Some idea of what is included in the entire number can be gained from the following tabulation of their contents. In the 70 containing such items as the foregoing, spinning-wheels were mentioned 50 times; sheep's wool, 30; flax, dressed and undressed, 30; cards, 24; leather, 20; woolen yarn, 16; yarn (kind not designated), 14; loom and tackling, 9; linen cloth, 13; cotton cloth (kind not designated), 11; cotton wool and woolen cloth, 8 each; hatchel and worsted, 7 each; cotton yarn and hemp on stalk or dressed, 6 each; shoemakers' tools, combs, and cloth of cotton and linen, 5 each; tow, 4; cider-mill and press, reel, and cloth of cotton and wool, 3 each; tow yarn, homespun cloth, sheepskins, worsted combs, combed wool, 2 each; and coopering tools, weaver's shuttle, apple beer, cider, cotton tow, flax brake, quill wheel, tallow, cloth of wool and flax, tow cloth, warping tackle, and calfskin, 1 each.

Certain conclusions are obvious from this tabulation. The fact that a loom is listed in but nine inventories, while spinning-wheels appear in fifty, hints that most of the weaving must have been done by professional weavers.[1] It is

[1] The following are some interesting facts relative to spinning-wheels. In all, one hundred wheels were listed. Two, without any designation of the kind, were mentioned in 20 inventories; three, in 5; four and five, in

also clear that wool and flax were the raw materials in most common use, cotton appearing but 8 times. The appearance of leather 20 times and shoemaker's tools but 5 suggests the itinerant shoemaker. From the entire absence of candles one is led to conclude that candle-making in the home was not an industry at this time in Providence. And finally, the appearance of but three cider-mills and presses implies that cider-making was not a common industry during the time covered by the inventories.

The enthusiasm in New England for household manufactures at times expressed itself in the form of a modern "craze." Between 1700 and the breaking out of the Revolution there was going on in this region an economic revolution of which the mother-country seemed unaware. Some outward signs of this revolution were the periodic "spinning crazes" that swept over this section during these years. Such movements were responsible for originating and sustaining the emotional stimulus needed to keep the women busy at their wheels and looms and the men at making all sorts of necessary utensils during a time in which they were unable to secure the requisite medium of exchange to buy English manufactured goods. It was this region that felt most keenly the adverse effects of the mercantile system which the king and Parliament attempted to foist upon the colonies.

2 each; and one, in 7. Linen wheels were designated in 13 cases and woolen in 12, a total of 16 of the former and 13 of the latter. The mentioning of two wheels 20 times without designating the kind leads one to suspect that in most cases one was a linen and one was a woolen wheel. The appearance of raw wool and flax an equal number of times suggests the same thing.

The first "spinning craze" of any note occurred in Boston in 1721. The coming of the Scotch-Irish in August, 1718,[1] stimulated much interest in the raising of flax and the manufacture of linen cloth. So, on September 28, 1720, at a town meeting called especially to consider the question of spinning, a committee was appointed to "Consider abt promoting of a Spinning School or Schools, for the Instruction of the children of this town, in Spinning."[2] On the recommendation of this committee such a school was established, the selectmen appropriating £300 for the purpose.[3] To house it, a large building was erected on what was then Longacre Street; and on the occasion of its opening, the women, rich and poor, appeared on the Common with their wheels and vied with each other in their skill in using them.[4] While the school continued but three or four years, yet the interest stimulated by the movement did not die so soon. Ten years later (1731) one Daniel Oliver bequeathed to the town a large house valued at £600 to be used for a spinning school where poor children were to be taught gratis.[5]

Another "craze" spread over Boston and vicinity in 1753 and 1754. The interest in spinning manifested during these years was largely the result of work done by the

[1] Hanna, *Scotch-Irish*, II, 17.

[2] *Bost. Town Rec.* (1700–1728), p. 147.

[3] *Reç. of the Bost. Selectmen* (1716–36), p. 80.

[4] Drake, *Hist. and Antiq. of Bost.*, pp. 560 f.

[5] *Ibid.*, p. 591, note. Oliver was chairman of the committee to provide a spinning school. Bagnall thinks that the house he bequeathed to the town was one he had probably built for the school (*Textile Industries*, I, 19).

Boston Society for Promoting Industry and Employing the Poor, which was formed in 1751.[1] On the second anniversary of this society a public celebration was held. "In the afternoon about three hundred spinsters, cleanly dressed, appeared on the Common at their spinning-wheels. The wheels were placed regularly in three rows and a female was seated at each wheel. The weavers also appeared, cleanly dressed, in garments of their own weaving. One of them, working at a loom on a stage, was carried on men's shoulders, attended with music. An immense number of spectators was present at this interesting spectacle."[2] This enthusiasm bore fruit in the law of 1753 appropriating £1,500 to establish a spinning school in Boston, and a tax on coaches, chariots, etc., to raise this amount.[3] The school was established, but the interest in it was short-lived. Upon the breaking out of the war in 1754 the enthusiasm of the people for spinning was turned in another direction. The young ladies were now kept busy making garments for the men at the front. After the soldiers from Boston had been in the field four months, word of their suffering from want of clothing reached their friends. Immediately a number of young ladies volunteered their services to the town authorities, offering gratuitously to make garments for those engaged in their country's service.[4] The records indicate that these industrious ladies really made more homespun than was needed

[1] Bagnall, *op. cit.*, p. 35. This date is given as 1749 by Holmes, *Am. Annals*, II, 180, and in *Mem. Hist. of Bost.*, II, 462.

[2] Holmes, *op. cit.*, II, 196.

[3] Cf. pp. 35 ff.

[4] Drake, *op. cit.*, p. 639.

by their own people. In a cargo of goods sent from Boston to Albany, New York, in 1756, there appeared two hundred homemade jackets.[1] While local traffic in homespun had long been a common custom in many of the older New England towns,[2] the export business seems to have been a new venture.

The interest in the spinning school in Boston was revived in 1762. Notice was given this year that the school in the "Manufacturing House was again open and that any one could learn to spin gratis." After the first four months the spinners were to receive pay. A premium of £18 was also offered to the four best spinners.[3] This revived interest, however, was of short duration; for in 1767, in the midst of the rejoicing over the repeal of the Stamp Act, the building was ordered sold, since trade was reopened with England and the economic outlook seemed brighter.[4] But the rejoicing was brief, and ere long another "spinning craze" was on. This enthusiasm was the direct result of England's taxing measures and marks the beginning of an important era in the struggle for economic independence—but more of this in a subsequent section.

In order to substantiate the statement made above that the status of household manufactures was much the same during most of the colonial period in all of the territory north of Maryland, a brief presentation of conditions in the

[1] Weeden, *op. cit.*, II, 679.

[2] Judd, *Hist. of Hadley*, p. 359; also Temple, *Hist. of Whately*, p. 70.

[3] Drake, *op. cit.*, p. 660.

[4] *Ibid.*, p. 719.

middle colonies seems necessary. In 1708 Caleb Heathcote, then a member of the Council in New York, wrote to the Board of Trade that three-fourths of the linen and woolen goods used by the people were made among them, and that if some speedy and efficient way was not found to put a stop to it they would carry it on a great deal further, and perhaps in time to the prejudice of the goods manufactured in England.[1] Governor Hunter wrote in 1715, in answer to queries concerning the extent to which homespun was used, that the people in the cities of New York and Albany wore no clothing of their own manufacture, but that the planters and poorer sort were clothed by their own efforts and work, and that the few who could not afford English manufactures wore homespun. It was his belief that a law forcing the people to wear English-made goods would be equivalent to one compelling them to go naked, for goods sold at 100 per cent advance in New York over what they sold for in England. He had no knowledge that any homespun had every been sold in shops.[2] The general report submitted in February, 1731/32, to which reference has already been made, included all the middle region in the generalization regarding the amount of goods made in the homes. Subsequent reports attest the truth of the generalization. It was asserted of New York, in 1737, that the country people for many years had been making in their homes from flax and wool enough clothing to supply their needs.[3] Similar statements were made in reports dated January, 1746/47, and May, 1749.[4]

[1] *Docs. Rel. Col. Hist. N.Y.*, V, 63.

[2] *Ibid.*, p. 460.

[3] *Ibid.*, VI, 127.

[4] *Ibid.*, pp. 393, 511.

Conditions in the other middle colonies were not unlike those in New York. In 1728 Governor William Keith, of New Jersey, wrote that "every Farmer is by Industry led to employ his spare time in working up the wool of the few sheep he is obliged to keep on his Farm, for the Improvement of his Land, for the use of his Family, and in like manner he often Raises a small Quantity of Flax, which is broke or dress'd commonly in the Winter Season, and Spun up into Course Cloth by the old Women and children, for the same use."[1] Acrelius, writing of conditions in Delaware from about 1725 to 1758, said: "The articles of dress are very little different among the city and country people, except that the former procure them from merchants' shops, and the latter make them for themselves, and usually of coarser stuff. Wool-, weaving-, and fulling-mills are not used for manufacturing broadcloth, camelot, and other woolen cloths, which might be finer, if more carefully attended to. The coloring of certain stuffs is very inferior. Silks are rare even in the towns. Plush is general, and satin is very widely used all over the country."[2] Referring chiefly to Pennsylvania, Douglas, in 1753, said that perhaps the farmers made nine-tenths of all their wearing apparel.[3] Of the Dutch he remarked: "Most of the Dutch Husband-men have Stills, and draw a Spirit from Rye malted, from Apples and Peaches. There may be from 7,000 to 8,000 Dutch Waggons with four Horses each, that from Time to Time bring their Pro-

[1] *N.J. Archives*, 1st ser., V, 203 f.

[2] *Hist. of New Sweden* (ed. 1759, Eng. tr. Reynolds, 1874), p. 157.

[3] *A Summary, Historical and Political* (ed. 1753), II, 332.

duce and Traffick to Philadelphia, from 10 to 100 Miles Distance."[1]

One has an indirect check on the foregoing general statements in certain facts revealed in the notices of runaway servants and slaves appearing in the newspapers of

TABLE VI

CLOTHING WORN BY RUNAWAY SERVANTS AND SLAVES IN NEW JERSEY, 1704–79*

Years	No. of Cases		Part of Clothing Designated as Homemade		None of Clothing Designated as Homemade		Clothing Made of Buckskin, Leather, Bearskin		Osnaburg		Linsey-Woolsey	
	Servants	Slaves	Servants	Slaves	Servants	Slaves	Servants	Slaves	Servants	Slaves	Servants	Slaves
1704–39	89	8	50	5	39	3	32	2	25	1	8	0
1740–50	129	18	49	2	80	16	35	1	45	5	3	3
1751–55	120	23	30	10	91	13	55	9	37	6	4	2
1755–61	34	15	5	0	29	15	15	5	8	1	0	0
1762–65	80	22	13	4	67	18	30	9	17	7	3	0
1766–67	43	23	12	9	31	14	9	5	13	3	1	0
1768–69	61	24	14	6	47	18	15	6	15	3	0	0
1770–71	61	14	14	4	47	10	26	7	7	2	1	0
1776–77	44	14	15	3	29	11	12	4	7	0	0	0
1778	5	14	2	6	3	8	2	4	1	3	0	0
1779	7	14	2	3	5	11	3	8	1	0	0	0
Totals	673	189	206	52	468	137	234	60	176	31	20	5

* A few cases of apprentices are included with the servants. The table is based on 863 notices of runaway slaves and servants. These notices are published in *N.J. Archives*, 1st ser., Vols. XI, XII, XX, XXIV, XXV, XXVI, XXVII, and 2d ser., Vols. I, II, III, IV. No data were given in the extracts for the years 1771–76.

the period to which such statements relate. These advertisements usually gave in considerable detail a description of the clothing worn by the fugitives. Table VI exhibits

[1] *Ibid.*, p. 333.

facts revealed by 863 announcements of runaway servants and slaves in the New Jersey colony during seventy years of its history.

Counting the sum of all cases in each of the eleven different periods included in Table VI, the percentage of cases for each in the order given in which a part of the clothing was specifically designated as homespun is as follows: 57, 34, 28, 10, 17, 32, 24, 24, 31, 42, and 24; for the entire period covered by all cases, 30 per cent. If to the number of cases in which homespun was specified there were added those in the last three columns, all of which could have been made in the home, these percentages would be considerably increased. Since such items are not clear cases, they will be left to tell their own story. The indisputable ones show that quite a considerable amount of the apparel of servants and slaves in colonial New Jersey must have been homemade.

The discussion of household manufactures in the South during the period under consideration will be prefaced by a brief treatment of the same subject in the back-country of this section. Such a statement will serve as an admirable transfer from our lengthy canvass of the northern section where household manufacturing was more or less permanent, to the southern, where it was sporadic. These back-country districts were southern only in location. In respect to the status of home industries, as well as other phases of their industrial life, they were strictly northern—a fact which must always be kept in mind in thinking of the southern colonies during much of their history.

The filling up of the back-country in the South with Germans and Scotch-Irish during the second quarter of the eighteenth century greatly diversified the general economic life of the section as a whole.[1] These people were small farmers. On account of their remoteness from the coast, their lack of facilities to market their crops, and the traditions they brought with them, they turned their attention to household manufacturing from the beginning of their settlement. In fact, for many years they were almost economically independent of the outside world. They raised their wool, cotton, flax, hemp, and hides, and made them into clothing, shoes, and harness. Their mines, mills, and forges supplied them with utensils and implements, which were usually made by the farmers themselves. Speaking of the pioneer settlers who came into Rockingham County, Virginia, between 1730 and 1750, a careful writer says: "When the pioneer settlers came to Rockingham County from 1730 to 1750 to make their homes, one of the first machines they set up was the old loom. It found its abiding place in one of the rooms of the main house or in a shed attached to the house; sometimes in the attic; and often a house was built especially for the loom."[2] Doddridge, whose father was one of the pioneer settlers of Washington County, Pennsylvania, where conditions were similar to those in western Virginia, informs us that the clothing was practically all of household manufacture

[1] See Faust, *German Element in U.S.*, I, chaps. ii., vi, vii, viii; also Hanna, *Scotch-Irish*, II, chap. ii.

[2] Heatwole, "Hand-Weaving in Rockingham County, Va."; Wayland, *Hist. of Rockingham Co., Va.*, p. 381.

and that every house contained a loom and almost every woman was a weaver. From him we also learn that practically every family had its tailors and its shoemakers and that both shoes and shoepacks were made, the latter by those who could not make the former. In almost every household hominy blocks and handmills were in use. With the mortar and pestle, handmill or grater, these early settlers pounded, ground, or grated their corn so that it could be made into mush or cakes. Besides the immediate necessities of life, plows, harrows, sleds, cooper-ware, cedar-ware, and looms were made.[1] All these were manufactured on the farms, since few persons in the early stages of the settlements could make a living by depending solely upon any one of the mechanic arts. Under such a régime men became mechanical geniuses of the highest order. Doddridge's father was one of these. He was an expert on the loom of his own construction; spun his own shoethread; made all the shoes for the family; made his own cooperware; did his own carpentering; and during his later life, when unable for service on the scouts and campaigns, did the rifle repairing for the whole neighborhood.[2] This régime remained thus in the newer settlements throughout the eighteenth century.

It has already been suggested that the southern colonies (the back-country excepted) never gave the mother-country much concern regarding the working out of her mercantile policy. They were content to have supplies of all kinds from England in return for their tobacco, tar, pitch, rice,

[1] Doddridge, *Notes* (ed. 1912), pp. 110 ff.

[2] *Ibid.*, p. 114.

indigo, flax, hemp, silk, wool, and leather. The reliance upon the outside world for clothing and other supplies was so great that much suffering ensued among them when this supply was temporarily cut off. Of this dependence, Beverly, speaking of Virginia about 1703, remarked:

> They have their Cloathing of all sorts from England, as Linnen, Woolen, Silk, Hats, and Leather. Yet Flax, and Hemp grow no where in the World, better than there; their Sheep yield a mighty Increase, and bear good Fleeces, but they shear them only to cool them. . . . . The very Furrs that their Hats are made of, perhaps go first from thence; and most of their Hides lie and rot, or are made use of, only for covering dry Goods, in a leaky House. Indeed some few Hides with much adue are tann'd, and made into Servant's Shoes; but at so careless a rate, that the Planters don't care to buy them, if they can get others; and sometimes perhaps a better manager than ordinary, will vouchsafe to make a pair of Breeches of a Deer-Skin. Nay, they are such abominable Ill-husbands, that tho' their Country be overrun with Wood, yet they have all their Wooden-Ware from England; their Cabinets, Chairs, Tables, Stools, Chests, Boxes, Cart-Wheels, and all other things, even so much as the Bowls, and Birchen Brooms, to the Eternal Reproach of their Laziness.[1]

While Beverly's account is doubtless an exaggerated one, yet the people as a general rule did not engage in household or plantation manufacturing to any considerable extent unless forced to do so by an inadequate supply of goods, caused by certain economic conditions over which they had no control. For example, it was said of Virginia in 1705: "The quantity of Goods and especially of Cloathing imported of late, not being sufficient for supplying the Country, Many of the Inhabitants, ... have this last

[1] *Hist. of the Present State of Va.* (1st ed., 1705), Book IV, Part II, p. 58.

year, planted a considerable quantity of Cotton."[1] Reference has already been made to the picture of conditions in Virginia in 1710 given by Governor Spotswood.[2] Even as early as 1697 the Council of Maryland reported to the Board of Trade that necessity had taught some of the inhabitants to use the native wool for coarse stockings and clothing for servants and slaves.[3] In petitioning the Board for relief in 1713 the Council said that, "had not many people Applyed themselves to Spinning the little wooll their Small fflocks of Sheep afford, and likewise some Small Quantitys of Flax, they would have Suffered very much for want of Necessary Cloathing."[4] The next year it was reported that many of the people were stark naked, which occasioned them to turn their hands to the manufacture of linen and woolen cloth.[5] These citations substantiate the statement that whatever manufacturing was done in the homes and on the plantations in the region under discussion was done more from necessity than from inclination—a fact truer of this section up to 1766 than any of those heretofore treated.

While household manufacturing was not an important element in the life and prosperity of the people in this southern region under discussion, yet there was some going on in the more or less remote districts between 1700 and 1766. Evidence of this is found in statements of contemporary writers. Lawson, speaking of North Carolina about 1714, said: "The women are the most Industrious Sex

[1] Cited by Morriss, *op. cit.*, p. 64.

[2] Cf. pp. 49 ff.

[3] *Archives of Md.*, XIX, 540.

[4] Morriss, *op. cit.*, p. 71.

[5] *Ibid.*, p. 65.

in that place, and by their good Housewifry, make a good deal of Cloath of their own cotton, Wool, and Flax; some of them keeping their families (though large) very decently apparel'd, both with linnens and Woolens, so that they have no occasion to run into the Merchant's debt or lay their money out on stores for cloathing.[1] Similar conditions still existed in 1728 in this colony. Describing the state of affairs as he saw it at this date while surveying the "dividing-line" between North Carolina and Virginia, William Byrd commented as follows on what he observed on Timothy Ivy's plantation:

> We saw no Drones there, which are but too Common, alas, in that Part of the World. Tho', in truth, the Distemper of Laziness seizes the Men oftener much than the Women. These last Spin, weave, and knit, all with their own Hands, while their Husbands, depending on the Bounty of the Climate, are Sloathful in everything but getting of Children, and in that only Instance make themselves useful Members of an Infant-Colony.
>
> There is but little wool in that Province, tho' Cotton grows very kindly, and, so far South, is Seldom nippt by the Frost. The Good Women mix this with their Wool for their outer Garments; tho', for want of Fulling, that kind of manufacture is Open and Sleazy.[2]

It is not the aim, in citing such sources, to leave the impression that manufacturing was carried on in the homes of this southern seaboard region to any considerable extent

[1] *Hist. of N.C.* (reprint of ed. 1714, Charlotte, N.C., 1903), p. 47. Lawson made extensive travels in North and South Carolina before writing his history. He had the opportunity of gaining first-hand knowledge. He was general surveyor of North Carolina when he gathered the material for his book.

[2] Bassett (editor), *Writings of Col. William Byrd*, p. 56.

before 1766. In fact, the evidence leads one to conclude that the amount generally done was rather inconsiderable. A few citations will substantiate this statement.

A report on Maryland in 1721 said: "The Inhabitants wear the like Cloathing and have the same furniture within their houses with those in this Kingdom. The slaves are cloathed with Cottons, Kerseys, flannels, & coarse linnens, all imported; & it is computed that this province consumes of British Manufactures to the value of £20,000 per annum."[1] In commenting on industrial conditions in Virginia in 1759 as he noted them on traveling through the colony, Burnaby remarked: "Their manufactures are very inconsiderable. They make a kind of cotton cloth which they clothe themselves with in common, and call it after the name of their country; and some inconsiderable quantities of linen, hose, and other trifling articles; but nothing to deserve attention."[2] It was said of South Carolina in 1760 that cloths, broad and narrow of all sorts, from the finest broadcloth down to negro-cloth, came from without, none having been manufactured there except a little negro-cloth and that only when the produce of the province bore but a low price. Small quantities of linen were imported from the vicinity of Williamsburg, Virginia. It was made by the Scotch-Irish living there.[3] As early as 1740 Georgia was making a few stockings from the native

[1] *Docs. Rel. Col. Hist. N.Y.*, V, 606.

[2] *Travels through the Middle Settlements in N.A.* (2d ed., London, 1775), p. 21.

[3] *A Description of S.C.* (London, 1761), attributed to Governor James Glen. See also Carroll, *Hist. Colls. of S.C.*, II.

cotton, but depended upon the outside world for the greater part of her supplies.[1] Some of these came from Frederick, Maryland, where a band of Germans from the Palatinate had settled in 1749. These people carried on a rather extensive trade with the people of Georgia, sending them boots, shoes, saddles, all kinds of harness, fine woolen goods, sheetings and table linen, counterpanes, made of flax and woolen thread.[2] Thus, except in specific localities where a group of Quakers, Germans, or Scotch-Irish had settled, no consistent policy of household manufacturing was followed in the low-country districts of the South before the agitation caused by the Stamp Act and the other taxing measures following it.

An excellent summary of the status of household manufactures in the various sections of the country during the last half of the period under discussion is contained in certain reports made to the Lords of Trade by the colonial governors on the general state and progress of manufactures in their respective jurisdictions. On August 1, 1766, letters were addressed to all the colonial governors demanding a report on the manufactures set up and carried on in the colonies since 1734.[3] A second copy of the letter was

[1] *Col. Rec. of Ga.*, V, 443.

[2] Tyson, "A Brief Account of the Settlement of Ellicott's Mills," *Md. Hist. Soc. Pubs.*, I–VI, No. 4, p. 55.

[3] These reports seem to overlap the discussion given in the opening of the following section. It should be kept in mind that the governors were reporting on conditions since 1734. Furthermore, the climax of the boycotting of English goods did not come until 1768, hence the full effects of the factors mentioned below were not yet felt when the reports were made.

sent out in February, 1768, with the injunction to furnish the required information made even stronger than in the first copy.[1] Governor Wentworth, of New Hampshire, in response to these circulars, reported that in his jurisdiction there were manufactured annually from native flax 25,000 yards of linen, which freely sold for 37 cents a yard. This was from 20 to 40 per cent higher than the price of corresponding imported linen. In the farmers' families much native wool was also manufactured, and nearly enough saddles were made to supply the home demand.[2]

Since a report made in 1763 by Governor Bernard, of Massachusetts, contained about all there was to say concerning manufactures in his colony, there was little need for an elaborate account in 1768. At the former date the governor reported:

> The inhabitants of the trading towns, men, women, children, have their whole supply of clothing from Great Britain. Most of the women in all other towns have the principal part of their clothing of British manufacture; the men have more or less. The poor laboring people in the country towns wear their own common clothes principally of coarse homespun linens and woolens. Shoes are to be excepted, the men's being generally made here, the women's partly only. Most of the furniture of the houses in the trading towns is of British manufacture. Nails, glass, lead, locks, hinges, and many other materials for houses are wholly imported from Great Britain. Canvas, cordage, ship chandlery wares for vessels and in general such manufactures as are exported to the plantations are consumed here, and by the best information I can get the consumption increases rather than decreases.[3]

[1] Clark, *Hist. of Manufactures in the U.S.*, p. 207.

[2] *Ibid.*

[3] Quoted *ibid.*, pp. 207 f.

Governor William Pitkin, of Connecticut, on December 5, 1766, wrote to the Board, in answer to the inquiry concerning the several manufactures set up and carried on in his colony, in part as follows:

There are in sundry Towns in this Colony some small Buildings erected for the manufacture of Ashes, for making Pot Ash, and this by Ashes almost entirely collected from the House Hearths of the inhabitants. . . . . The Inhabitants of this Colony are chiefly Employed in subduing and Improving Land, do nothing more at the Woolen & Linen Manufactures than to supply the Deficiencies of what our produce Enables us to purchase of Great Britain, and what is wrought of that Kind, is principally of the Courser Sort for Laborers & Servants which is done by particular Families for their Necessary use.[1]

Governor Moore, of New York, reporting on January 12, 1767, portrayed conditions in his province in language as follows:

The custom of making these coarse cloths [woolen and linsey-woolsey] in private families prevails throughout the whole Province, and in almost every House a sufficient quantity is manufactured for the use of the Family, without the least design of sending any of it to market. This I had an opportunity of seeing during the late Tour I made, and had the same Accounts given me by all those persons, of whom I made any inquiry, for every home swarms with children, who are set to work as soon as they are able to Spin and card; and as every family is furnished with a Loom, the Itinerant Weavers who travel about the Country, put the finishing hand to the work.[2]

[1] *Board of Trade Papers*, "Proprieties," XXII, 129; transcript in *Hist. Soc. Pa. Library*. The report of the governor of Rhode Island made no mention of household manufactures (Clark, *op. cit.*, p. 208).

[2] *Docs. Rel. Col. Hist. N.Y.*, VII, 888.

Deputy Governor Penn, of Pennsylvania, made no mention of household manufactures in his report.[1] Governor Franklin, of New Jersey, answered as follows:

> As to Manufactures in this Colony, I can assure your Lordship [Earl of Hillsborough] that there are none either of woolen or Linen which deserve to be call'd by that Name. It is true that many Families who live on Farms make some coarse Cloathing for themselves or Servants, but it is by no means sufficient for their consumption.[2]

These statements indicate that the people of New York in about 1767 were very active in making goods in their homes, while in the other colonies reporting there was nothing unusual about such manufacturing. People were engaging in it as an industry from which there was no escape, because of their inability to secure such articles from other sources. Such was also true of the people in Maryland, as evidenced by Governor Sharpe's report in 1768, which contained the following paragraph relative to household manufactures:

> A great many Families however throughout the Province make both Linen & Woolen Cloathing for their own use, & in order to encourage the making Linen Acts of the Assembly have from time to time been made granting Bounties to those Persons that annually produce to the several County Courts the Best Pieces of Linen manufactured by White inhabitants in the respective Counties. The Act under which Bounties are now paid was made three years ago & is to continue in force till the year 1770, but it is not supposed to have any great Effect nor do I apprehend that the Inhabitants will think much of Manufacturing for themselves while they can with the produce of their Lands purchase such Goods as they may have occasion for.[3]

[1] *Pa. Archives*, 4th ser., III, 332.

[2] *N.J. Archives*, 1st ser., X, 30.

[3] *Archives of Md.*, XIV, 496 f.

The conditions in parts of North Carolina were much similar to those in Maryland. Governor Tryon's report, dated January 30, 1767, contained the following on the subject:

> There are dispersed over this colony more particularly in the northern and western settlements some spinning wheels and looms for the manufacture of cotton, wool and flax, but no greater quantities of stuffs or coarse cloths are made than will supply the respective families in which they are worked; very few indeed make sufficient for their own wear. I have not heard of a piece of woolen or linnen cloth being ever sold that was the manufacture of this province. It is the usage of some families who from poverty or other circumstances have no looms, to send their woolen and linnen yarn to their neighbours to weave. Sheep are not yet become a staple of this country tho' they thrive well here; the wool therefore being very inconsiderable in quantity, is generally mixed with cotton in the manufacture.[1]

Governor Wright, of Georgia, on November 18, 1766, wrote:

> Some few of the poorer and more industrious people make a trifling quantity of coarse homespun cloth for their own families, and knit a few cotton and yarn stockings for their own use, and this done but by a very few, and I don't know that there is or has been a yard of linen cloth of any kind manufactured in this province.[2]

These official reports[3] warrant the general conclusion that, long before the breaking out of the excitement caused

[1] *Col. Rec. of N.C.*, VII, 429.

[2] Quoted by Jones, *Hist. of Ga.*, II, 24. Original in *Marquis of Lansdowne's Colls. Answers to Am. Cir.*, Vol. LV.

[3] There seems to be no good reason for questioning the reliability of the foregoing reports. Household manufacturing was not against any English law or regulation, and the Board of Trade had gone on record as opposing

by the Stamp Act controversy, household manufacturing was a common industry among the country people and was carried on not so much from desire as from necessity. In some instances families made enough for their own use and no more. Homemade goods were rarely exported or sold in shops, especially outside of New England. The household manufactures reported in the district south of Maryland were carried on principally in the back-country, which was settled by people more or less mechanically inclined.

NEW INFLUENCES AND TENDENCIES

Of all the factors affecting household manufactures during the colonial period, the political controversies following 1765, and the Revolution in which these culminated, were the two most potent ones. Up to the beginning of the Stamp Act controversy and the non-importation, non-exportation, and non-consumption agreements growing out of it and subsequent events, household manufactures were local. By this is meant that they were carried on in certain localities where the economic status required such a supplement to the other regular labors, or merely as a temporary relief from an inadequate supply of foreign goods, or from a dull or obstructed market for certain

any restrictions upon it other than those contained in the act of 1699. While a governor might have colored his report favorably or unfavorably to his colony in regard to manufactures carried on contrary to the laws of England, there was seemingly no reason why he should fail to report conditions just as they existed in respect to family manufactures. Of course one governor might have reported conditions in milder terms than another. The report from Connecticut seems to have been one of the more moderate ones.

staple products. But along with, and in consequence of, the disputes over the right of England to tax the colonies came the generalizing of an industry which had heretofore been both local and sporadic. There arose out of this controversy a definite notion among the colonies as a whole that closely connected with political was economic independence. This belief led the people, north and south alike, to rely mainly upon the home factory to establish this industrial self-sufficiency, since no adequate system of factory manufacturing had been permitted to grow up under England's restrictive colonial policy.

The trouble caused by the Stamp Act created both a desire for American goods and a determination to use no other. This determination found expression in the non-importation, non-consumption, and non-exportation resolutions discussed in chapter ii. These resolves were the tools used by the radical element to carry out a growing desire for economic independence as well as to bring the influence of the English merchants to bear in their favor against laws of a similar nature. Now, to carry out measures so radical and that demanded so much sacrifice on the part of so many, required considerable pressure from various sources. Much of the social pressure, especially in New England, was furnished by the Daughters of Liberty, a society whose members pledged themselves not to buy goods from British importers and shopkeepers.[1] This society had organizations in many sections of New England

[1] Jameson says that this society was formed in Boston in 1769–70 (*Dict. of U.S. Hist.*, p. 185). The society certainly existed before this date, for the meeting, an account of which is given on p. 106, was held in March, 1766.

and did effective work in creating sentiment in favor of the production and consumption of American rather than English goods.

The effective tool for crystallizing sentiment in favor of homemade goods used by the Daughters of Liberty was the "spinning bee." While this was not a new form of social gathering in New England, yet it was probably used at this particular time more generally and more effectively than ever before. From early in 1766 to about 1771 "spinning bees" were the rage in this region. On March 4, 1766, one of these revived gatherings was held in Providence, Rhode Island. The spirit displayed by the women who attended the meeting was vividly portrayed by the author of the following account, which appeared in the *Boston Chronicle*, April 7, 1766:

> On the 4th instant, *eighteen daughters of liberty*, young ladies of good reputation, assembled at the house of doctor *Ephraim Bowen*, in this town, in consequence of an invitation of that gentleman, who had discovered a laudable zeal for the introducing *Home Manufactures*. There they exhibited a fine example of industry, by spinning from sunrise until dark, and displayed a spirit for saving their sinking country, rarely to be found among persons of more age and experience.[1]

The next assemblage of the society was held in the courthouse, when a handsome piece of linen was made and given as a premium for the largest amount of flax raised in Providence County during the year.[2] Similar gatherings were held in other parts of New England. For example,

[1] The communication was dated March 12, 1766; quoted in *Niles' Register*, XXXIX, 195.

[2] Arnold, *Hist. of R.I.*, II, 266.

forty-five young women met at the house of Rev. Samuel Webster, of Salisbury, on August 17, 1767, and spun from about five o'clock in the morning until five in the afternoon. They carded and spun over 101 single skeins of cotton yarn and 100 of linen.[1] The ladies of Byfield were likewise busy with their wheels. In August, 1768, they met, twenty-five strong, at the minister's home, where they carded and spun twenty double skeins of cotton yarn and sixty of linen, each skein containing forty threads two yards long to a knot.[2] On April 20, 1768, twenty-five ladies of Newbury assembled at the home of Rev. Mr. Parsons and spun 270 skeins of good yarn.[3] As late as May 21, 1770, the following account appeared in the *Boston Gazette:* "Last Wednesday forty-five Daughters of Liberty met in the morning at the house of the Rev. Mr. Moorehead in this town; and in the afternoon they exceeded fifty. By the evening of said day they spun two hundred and thirty-two skeins of yarn—some very fine. Their labors and materials were all generously given to the worthy pastor. . . . . [4]

[1] *Essex Gazette*, August 22–29, 1769; quoted in *Essex Antiquarian*, XII, 57.

[2] *Essex Gazette*, August 23, 1768; quoted in *Essex Antiquarian*, I, 51. Similar gatherings in other towns of Essex County were reported in the *Gazette*, December 20–27, 1768, and August 15–22, 1769 (quoted in *Essex Antiquarian*, IV, 38, and XII, 40). *The Boston News Letter* of June 22 and July 6, 1769, contained reports of spinning bees at Rowley, Ipswich, and Beverly. These are quoted by Bagnall, *op. cit.*, p. 58.

[3] Coffin, *Hist. of Newbury*, p. 234.

[4] Quoted in *Mem. Hist. of Bost.*, III, 150. Besides the general enthusiasm produced by the "spinning bees" and "matches," the minister often preached a sermon to the ladies in which he admonished them to cast aside

The result of all this agitation is seen in the actual output of some of the homes. In 1767 a small country town in Massachusetts manufactured 30,000 yards of cloth.[1] Ebenezer Hurd, of Saybrook, Connecticut, made in the same year, by the help of his wife and children, 500 yards of linen and woolen cloth, the whole from flax of his own raising.[2] From 500 to 700 yards of cloth in a year were made by families in Newport, Rhode Island.[3] In generalizing on the effects of these social gatherings upon the production of textile fabrics for ordinary clothing, Weeden says: "These impressed the popular mind exceedingly, and turned the skill and industry of the women of all classes to the production of cloth as a domestic business. This social movement was so effective that it ceased to be a matter of record. The people were now clothed in their own garments as naturally as they were fed by their own Indian corn."[4]

the English goods for the product of their own hands. Sometimes an enthusiast would clothe his appeal in poetical language. In the *Massachusetts Gazette* of November 9, 1767, may be found the following lines (cited by Crawford, *Soc. Life in Old N. Eng.*, p. 268; also Bagnall, *op. cit.*, p. 57):

Young ladies in town and those that live round
  Let a friend at this season advise you.
Since money's so scarce and times growing worse,
  Strange things may soon hap and surprise you.
First then throw aside your high top knots of pride,
  Wear none but your own country linen.
Of economy boast. Let your pride be the most
  To show cloaths of your own make and spinning.

[1] *Bost. Eve. Post*, November 2, 1767; cited by Weeden, *op. cit.*, II, 732.

[2] *Bost. News Let.*, January 7, 1768; Weeden, *op. cit.*, 733.

[3] *Bost. News Let.*, January 21, 1768; Weeden, *op. cit.*, 732.

[4] *Op. cit.*, II, 789.

This outward opposition to English manufactures and the movement to encourage the production and use of homemade goods were by no means confined to New England. Since the colonies were practically a unit in opposing the Stamp and other acts of Parliament, there followed a similar unity in resisting them. While efforts equally strenuous as those in New England were not put forth in all of the colonies, yet there is evidence that the problem of encouraging the production of goods in the home was not entirely neglected. Soon after the passage of the Stamp Act a market was established in Philadelphia for the sale of home-manufactured goods. This market was kept open from nine o'clock until noon every Monday, Wednesday, and Saturday.[1] The people of New Jersey were none behind their neighbors. As evidence of this, the following is cited from the *New York Journal*, January 21, 1768: "As a further Specimen of the Practicability of manufacturing our own clothes in this Country, we can assure the Public of the following Persons in Woodbridge in New Jersey, making in their respective Families, within the Year past, both Woolen and Linen of their own raising, the quantities following, viz. Mr. Isaac Freeman, 599 Yards, Mr. James Smith, 567 Yards, and Mr. Nathaniel Heard, 414 Yards."[2] Even South Carolina fell into line with her northern sister colonies. A news letter from Charleston, dated November, 1768, and printed in the *Boston Chronicle*, December 5–12, 1768, said in part: "We are informed, the quantity of Hemp made last year is nearly

[1] Scharf and Westcott, *op. cit.*, III, 2227.

[2] *N.J. Archives*, 1st ser., XXVI, "Newspaper Extracts," VII, 16.

double this; that the inhabitants now manufacture most of their linens (such as cost in England from 12 to 18*d.* a yard) Linsey-Woolsey, and even coarse cloths."[1]

Virginia's response to the movement to encourage the production and consumption of homemade goods is well illustrated by the spinning and weaving operations on Washington's plantation, where they were carried on in a house built especially for the purpose. An idea of what was done in this establishment[2] is gained from an account of the output for the years 1767 and 1768. In the former year weaving was done for twenty-eight different individuals living in the neighborhood. The returns for this work amounted to £18 8*s.* 6*d.*; the weaving for the plantation this same year totaled £38 2*s.* 7*d.*, making £56 11*s.* 1*d.* for the year's output. The number of yards woven for the use of the plantation was 1,059, for the neighbors, 499, total, 1,558 yards. The cloth fabricated consisted of striped, plaided, and plain woolen, linsey-woolsey, striped and plain cotton, and plain linen.[3] During the year 1768 the establishment put out 1,355½ yards of linsey-woolsey and linen. The weaving of this amount totaled £30 15*s.* 10*d.* rated at the customary prices.[4] According to

[1] Commons (editor), *Doc. Hist. of Am. Indust. Soc.*, II, 274.

[2] This establishment with its equipment is still (1917) to be seen at Mount Vernon. The writer was much disappointed in its size when he saw it for the first time in February, 1914. From the accounts he had read of the work carried on in it he expected to see quite an establishment, instead of a little, low building of rather small dimensions.

[3] "Record of the Operations in George Washington's Weaving Establishment for the Year 1767," in Commons, *op. cit.*, II, 322.

[4] These rates were: for woolens, the price averaged 5½*d.* a yard; for cotton, 14 7/10*d.*; for linsey, 5*d.*; and for linen, 4 8/10*d.* (*ibid.*, II, 324).

Washington's somewhat ambiguous bookkeeping his establishment was run on a losing basis. The output for the year 1767–68 could have been imported at a total cost of £105 7*s*. 3*d*. The raw material necessary to make the cloth that this amount would buy and the weaving of it amounted to £76 15*s*. 4*d*., leaving but £28 11*s*. 11*d*. for the expense of the spinning, which in this case consisted of the hire of one white woman and of the boarding and clothing of five negro girls.[1] Even though it was run at a loss, as no doubt were those on many other plantations, the years of controversy with England over taxation and the war that followed made necessary an increase, regardless of cost, of the output of all such establishments.[2]

The boycott of the English goods during the year 1768–69 in the territory north of Maryland was of short duration. The very next year imports returned to their normal condition, and in the year 1771–72 they reached a value, in all the colonies but New York, never before equaled.[3] During the next two years they returned to a little above normal,

[1] "Summary by Washington of the operations of his weavers in the year 1768," *ibid*., II, 324.

[2] It would certainly be wrong to conclude that the sentiment in the South against the use of English goods was as strong as it was in the North. The table of imports from Great Britain for the years 1767–68 and 1768–69 cited in chap. ii clearly shows that, while there was a considerable decline in the imports into the territory north of Maryland during the latter year, there was also a slight increase in all the territory south of Pennsylvania. In fact, the boycott of English goods did not become effective in North and South Carolina, Maryland, and Virginia until 1774–75, and not until 1775–76 in Georgia (see Table II).

[3] Macpherson, *op. cit*., III, 508, 533.

and not until 1774–75 did another falling off occur. What happened after this date is shown by the tables in chapter ii.[1]

Certain facts exhibited by these tables should be recalled before entering the period of the Revolution proper. They are: (1) that the people of New England, Pennsylvania, Maryland, and Virginia were almost completely cut off from the English supply of goods during the war; (2) that New York, beginning with the year 1779, had almost a normal supply, and that the supply was entirely cut off but one year, Christmas, 1775, to Christmas, 1776; (3) that the Carolinas and Georgia, after Christmas, 1779, had almost a normal supply during the remainder of the war, except Georgia in 1782.

There is little danger of exaggerating the amount of manufacturing done in the homes and on the plantations during the first three or four years of the Revolutionary War. Bishop estimates that the household industry in New England and some parts of the middle colonies was nearly or quite equal to the ordinary wants of the inhabitants for clothing.[2] The patriotic sentiment which expressed itself in the making and wearing of homemade goods during the decade beginning in 1765 prepared the people for the real emergency which came with the sudden stoppage of a large supply of English goods that they had previously depended upon. Long before the actual cutting off of this supply the family textile manufactures had come to be a positive factor in the common life and prosperity of the people in New England, the middle colonies, and in the back-country of the South. In the absence of adequate

[1] Pp. 58 f.

[2] *Op. cit.*, I, 390.

textile manufacturing establishments, the homes were the main reliance for this type of goods until the privateers began to bring in their rich prizes and trade relations were established with countries other than England.[1]

Besides providing for their own immediate needs, the homes were called upon to assist in furnishing necessary supplies for the army. Wearing apparel of all kinds was the one great item in these supplies that seemed to be in constant demand throughout the Revolution. The Continental Congress realized quite early in the war that one of the most difficult problems to be met was a sure and ample supply of such necessities. In June, 1776, each state was asked to furnish a suit of clothes, a blanket, a felt hat, two shirts, two pairs of hose, and two pairs of shoes for each soldier enlisted therein.[2] The general supervision of the collection of these was intrusted to agents in the states, working under the directions of the Clothier-General with headquarters at Lancaster, Pennsylvania.[3] While all states were requested to do their part in this important matter, yet the main dependence for clothing seems to have been on the region north of Maryland. In

[1] The great amount of goods supplied through privateering should not be overlooked when one is thinking of the sources of manufactured supplies during the latter half of the Revolution. In discussing this point Weeden remarks: "The former commerce of the country was largely superseded by this trade in irregular but abundant supplies of wares taken from the rich commerce of the enemy. Articles actually needed for the comforts of the household were generally to be had in the marts of trade, and luxuries were not wanting" (*op. cit.*, II, 779).

[2] *Jour. Cont. Cong.* (Library of Congress ed.), V, 467. If the state so desired, the breeches and waistcoat could be made of deerskin.

[3] *Ibid.*, VII, 120.

August, 1777, the Clothier-General was directed by Congress to make an estimate of the number of blankets, shoes, hose, shirts, etc., that would be needed in the field the coming winter and to apply to the assemblies and to the executive authorities of New Hampshire, Massachusetts Bay, Rhode Island, Connecticut, Pennsylvania, and Delaware for the amounts needed in proportion to the number of inhabitants in each.[1]

The manner of procuring the requisite amount was left to each state. Several methods were used. The general plan followed in Connecticut after 1777 was to request the towns to supply a complete outfit for each of their non-commissioned officers and soldiers in the army.[2] Massachusetts asked each town for a certain number of blankets, coats, shirts, etc.[3] At first the selectmen in the towns in New Hampshire were asked to procure blankets and clothing;[4] later the state voted a certain amount of taxes and permitted them to be paid in clothing suitable for the soldiers.[5]

[1] *Jour. Cont. Cong.*, VIII, 611.

[2] *Pub. Rec. of State of Conn.* (1776–78), I, 396.

[3] Taylor, *Hist. of Great Barrington, Mass.*, 252.

[4] *Docs. and Rec. Rel. to State of N.H.*, VIII, 837 f.

[5] For example, in 1782 New Hampshire voted a tax of £110,000 and received homemade goods in payment therefor at the following values: cotton or cotton and linen cloth ⅞ yard wide, 2*s.* a yard; good tow and linen cloth one yard wide, 1*s.* 6*d.* a yard; good white woolen cloth ¾ yard wide, well milled and sheared once, 7*s.* a yard and poorer quality in proportion; good eight-quarter blankets for soldiers, 21*s.*; linen cloth ⅞ yard wide for shirting, 5*s.*, and linen cloth of an inferior quality in proportion; men's yarn hose of best quality, 5*s.* a pair, and others in proportion; men's neat leather shoes, good, 6*s.* a pair; good felt hats, 5*s.* each (*ibid.*, p. 927).

Rhode Island followed a plan similar to that of Massachusetts.[1]

Two or three examples will illustrate how these plans worked out and at the same time show that the homes must have furnished much of the clothing for the soldiers. For instance, Rhode Island about the same date apportioned 3,622 yards of tow cloth and 518 pairs of stockings to the towns, as shown in the following tabulation:[1]

Towns	Yards of Tow Cloth	Pairs of Stockings	Towns	Yards of Tow Cloth	Pairs of Stockings
Newport	182	26	North Kingston	182	26
Portsmouth	70	10	South Kingston	308	44
Jamestown	28	4	Charleston	98	14
Middletown	42	6	Westerly	125	18
Teverton	140	20	Richmond	81	12
Little Compton	112	16	Hopkinton	112	16
Providence	252	36	Exeter	126	18
Smithfield	238	34	Bristol	84	12
Scituate	140	20	Warren	56	8
Glocester	210	30	Barrington	28	4
Cumberland	112	16	Warwick	196	28
Cranston	140	20	East Greenwich	98	14
Johnston	84	12	West Greenwich	98	14
North Providence	56	8	Coventry	126	18
Foster	98	14	Total	3,622	518

In 1781 supplies were furnished the army by the following citizens of Dover, Massachusetts: Eleazer Allen, eight shirts; Joseph Draper, one pair of socks; John Jones, three pairs of stockings; Joseph Haven, two pairs of socks; Ebenezer Smith, sixteen pairs of shoes; Ebenezer

[1] *Rec. of R.I. and Providence Planta.* (1780–83), IX, 534.

Battle, five pairs of socks; Ebenezer Newell, four blankets; John Battle, four pairs of socks; Timothy Allen, one pair of socks; James Draper, stockings; and Captain Ebenezer Battle, sixteen pairs of shoes.[1] The records of North Brookfield, Massachusetts, show that in February, 1781, 30 blankets, 67 shirts, 67 pairs of shoes, and 67 pairs of hose were sent to the army; and in October, 31 blankets, 62 shirts, and 62 pairs of hose. In February, 1782, 31 blankets, 62 shirts, 62 pairs of shoes, and 62 pairs of hose were sent.[2]

These supplies were purchased by the towns from the inhabitants—a policy that was much encouraged during the later years of the war. This method kept the money within the state and enabled the people to bear their burdens somewhat more easily. Governor Greene was an ardent advocate of such a procedure.[3]

The foregoing examples are sufficient to show that household manufactures were in reality a factor in furnishing the Continental army with a supply of clothing, especially in the New England states. Exactly to what extent this was true one cannot estimate from the sources at hand,

[1] Smith, *Hist. of Dover, Mass.*, p. 108.

[2] Temple, *Hist. of North Brookfield, Mass.*, pp. 244 f.

[3] *Ibid.*, p. 503, note. Occasionally a bounty was offered for cloth made within the town. On March 7, 1775, the town of Harvard, Massachusetts, voted a bounty on cloth made as follows: "One peney half peney pr. yard for alwool cloth men's wair . . . . being over and above what is intended for the use of the Familyes where it is made. . . . . Likewise one penney pr. yard for woman's all wool . . . . and for linnen, and tow, half penney pr. yard" (quoted by Nourse, *Hist. of Harvard, Mass.*, p. 315).

since no distinction was ever made in the records between that furnished by the tradesmen in a town and the inhabitants not so classed.

Supplying clothing to the soldiers in the field was but one of the many demands upon the home factory during the years of warfare. There were approximately two and one-half millions[1] of citizens to be housed, clothed, and fed throughout the period of actual war. The artful policy impressed upon the king and Parliament by the English manufacturers had kept the textile industry in the colonies far behind other industries. Thus, when war came, the homes were still the main reliance for clothing and household textiles. The ten years of agitation following 1765, during which time household textile manufactures were greatly augmented, were an excellent preparation for the strenuous times which the first few years of the war brought. The fact that the people had within their own homes the means of supplying their needs for wearing apparel was one of the big factors which enabled them to continue their struggle to a successful termination. To show their response to the demands for ordinary clothing and household fabrics, but a few examples are necessary.

Anburey, one of the Saratoga prisoners, was taken through Pennsylvania in 1778. According to his testimony there was little suffering at this date in this section. "The Pennsylvanians," he said, "are an industrious and hardy people, they are most of them substantial, but

[1] Dexter, "Estimates of Population in the American Colonies," *Proc. Am. Ant. Soc.*, N.S., V, 50 ff.

cannot be considered rich, it being rarely the case with landed people. However, they are well lodged, fed, and clad, and the latter at an easy rate, as the inferior people manufacture most of their own apparel, both linens and woollens and are most industrious of themselves, having but few blacks among them."[1] Speaking of the women on Nantucket Island in about 1780, Crevecouer remarked: "They spin, or cause to be spun in their homes, abundance of wool and flax; and would be forever disgraced, and looked down upon as idlers, if all the family were not clad in good, neat, and sufficient homespun."[2] In fact, these industrious women did more than simply supply their own households with wearing apparel. During the year 1781 Theodora Orcutt, wife of Stephen Orcutt, of Whately, Massachusetts, sold to Parson Wells in exchange for groceries and other household supplies the following:[3]

[1] *Travels through the Interior Parts of Am.* (London, 1791), II, 251. While the above sounds much like Edmund Burke's statement written twenty years earlier, yet there is no indication that Anburey copied from him in a wholesale fashion. Here is Burke's account: "The Pennsylvanians are an industrious and hardy people; they are most of them substantial, though but few of the landed people can be considered rich; but they are well lodged, well fed, and for their condition, well clad, too; and this at a more easy rate, as the inferior people manufacture most all of their own wear both linens and woollens" (*An Account of the European Settlements in Am.* [London, 1757], II, 199).

[2] *Letters from an Am. Farmer* (Philadelphia, 1793), p. 155.

[3] Temple, *Hist. of Whately, Mass.*, p. 71. A "run" of yarn consisted of twenty knots. A knot was composed of twenty threads, and a thread was seventy four inches in length, or once around the reel. A "skein" consisted of seven "knots." An ordinary days work for a spinner was four skeins when she carded her own wool; when the wool was carded by a machine, she could spin six skeins a day (*ibid.*, p. 72).

Sept.		11	runs at 7/4—3 runs at 7*d*	£0	9*s*.	1*d*.
Feb.	11	4	" for handkerchiefs	0	2	4
Mch.	2	8	" linen yarn at 7*d*	0	4	8
"	2	5	" tow yarn	0	2	8
"	6	1	" fine tow yarn at 7*d*	0	0	7
"	13	2	" woolen yarn	0	1	4
Apr.	8	13	" tow yarn	0	6	11
"	"	14	" linen yarn at 8*d*	0	9	4
"	29	9½	" fine tow yarn at 8*d*	0	6	4
May	13	2	" fine thread for stockings at 8*d*	0	1	4
"	13	4	" fine tow yarn at 8*d*	0	2	8
"	13	3	" coarse tow yarn at 4*d*	0	1	7
"	13	3	" coarse linen yarn at 6*d*	0	1	6
June	19	8	" fine yarn for lawn	0	8	0
"	19	22	" coarse linen yarn at 6*d*	0	11	0
"	24	2	" linen yarn at 8*d*	0	1	4
July	5	10	" tow yarn at 4	0	5	4
"	9	3½	" tow yarn at 4	0	1	10
"	11	10	" tow yarn at 6*d*	0	5	0
"	25	3	" fine linen yarn at 8*d*	0	2	0
"	25	2	" coarse linen at 6*d*	0	1	0
"	25	2	" fine tow yarn at 8*d*	0	1	4
"	31	1	" fine tow yarn at 8*d*	0	0	8
Aug.	24	19	" coarse linen chain	0	9	6
Sept.	11	11	" coarse tow yarn	0	1	1
"	11	12	runs tow, 8 runs tow	0	6	5
				£5	4*s*.	10*d*.

The people on the frontier from Maine to Georgia were driven by necessity during the years of the Revolution to supply themselves in their homes with practically every necessity of life. Mills for grinding grain, tanneries for making leather, smiths for making and repairing their farming utensils, carpenters, tailors, cabinetmakers, shoemakers, brewers, and weavers did not generally exist. Professional tradesmen as such were almost unknown. Because of such primitive conditions, each family tanned its own leather and made shoes, shoepacks, hunting-shirts, and leggings for its own use; spun, wove, and tailored its textile clothing from wool, flax, or cotton; and supplied itself with farming implements, household furniture, harness, wagons, sleds, cooper-ware, etc. While the towns on the coast and along the rivers had access occasionally to supplies from the prize ships and from French shipmasters, the people on the frontier, during the entire period of the war, were practically economically independent. This independence was one of the home rather than of the town or community, as was the case in the older settlements. The amount of all kinds of manufactures produced in the homes can be stated in terms of the actual needs of the family, for its chief dependence was upon the household factory.[1]

As already suggested, the southern planter, prior to 1765, accepted the British policy of maintaining the American settlements in economic dependence without serious complaint. It took the Stamp Act controversy and the reign of the non-importation leagues to convince the people of the close connection that existed between industrial and political independence. While the trade between the South and Great Britain during the decade next following 1765 does not indicate that the idea of industrial independence had been unconditionally accepted at the outbreak of the war, yet when the war actually came the planters accepted the situation and began providing on their plantations the necessary articles that they had formerly acquired from England in exchange for their staple products. The beginning of such manufacturing on one plantation is thus related by a contemporary writer in his diary:

[1] Doddridge, *op. cit.*, pp. 110 ff.

Monday, (October) 16th (1775). This morning 3 men went to work to break, swingle and heckle flax and one woman to spin in order to make course linnen for shirts to the Nigers, This being the first of the kind that was made on the Plantation. An before this year there has been little or no linnen made in the Colony. Tuesday (October), 17th, (1775). Two women spinning wool on the bigg wheel and one woman spinning flax on the little wheel all designed for the Nigers.[1]

This beginning mentioned by Harrower grew to such proportions that by the end of the war Jefferson could say that "in almost every family some [cotton stuffs] is manufactured for the use of the family, which is always good in quality & often tolerably fine. In stockings of cotton, weaving is in like manner carried on principally in the family way; among the poor the wife weaves generally, & the rich either have a weaver among their servants or employ their poor neighbors."[2] Of the entire southern region, he commented as follows:

The four Southernmost states make a great deal of cotton. Their poor are almost entirely clothed in it in winter & summer. In winter they weave shirts of it, & outer clothing of cotton & wool mixed. In Summer their shirts are linnen but the outer clothing cotton. The dress of the women is almost entirely of cotton, manufactured by themselves, except the richer class, and even many of those wear a good deal of homespun cotton. It is as well manufactured as the calicoes of Europe.[3]

[1] "Diary of John Harrower, Virginia, 1774, 75," *Am. Hist. Rev.*, VI, 103.

[2] "Jefferson to Thomas Digges," *Works* (Fed. ed.), V, 409. The young negroes on the plantation were often employed in weaving. In 1782 Robert Carter, a planter living in the northern neck of Virginia, had six negro weavers in his weaving establishment, also four negro winders, none over nineteen years old (Commons, *op. cit.*, II, 315).

[3] "Jefferson to Jean Pierre Brissot de Warville," *Works*, V, 166.

A modern writer on southern colonial manufactures concludes thus:

> The account books and letters of the period show how frequently the planters employed their poorer white neighbors, at spinning and weaving cloth, and how they themselves built loom houses and trained their slaves in the household arts.[1]

Hence it becomes evident that household and plantation manufactures must have been very important factors in the struggle for both political and economic independence from the mother-country, on whom so much reliance had been placed for all sorts of manufactured commodities before the opening of the war.

[1] Clark, "Colonial Manufactures," *South in the Building of the Nation*, V, 311.

CHAPTER IV

A QUARTER-CENTURY OF DEVELOPMENTS, 1784–1809

Between 1784 and 1810 household manufactures passed through the following three important stages: (1) a sudden decline of interest in and devotion to them; (2) a quick recovery of this interest and devotion; and (3) the stage in which they became the dominant factor in the struggle for industrial independence. The first few years next following the Treaty of Paris saw a sudden decline in the interest of the people in goods of their own fabrication. However, as soon as they realized the full effects of their "madness for foreign finery," they returned to their former simplicity and economy in life's necessities. This return is evidenced by the amount of commodities of all sorts made in the homes and on the plantations about 1790. As a result of their experience during the hard times following the establishment of their political independence, the people began to see the need of industrial independence as well. To establish this much-desired condition great reliance was placed in the system of household manufacturing. In fact, prior to the economic changes brought about by the chain of events which culminated in the War of 1812, this system was the dominant factor in an earnest struggle for economic freedom; for without factories and mills sufficient to supply their needs the inhabitants of this newly born nation were forced to rely mainly upon the home and the small shops for many of their manufactured necessities. This was especially true of the southern and western sections of the country during the twenty-five years prior to 1810.

A SUDDEN DECLINE AND A QUICK RECOVERY

Even before the Treaty of Paris was signed, foreign manufactured commodities began to flood the country. During the year ending at Christmas, 1783, wares were imported from England to the official value of £1,435,407. The same value in pounds for 1784 was 3,697,467; for 1785, 2,308,023; and for 1786, 1,603,466. Not until 1791 did the imports again equal those of 1784.[1] Since these values were official, they were considerably less than the real values, which Pitkin estimated for the years 1784 and 1785 at $30,000,000.[2] The sudden drop in 1786 is significant. The people had bought beyond their means. Such a vast influx of goods soon took from them a large amount of the specie which they had when the war closed. Hard times followed, all of which brought about a considerable decline in the amount of English as well as other foreign goods consumed.

The influx of this large quantity of foreign supplies had a direct effect on household manufactures. The women gave up their wheels and looms, and foreign fabrics took the place of those made in the homes. In the sections of the country where commercial communication made it possible to acquire such luxuries the whole domestic life

[1] Macpherson, *Annals of Commerce*, IV, 40, 68, 99, 120, 231.

[2] *Statistical View of the Commerce of the U.S.* (ed., 1816), p. 30.

was entirely changed. Speaking of this matter in his message to the legislature in February, 1786, Governor Bowdoin, of Massachusetts, said: "The quantity of woolens imported, their superior fabric, and the cheapness of them, have not only in a great measure put a stop to our looms, and to the several other modes of manufacturing our wool, but have thereby been a principal cause of the decrease of sheep in this Commonwealth."[1] The governor asked the Assembly to remedy these conditions. This body, however, must have felt that they would adjust themselves without legislative interference, since no action was taken regarding the governor's request.

Massachusetts was not alone in this superabundant supply of foreign manufactures. Similar situations existed in other parts of the country. In addressing an assembly of the friends of American manufactures in Philadelphia on August 9, 1787, Tench Coxe, in speaking of the use and plentifulness of foreign goods, said:

> An extravagant and wasteful use of foreign manufactures has been too just a charge against the people of America, since the close of the war. They have been so cheap, so plentiful, and so easily obtained on credit, that the consumption of them has been absolutely wanton. To such an excess has it been carried, that importations of the finer kinds of coat, vest, and sleeve buttons, buckles, brooches, breast-pins and other trinkets into this colony [Pennsylvania], is supposed to have amounted in a single year to ten thousand pounds sterling, which cost wearers above 60,000 dollars. . . . . [2]

While Coxe felt that it was only "in the towns that the madness for foreign finery raged and destroyed," yet,

[1] *Acts and Laws of the Commonwealth of Mass.* (1784–85), p. 840.

[2] Coxe, *A View of the U.S. of Am.*, pp. 49 f.

according to the testimony of a farmer living near Philadelphia, the people in rural districts too had given up their homemade stuffs for the foreign finery. This farmer illustrated the cause of the hard times that were then upon them by citing the change in the "setting out" given each of his three daughters. In 1780, when the first daughter married, she was permitted to take the best wool and flax and make for herself gowns, coats, stockings, and shifts. She was also allowed to buy some cotton and make it into sheets. Two years afterward his second daughter married. For her "setting out" the mother went to town and purchased a calico gown, a calamanco petticoat, a set of stone teacups, a half-dozen pewter teaspoons, and a teakettle—things that had never entered this farmer's house before. Three years later the third daughter married. She had to have a silk gown, silk for a cloak, a looking-glass, china, tea-gear, and other finery.[1]

The change that took place in this farmer's household is representative of what happened between 1780 and 1786 in many sections of the country. In this particular case the mother simply wished to have the "settings out" of her daughters equal to those of other girls in the community. Up to 1780 this farmer had never spent more than ten dollars a year for clothing and household supplies. Nothing to eat, drink, or wear was purchased, as his farm provided all of these necessities. It was his belief that the hard times, of which so many complained in 1787, were caused by the drifting away of the people from their mode of living in 1780. The wheel and loom had come to be used

[1] Carey, *Am. Museum*, I, 11.

only for the purpose of exchanging the substantial cloth of flax and wool for gauze, ribbon, silk, tea, and sugar, instead of providing textile fabrics for the family's own use.[1]

The "unextinguishable rage for foreign finery" even invaded the Valley of Virginia. In speaking of imports into this section on the close of the war, Kercheval said:

> Immense quantities of British and French goods were soon imported; our people imbibed a taste for foreign fashions and luxury; and in the course of two or three years, from the close of the war, such an entire change had taken place in the habits and manners of our inhabitants, that it almost appeared as if we had suddenly become a different nation. The staid and sober habits of our ancestors, with their plain home-manufactured clothing, were suddenly laid aside, and European goods of fine quality adopted in their stead.[3]

The Quakers then living in the Valley were not included in the term "our ancestors." They still continued their ancient custom of depending upon household manufactures for their clothing.[3]

Special efforts were made in some states to call the people back to their former primitive custom of manufacturing their own clothing and household textiles. In March, 1786, the General Assembly of Rhode Island passed an act for encouraging the growth of hemp and flax within the state. The Assembly took this action because of the great importance to the state of encouraging the growth of all raw materials, more especially, as the

[1] *Ibid.*, p. 12.

[2] Kercheval, *Hist. of the Valley of Va.* (1st ed., 1833), pp. 199 f.

[3] *Ibid.*, p. 202.

preamble claimed, of those that supplied clothing to the inhabitants. One penny a pound was offered for every pound of good merchantable hemp or flax raised in the state during the years 1786 and 1787. At the same session a law was enacted to encourage the growth of sheep in the state.[1] Connecticut in the same year provided that there should be deducted from the sum of the total lists of all owners of sheep an amount equal to 4*s*. a head for all sheep owned. By the same act sheep up to the number of twenty were exempted from executions.[2] Governor Livingston, of New Jersey, an ardent advocate of homespun, communicated his views on the subject to the public through the pages of the *American Museum*. In an article published in July, 1791, he made a strong plea to induce the people to stand firmly by their homespun and leave off the European finery. He said in part:

> By what strange fatality, by what unaccountable, fortuitous concourse of atoms, has our *homespun* gone out of fashion, in a country that ought to glory in it; and in which its perpetuity annually would have saved thousands of pounds? O, how I have delighted to behold, in the county of Bergen, piles of this home wrought woollen not only for the dress of my male compatriots, but for the future investment of the delicate limbs of my fair country women. . . . . This laudable economy was not peculiar to Bergen. It is not long since that the manufacture of our own cloth was very general among the farmers. Why is this practice so generally discontinued at present? Must we necessarily determine upon a domestic, because we have acquired a political revolution? And the former as ruinous, as the latter is or may be made advantageous?

[1] *R.I. Col. Rec.*, X, 180, 182.

[2] *Acts and Laws of Conn.* (1786), p. 345.

The governor attributed the decline of home manufacturing to what he termed "the unextinguishable rage for foreign finery." He felt that the people had simply gone mad over the fashions of Paris and London. His plea to them to return to their homespun was as follows:

> To your home-spun, my fellow citizens. Have the patriotism to disappoint both Gaul and Albion in their arts to drain your every copper for their trifles and baubles. Disappoint both of them in their contest who shall make most of you; and which of them shall soonest ruin you. To your home-spun, I say. And in order to facilitate its fabric, I would advise our farmers to desist from their present practice of selling their best lambs to the butcher; and at the same time urge the utility of exchanging their rams with some distant farmer, every year.[1]

Influenced partly by such pleas as this one of Governor Livingston and the one by the citizen of Massachusetts, cited below, but more by the lack of means to supply themselves with foreign goods, many of those who had gone off after the "foreign finery" returned to their homespun before 1790. The spinning bees of 1768 were revived and again became the rage in New England. Sometimes more than a hundred married and single ladies would attend one of these bees, which was usually held at the minister's house. On account of both their social and their economic importance, a full account of one held in Falmouth (now Portland), Maine, on May Day, 1788, follows:

> On the 1st instant, assembled at the house of Rev. Samuel Deane, of this town, more than one hundred of the fair sex, married and

[1] "Homespun," *Am. Museum,* X, 17 f. For a similar plea made to the citizens of Massachusetts, see extracts from an essay entitled "National Arithmetic or Observations on the Finance of the Commonwealth of Massachusetts," *ibid.*, V, 358. This was written in 1789.

single ladies, most of whom were skilled in the important art of spinning. An emulous industry was never more apparent than in this beautiful assembly. The majority of fair hands gave motion to not less than sixty wheels. Many were occupied in preparing the materials, besides those who attended to the entertainment of the rest—provisions for which was mostly presented by the guests themselves, or sent in by other generous promoters of the exhibition, as were also the materials for the work. Near the close of the day, Mrs. Deane was presented by the company with two hundred and thirty-six seven-knotted skeins of excellent cotton and linen yarn, the work of the day, excepting about a dozen skeins which some of the company brought in ready spun. Some had spun six and many not less than five skeins apiece.[1]

The effect of the social movement represented by the spinning bees and the general agitation for economy and frugality throughout the country about 1790 can be seen in the actual output of the home factory at this time. Fortunately some rather definite data were collected on household manufactures about the time the first census was taken. These data are very significant and worth presenting in considerable detail. The following section is devoted to such a presentation.

A CROSS-SECTION VIEW ABOUT 1790

Two of the best-informed men on the general economic state of the country in 1790 were Tench Coxe and Alexander

[1] *Cumberland Gazette,* May 8, 1788; quoted by Kittredge in *The Old Farmer and His Almanack*, pp. 18 f.; Smith, in his *Hist. of Pittsfield, Mass.* (1800–1876), pp. 53 f., quotes from the *Pittsfield Chronicle* accounts of bees held in July and October, 1788, similar to the one above. Forty-five young ladies were present at the first bee reported, and twenty-four married women at the second. Fifty-five runs of yarn were spun at the former and twenty-six at the latter.

Hamilton. In speaking of household manufactures at this date, Coxe said:

> The progress and present state of the invaluable branch of the national industry, exceeds every idea of it, it is believed, that has been formed of it, either in this country or in Europe. In all the states inhabited almost entirely by white people, domestic manufactures are known to be considerable, yielding a considerable surplus for use of other parts of the union.[1]

Hamilton, in his famous report on manufactures in 1791, after enumerating seventeen of the most considerable articles of manufactories, concluded thus:

> Besides manufactories of these articles, which are carried on as regular trades, and have attained to a considerable degree of maturity, there is a vast scene of household manufacturing which contributes more largely to the supply of the community than could be imagined, without having made it an object of particular inquiry. This observation is the pleasing result of the investigation to which the subject of this report has led, and is applicable as well to the Southern as to the Middle and Northern States. Great quantities of coarse cloths, coatings, serges, and flannels, linsey woolseys, hosiery of wool, cotton, and thread, coarse fustians, jeans, and muslins, checked and striped cotton and linen goods, bed ticks, coverlets and counterpanes, tow linens, coarse shirtings, sheetings, toweling, and table linen, and various mixtures of wool and cotton, and of cotton and flax, are made in the household way, and in many instances, to an extent not only sufficient for the supply of the families in which they are made, but for sale and, even, in some cases, for exportation. It is computed in a number of districts that two-thirds, three-fourths, and even four-fifths, of all the clothing of the inhabitants, are made by themselves. The importance of so great a progress as appears to have been made in family manufactures, within a few years, both in a moral and political view, renders the fact highly interesting.[2]

[1] *Op. cit.*, p. 260.

[2] *Am. State Papers*, "Finance," I, 132.

These generalizations were based upon letters and statements sent to Hamilton and Coxe when they were collecting data for the report mentioned above. While no house-to-house canvas was made by those who sent in the accounts, yet, judging from their character, they must have been made by well-informed individuals. Since they are the result of the first systematic attempt to gather statistics on household manufactures in the country at large, and at the same time furnish concrete data to substantiate the generalizations made by the Secretary of the Treasury and his assistant, they are worth presenting in some detail, along with certain facts from other sources which serve to validate them and at the same time furnish additional data to justify the generalization cited above.

On general conditions in New England, Phineas Bond, consul at Philadelphia to the British Foreign Office, in a special report on manufactures in 1789, said:

> In the 4 Eastern States viz. New Hampshire, Mass. Bay, Rhode I. and Connect. the people manufacture much larger quantities of woollens for their own use than they did before the war. . . . . 40,000 yards of coarse New England linen have been sold in Philada within the last year; . . . . Among the country people coarse linens in Mass. Bay of their own making are in such general use as to lessen the importations of checks and even coarse Irish linens nearly ⅔ds. . . . . Pearl and potashes are made in great quantities throughout these States.[1]

Such conditions, according to Bond, existed at this time only among the farmers, the people in the towns wearing the European and British goods in preference to

[1] "Letters of Phineas Bond," edited by Jameson, in *Am. Hist. Ass'n Report*, 1896, I, 651.

all others.[1] A few scattering statistics will show that Bond's statement was a fair estimate of household manufactures in New England in about 1790.

In the town of Ipswich, Massachusetts, from August, 1789, to August, 1790, there were 28,496 yards of lace and 13,483 yards of edging manufactured in the family way.[2] The population of the town at this time was 4,562.[3] In 1793 Whittemore and Richards of Boston were making 12,000 dozens of cotton and wool cards yearly; and from 2,000 to 3,000 dozens were made annually in other parts of the state.[4] These cards were sold to the country people for carding wool and cotton, as carding-machines had not yet come into general use in this country. In the year 1790, 30,000 yards of woolen cloth were made in the town and vicinity of Providence, Rhode Island, in factories and private families, and in the first nine months of 1791 there were manufactured in a family way in the same town 25,262 yards of linen cloth, 5,858 of cotton, 3,165 of woolen, 512 of carpeting, 4,093 pairs of stockings, 859 pairs

[1] *Ibid.*, p. 634. The Manchester cotton goods were selling at this time (1789) at 25 per cent less than Philadelphia cotton goods. Bond gave the following reasons for the New England preference for home goods: populousness of the country, cheapness of living, and activity and punctuality of the people (*ibid.*, p. 365).

[2] *Hamilton Papers for 1790–1791*, L.C., No. 1545; this is the number of the manuscript in the Library of Congress. Joseph Dana, who reported the above, said that most of the families were waited upon twice by the young ladies who undertook the inquiry. Twenty-two samples of black lace and edging were sent along with the report. These are still in an excellent state of preservation.

[3] Coxe, *op. cit.*, p. 266.

[4] Fessenden, *The Register of Arts*, p. 294.

of gloves, and 260 yards of fringe.[1] In Northfork, Connecticut, in 1790, twenty-nine families raised and spun 1,200 runs of silk.[2] The reports from the various towns in this state sent to Hamilton indicated that family manufacturing was carried on to a very great extent. For example, 9,800 yards of linen and woolen cloth were made in 1790 in the town of Southington.[3] Norwich, Middleton, Montville, and Stamford were making in the family way considerable more cloths of various kinds than they used. Some of the surplus was bartered at the village stores and the remainder was sent to the southern states.[4] In Suffolk four hundred families worked up annually about 10,000 pounds of wool and 20,000 pounds of flax;[5] and in New London and Cornwall every family wove enough coarse linens and woolens for its own consumption.[6] Besides clothing, such necessities as sailcloth, bedticks, thread, fringe, silk buttons, hosiery, nails, spikes, sewing-silk, pot and pearl ashes were made. Whatever surplus of these articles existed was sent to the middle and southern states. Commenting on this, Coxe said: "Here then is *a surplus* of household manufactures sold *out of the state.* It is an acknowledged fact that New England linens have affected the price and importation of that article from New York to Georgia."[7]

There was as much, or even more, household manufacturing in the northern part of New England about 1790

[1] Coxe, *op. cit.*, p. 267.

[2] *The American Pioneer*, I, 146.

[3] *Hamilton Papers*, No. 1865.

[4] *Ibid.*, Nos. 1813, 1882–83, 1841, 1871–72.

[5] *Ibid.*, No. 1853.

[6] *Ibid.*, Nos. 1809–10, 1859.

[7] *Op. cit.*, p. 265.

as in the southern. A great deal of tow cloth was made in the country towns of New Hampshire, much of which was sent south to clothe the slaves. Pot and pearl ashes were also exported in large quantities.[1] Every family in Vermont raised a quantity of flax and carried on a small manufacture of linen, and from the wool of their own raising the "bigger part of the farmers manufactured their woolens."[2] Much maple sugar was likewise made, forty families in Orange County making 13,000 pounds in 1791.[3] The average yearly amount made by every family in the outer district was about 250 pounds.[4] The farmers made much of their corn into spirits.[5] In Maine "almost every family manufactured wool and flax into cloth, and made farming utensils of evey kind for their own use."[6] From these concrete data concerning actual conditions in this region it can be observed that the generalizations cited above were not overdrawn, especially in so far as they related to the New England states.

Bond made no general summary of the condition of household manufactures in the middle states as a whole in his report on manufactures to the home office in 1789.[7] Comments on each state separately were made instead. Regarding New York he said: "Coarse woollens and some linens are made among the farmers but these fall infinitely

[1] Winterbotham, *View of the U.S.*, II, 118.

[2] Williams, *Nat. and Civ. Hist. of Vt.* (ed. 1794), pp. 315 f.

[3] Winterbotham, *op. cit.*, II, 54.

[4] Williams, *op. cit.*, p. 319.

[5] Winterbotham, *op. cit.*, II, 53.

[6] *Ibid.*, II, 221.

[7] This is the report mentioned on p. 132.

short of their own consumption." On conditions in New Jersey he commented as follows: "The manufactures in N. Jersey made in private families are now increasing and the farmers in general paying infinitely more attention to domestic manufactures than they have done since the war. Coarse woollens and coarse linens are made in private families fit only for the use of servants and not in a quantity to supply even them." Of what was being done in Pennsylvania he remarked: "In this state also the farmers raise large quantities of flax and hemp and some wool; their domestic manufactures are of a coarser sort and seldom seen in cities and towns. Tow linens, lindseys, and some sort of coarse linens are attended to with more care and industry than formerly, and in some small quantities offered for sale."[1] It was said of Delaware: "In this state as in the neighboring State of Pennsylv^{a}, the advancement of domestic manufactures is encouraged, attention is payed to the raising of hemp flax and wool but the articles manufactured bear no sort of proportion to the wants of the laboring part of the people."[2]

The raw materials, implements, and finished products connected with manufacturing in the household, listed in 44 out of 49 inventories of Ulster County, New York, covering the period from 1788 to 1792, indicate that Bond's estimate was correct, at least for one county. For example, in the 44 itemized inventories, spinning-wheels (kind not designated) appeared 23 times, with total of 44 wheels; woolen wheels, 21 times; small wheels,

[1] Letters, *op. cit.*, p. 652, for New York, New Jersey, and Pennsylvania.

[2] *Ibid.*, p. 654.

9; sheep, 20; flax, 11; weaver's loom, 16; sheep's wool, hatchels, shoe leather, and linen yarn, 3 each; wool cards, reels, and quill wheels, 4 each; yarn (kind not designated) and woolen yarn, 5 each; reeds and spool wheels, 6 each; hemp, linen cloth, and warping bars and spools, 2 each; and flannel cloth, wool combs, shoemaker's tools, woolen cloth, cotton yarn, tow yarn, homespun cloth, homespun coats, tow cloth, clock reel, weaver's brushes, spooling-wheel, weaver's spools, weaver's wheel, shuttles, and checks, 1 each.[1] Such data show that the people in Ulster County had in their homes both the raw products and the implements necessary to supply their needs for clothing and household textile supplies.

The Revolution changed the South from a region depending almost wholly upon the outside world for manufactured commodities to one in which many of such commodities were made by the people in their homes or on their plantations. A few facts from letters written to Hamilton when he was collecting data for his report will substantiate this. For example, the individual reporting on conditions in the two counties on the Eastern Shore of Virginia said: "I suppose that $\frac{3}{4}$ of the people are clothed in their own Manufactury; Leather Shoes we make cheafly within ourselves and Common Stockings. . . . ."[2] Similar conditions existed in other counties of this state. The inhabitants of Princess Anne, Norfolk, and Nansemond counties made most of their negro clothing and their coarse cloth. Each family within a radius of ten miles of

[1] Anjou, *Ulster County, N.Y., Probate Records*, "Wills," II.

[2] *Hamilton Papers*, No. 1886.

Surry made annually about 200 yards of cloth. At least five-sixths of all the cloth, shoes, and stockings used in these families were homemade.[1] In the counties adjacent to Culpeper the rich planters made a great deal of linen cloth for slaves, as did the middle classes also, while the poorer sort made it for their own wear. The first two classes also made cloth for coverlets, bedticks, and jeans. The rich bought most of their fine shoes and stockings.[2] The amount manufactured by each of twenty families in twelve months in King William County (rich and poor indiscriminately taken) is exhibited in Table VII.

To show that King William County was not alone in the attention given to household manufactures, an account of the output for one year in another county is submitted (Table VIII). The total value made by the twenty families included in this account was slightly less than that made by the families included in the preceding tabulation.

The value of the cloth, stockings, and shoes made by the twenty families included in Table VIII was as follows: linen cloth, \$273.75; yarn cloth, \$143.33; cotton cloth, \$980.83; stockings, \$130.50; and shoes, \$263.33—making a total of \$1,791.74, and an average of \$89.59 in each family. The average value in each of the forty families represented in the foregoing tables was \$91.75. There were in Virginia (exclusive of Kentucky) in 1790, 70,825 families. On the basis of what was made in the forty families from which definite statistics were collected,

[1] *Ibid.*, Anselm Bailey's report.

[2] *Hamilton Papers*, No. 1912.

the value of goods made in homes during the year 1790 in this state was $6,498,183.75. If, as was claimed by those reporting,[1] the situation in the families included in

TABLE VII

QUANTITY AND VALUE OF CLOTH AND STOCKINGS MADE BY TWENTY FAMILIES IN KING WILLIAM COUNTY, VIRGINIA, FROM JANUARY 1, 1790, TO JANUARY 1, 1791*

HEADS OF FAMILIES	NO. IN FAMILY			CLOTH MADE		STOCKINGS MADE		VALUES OF CLOTH AND STOCKINGS	
	White	Slave	Total	Yards	Value	Pairs	Value	Total	Per Capita
T. Avera....	4	9	13	263	$ 152.25	15	$ 10.17	$162.42	$12.49
J. Ruffin....	7	36	43	468	266.83	37	22.85	289.68	6.73
S. Ruffin....	4	31	35	287	164.50	25	13.94	178.44	5.09
D. Pannell ..	8	23	31	400	232.75	29	19.06	251.81	8.12
J. King.....	3	5	8	127	74.25	7	5.09	79.34	9.91
H. Bagwell ..	3	1	4	69	43.50	7	5.52	49.02	12.25
N. Fox Inn..	6	14	20	200	112.50	15	9.31	121.81	6.09
Wm. Tawler.	4	1	5	68	41.00	6	5.10	46.10	9.22
B. Lipscomb.	5	13	18	130	70.83	6	5.10	75.93	4.21
M. Towler ..	10	0	10	56	34.33	8	6.80	41.13	4.11
J. Howard...	4	5	9	52	29.17	3	2.55	31.72	3.52
S. Howard ..	4	0	4	39	24.08	4	3.40	27.48	6.87
Wm. Starke .	3	8	11	00	00.00	0	0.00	00.00	0.00
J. Hollins ...	5	0	5	33	21.58	4	3.40	24.98	4.99
Mrs. Aawse .	3	6	9	40	25.75	8	5.51	31.26	3.47
C. Lipscomb.	3	2	5	50	32.08	7	5.42	37.50	7.50
P. Richeson .	8	8	16	147	95.33	21	15.70	111.03	6.93
E. P. Chamberlayne ..	3	14	17	70	32.50	8	3.36	35.86	2.10
W. Newman.	5	14	19	145	86.67	21	13.98	100.65	5.29
D. Ragsdale.	4	15	19	270	163.75	29	18.22	181.97	9.57
Totals ..	96	205	301	2914	$1703.65	260	$174.48	$1878.13	$ 6.23

* Based on the report of Drury Ragsdale, *Hamilton Papers*, No. 1892. The values in the report are given in pounds, shillings, and pence. In expressing these amounts in dollars the values used by Coxe in his *View of the United States* (p. 261) were adopted—£1 equaling $3.33⅓.

[1] *Hamilton Papers*, No. 1903.

the two foregoing tabulations was applicable to the whole of Virginia, this computation is a fair one. It must, however, stand as merely an estimate, since the first census included no statistics on manufactures of any kind, making the checking of such calculations an impossibility.

TABLE VIII

ACCOUNT OF MANUFACTURES MADE IN SURVEY NO. 2 BY TWENTY FAMILIES FROM THE RICHEST AND THE POOREST IN THE PERIOD FROM JANUARY 1 TO DECEMBER 31, 1790*

Classes of Four Families in Each Class	Linen Cloth (Yards)	Yarn Cloth (Yards)	Cotton Cloth (Yards)	Stockings, Different Kinds (Pairs)	Shoes, Different Kinds (Pairs)
First	187	225	700.5	51	112
Second	225	95	440	46	57
Third	320	24	296	40	38
Fourth	254	24	177	28	17
Fifth	109	24	68	9	13
Totals	1,095	392	1,681.5	174	237

* *Hamilton Papers*, No. 1909. On the reliability of the data included in this and the preceding table, Coxe commented as follows: "These papers have been obtained under circumstances that justify a reliance on their truth and are believed to be very little variant from the medium of the state of Virginia" (*op. cit.*, p. 262). To justify the last half of this statement Coxe cited the facts that during the year 1790 in the counties of Accomac and Northampton 315,000 yards of flaxen cloth, 45,000 of woolen, 30,000 of cotton, and 45,000 of linen and woolen, and a quantity of coarse stockings equal to the demand were made in the 2,729 families living in these counties at this date (*ibid.*, pp. 262 f.).

The reports from the other southern states indicated that they too were quite generally engaged in household manufacturing. Generalizing on the basis of the reports sent him in 1791 from the South, Coxe said: "The family manufactures of the middle and interior counties of Virginia, North Carolina, and the interior counties of Georgia, South Carolina, and Maryland, are said to be greater in value than the articles of foreign manufacture which they use."[1] The reports from the interior of South Carolina stated that the inhabitants manufactured entirely in the family as much as they had occasion for of cotton, flaxen, hempen, and woolen goods. It was also evident from the reports from North Carolina and Georgia that these two states did as much as Virginia and South Carolina.[2]

But brief mention need be made here of conditions on the frontier settlements of Kentucky and Tennessee about 1790. In the principal stations and towns there were stores in which were kept such articles as nails, calicoes, axes, broadcloth, delftware, silks, furniture, bonnets, lumber, hats, sugar, medicine, whisky, and books, all jumbled together. The women of the country brought their linen, linsey, and jeans and bartered them for tea,

[1] *Op. cit.*, p. 298. A similar statement was made by the editor of the *American Museum* in 1791. This statement occurs in Vol. XI, 231, in the first of a series of articles on "Reflection on the State of the Union." Carey, the editor of the *Museum*, no doubt based his conclusions on Coxe's statement quoted above.

[2] *Ibid.*, p. 264. Both Bishop and Winterbotham give similar statements regarding South Carolina. The former states that in about 1790 the planters began generally to clothe their slaves with homespun from the produce of their cotton fields. The material was prepared for the spindle by the field hands, spun in the family, and then sent to the nearest weaver (*Hist. of Am. Manufactures*, II, 27). Winterbotham says: "Late accounts from the interior parts of this State inform us, that the inhabitants manufacture, entirely in the family way, as much as they have occasion for; that cotton hemp and flax are plenty; that they have a considerable stock of good sheep; that great exertions are made, and much done in the household way; that they have long been in the habit of doing something in family manufactures, but within a few years past, great improvements have been made. The women do the weaving and leave the men to attend to agriculture" (*op. cit.*, III, 255).

coffee, and such articles as they could not make themselves. The store sold few things that could be produced in the home.[1] These conditions were common on the older frontier everywhere. Since they will be treated separately elsewhere, no further note will be made of them here.

From the concrete data presented above it is evident that the general statements of Coxe and Hamilton quoted at the beginning of this section were not overdrawn. When the people returned to their home manufactures after their sad experience with foreign commodities, they did it with a conviction that industrial dependence was as detrimental to their prosperity and happiness as political. Before the general establishment of mills and factories the household was the big factor in attaining the industrial independence so much needed and desired. During the two decades next following 1790 the family factory was certainly the dominant element in the struggle for independence of foreign mills, especially in the matter of clothing and household textile supplies.

HOUSEHOLD MANUFACTURES THE DOMINANT FACTOR IN THE STRUGGLE FOR INDUSTRIAL INDEPENDENCE

Industrial and political conditions in the two decades next preceding 1810 were on the whole conducive to sustaining and increasing household manufacturing. The uncertain trade relations between the United States and England, the quasi-war with France in 1798, the unfavor-

[1] Durrett, "Condition of Kentucky When She Began Statehood," *Filson Club Pubs.*, No. 7, p. 84.

able balance of trade,[1] Jefferson's embargo policy,[2] and the westward movement of population, all tended to force the people to depend more or less upon the homes and plantations for many of the necessities of life. Of all these influences the last two were the most potent. The embargo policy cut off, not only the manufactured supplies which had been coming from England and France, but also the proceeds from the staple articles that the farmers had been sending to these countries. As the frontier moved westward the distance to a market both for raw materials and for manufactured goods became greater and greater. In reality it was as far from the Ohio, Indiana, Kentucky, and Tennessee frontiers in 1810 to the eastern markets as it was from the colonies to the English markets during the colonial period. The lack of a market for the products of the frontier and the high cost of imported articles forced the people to become almost industrially independent. At first this was a household independence, later a community one. The condition at

[1] During the seven years next following 1795 there was a balance of trade against the United States amounting to $106,609,363, or $15,229,909 per annum (Seybert, *Statistical Annals*, p. 277). For the trade relations of the United States with each of the important countries of the world during these seven years, see *ibid.*, pp. 276 f.

[2] During the early stages of the embargo and non-intercourse policy the inhabitants of Richmond, in a public gathering, adopted, among other patriotic resolutions, one saying that they would dress in domestic fabrics. Mordecai, commenting on this, said: "As homespun 'was the only wear,' the price of coarse mixed *Virginia cotton cloth* was a dollar or more a yard for such now [1860] is worth twelve or eighteen cents, and many of our citizens who could afford it . . . . were thus arrayed from head to foot" (*Va., Especially Richmond, in By-gone Days*, p. 320).

any one time in a community was determined by the status of the handicraft system and by the character of the frontiersmen.

Except in extreme frontier communities separated from the base of supplies by inadequate transportation facilities, New England before 1810 had passed into the shop stage of manufacturing in most every manufactured article except clothing. The women of the household refused to permit the professional spinners and weavers to usurp the traditional adjunct to their household duties. Goodrich's account of general industrial conditions in Ridgefield, Connecticut, in 1800, which, as he asserted, was a typical New England town containing about two hundred families, nearly all farmers, portrays fairly well the amount of manufacturing going on in the homes and the amount done by the tradesmen at this date in this entire region. There was a butcher who went from house to house to slaughter the cattle and swine of his neighbors. There were a tanner, a tailor, a weaver, and a shoemaker, all in the itinerant stage. The weaver went from house to house, put up his loom, and threw his shuttle till the season's work was done; twice a year the tailor came to the house and made the semiannual stock of clothes for the men and boys; upon due notice the circulating shoemaker came with his bench, lapstone, and awl, converted some room into a shop until the household was duly shod, the leather used being that sent back from the tanner from the hides of the cows and calves that the family had killed for meat. The hatter, whose craft was one stage in advance of the foregoing ones, had a place of business and made hats to order in exchange for skins of foxes, rabbits, muskrats, and other chance peltry. The furniture was made by the village cabinetmaker and the fuller dyed and fulled the woolen cloth.

Of the manufacturing done in the homes, Goodrich tells us that the people raised their own flax, rotted it, hackled it, dressed it, and spun it. The little wheel, turned by foot, had its place, and was as familiar as if it had been a member of the family. The wool was also spun in the family, partly by his sisters and partly by Molly Gregory, daughter of their neighbor, the town carpenter. Sugar was often made, but most of the supply came from the West Indies. The carpets were all homemade. Soap and candles were also made in the home. The woolen cloth was sent to the fuller to be dyed and fulled, while the linen was bleached and made up in the family.[1]

[1] *Recollections of a Life Time*, I, 64, 71, 72, 74. The picture of North Brookfield, Massachusetts, quoted from Dr. Snell's description of the town in 1798, when he settled in it, by Temple (*Hist. of North Brookfield*, pp. 267 ff.), shows that the foregoing was not an isolated case. There were about a thousand people in the town at this date. These were nearly all husbandmen. What few mechanics there were, were also farmers upon a large or small scale. Among these half-mechanics and half-farmers were a blacksmith, a nail-maker, a gunsmith, wheelwrights, carpenters, coopers, cobblers, peeled broom-makers, and tailors. The cobblers had a bench in their kitchen and would also go around to the farmers' houses in the fall with their kit and stay a week or so, mending and making the family supply of shoes. The father or grandfather was still making most of the brooms. The wheelwright made ox-cart wheels, axles, and tongues, the remainder of the cart being made by the farmer. The carpenter had little to do, because every thriving man could hew, mortise, and lay shingles. The spinning, weaving, and dyeing were still done in the households. Every family owned a great and a little wheel as well as a loom. The dyepot was still in the chimney corner. Soap was made in every family. There were

In going through New England in 1806, Melish made note of the household manufactures. According to his observations, the farmers of Connecticut and their families were generally dressed in cloth of their own manufacture, which was both substantial and good.[1] In the interior of Massachusetts there was a vast variety of family manufactures.[2] Of New Hampshire he remarked: "The country people generally manufacture their own clothing,

also at this time, a potter, a sieve-maker, and four cider-mills. For conditions in Maine from 1800 to 1810, see Bourne, *Hist. of Wells and Kennebunk;* and Emery, *Hist. of Sanford.* Memories of the conditions portrayed were yet fresh when Bourne wrote his account.

[1] *Travels in the U.S. of Am.*, p. 101.

[2] *Ibid.*, p. 93. That Melish's general statements are substantiated by the actual conditions is seen by what was made in Berkshire County, Massachusetts, in 1808. Of woolen goods there were 55,212 yards made in ten of the thirty towns of the county. The towns were: Lenox, 3,030 yards; Lanesboro, 5,000 yards; Hinsdale, 2,000; Sandisfield, 5,441; Cheshire, 6,960; Pittsfield, 15,270; Great Barrington, 4,400; Stockbridge, 3,250; Tryingham, 5,450 (estimated); Alford, 4,400 (estimated). It was estimated by the *Pittsfield Sun*, which gathered this information, that the total product of the Berkshire looms was at least 100,000 yards. In commenting on this fact the editor said: "Here then in a single branch of manufacture, carried on principally in the private families, at a very trifling expense, and interfering very little with the great business of the farmer, which yields to this small county—consisting by the last census of about 33,000 souls—more than $100,000, being more than three dollars to each person of all ages and sexes. It is easy to see how greatly the wealth, comfort and happiness of our country are promoted by pursuits of this sort, and how far they tend to increase and invigorate the solid sinews of national wealth. It is equally obvious to see how easy it would be for our farmers to double the amount of this branch of manufactures in *quantity*, even by the increase of the common wool of our country; and equally to quadruple it in *value*, by cultivating the finer species of wool, which is not happily brought within the reach of everyone" (quoted by Smith, *Hist. of Pittsfield*, p. 177).

and make considerable quantities of tow cloth for exportation";[1] and of Vermont: "The principal manufactures are of the domestic kinds, consisting of wool and flax, for the family use."[2]

The people in the middle states were probably as active as those in New England in household manufacturing during the two decades under consideration. In going through New Jersey in 1807, Melish was led to remark: "The inhabitants of New Jersey, except in the towns, make the greater part of their clothing."[3] Of Pennsylvania

[1] *Travels in the U.S. of Am.*, p. 84.

[2] *Ibid.*, p. 86. This statement is substantiated by facts gathered in 1809. In October of this year the General Assembly of Vermont appointed a committee composed of one member from each county to prepare a statement of the manufactures of the state. The following is the report of the committee on cotton, linen, and woolen goods made in the homes during the year ending October, 1809:

Counties	Cotton and Linen Goods (Yards)	Woolen Goods (Yards)	Clothier's Works (Number)	Carding-Machines (Number)
Bermington	84,110	62,900	11	9
Windham	120,000	100,000	24	16
Rutland	170,000	143,040	26	18
Windsor	269,090	134,045	34	25
Addison	127,600	107,200	15	13
Orange	177,000	177,000	19	19
Chittenden	128,000	110,000	8	8
Caledonia	135,000	110,000	12	10
Franklin	32,600	40,400	7	10
Orleans	33,000	30,000	4	4
Essex and Grand Isle	28,960	28,960	3	3
Totals	1,305,360	1,043,545	160	135

The committee omitted hosiery from the above. It was claimed that every article made from wool, cotton, or flax was made in nearly sufficient quantities for the common use of the family (*Rec. Gov. and Council of Vt.*, V, 500).

[3] *Op. cit.*, p. 113.

he said: "Domestic [family] manufactures are general throughout the state."[1] In his message to the General Assembly in 1808, Governor Mitchell, of Delaware, recommended the countenancing by law, so far as it could be done without too much interference and regulation, every species of family manufacture.[2] While the Delaware legislature took no action respecting this recommendation, yet the Assembly of New York this same year did take up the matter and passed a law to encourage rather than regulate the industry.[3] This law provided for a premium of $80 to any person who in his family manufactured within any of the counties of the state the best specimen of woolen cloth of uniform texture and quality containing not less than 30 yards and not less than three-quarters of a yard in width. The county judges were to determine by a majority vote to whom the premium should be awarded each year.[4] In 1810 this law was enlarged to include premiums for the three best pieces of the same kind of cloth. The premiums were $40, $35, and $30. The amount of cloth required for each was 30, 25, and 20 yards.[5] The effects of these acts are seen in Tables IX and X (pp. 150–51 and 152).

[1] *Travels in the U.S. of Am.*, p. 132.

[2] *Jour. of the H.R., Del.*, 1808, p. 16.

[3] It should be said for Delaware that in 1809 sheep were exempted from taxation. Ten or less could not be seized for debt. The act was to continue for five years (*Laws of Del.* [printed by M. Bradford and R. Porter], IV, 267).

[4] *Laws of N.Y.*, 31st Sess., c. 360.

[5] *Ibid.*, 33d Sess., c. 108. In June, 1812, the act of 1810 was renewed for three years (*ibid.*, 35th Sess., c. 230), and in 1817 the act of 1812 was revived, but was repealed in 1819 (*ibid.*, 40th Sess., c. 240, and 42d Sess.,

These two tables furnish evidence of the interest in, and results of, household manufactures in New York during a period of more or less forced economic independence. While they do not exhibit the *amount* made in each county, yet they do show that the custom was common throughout the state. The few general citations respecting the extent to which the industry was carried on in the other middle states and New England suggest that the facts indicated by the tables were not restricted to New York.

Household manufactures were in a flourishing condition in the southern states during most of the two decades next preceding 1810, the embargo policy and the general trade conditions being conducive to the fostering of them during this period. As Isaac Weld passed through the Upper Neck of Virginia (between the Potomac and the Rappahannock) in 1796 he noticed that nearly every article that could be wanted by the planters was made or produced upon the principal estates. In this region the slaves were instructed in the business of smiths, carpenters, wheelwrights, turners, tanners, weavers, etc. From the cotton grown on the plantations a sort of nankeen was made by the negroes.[1] Other regions of the South were

c. 230). These laws were the result of work done by the Society for the Promotion of Arts in New York. In 1807 this society voted one Walter Briggs, of Schoharie County, a piece of silver plate in consideration of his having laid before the society five specimens of woolen cloth of superior quality, made from the wool of his flock, consisting of about 300 sheep. About 1,200 yards of cloth were made annually by the daughters of Mr. Briggs (*Trans. Albany Inst.*, IV, 114). Out of this incident grew the notion of having the state offer money premiums for similar products; hence the law of 1808 mentioned above.

[1] *Travels through the U.S. and N.A.* (4th ed., 1800), p. 114.

TABLE IX

DISTRIBUTION BY COUNTIES OF PREMIUMS AWARDED IN NEW YORK STATE UNDER THE ACTS OF APRIL 8, 1808, APRIL 5, 1810, AND JUNE 19, 1812*

Counties	Number of Premiums In					Amount of Premiums In				
	1809	1810	1811	1813	1814	1809	1810	1811	1813	1814
Albany	1	1	3	3	3	$ 80	$ 80	$ 105	$ 105	$ 105
Allegany	1	....	3	....	....	80	.....	105	.....	.....
Broome	1	1	3	1	....	80	80	105	30	.....
Cayuga	1	1	3	....	3	80	80	180	.....	105
Chenango	1	1	3	....	....	80	80	105	.....	.....
Clinton	1	1	3	....	1	80	80	105	.....	30
Columbia	....	1	3	....	....	.....	80	105	.....	.....
Cortland	....	1	3	3	3	.....	80	105	105	105
Delaware	....	1	1	3	3	.....	80	(?)	105	105
Dutchess	1	1	2	1	4	130	230	165	40	235
Essex	....	1	3	2	2	.....	80	105	65	70
Franklin	....	1	3	....	....	.....	80	105	.....	.....
Genesee	....	....	3	....	....	.....	.....	105	.....	.....
Greene	1	1	3	3	3	80	130	105	105	105
Herkimer	1	1	3	3	2	80	80	105	105	75
Jefferson	1	1	3	....	....	80	80	105	.....	.....
Kings	....	1	....	....	1	.....	80	.....	.....	40
Lewis	1	1	3	....	3	80	80	105	.....	105
Madison	1	1	3	3	1	80	80	105	105	40
Montgomery	1	1	3	3	....	80	80	105	105	.....
Oneida	....	1	3	....	1	.....	80	105	.....	40
Onondaga	1	1	3	....	3	80	80	105	.....	105
Ontario	....	1	3	2	3	.....	80	105	75	105
Orange	1	1	3	2	4	80	80	105	75	225
Otsego	1	....	2	3	3	80	.....	75	105	105
Queens	1	1	3	3	3	80	80	105	105	105
Rensselaer	1	1	3	3	3	80	80	105	105	105
Rockland	....	1	3	....	3	.....	80	105	.....	105
St. Lawrence	1	....	1	2	3	80	.....	40	75	105
Saratoga	1	1	3	3	4	230	180	105	345	215
Schenectady	....	1	1	3	3	.....	80	40	105	105
Schoharie	1	1	3	3	3	80	80	105	105	105
Seneca	1	1	3	1	3	80	80	105	35	105
Steuben	1	....	3	3	....	80	.....	105	105	.....
Suffolk	....	1	3	1	2	.....	80	105	40	75
Sullivan	....	....	1	....	3	.....	.....	40	.....	105

TABLE IX—*Continued*

Counties	Number of Premiums In					Amount of Premiums In				
	1809	1810	1811	1813	1814	1809	1810	1811	1813	1814
Tioga........	1	1	3	3	....	80	80	105	105	.....
Ulster.......	1	....	3	3	....	180	.....	105	105	.....
Warren......	....	....	....	....	3	.....	.....	.....	.....	105
Washington..	....	1	1	3	2	.....	80	(?)	105	75
Westchester ..	....	....	1	....	2	.....	.....	40	.....	75
Total....	25	32	103	63	80	$2,300	$2,860	$3,695	$2,460	$3,085

* *Trans. of the Albany Inst.*, IV, 124. For a list of the persons who received the premium awarded by the county judges, see *ibid.*, pp. 117 ff. The specimens are preserved in the Institute library. They are arranged in five volumes. Each volume contains the returns for one year. The law of 1810 expired at the end of 1811. There were no premiums for the year 1812. There were no premiums awarded in Cattaraugus, Chautauqua, New York, Niagara, Putnam, and Richmond counties.

equally as busy as Virginia in this plantation manufacturing. Maryland in 1803 exempted from public assessment all homemade wares in the hands of the makers. Plantation utensils and working tools of mechanics and manufacturers were exempted at the same time.[1] Nor was South Carolina behind Virginia and Maryland. In his view of this state about 1800, Drayton said:

> Hence, where the population of the state is convenient to commerce, the manufacturing business is not at all entered into; importations from abroad supplying all the necessary wants. But, as transportation is more difficult to, and from, the middle and upper country; so necessity has, in a proportionate degree, compelled the inhabitants to provide for their respective wants. And thus a domestic spirit of manufacturing has arisen, which must prevail in those parts of the state. The traveller there, soon becomes accustomed to the humming music of the hand spinning-wheel; and the industry of the loom often meets his eye. Cottons are thus made, both striped, figured

[1] Maxcy, *Laws of Md.*, III, 110.

and plain, of ingenious fabrications; as well for clothes, and the table, as for house use; woollens also of strong nature and decent appearance, are woven and dressed by suitable fulling-mills; coarse linens, blanketing, woollen bed covers and cotton rugs, are also manufactured. With the exception of salt and sugar, the people, in the upper part of the state may be considered independent of foreign support.[1]

TABLE X

GENERAL SUMMARY OF PREMIUMS AWARDED BY THE SOCIETY FOR THE PROMOTION OF USEFUL ARTS IN NEW YORK AND BY THE COUNTY JUDGES, UNDER THE ACTS OF 1808, 1810, AND 1812*

Years	Premiums Awarded by the Society		Premiums Awarded by the County Judges				Total by Society and County Judges	
			Number Of			Amount		
	Number	Amount	Firsts	Seconds	Thirds		Number	Amount
1809........	4	$ 450	25	0	0	$ 2,300	29	$ 2,750
1810........	4	450	32	0	0	2,860	36	3,310
1811........	6	420	39	33	31	3,695	109	4,115
1813........	5	370	22	22	19	2,460	68	2,830
1814........	5	240	32	25	23	3,085	85	3,325
Total...	24	$1,930	150	80	73	$14,400	327	$16,330

* *Trans. of the Albany Institute,* IV, 123. The form used by the Society in awarding premiums was as follows:

"STATE OF NEW-YORK
"181–

"By the Society for the Promotion of Useful Arts, This premium is warded to . . . . of the County . . . . for the best (or as the case may be) specimen of Woollen Cloth, of family manufacture, exhibited the present year" (*Trans. Soc. for the Promotion of Useful Arts,* III, 249).

In going through North Carolina in 1807, Melish noted that practically all of the families in the country manu-

[1] *A View of S.C.* (Charleston, 1802), p. 150. Ramsay in his *History of South Carolina* gives a similar word-picture of the conditions about 1808. He says: "Where slaves abound and the staple commodities are raised in the greatest plenty, the least attention is paid to the domestic manufacture

factured their own clothing, so that the "British trade," as he remarked, "to this state is not great or important."[1] Similar conditions were observed in Georgia. After a day and a half's journey out of Savannah toward Augusta a stop was made at a farmhouse for dinner. On hearing the noise of a wheel upstairs the traveler went up and found the daughter of the landlord spinning the rolls of cotton which a negro girl was busy carding. On inquiry of the mistress of the house he found that this family, as well as all other families in the neighborhood, spun cotton all the year round and got the yarn woven into every article necessary for family use, such as sheeting, shirting, toweling, tablecloths, gowns, petticoats, aprons, caps, pantaloons, vesting, and summer coats for the men's use—besides sofa-cloths, fringes, tassels, hosiery, etc. "I examined," said he, "the yarn and cloth and found the fabrics substantial and durable. The cloth was neatly manufactured, and some of the articles were handsome. I saw

of articles of clothing. If the crop succeeds and afterwards sells for a good price, there is money to buy clothing; but if either fails, the reverse takes place, and no provision is made against the pinching of a cold winter. The least wealthy are generally the most provident. The loom and the wheel are most steadily plied among the minor planters or farmers. . . . . Among such domestic manufactures now are and for a long time have been carried on for almost every necessary family purpose. . . . . Wool, cotton, and flax, either combined or separate, are worked up into plain garments for warmth, but are seldom made of so fine a texture as to be suitable for summer wear. Though domestic manufactures are daily increasing in quantity and improving in quality, and are carried on, especially in the interior parts of the state, to so considerable an extent that their aggregate is very great, yet they are far short of a sufficiency for the supply of the inhabitants" (II, 257 f.).

[1] *Op. cit.*, p. 189.

that this family was 'independent of commerce,' and this was the first impression that I had received as to the importance of the domestic manufactures of America."[1] At Sparta he was informed that there was no demand at all for British goods and that all the people were clothing themselves in homespun.[2] Victor Clark summed up conditions in the South a decade or so prior to 1810 very adequately when he said:

> Therefore prior to the War of 1812, the advance of Southern manufacture was principally in what were then household arts—those that produced for the subsistence of the family rather than for an outside market. These manufactures continued generalized and dispersed rather than specialized and integrated. There is little evidence even of that rudimentary localization that for a century and a half had characterized some industries in New England and Pennsylvania. This did not indicate stagnation but rather an adaptation of manufactures to the economic constitution of Southern society. In their aggregate these manufactures were for a time considerable; but they were so distributed and combined with other productive activities as to lose their identity in contemporary records.[3]

The people west of the Alleghany Mountains during the period under discussion were forced by the exigencies of the times and the general inconveniences connected with pioneer life to make in their homes or small com-

[1] *Ibid.*, p. 40.

[2] *Ibid.*, p. 263. Melish spent a night at a farmhouse about half-way between Sparta and Greensburg. Of his experiences here he said: "On reaching the house, I found the family all busily employed in manufacturing, and they showed me a number of articles, which were very good, some of them handsome. They told me that, besides supplying the family, they made a considerable quantity of goods for sale."

[3] "Colonial Manufactures," *op. cit.*, V, 312.

munities nearly all the necessities of life. Imports into the country were attended with difficulty, great expense, and risk. The impossibility of getting their raw materials to the Atlantic states from which they had their supply of European goods made the balance of trade continually against them.[1] In 1805 it cost fifty cents to carry a hundred pounds twenty miles.[2] For this reason there was not a single species of product except ginseng, beeswax, and saltpeter that would justify the expense of land carriage to the eastern market.[3] From the period of the first settlement down to 1803 this region was in almost complete isolation so far as commercial relations were concerned. As long as the Spaniards held the mouth of the Mississippi, it was practically useless for the farmers to cultivate the soil beyond what was needed for their own consumption. But after the purchase of Louisiana trade conditions became more favorable when the inhabitants found an unobstructed market for their ginseng, flax, hemp, iron, pork, lard, lumber, furs, cotton, deerskins, and flour down the Mississippi. With the proceeds from the sale of these staples they could buy European goods from the eastern markets. This favorable situation was somewhat upset by the Embargo Act and the trade conditions following it. From the passage of this act in 1807 to the close of the War of 1812 these western people had to shift largely for themselves. They were forced to manufacture in their homes sufficient to supply their daily

[1] Ellicott, *Journal*, p. 24.

[2] Lippincott, "Pioneer Industry," *Jour. Pol. Econ.*, XVIII, 270.

[3] Reynolds, *My Own Times*, p. 13.

needs or to set up manufactures in small villages. The latter was done on a considerable scale in Cincinnati, Lexington, Louisville, Nashville, and Pittsburgh.[1]

Until there were set up in these local communities beyond the mountains gristmills, sawmills, hat factories, fulling-mills, distilleries, breweries, blacksmith-shops, wagon-shops, shoeshops, etc., the pioneer farm was a little world of its own. There was nothing in daily use except salt, lead, and powder that was not made from the products of the farm. The food, clothing, furniture, and agricultural implements were the products of this independent household. The farmer was his own cabinetmaker, tanner, brewer, distiller, shoemaker, harness-maker, hatter, tailor, and blacksmith. His tools were simple and often rude. At first he had only the ax and the auger. Later he added the drawing-knife, broadax, cross-cut saw, and awl and last. With these he made everything he needed on the farm. He stocked his plow, mended or made his wagon, made his ox-yokes, harness, shoes, tables, bedsteads, and chairs.[2] His whole life for the first dozen or so years was taken up with providing for himself and his family food, clothing, and shelter. The history of a typical pioneer community is chiefly an account of the efforts to provide these necessities. Until trade relations were established with older communities the household was practically self-supporting. Ways and means had to

[1] For an account of these manufactures in Lexington in 1806, see Cuming, *Tour of the West;* in Thwaites, *Early Western Travels*, IV, 185 ff. See also Melish, *op. cit.*, pp. 315, 361, 403.

[2] Hall, *Romance of Western History*, p. 239.

be thought out and operated on the farm to supply the daily needs.

Of the trinity of pioneer necessities, clothing was the most difficult to secure. The duty of transforming the raw materials into suitable wearing apparel and household supplies fell principally upon the women. A pioneer woman's work was never done. The day was not sufficient for her to perform all her duties. She was often compelled to work late into the night. The product of her strenuous labors was much the same in all new communities, for the dress of the American pioneers bore a striking similarity. This dress has been minutely described by one whose knowledge was first-hand, as follows:

> Home-made wool hats were the common wear. Fur-hats were not common and scarcely a boot was ever seen. The covering of the feet in winter was mostly moccasins made of deer-skin, and shoe-packs of tanned leather. Some wore shoes, but not common in very early times. In the summer, the greater portion of the young people, male and female, and many of the old, went barefooted. The substantial and universal outside wear was the blue linsey hunting shirt. . . . . It is made with wide sleeves, open before, with ample size, so as to envelop the body in its folds, almost twice around. Sometimes it has a large cape, which answers well to save the shoulders from the rain. A belt is mostly used, to keep the garment close and neatly around the person, and nevertheless, there is nothing tight in it to hamper the body. It is often fringed, and at times the fringe is composed of red, and other gay colors. The belt frequently is sewed to the hunting-shirt. At times, a belt of leather with a buckle sewed to one end is used. Many pioneers wore the white blanket-coats in winter. . . . . They are made loose, and a cap or cape to turn over the head in extreme cold weather. . . . . The vest was mostly made of striped linsey. The colors were made often with alum, copperas, and madder, boiled with the bark of trees, in such a manner

and proportion as the old ladies prescribed. The shirts wore by the Americans were usually home-made of flax and cotton material. . . . . The flax and cotton were raised at home, and manufactured into shirts. Looms and flax brakes were at that day quite common, and cotton-gins made of wooden rollers. . . . . The pantaloons of the masses were generally made of deer-skins and linsey. Coarse blue cloth was at times made into pantaloons. At that day, the factory-goods did not exist.[1]

The foregoing description of the clothing of the pioneer is applicable mainly to the first few years of his life on the frontier. Phelan says that by 1800 in some parts of Tennessee calico, chintzes, coarse woolen cloths, and bleached linen had taken the place of the leathern apron and the moccasin among the women. The men were a little slower, yet after a time vests, pants, and shirts, made of deerskin worn next to the person were discarded, and also the coonskin and other fur caps. The hunting-shirt

[1] Reynolds, *op. cit.*, pp. 43 f. Reynolds came from Tennessee to the region around Cahokia and Kaskaskia, Illinois, about 1800. He describes things as he himself saw them. Other accounts of the clothing of the time substantiate his description. In speaking of the early conditions of the settlement on the Little Hockhocking River at Belpre, Ohio, Hildreth says: "Whole households from the oldest to the youngest, were clad in dressed deer skins. Some of them possessed great skill in making them soft and pliable, equal to the finest cloth. Before the introduction of sheep, buckskin pantaloons were in general use by all the farmers' boys. The New England settlers, with most of the frontier inhabitants, made cloth of various materials. For the first two or three years, hemp was raised in small quantities, water rotted, and manufactured into cloth by the industrious females of the garrison. Flax was also raised. Nearly every family had their spinning-wheels and looms. With these the girls and young women used to congregate in companies of ten or fifteen in the spacious rooms of the block houses, and cheer each other at their labors, with song and sprightly conversation" (*Pioneer History*, p. 392).

lingered for some time yet, as did the leggings and moccasins. Leather thread for leathern garments gave place to cotton and flax thread.[1] When F. A. Michaux went through Kentucky and Tennessee in 1802 he noted that in Kentucky the women were exchanging their homemade linen for goods imported from Europe. It was his observation that these linens, though coarse, were of a good quality, and worn principally by the inferior inhabitants, the others giving a preference to Irish linens, which at that time comprised a considerable share of their commerce.[2] Of Tennessee he said:

> The cottons that are manufactured in West Tennessee are exceedingly fine, and superior in quality to those I saw in the course of my travels. In this part as well as in Kentucky, the higher circles wear in summer time, as much from patriotism as from economy, dresses made of the cottons manufactured in the country. At the same time they are convinced that it is the only means of preserving the little specie that is in the country, and of preventing its going to England.[3]

By 1810 the older settlements in these two states and those in Ohio had settled down to a life much like that beyond the mountains whence they had come. Cincinnati, Lexington, and Nashville had developed to thriving trading centers. Manufactured goods were brought into these states from Baltimore and Philadelphia, while most of their raw products found a market down the Mississippi River. Even as early as 1806, when Ashe visited

[1] *Hist. of Tenn.*, p. 180.

[2] *Travels to the West of the Alleghany Mountains*, Thwaites, *op. cit.*, p. 241.

[3] Thwaites, *op. cit.*, p. 278.

Lexington, Kentucky, he found that the chief business was ordering "immense quantities of goods from Philadelphia and Baltimore, and in bartering the same through the state for produce which was forwarded to Frankfort and Louisville by land, and from thence to New Orleans by water." At this time, according to Ashe's observations, "the people in these regions were furnished with an abundant supply of every article found in the first markets of Europe, except fish."[1] Ashe probably saw these settlements at a most favorable time—just before the passage of the Embargo and Non-Intercourse acts, which cut off the supply of European goods. Yet it should be said that on the cutting off of this European supply the towns mentioned above set to manufacturing many of the most needful articles, hence the reversion to the household industries was necessary chiefly in the line of wearing apparel and household textile supplies.

But brief mention need be made here of the newly acquired territory of Louisiana. According to Stoddard, at the time of the transfer of this territory to the United States a small quantity of cotton was manufactured along the coast into quilts and cottonades. Most families in the neighborhood of New Orleans and in the settlements, especially at Point Coupee, on the Red River, and in the Attakapas and Opelousas, spun and wove such articles of clothing as were necessary for their slaves. The people found on experiment that this sort of manufacturing was of great value, and began pretty generally to train some of their women and girl slaves to spin and weave and some

[1] *Travels*, p. 193, both references.

of their men to do blacksmith and carpenter work.[1] In the upper part of what is now Louisiana, according to the same author, "the inhabitants generally cultivated a sufficient quantity of cotton for family purposes, spun and wove it into cloth. They were unable to defray the expense of foreign manufactures; the prices of which in these upper regions were very exorbitant."[2] These foreign manufactures were plentiful in New Orleans at this time. The imports into this city in 1802 consisted of some 202 different items, including everything anyone could wish either for comfort or for luxury.[3] It was only a lack of the means of exchange for factory-made goods that forced home manufacturing upon these people. In this they differed from the people on the extreme frontier.

The general conditions of household manufactures during the closing days of 1809 is exhibited in a report on the subject, "American Manufactures," sent to the House of Representatives on April 19 of this year by Secretary of the Treasury Gallatin, in compliance with a resolution of this body.[4] The brief time allowed for compiling such a report prevented an exhaustive investigation, yet from certain sections of the country considerable data were secured by the Secretary. For example, the report from

[1] *Sketches of La.*, p. 304.

[2] *Ibid.*, p. 305. Speaking of conditions in this region at the same date, Martin said: "There were but few domestic manufactures. The Acadians wrought some cotton into quilts and homespun, and in the more remote parts of the province, the poorer kind of people spun and wove the wool mixed with cotton, into coarse cloth" (*Hist. of La.*, p. 317).

[3] For an itemized list with quantity for each, see Martin, *op. cit.*, p. 311.

[4] For the text of the report, see *Am. State Papers*, "Finance," II, 426 ff.

New Hampshire said that in almost every town (of six miles square or a district containing one or more towns) having a population of 200 or 300 families there were a fulling-mill and a carding-machine. Every farmer's house was provided with one or more wheels, according to the number of women. Every other house had a loom for weaving linen, cotton, and coarse woolen cloths. Manufactures of this kind amounted on the average in each family to from 100 to 600 yards a year. Considerable quantities of coarse flaxen cloth worth from 15 to 20 cents a yard, thus manufactured in families, were sold to traders in villages or in towns and sent to markets in the southern states.[1] Similar returns came from other sections of the country. It was reported that in Delaware 150,000 pounds of wool were annually spun and woven in private families. Large exportations of linen from the western counties of Pennsylvania and some from Kentucky and several places in the eastern and middle states were annually made. Eighty thousand yards were brought for sale in 1809 to Pittsburgh alone. The number of looms in Pittsburgh increased from 17 in 1807 to 44 in 1810. In the lower counties of Virginia, North Carolina generally, and the upper counties of South Carolina and Georgia almost all the summer clothing, for every description of persons, was of household manufacture; and almost all the slaves were clothed entirely in the same manner. The scarcity of wool prevented an adequate supply from the same source for winter clothing. The number of stores for the sale of foreign goods in Mathews County, Virginia,

[1] *Am. State Papers*, "Finance," II, 435.

decreased from 15 to 1 between 1802 and 1810. In North Carolina, at a general militia review, out of 1,500 persons present there were less than 40 who were not entirely clothed in homespun.[1]

Generalizing on the basis of the foregoing and similar facts, Gallatin spoke as follows:

> By far the greater part of goods made of cotton, flax or wool, are manufactured in the private families, mostly for their own use, and partly for sale. They consist principally of coarse cloth, flannel, cotton stuffs, and stripes of every description, linen and mixtures of wool with flax and cotton. It is probable that about two-thirds of the clothing, including hosiery, and of the house and table linen worn and used by the inhabitants of the United States, who do not reside in cities, is the product of family manufacture.[2]

The results of the census of manufactures taken in the fall of 1810 revealed the truth of this generalization. These are analyzed in the following chapter.

[1] *Ibid.*, p. 435.

[2] *Ibid.*, p. 427.

CHAPTER V

A YEAR'S OUTPUT OF THE FAMILY FACTORY

THE RETURNS OF THE MARSHALS IN THE AUTUMN OF 1810

In April, 1810, Gallatin, in obedience to a resolution of the House of Representatives, sent to that body a report on American manufactures. The introduction of this report suggested the feasibility of collecting data on every phase of manufacturing through the marshals and assistants when they were taking the third census.[1] Acting upon this suggestion, Congress, on May 1, 1810, altered the act providing for the taking of the census so that it would include statistics on manufacturing establishments and manufactures.[2] The bill altering the original act gave the Secretary of the Treasury power to formulate the instructions to the marshals regarding the desired data along these lines. His instructions to them included questions on household manufactures.

The reports which came in in the fall of 1810 were sharply criticized on account of their omissions. It was felt that they did not represent anything like a reliable and complete account of all the manufactures carried on in the country. This discussion is not concerned with the returns as a whole, but only with those dealing with goods made in the homes. The character of the information demanded regarding this phase of the subject was of

[1] *Am. State Papers*, "Finance," II, 426.

[2] *U.S. Statutes at Large*, II, 605.

such a nature as to lead to many indefinite estimates. At best, the people could make but a gross calculation of the amount and value of what had been made in their homes during the year next preceding the date of the taking of the census. Many admitted that they were unable to give an accurate statement; others were afraid that the object of the government was to tax the industry, hence they either refused to give any account whatever or gave certainly not a full one. The marshal of Rhode Island informed the Secretary of the Treasury that much patience and forbearance were required by his assistants, "from the prejudice of the people, who in many instances refused to give any account of their manufactured articles, and perhaps not any article to the full amount of value from an opinion that the returns were demanded by the government with a view of taxing the industry." The marshal was of the opinion that from 20 to 25 per cent should be added to the amount returned in order to get the real value of what was made in the homes. It was felt at the time the census was taken that the amounts reported from Pennsylvania, Connecticut, Massachusetts, New Jersey, and Virginia were close approximations to the real ones. The errors in the remaining states and territories were on the side of omissions.[1]

On account of the admitted inadequateness of the returns, no full and complete exhibit of household manufactures in 1810 is possible. Table XI, based on Coxe's digest of the marshals' returns, shows what was done in the families in the way of textile manufactures in all

[1] Pitkin, *Statistics of the U.S.* (ed. 1835), p. 470.

TABLE XI

THE KINDS, TOTAL YARDS, TOTAL AND PER CAPITA VALUES OF HOUSEHOLD MANUFACTURES IN EVERY STATE AND TERRITORY OF THE UNITED STATES FOR THE YEAR ENDING IN THE AUTUMN OF 1810*

STATES AND TERRITORIES	YARDS OF THE FOLLOWING GOODS					VALUE OF FOREGOING	VALUE OF MISCELLANEOUS ARTICLES†	TOTAL VALUE	POPULATION, 1810‡	PER CAPITA VALUE
	Cotton	Flaxen	Woolen	Mixed and Unnamed	Total					
Maine district	811,912	....	812,796	1,021,047	2,645,755	$ 1,067,703	....	$ 1,067,703	228,709	$4.67
New Hampshire	515,985	1,811,309	900,273	1,043,588	4,271,155	1,760,417	$ 216,297	1,976,714	214,360	9.22
Vermont	67,614	1,366,483	907,568	85,198	2,426,863	1,268,263	53,164	1,321,427	217,913	6.06
Massachusetts	....	60,000	....	4,048,209	4,108,209	2,093,576	61,453	2,155,029	437,659	4.92
Connecticut	....	2,362,078	1,119,145	605,675	4,086,898	2,130,825	111,022	2,241,847	261,942	8.52
Rhode Island	460,989	229,699	145,618	481,841	1,318,147	895,923	4,096	900,019	76,931	11.70
New York	216,013	5,394,186	3,257,812	180,659	9,048,670	5,022,251	7,644	5,029,895	959,220	5.24
New Jersey	....	847,469	374,313	719,395	1,941,177	1,268,241	25,939	1,294,180	245,562	5.27
Pennsylvania	611,481	2,990,622	997,351	1,801,025	6,400,497	4,250,773	362,206	4,612,979	813,091	5.67
Delaware	661	280,369	63,943	17,820	362,793	207,822	4,759	212,581	72,674	2.92
Maryland	....	....	....	1,755,963	1,755,963	1,013,320	23,546	1,036,866	372,541	2.78
Virginia	2,998,255	4,918,273	408,224	1,298,793	9,623,545	4,643,929	241,673	4,885,602	909,670	5.37
North Carolina	....	....	....	7,376,154	7,376,154	2,989,140	....	2,989,140	552,213	5.41
South Carolina	3,083,188	690	72,636	110,627	3,267,141	1,677,228	....	1,677,228	296,765	5.65
Georgia	3,688,534	11,253	5,591	483,925	4,189,303	2,143,348	5,685	2,149,033	248,492	8.65
Kentucky	....	....	....	4,685,205	4,685,205	2,057,081	308,932	2,366,013	406,511	5.82
Tennessee§	1,790,514	....	34,141	228,193	2,052,848	1,675,314	16,234	1,691,548	261,727	6.46
Ohio	56,072	1,093,031	93,074	701,156	1,943,333	1,032,235	302,280	1,334,515	216,164	6.17
Mississippi Ter.	342,472	450	7,898	....	350,820	266,493	....	266,493	40,352	6.60
Orleans Ter.	133,180	....	....	....	133,180	106,941	300	107,241	43,154	2.48
Illinois Ter.	....	....	....	90,039	90,039	54,023	1,950	55,973	12,282	4.56
Indiana Ter.	54,977	92,740	19,378	77,171	244,266	166,813	11,000	177,813	24,520	7.25
Michigan Ter.	....	1,216	2,405	....	3,621	3,470	....	3,470	4,147	0.84
District of Columbia	26,000	....	....	20,000	46,000	39,500	....	39,500	24,023	1.64
Total	14,857,847	21,450,868	9,222,166	26,831,683	72,371,564	$37,834,629	$1,758,180	$39,592,809	6,940,622	$5.70

*Based on Part IV of Coxe's "Digest of Manufactures," *Am. State Papers*, "Finance," II, 719 ff.

†Under miscellaneous articles are included stockings, thread, web lace, fringe, blankets, carpets, coverlets, maple sugar, tow cloth, yarn, and wines. Not all counties reported on these. They are included only where it was evident that they were made in the homes. Such articles as pot and pearl ashes, boots, shoes, hats, caps, beer, spirits, candles, soap, harness, and cabinet wares were not included because it was impossible to tell what proportion of them was made in the homes and in the shops. Except in frontier communities, most of such articles were made in shops and by persons regularly engaged in the business.

‡See Table XII for details of population statistics. Counties from which there were no reports have been omitted. These are enumerated in the footnotes to Table XII.

§Sixteen counties reported values only. See p. 180.

the states and territories. Unfortunately other things evidently made in the family were not reported with such uniformity. All these are included under miscellaneous articles. For general estimates it is probably fair to assume that in textile manufactures omissions were about as common in one part of the country as in another. On account of this possible uniformity one gets a fair calculation of the relative amounts of such manufactures in the different parts of the country.[1]

The total value of all textile manufactures in 1810, according to the returns of the marshals, was $41,549,177. Table XI shows that $37,834,629 worth was made in the homes, leaving but $3,714,584 worth made otherwise. The total value of all manufactures (doubtful articles excluded) was, by the same returns, $127,694,602. Coxe estimated, when he made his digest, that the actual value was probably $172,762,676.[2] Based on the supposition

[1] The writer is fully conscious of the fallibility of materials of this type and the consequent danger of basing conclusions on them. However, since the census of manufactures taken in 1810 in connection with the taking of the census of population was the first and only detailed account of household manufactures ever secured by the national government, it is quite evident that no account of such manufactures would be at all complete without a presentation of such statistics even though they are fallible and fragmentary. In reading Table XI and the one exhibiting the same facts by counties, the reader must always keep in mind the circumstances under which the materials were collected.

[2] "Digest of Manufactures," *op. cit.*, 712 f. It has been estimated that in 1810 the factories of America were producing less than 4 per cent of the woolen goods made in the country. When this fact is considered along with another one of equal significance, namely, that the imports of woolen cloth from all sources did not exceed 5,000,000 yards, the importance of the 9,222,166 yards woven in the homes becomes more evident (Clark, *Hist. of Manufactures in U.S.*, p. 253).

that the counties from which there were no returns made a per capita value equal to that of the whole country, the household textile manufactures reached a total value of $39,457,471. The table certainly shows that the homes were doing their part in establishing an independence in common wearing apparel and general household textile supplies.

In order to see what the different sections of the various states were doing, it is necessary to analyze the returns from each county. By such an analysis one is able to determine the probable influence of locality, transportation, occupation, and other similar factors on the household production. The accompanying elaborate Table XII exhibits the amount and value of homemade textiles in each county and district in the Union as returned by the marshals. Only textile manufactures are included because other articles were not returned with sufficient uniformity to justify their inclusion when the county is made the unit. Within each state the counties are grouped according to location on the basis of transportation facilities in so far as they existed at that date.

Table XII reveals several interesting facts concerning household manufactures, the most striking one being the extent and uniformity of the system throughout the United States in 1810. The inhabitants in all sections of the country, regardless of locality, economic status, and transportation facilities, were deliberately trying to establish an independence from the outside world, especially in wearing apparel and household textile supplies. The more or less uniformity in the per capita value reveals

TABLE XII

THE KINDS, TOTAL YARDS, TOTAL AND PER CAPITA VALUES OF HOUSEHOLD TEXTILE MANUFACTURES IN EVERY STATE, TERRITORY, AND COUNTY IN THE UNITED STATES FOR THE YEAR ENDING IN THE AUTUMN OF 1810*

STATES, TERRITORIES, AND COUNTIES	YARDS OF THE FOLLOWING KINDS OF GOODS					VALUE OF ALL KINDS OF GOODS	POPULATION, 1810	PER CAPITA VALUE
	Cotton	Flaxen	Woolen	Mixed and Unnamed	Total			
						Dollars		Dollars
MAINE DISTRICT....	811,912	....	812,796	1,021,047	2,645,755	1,067,703	228,709	4.67
Cos. on Coast.....	*597,096*	....	*560,337*	*736,466*	*1,893,899*	*759,156*	*165,605*	*4.58*
Cumberland....	162,198	....	151,082	198,733	512,013	205,211	42,835	4.56
Hancock.......	66,746	....	104,460	62,747	233,953	105,061	30,031	3.50
Lincoln.........	122,389	....	170,989	134,713	428,091	185,227	42,992	4.31
Washington.....	43,766	....	42,534	45,000	131,300	54,277	7,870	6.90
York...........	201,997	....	91,272	295,273	588,542	209,380	41,877	5.02
***Inland** Cos*........	*214,816*	....	*252,459*	*284,581*	*751,856*	*308,547*	*63,104*	*4.89*
Kennebeck.....	108,266	....	122,107	139,281	369,654	151,391	32,564	4.65
Oxford.........	49,678	....	72,859	90,857	213,394	86,301	17,630	4.90
Somerset.......	56,872	....	57,493	54,443	168,808	70,855	12,910	5.49
NEW HAMPSHIRE....	515,985	1,811,309	900,273	1,043,588	4,271,155	1,760,417	214,360	8.21
Cheshire.......	50,000	220,000	248,000	300,000	818,000	383,000	40,988	9.34
Hillsborough....	221,000	512,000	243,000	180,770	1,156,770	568,350	49,149	11.56
Rockingham....	180,000	600,757	113,902	237,540	1,132,199	351,391	50,175	7.00
Coos..........	23,000	17,000	24,000	40,000	104,000	41,600	3,991	10.42
Grafton........	20,000	153,000	132,000	98,000	403,000	169,900	28,462	5.97
Strafford.......	21,985	308,552	139,371	187,278	657,186	246,176	41.595	5.92
VERMONT...........	67,614	1,366,483	907,568	85,198	2,426,863	1,268,263	217,913	5.82
Cos. on Conn. R...	*55,102*	*787,122*	*448,054*	*52,871*	*1,343,149*	*691,802*	*108,711*	*6.36*
Caledonia......	12,909	216,734	130,873	....	360,516	201,331	18,740	10.74
Essex..........	745	23,308	12,576	5,440	42,069	19,881	3,087	6.44
Orange.........	15,857	125,763	93,707	40,810	276,137	115,413	25,247	4.57
Windham†	15,491	119,133	60,605	6,621	201,850	94,509	26,760	3.53
Windsor‡.......	10,100	302,184	150,293	....	462,577	260,668	34,877	7.47
Inland Cos........	*12,512*	*579,361*	*459,514*	*32,327*	*1,083,714*	*576,461*	*109,202*	*5.28*
Addison........	1,473	131,958	118,638	8,347	260,416	134,106	19,993	6.71
Bennington.....	800	68,895	66,834	2,222	138,751	78,446	15,893	4.94
Chittenden.....	3,572	129,590	92,835	....	225,997	116,053	18,120	6.40
Franklin.......	....	70,492	50,991	2,500	123,983	87,487	16,427	5.33
Grand Isle......	....	13,617	18,154	7,373	39,144	21,081	3,445	6.12
Orleans.........	....	34,436	22,614	11,885	68,935	30,236	5,838	5.18
Rutland........	6,667	130,373	89,448	....	226,488	100,052	29,486	3.70

* This table was compiled from data in Coxe's "Digest of Manufactures." By order of Congress, Coxe made an elaborate digest of the census of manufactures taken by the marshals in 1810. Part IV of the digest contained statistics on household manufactures. This part was printed separately in 1814.

The population statistics were copied from *Niles' Register*, I, 264, 289, 358, 388. Carey and Lea's *American Atlas* (1823) was used for the county locations and to check the population statistics in Niles. It was thought best to adopt Coxe's spelling of the counties in order to facilitate the matter of checking the material in the table.

† Nine townships not returned. ‡ Four townships not returned.

TABLE XII—*Continued*

States, Territories, and Counties	Yards of the Following Kinds of Goods					Value of All Kinds of Goods	Population, 1810	Per Capita Value
	Cotton	Flaxen	Woolen	Mixed and Unnamed	Total			
						Dollars		Dollars
Massachusetts*	....	60,000	....	4,048,209	4,108,209	2,093,576	437,659	4.79
Coast and Island	....	....	....	*1,309,800*	*1,309,800*	*678,485*	*223,399*	*3.05*
Barnstable	....	....	....	41,720	41,720	20,860	22,211	0.94
Dukes	....	....	....	17,775	17,775	12,442	3,290	3.78
Essex	....	....	....	259,053	259,053	103,813	71,888	1.44
Middlesex	....	....	....	448,661	448,661	246,709	52,789	4.67
Nantucket	....	....	....	4,300	4,300	2,980	6,807	0.44
Norfolk	....	....	....	190,593	190,593	129,397	31,245	4.14
Plymouth	....	....	....	347,698	347,698	162,284	35,169	4.61
Inland Cos	....	*60,000*	....	*2,738,409*	*2,798,409*	*1,415,091*	*214,260*	*6.60*
Berkshire	....	....	....	527,226	527,226	181,058	35,907	5.04
Bristol	....	....	....	319,905	319,905	144,452	37,168	3.89
Hampshire	....	60,000	....	1,054,558	1,114,558	599,941	76,275	7.87
Worcester	....	....	....	836,720	836,720	489,640	64,910	7.54
Connecticut	....	2,362,078	1,119,145	605,675	4,086,898	2,130,825	261,942	8.14
On Long Island Sd.	....	*1,121,654*	*452,448*	*284,761*	*1,858,863*	*943,015*	*133,444*	*8.13*
Fairfield	....	412,006	139,572	10,054	561,632	298,955	40,950	7.30
Middlesex	....	150,839	67,062	42,655	260,556	149,687	20,723	7.22
New Haven	....	292,561	131,054	64,864	488,479	258,336	37,064	6.97
New London	....	266,248	114,760	167,188	548,196	245,037	34,707	7.06
Inland Cos	....	*1,240,424*	*666,697*	*320,014*	*2,228,035*	*1,187,810*	*128,498*	*9.25*
Hartford	....	300,169	188,663	7,234	586,066	329,359	44,733	7.36
Litchfield	....	431,104	281,184	16,700	729,078	441,304	41,375	10.67
Tolland	....	165,479	86,998	5,000	257,477	130,012	13,779	9.44
Windham	....	253,582	109,852	291,980	655,414	287,135	28,611	10.04
Rhode Island	460,989	229,699	145,618	481,841	2,318,147	895,923	76,931	11.65
Providence	63,159	35,940	50,957	107,860	257,916	101,197	30,769	3.29
Bristol	21,500	3,200	5,000	....	29,700	13,560	5,072	2.67
Kent†	313,271	7,006	16,624	352,742	689,643	613,631	9,834	62.11
Newport	11,373	33,345	16,791	17,741	79,250	55,052	16,294	3.04
Washington	51,686	150,208	56,246	3,498	261,638	112,483	14,962	7.52
New York	216,013	5,394,186	3,257,812	180,659	9,048,670	5,022,251	959,220	5.24
Cos. on Hudson R.‡	*90,445*	*2,622,995*	*1,717,590*	*49,483*	*4,480,513*	*2,549,012*	*528,871*	*4.82*
Albany	....	145,282	87,272	....	232,554	130,843	34,661	3.77
Clinton	....	24,068	23,795	....	47,863	29,846	8,002	3.73
Columbia	20,500	341,530	254,750	....	616,780	357,540	32,390	11.04
Dutchess	....	230,404	128,655	....	359,059	198,975	51,434	3.87
Essex	....	34,428	69,857	....	104,285	74,035	9,477	7.81
Green	868	32,265	22,189	....	55,322	31,140	19,536	1.54
Kings	....	32,233	4,301	3,931	40,465	18,023	8,303	2.16
New York (city and Co.)	....	217	2,540	....	2,757	2,304	96,373	0.23
Orange	4,182	212,429	95,611	3,859	316,081	166,007	34,347	4.83

* Nothing reported from Suffolk County.

† The high per capita value in Kent County resulted from 352,742 yards of blended goods valued by the marshal at $472,921.80. This value was considerably higher than that placed on similar goods by the marshals in other counties.

‡ Also on Atlantic Ocean and Lake Champlain.

TABLE XII—*Continued*

States, Territories, and Counties	Yards of the Following Kinds of Goods					Value of All Kinds of Goods	Population, 1810	Per Capita Value
	Cotton	Flaxen	Woolen	Mixed and Unnamed	Total			
New York—*Continued*						Dollars		Dollars
Queens	....	132,936	51,292	2,913	187,141	95,751	19,336	4.95
Rensselaer	2,263	222,049	157,862	....	382,174	222,123	36,309	6.12
Richmond	....	23,100	2,000	7,000	32,100	12,863	5,347	2.41
Rockland	....	36,792	8,008	....	44,800	19,457	7,758	1.87
Saratoga	....	194,976	171,789	....	366,765	223,431	33,147	6.74
Schenectady	....	5,000	2,500	....	7,500	4,063	10,201	0.40
Suffolk	4,087	158,390	51,220	....	213,697	122,146	21,113	5.78
Ulster	7,404	222,042	87,400	31,780	348,626	173,232	26,576	6.52
Washington	51,141	350,754	384,359	....	786,254	484,212	44,289	10.93
Westchester	....	224,280	112,190	....	336,470	183,021	30,272	6.04
Cos. on Great Lakes	*9,072*	*899,968*	*463,728*	*10,815*	*1,383,583*	*749,904*	*125,183*	*5.99*
Niagara	3,218	43,039	17,585	....	63,842	32,554	3,971	8.19
Ontario	....	329,226	195,551	....	524,777	294,567	42,032	7.01
Seneca	2,035	115,585	49,473	5,620	172,713	89,221	16,609	5.37
Cayuga	....	216,805	120,346	3,720	340,871	187,905	29,843	6.30
Genesee	2,427	88,690	29,760	....	120,877	60,075	12,588	4.77
Jefferson	1,392	106,623	51,013	1,475	160,503	85,582	15,140	5.65
Inland Cos	*116,496*	*1,871,223*	*1,076,494*	*120,361*	*3,184,574*	*1,723,335*	*305,165*	*5.64*
Alleghany	307	11,679	3,162	....	15,148	7,243	1,942	3.73
Broom	....	63,455	22,816	19,939	106,210	50,738	8,130	6.24
Chenango	3,278	149,510	64,783	3,278	220,849	114,948	21,704	5.30
Cortlandt	2,826	39,000	25,400	....	67,226	37,754	8,868	4.26
Delaware	724	130,801	70,571	....	202,096	111,029	20,303	5.46
Franklin	....	9,913	5,138	859	15,010	8,512	2,717	3.13
Herkimer	10,000	190,945	95,590	....	296,535	158,445	22,046	7.19
Madison	5,026	225,297	120,452	....	350,775	191,490	25,144	7.62
Montgomery	1,255	150,136	85,861	....	237,252	131,831	41,214	3.20
Oneida	80,817	12,791	159,622	80,405	333,635	198,468	33,792	5.76
Onondaga	3,009	196,106	107,470	....	306,585	168,638	25,987	6.49
Otsego	....	327,088	153,728	....	480,816	257,170	38,802	6.63
St. Lawrence	....	36,000	19,047	1,926	56,973	30,841	7,885	3.91
Schoharie	2,823	112,128	53,093	3,909	171,953	90,776	18,945	4.79
Steuben	4,416	63,687	25,937	....	94,040	48,192	7,246	6.65
Sullivan	....	35,347	13,587	1,057	49,991	25,510	6,108	4.18
Tioga	2,015	67,340	24,737	7,988	112,080	50,337	7,899	6.37
Lewis	....	50,000	25,500	1,000	76,500	41,413	6,433	6.44
New Jersey*	....	847,469	374,313	719,395	1,941,177	1,268,241	245,562	5.16
Bergen	....	139,035	11,739	29,137	170,911	98,759	14,728	6.71
Burlington	....	....	34,123	32,196	66,319	50,221	24,553	2.04
Cape May	....	....	....	19,482	19,482	9,741	3,632	2.68
Cumberland	....	68,467	29,552	....	98,019	55,491	12,670	4.38
Essex	....	....	43,000	201,836	244,836	200,000	24,979	8.01
Glouchester	....	....	....	149,094	149,094	198,295	19,744	10.04
Hunterdon	....	152,905	48,477	20,580	221,962	107,799	25,984	4.19
Middlesex	....	108,720	35,831	....	144,551	126,628	20,381	6.21
Monmouth	....	....	....	18,749	18,749	11,705	22,150	0.53
Morris	....	164,240	60,830	14,063	239,133	107,405	21,823	4.92
Salem	....	44,200	13,200	36,000	93,400	57,560	16,603	3.47
Somerset	....	....	....	120,048	120,048	59,819	12,761	4.69
Sussex	....	169,902	97,561	78,210	345,673	184,818	25,549	7.23

* All counties run east and west across the state; no classification necessary.

TABLE XII—*Continued*

States, Territories, and Counties	Yards of the Following Kinds of Goods					Value of All Kinds of Goods	Population, 1810	Per Capita Value
	Cotton	Flaxen	Woolen	Mixed and Unnamed	Total	Dollars		Dollars
PENNSYLVANIA	611,481	2,990,622	990,346	1,801,025	6,400,479	4,250,773	813,091	5.23
*Cos. on Del. R.**	*544,099*	*2,024,217*	*743,341*	*830,195*	*4,148,857*	*3,043,156*	*614,569*	*4.95*
Adams	12,429	75,212	18,639	11,207	117,487	70,831	15,152	4.67
Bedford	12,745	78,422	31,422	6,321	128,910	77,947	15,746	4.95
Berks	20,022	238,016	71,812	....	329,850	289,790	43,146	6.72
Bucks	7,552	113,293	30,211	....	151,056	378,515	32,371	11.69
Centre	10,648	17,675	28,767	814	57,904	30,742	10,681	2.88
Chester	7,441	170,604	74,996	....	253,041	163,274	39,596	4.12
Cumberland	24,504	255,385	48,786	1,994	330,669	171,078	26,757	6.39
Dauphin	22,776	81,660	77,451	245,304	427,191	265,410	31,883	8.32
Delaware	....	....	....	79,250	79,250	79,250	14,734	5.38
Franklin	9,793	83,121	36,731	7,571	137,216	77,774	23,083	3.37
Huntingdon	12,001	70,029	25,030	4,600	111,660	66,684	14,778	4.51
Lancaster	23,336	106,482	32,744	71,214	233,776	152,381	53,927	2.83
Luzerne	3,154	80,703	28,232	56,411	168,500	87,975	18,109	4.80
Lycoming	19,973	70,172	20,108	752	111,005	75,200	11,006	6.83
Mifflin	13,563	75,429	30,927	5,471	125,390	77,397	12,132	6.38
Montgomery	....	....	38,800	40,000	78,800	94,200	29,703	3.17
Northampton	....	....	....	113,175	113,175	56,587	38,145	1.48
Northumberland	73,566	197,901	71,437	....	342,704	159,510	36,327	3.84
Philadelphia	233,232	77,788	16,168	157,784	484,972	399,979	111,210	3.59
Wayne	1,130	16,312	7,905	....	25,347	16,613	4,125	4.03
York	36,234	216,213	60,180	28,327	340,954	252,019	31,958	7.89
Cos. N.W.†	*67,382*	*966,405*	*247,005*	*970,830*	*2,251,622*	*1,207,617*	*198,522*	*6.08*
Alleghany	....	....	....	230,756	230,756	115,379	25,317	4.56
Armstrong	....	61,725	5,531	22,070	89,326	46,781	6,143	7.62
Beaver	17,362	120,563	28,274	....	166,199	83,493	12,168	6.86
Butler	15,948	82,501	13,030	....	111,479	60,659	7,346	8.26
Cambria	850	12,900	930	....	14,680	7,750	2,117	3.66
Clearfield	1,306	4,300	....	3,461	9,067	4,725	875	5.40
Crawford	3,250	53,330	16,819	....	73,399	37,706	6,178	6.10
Erie	1,037	20,217	7,979	15	29,248	19,032	3,758	5.06
Fayette	....	183,392	67,897	33,796	285,085	164,453	24,714	6.65
Greene	5,000	39,181	5,112	5,062	54,355	28,273	12,544	2.25
Indiana	1,000	50,000	10,000	1,000	62,000	31,500	6,214	5.07
Jefferson	....	1,318	200	....	1,518	811	161	5.03
M'Kean	54	125	52	....	231	129	142	0.91
Mercer	6,016	28,312	5,499	10,910	50,737	35,563	8,277	4.30
Somerset	....	....	....	136,545	136,545	68,273	11,284	6.05
Venango	....	21,119	2,860	7,346	31,325	19,745	3,060	6.45
Warren	578	6,549	160	1,811	9,098	5,690	3,827	1.49
Washington	....	....	....	515,129	515,129	270,342	36,289	7.45
Westmorland	14,552	270,803	81,159	2,929	369,443	200,829	26,392	7.61
Tioga and Potter	429	10,070	1,503	....	12,002	6,484	1,716	3.78
DELAWARE‡	661	280,369	63,943	17,820	362,793	207,822	72,674	2.86
Kent	....	38,427	4,269	....	42,696	23,482	20,495	1.15
New Castle	661	75,440	11,524	17,820	105,445	52,939	24,429	2.17
Sussex	....	166,502	48,150	....	214,652	131,401	27,750	4.74

* Also in lower Susquehanna valley and southeast of the Alleghany Mountains.

† Northwest of the Alleghany Mountains.

‡ All counties on the Bay.

TABLE XII—*Continued*

States, Territories, and Counties	Yards of the Following Kinds of Goods: Cotton	Flaxen	Woolen	Mixed and Unnamed	Total	Value of All Kinds of Goods	Population, 1810	Per Capita Value
						Dollars		Dollars
MARYLAND*	....	....	....	1,755,963	1,755,963	1,013,320	372,541	2.71
Cos. on Potomac†	....	....	....	*1,284,853*	*1,284,853*	*664,096*	*294,485*	*2.22*
Anne Arundel	....	....	....	30,155	30,155	14,689	26,668	0.55
Baltimore	....	....	....	182,517	182,517	78,297	75,810	1.03
Caroline	....	....	....	50,490	50,490	23,565	9,453	2.49
Cecil	....	....	....	75,531	75,531	67,076	13,066	5.13
Charles	....	....	....	203,810	203,810	81,524	20,245	4.03
Dorchester	....	....	....	43,719	43,719	23,347	18,108	1.29
Harford	....	....	....	102,387	102,387	65,528	21,258	3.08
Kent	....	....	....	39,244	39,244	20,240	11,450	1.77
Prince George	....	....	....	82,951	82,951	41,475	20,589	2.01
QueenAnne	....	....	....	55,000	55,000	27,500	16,648	1.65
Saint Marys	....	....	....	90,000	90,000	45,000	12,794	3.52
Somerset	....	....	....	80,000	80,000	50,000	17,195	2.91
Worcester	....	....	....	177,920	177,920	88,960	16,971	5.24
Talbot	....	....	....	71,129	71,129	36,895	14,230	2.59
Cos. on Potomac‡	....	....	....	*471,110*	*471,110*	*349,224*	*78,056*	*4.47*
Alleghany	....	....	....	56,702	56,702	23,109	6,909	3.34
Frederick	....	....	....	209,944	209,944	152,583	34,437	4.43
Montgomery	....	....	....	71,647	71,647	40,715	17,980	2.26
Washington	....	....	....	132,817	132,817	132,817	18,730	7.09
VIRGINIA§	2,998,255	4,918,273	408,224	1,298,793	9,623,545	4,643,929	909,670	5.14
Cos. in Tide‖	*1,662,084*	*1,248,262*	*79,099*	*349,193*	*3,338,638*	*1,456,033*	*341,358*	*4.32*
Essex	53,978	....	11.087	....	65,065	32,533	9,376	3.35
Accomack	....	82,000	....	82,000	164,000	56,958	15,743	3.62
Brunswick	155,665	....	....	31,257	186,922	98,413	15,411	6.39
Caroline	124,283	....	....	26,709	150,992	50,331	17,544	2.89
Charles City	....	33,766	....	....	33,766	13,889	5,186	2.68
Chesterfield	....	93,764	....	....	93,764	31,225	9,979	3.13
Dinwiddie	....	115,376	....	....	115,376	57,688	12,524	4.61
Elizabeth City	29,500	....	....	....	29,500	17,700	3,608	4.91
Fairfax	....	87,692	....	....	87,692	45,840	13,111	3.50
Gloucester	187,696	....	....	....	187,696	93,848	10,427	9.00
Hanover	113,462	....	34,063	....	147,525	64,344	15,082	4.27
Henrico	....	....	....	67,000	67,000	33,500	9,945	3.37
Isle of Wight	101,875	....	....	....	101,875	50,937	9,186	5.54
James City	34,236	....	....	8,559	42,795	21,397	4,094	5.22
King George	40,746	....	....	15,288	56,034	18,678	6,454	2.89
King and Queen	98,400	....	....	20,500	118,900	59,450	10,988	5.41
King William	84,000	....	....	14,000	98,000	32,667	9,285	3.52
Lancaster	....	75,560	....	....	75,560	32,987	5,592	5.90
Matthews	....	35,897	....	....	35,897	11,965	4,227	2.83
Middlesex	....	51,125	....	....	51,135	17,045	4,414	3.86

* Nothing reported from Calvert County.

† On Potomac River below the Fall Line.

‡ On Potomac River above the Fall Line.

§ Nothing reported from Greenville, Amherst, Fluvana, Pendleton, Mason, Hampshire, and Prince William counties.

‖ In the tidewater region.

TABLE XII—*Continued*

States, Territories, and Counties	Yards of the Following Kinds of Goods					Value of All Kinds of Goods	Population, 1810	Per Capita Value
	Cotton	Flaxen	Woolen	Mixed and Unnamed	Total			
Virginia—*Continued*						Dollars		Dollars
Nansimond	....	70,005	....	....	70,005	23,334	10,324	2.26
New Kent	51,792	....	....	24,923	76,715	38,350	6,478	5.92
Northampton	68,618	....	....	....	68,618	22,872	7,474	3.06
Northumberland	86,790	....	....	....	86,790	28,930	8,308	3.48
Prince George	122,382	....	....	....	122,382	40,794	8,050	5.07
Princess Anne	11,866	36,295	22,383	....	70,544	30,377	9,498	3.20
Richmond	....	69,927	....	7,860	72,787	49,297	6,214	7.93
Southampton	....	315,140	....	....	315,140	105,047	13,497	7.78
Spotsylvania	100,000	....	....	30,000	130,000	68,400	13,296	5.14
Stafford	....	97,422	....	....	97,422	49,028	9,830	4.99
Surry	73,220	948	11,566	....	85,734	42,867	6,855	6.25
Sussex	117,575	....	....	21,097	138,672	69,336	11,362	6.10
Warwick	....	1,790	....	....	1,790	7,347	1,835	4.00
Westmorland	....	56,525	....	....	56,525	23,740	8,102	2.93
York	....	25,020	....	....	25,020	12,519	5,187	2.41
Norfolk	6,000	....	....	....	6,000	2,400	22,872	0.11
*From Fall Line**	*1,162,770*	*1,984,818*	*150,113*	*469,924*	*3,767,625*	*2,033,290*	*335,519*	*6.04*
Albemarle	176,769	32,794	5,578	....	215,141	95,564	18,268	5.23
Amelia	....	151,418	....	....	151,418	75,709	10,594	7.15
Bedford	60,240	21,830	32,830	33,360	148,260	74,160	16,148	4.59
Buckingham	106,000	14,401	32,401	....	152,802	79,052	20,059	3.94
Campbell	....	77,823	....	....	77,823	38,936	11,001	3.54
Charlotte	....	15,900	....	....	15,900	79,500	13,161	6.04
Culpeper	51,180	37,659	32,860	78,337	200,036	117,314	18,967	6.19
Cumberland	....	112,344	....	....	112,344	56,172	9,992	5.62
Fauquier	53,629	39,277	1,931	49,217	144,054	48,822	22,689	2.15
Franklin	57,285	28,687	375	47,650	133,997	70,592	10,724	6.58
Goochland	87,718	409	15	24,466	112,608	62,359	10,203	6.11
Halifax	....	242,493	....	....	242,493	80,831	22,131	3.65
Henry	....	70,936	....	....	70,936	35,468	5,611	6.32
Loudoun	....	167,655	....	....	167,655	112,915	21,338	5.29
Louisa	140,068	....	40,440	....	180,508	187,095	11,900	15.72
Lunenburg	....	118,657	....	....	118,657	50,328	12,265	4.10
Madison	....	38,815	1,439	61,576	101,830	34,507	8,381	4.12
Mecklenburg	....	234,908	....	....	234,908	117,454	18,453	6.37
Nelson	9,656	21,810	....	9,046	40,512	34,892	9,684	3.60
Nottaway	90,705	....	....	....	98,705	48,543	9,278	5.23
Orange	37,024	30,152	2,244	47,490	116,910	56,714	12,323	4.60
Patrick	....	526,850	....	....	526,850	263,425	4,695	56.11
Pittsylvania	179,606	....	....	....	179,606	89,803	17,172	5.23
Powhatan	14,994	....	....	53,655	68,649	41,624	8,073	5.16
Prince Edward	97,896	....	....	65,127	163,023	81,511	12,409	6.57
Between Mts.†	*160,583*	*1,034,913*	*131,963*	*314,959*	*1,642,418*	*738,412*	*154,434*	*4.78*
Augusta	....	221,640	....	....	221,640	73,880	14,308	5.16
Bath	....	23,000	8,247	21,623	52,870	32,169	4,837	6.65
Berkley	....	10,300	6,200	17,710	34,210	21,739	11,479	1.89
Botetourt	13,953	46,884	3,322	48,414	112,573	57,358	13,301	4.31
Frederick	45,108	47,463	18,307	24,591	135,469	52,784	22,574	2.34

* From the Fall Line to the Blue Ridge Mountains.

† Between the Blue Ridge and Alleghany Mountains.

TABLE XII—*Continued*

States, Territories, and Counties	Yards of the Following Kinds of Goods: Cotton	Flaxen	Woolen	Mixed and Unnamed	Total	Value of All Kinds of Goods	Population, 1810	Per Capita Value
						Dollars		Dollars
Virginia—*Continued*								
Grayson	....	90,665	....	....	90,665	57,109	4,941	11.56
Hardy	....	45,777	....	....	45,777	18,850	5,525	3.41
Jefferson	....	....	13,255	77,481	90,736	35,768	11,851	3.02
Montgomery	....	65,534	14,352	26,471	106,357	41,452	8,409	4.93
Rockbridge	13,500	34,801	10,557	....	58,858	30,492	10,318	2.96
Rockingham	33,893	157,046	25,764	84,507	301,210	11,138	12,753	0.87
Shenandoah	....	145,960	....	....	145,960	70,813	13,646	5.19
Washington	35,941	96,946	21,281	14,162	168,330	104,490	12,136	8.61
Wythe	18,188	48,897	10,678	....	77,763	30,370	8,356	3.63
*West of Mts.**	*12,818*	*650,280*	*47,049*	*164,717*	*874,864*	*416,194*	*78,359*	*5.31*
Brooke	....	39,185	....	....	39,185	19,592	2,717	7.21
Cabell	....	17,715	....	....	17,715	886	5,843	0.15
Giles	2,279	26,642	591	16,727	46,239	23,835	3,745	6.36
Greenbrier	7,160	21,870	13,653	5,027	47,710	25,438	5,914	4.30
Harrison	....	80,412	989	24,782	106,183	44,270	9,958	4.44
Kenhawa	....	51,154	....	....	51,154	17,051	3,866	4.41
Lee	....	57,024	....	....	57,024	27,553	4,694	5.87
Monongalia	....	92,352	23,088	69,264	184,704	91,198	12,793	7.13
Monroe	....	48,440	....	26,471	74,911	24,796	5,444	4.55
Ohio	....	75,960	3,310	....	79,270	43,039	8,175	5.26
Randolph	....	18,481	4,734	....	23,215	10,726	2,854	3.76
Russell	3,379	53,395	684	22,446	79,904	50,122	6,316	7.94
Tazewell	....	37,874	....	....	37,874	23,178	3,007	7.89
Wood	....	29,776	....	....	29,766	14,510	3,036	4.78
North Carolina†	....	....	....	7,376,154	7,376,154	2,989,140	552,213	5.53
Low-country‡	....	....	....	*3,389,624*	*3,389,624*	*1,474,550*	*244,360*	*5.87*
Beaufort	....	....	....	76,500	76,500	38,200	7,203	5.30
Bertie	....	....	....	113,000	113,000	45,000	11,218	4.01
Bladen	....	....	....	66,000	66,000	29,000	5,671	5.11
Brunswick	....	....	....	28,700	28,700	14,300	4,778	2.99
Camden	....	....	....	103,000	103,000	58,000	5,347	10.87
Carteret	....	....	....	80,000	80,000	15,000	4,823	3.11
Columbus	....	....	....	43,500	43,500	12,000	3,022	3.97
Craven	....	....	....	133,000	133,000	66,000	12,676	5.21
Cumberland	....	....	....	175,000	175,000	70,000	9,382	7.46
Currituck	....	....	....	41,000	41,000	11,000	6,985	1.57
Duplin	....	....	....	126,500	126,500	42,000	7,863	5.34
Edgecomb	....	....	....	150,000	150,000	60,000	12,423	4.83
Gates	....	....	....	68,000	68,000	33,000	5,965	5.05
Greene	....	....	....	81,000	81,000	40,000	4,867	8.22
Halifax	....	....	....	215,000	215,000	86,000	15,620	5.51
Hertford	....	....	....	89,727	89,727	44,823	6,052	7.41
Hyde	....	....	....	158,000	158,000	45,000	6,029	7.46
Johnson	....	....	....	100,248	100,248	40,000	6,867	5.82
Jones	....	....	....	57,600	57,600	28,000	4,968	5.64
Lenoir	....	....	....	74,400	74,400	14,500	5,572	2.60
Martin	....	....	....	155,000	155,000	66,500	5,987	11.11

* West of the Alleghany Mountains.

† Nothing reported from Chowan County.

‡ In the low-country, extending from about sixty to eighty miles inland.

TABLE XII—*Continued*

States, Territories, and Counties	Yards of the Following Kinds of Goods: Cotton	Flaxen	Woolen	Mixed and Unnamed	Total	Value of All Kinds of Goods	Population, 1810	Per Capita Value
North Carolina—*Continued*						Dollars		Dollars
Nash	....	....	....	112,500	112,500	38,500	7,268	5.30
New Hanover	....	....	....	46,000	46,000	23,000	11,465	2.01
Northampton	....	....	....	200,400	200,400	100,000	13,082	7.64
Onslow	....	....	....	72,000	72,000	28,300	6,669	4.24
Pasquotank	....	....	....	168,600	168,600	137,000	7,674	17.85
Perquimans	....	....	....	66,000	66,000	32,000	6,052	5.29
Pitt	....	....	....	145,000	145,000	62,000	9,169	6.76
Robeson	....	....	....	66,200	66,200	46,900	7,528	6.23
Sampson	....	....	....	127,500	127,500	47,000	6,620	7.10
Tyrrel	....	....	....	58,524	58,524	14,000	3,364	4.16
Washington	....	....	....	57,725	57,725	28,827	3,464	8.32
Wayne	....	....	....	134,000	134,000	18,700	8,687	2.15
Back-country	....	....	....	*3,986,530*	*3,986,530*	*1,514,590*	*307,853*	*4.92*
Anson	....	....	....	111,000	111,000	44,400	8,831	5.03
Ash	....	....	....	221,000	221,000	103,000	3,695	27.90
Buncombe	....	....	....	95,800	95,800	10,100	9,277	2.06
Burke	....	....	....	77,000	77,000	45,000	11,007	4.09
Cabarras	....	....	....	39,550	39,550	13,000	6,158	2.11
Caswell	....	....	....	131,000	131,000	55,200	11,757	4.70
Chatham	....	....	....	199,000	199,000	84,000	12,977	6.47
Franklin	....	....	....	174,000	174,000	55,000	10,166	5.41
Greenville	....	....	....	261,780	261,780	120,000	15,576	7.70
Guilford	....	....	....	148,400	148,400	67,300	11,420	5.89
Haywood	....	....	....	17,000	17,000	5,540	2,789	1.99
Iredell	....	....	....	132,600	132,600	52,000	10,972	4.79
Lincoln	....	....	....	223,300	223,300	53,700	16,359	3.28
Mecklenburg	....	....	....	191,600	191,600	76,500	14,272	5.36
Montgomery	....	....	....	96,000	96,000	39,000	8,430	4.63
Moore	....	....	....	100,500	100,500	39,550	6,367	6.22
Orange	....	....	....	279,000	279,000	111,600	20,135	5.54
Person	....	....	....	79,000	79,000	15,000	6,642	2.26
Randolph	....	....	....	86,600	86,600	34,600	10,112	3.42
Richmond	....	....	....	141,000	141,000	40,300	6,695	6.02
Rockingham	....	....	....	85,000	85,000	16,500	10,316	1.60
Rowan	....	....	....	235,000	235,000	104,000	21,543	4.83
Rutherford	....	....	....	140,000	140,000	79,000	13,202	5.98
Stokes	....	....	....	68,000	68,000	28,000	11,645	2.40
Surry	....	....	....	142,000	142,000	71,000	10,366	6.85
Wake	....	....	....	276,400	276,400	55,300	17,086	3.24
Warren	....	....	....	151,000	151,000	65,000	11,004	5.91
Wilkes	....	....	....	84,000	84,000	22,000	9,054	2.43

TABLE XII—*Continued*

States, Territories, and Counties	Yards of the Following Kinds of Goods: Cotton	Flaxen	Woolen	Mixed and Unnamed	Total	Value of All Kinds of Goods	Population, 1810	Per Capita Value
						Dollars		Dollars
South Carolina*	3,083,188	690	72,636	110,627	3,267,141	1,677,228	296,765	5.36
Low-country†	*798,568*	....	*56,050*	*78,669*	*933,287*	*499,613*	*129,025*	*3.87*
Barnwell	74,879	....	....	6,000	80,879	41,700	12,280	3.40
Beaufort	55,471	....	....	....	55,471	27,736	25,887	1.07
Chesterfield	71,895	....	....	11,305	83,200	43,974	5,564	7.90
Darlington	125,091	....	....	40,431	165,522	91,252	9,047	10.09
Horry	42,560	....	....	....	42,560	21,280	4,349	4.89
Kershaw	73,718	....	....	....	73,718	36,859	9,867	3.74
Marion	55,950	....	56,050	....	112,000	72,815	8,884	8.20
Marlborough	43,423	....	....	7,000	50,423	26,312	4,966	5.30
Orangeburgh	20,061	....	....	....	20,061	10,031	13,229	0.76
Richland	45,986	....	....	....	45,986	22,993	9,027	2.55
Sumter	166,135	....	....	8,900	175,035	89,388	19,054	4.36
Williamsburg	23,399	....	....	5,033	28,432	15,273	6,871	2.22
Back-country	*2,284,620*	*690*	*16,586*	*31,958*	*2,333,854*	*1,177,615*	*167,740*	*7.03*
Abbeville	176,875	....	....	....	176,875	88,438	21,156	4.18
Chester	150,320	....	....	25,470	175,790	93,244	11,479	8.12
Edgefield	378,251	....	....	6,488	384,739	192,732	23,160	8.32
Fairfield	70,502	....	....	....	70,502	35,251	11,857	2.97
Lancaster	65,915	690	16,586	....	83,191	46,571	6,318	7.32
Laurens	169,236	....	....	....	169,236	84,618	14,982	5.65
Lexington	38,780	....	....	....	37,870	19,390	6,641	2.92
Newberry	154,420	....	....	....	154,420	77,210	13,964	5.53
Spartanburgh	427,440	....	....	....	427,440	213,720	14,259	14.99
Union	98,721	....	....	....	98,721	49,361	10,995	4.49
York	205,800	....	....	....	205,800	102,900	10,032	10.26
Pendleton	348,360	....	....	....	348,360	174,180	22,897	7.61
Georgia‡	3,688,534	11,253	5,591	483,925	4,189,303	2,143,348	248,492	8.62
Low-country§	*1,484,813*	*1,790*	*4,229*	*213,793*	*1,704,625*	*870,950*	*103,066*	*8.45*
Bryan	4,510	....	....	....	4,510	2,255	2,827	0.80
Bullock	266,000	....	....	134,000	400,000	216,750	2,305	9.40
Burke	86,350	....	....	5,255	91,605	47,116	10,858	4.34
Chatham	7,650	....	....	200	7,850	4,038	13,540	0.29
Columbia	165,977	1,790	20	18,421	186,208	103,140	11,242	9.02
Effingham	12,904	....	....	3,101	16,005	6,851	2,586	2.65
Glynn	4,250	....	....	....	4,250	2,125	3,417	0.62
Jefferson	34,695	....	....	3,855	38,550	19,275	6,111	3.15
Laurens	58,960	....	374	846	60,180	30,912	2,210	13.99
Liberty	7,800	....	....	3,000	10,800	5,662	6,228	0.91
McIntosh	3,000	....	....	....	3,000	1,500	3,739	0.40

* Nothing reported from Colleton, Charleston, Greenville, and Georgetown. Something must have been done in Colleton and Greenville, as there were 183 looms reported from the former and 500 from the latter.

† In the low-country, extending from about eighty to one hundred miles inland.

‡ Nothing reported from Camden County.

§ In the low-country, including pine barrens and the country of sand hills, sixty to ninety miles inland.

TABLE XII—*Continued*

States, Territories, and Counties	Yards of the Following Kinds of Goods: Cotton	Flaxen	Woolen	Mixed and Unnamed	Total	Value of All Kinds of Goods	Population, 1810	Per Capita Value
						Dollars		Dollars
GEORGIA—*Continued*								
Montgomery	99,000	....	....	....	99,000	49,500	2,954	16.76
Pulaski	408,825	....	....	....	408,825	204,413	2,093	97.67
Richmond	31,978	....	....	....	31,978	15,989	6,189	2.58
Scriven	51,882	....	....	5,422	57,304	28,652	4,477	6.40
Tattnall	35,196	....	....	....	35,196	17,598	2,206	7.98
Telfair	6,077	....	....	....	6,077	4,558	744	6.13
Warren	64,000	....	3,835	14,227	82,062	49,103	8,725	5.63
Washington	127,334	....	....	25,466	152,800	57,300	9,940	5.76
Wayne	8,425	....	....	....	8,425	4,213	676	6.23
Back-country	*2,203,721*	*9,463*	*1,362*	*270,132*	*2,484,678*	*1,272,398*	*145,425*	*8.75*
Baldwin	51,813	....	....	25,906	77,719	51,812	6,356	8.15
Clarke	155,900	....	....	15,311	171,211	85,606	7,628	11.22
Elbert	200,990	....	....	14,235	215,225	114,730	12,156	9.44
Franklin	167,687	1,203	....	5,783	174,673	89,083	10,815	8.23
Greene	120,135	....	....	50,500	170,635	85,318	11,679	7.30
Hancock	197,182	8,260	....	21,317	226,759	116,904	13,330	8.77
Jackson	182,594	....	....	8,083	190,677	97,359	10,569	9.21
Jones	100,000	....	....	30,000	130,000	70,625	8,597	8.22
Lincoln	65,452	....	....	....	65,452	32,726	4,555	7.18
Morgan	123,389	....	630	12,898	136,917	75,223	8,369	8.91
Oglethorpe	178,770	....	....	22,844	201,614	106,518	12,297	8.65
Putnam	162,250	....	....	20,248	182,498	73,509	10,029	7.33
Randolph	143,750	....	....	14,364	158,114	82,648	7,573	10.91
Twiggs	43,775	....	....	....	43,775	21,888	3,405	6.43
Walton	6,499	....	732	3,896	11,127	7,134	1,026	6.96
Wilkes	189,415	....	....	24,747	214,162	104,255	14,887	7.00
Wilkinson	114,120	....	....	....	114,120	57,060	2,154	26.49
KENTUCKY	....	....	....	4,685,205	4,685,205	2,057,081	406,511	5.06
*On or**	....	....	....	*1,402,568*	*1,402,568*	*648,561*	*138,434*	*4.61*
Bracken	....	....	....	35,510	35,510	14,204	3,706	3.83
Brackenridge	....	....	....	48,022	48,022	24,011	3,430	7.00
Bullet	....	....	....	46,183	46,183	18,473	4,311	4.29
Cardwell†	....	....	....	5,000	5,000	2,500	4,268	0.59
Campbell	....	....	....	40,060	40,060	15,813	3,473	4.55
Flemming	....	....	....	102,141	102,141	45,359	8,947	5.07
Gallatin	....	....	....	36,620	36,620	18,310	3,307	5.54
Grayson	....	....	....	17,890	17,890	8,850	2,301	3.84
Greenup	....	....	....	20,065	20,065	10,032	2,369	4.23
Hardin	....	....	....	66,473	66,473	31,076	7,531	4.14
Harrison	....	....	....	86,168	86,168	43,084	7,752	5.56
Henderson	....	....	....	28,838	28,838	14,419	4,703	3.28
Henry	....	....	....	48,980	48,980	18,367	6,777	2.70
Hopkins	....	....	....	27,178	27,178	13,589	2,964	4.58
Jefferson	....	....	....	114,290	114,290	47,731	13,399	3.56
Lewis	....	....	....	15,509	15,509	6,203	2,357	2.63
Livingston	....	....	....	47,113	47,113	23,556	3,674	6.41
Mason	....	....	....	139,871	139,871	75,813	12,459	6.08

* On or about fifty miles from the Ohio River.

† Output of 1 establishment included.

TABLE XII—*Continued*

States, Territories, and Counties	Yards of the Following Kinds of Goods: Cotton	Flaxen	Woolen	Mixed and Unnamed	Total	Value of All Kinds of Goods	Population, 1810	Per Capita Value
Kentucky—*Continued*						Dollars		Dollars
Nelson	....	....	....	190,880	190,880	95,440	14,078	6.78
Nicholas	....	....	....	58,898	58,898	23,862	4,898	4.87
Ohio	....	....	....	38,866	38,866	20,600	3,792	5.43
Pendleton	....	....	....	33,641	33,641	15,521	3,061	5.07
Shelby	....	....	....	154,372	154,372	61,748	14,877	4.15
All other Cos	....	....	....	*3,282,637*	*3,282,637*	*1,408,520*	*268,077*	*5.25*
Adair	....	....	....	92,790	92,790	37,767	6,011	6.28
Barren	....	....	....	128,490	128,490	64,222	11,286	5.69
Boone	....	....	....	30,993	30,993	16,174	3,608	4.48
Bourbon*	....	....	....	267,212	267,212	106,884	18,009	5.93
Butler	....	....	....	23,155	23,155	11,565	2,181	5.30
Casey	....	....	....	63,705	63,705	31,852	3,285	9.70
Christian	....	....	....	115,401	115,401	46,160	11,020	4.19
Clarke	....	....	....	121,434	121,434	45,537	11,519	3.95
Clay	....	....	....	11,320	11,320	5,660	2,398	2.36
Cumberland	....	....	....	68,605	68,605	32,584	6,191	5.26
Estill	....	....	....	25,536	25,536	10,640	2,082	5.11
Fayette†	....	....	....	207,687	207,687	83,074	21,370	3.88
Floyd	....	....	....	33,020	33,020	16,510	3,485	4.70
Franklin	....	....	....	82,609	82,609	33,079	8,013	4.13
Garrard	....	....	....	106,857	106,857	45,581	9,186	4.96
Greene	....	....	....	69,611	69,611	34,805	6,735	5.17
Jessamine	....	....	....	93,303	93,303	37,321	8,377	4.46
Knox	....	....	....	51,884	51,884	25,947	5,875	4.42
Lincoln	....	....	....	163,786	163,786	81,893	8,676	9.44
Logan	....	....	....	218,213	218,213	104,106	12,123	8.59
Madison*	....	....	....	236,569	236,569	97,333	15,540	6.26
Mercer*	....	....	....	163,653	163,653	65,461	12,630	5.18
Montgomery	....	....	....	196,630	196,630	78,652	12,075	6.06
Muhlenburg	....	....	....	43,197	43,197	21,275	4,181	5.09
Pulaski	....	....	....	56,411	56,411	26,651	6,897	3.86
Rockcastle	....	....	....	19,950	19,950	9,245	1,731	5.34
Scott*	....	....	....	133,669	133,669	49,457	12,419	3.98
Warren	....	....	....	127,104	127,104	63,469	11,937	5.32
Washington	....	....	....	135,473	135,473	47,905	13,248	3.61
Wayne	....	....	....	60,654	60,654	24,261	5,430	4.47
Woodford	....	....	....	133,626	133,626	53,450	9,659	5.53
Tennessee	1,790,514	....	34,141	228,193	2,052.848	1,675,314	261,727	6.40
Cos. on Miss.‡	*817,851*	....	*13,254*	*124,179*	*955,284*	*491,364*	*85,728*	*5.73*
Davidson	161,488	....	738	34,683	196,909	107,310	15,608	6.88
Dickson§	70,078	....	....	....	70,078	35,039	4,516	7.76
Humphreys	24,565	....	....	....	24,565	12,283	1,511	8.13

* Output of 2 establishments included.

† Output of 6 establishments included.

‡ On the Mississippi, lower Cumberland, and Tennessee rivers. Most of western Tennessee included.

§ The output of one establishment included. Same true of Bedford, Sumner, and Rutherford counties.

TABLE XII—*Continued*

States, Territories, and Counties	Yards of the Following Kinds of Goods					Value of All Kinds of Goods	Population, 1810	Per Capita Value
	Cotton	Flaxen	Woolen	Mixed and Unnamed	Total			
Tennessee—*Continued*						Dollars		Dollars
Montgomery....	125,540	....	....	20,000	145,540	77,770	8,021	9.70
Robertson......	63,012	....	2,680	7,998	73,690	39,421	7,270	5.42
Stewart........	34,796	....	....	....	34,796	17,396	4,262	4.08
Sumner........	40,660	....	1,700	4,550	46,960	24,305	13,792	1.77
Williamson.....	172,701	....	....	....	172,701	86,351	13,153	6.57
Wilson.........	65,084	....	8,136	56,948	130,168	61,525	11,952	5.15
Overton........	59,927	....	....	....	59,927	29,964	5,643	5.31
All other Cos......	*972,663*	....	*20,887*	*104,014*	*1,097,564*	*1,183,950*	*175,999*	*6.72*
Anderson*......	....	....	....	....	....	29,126	3,959	7.36
Bedford........	76,580	....	....	....	76,580	38,290	8,242	4.64
Bledsoe*†......	....	....	....	....	....	25,366	....	......
Blount*........	....	....	....	....	....	68,695	12,098	5.68
Campbell*......	....	....	....	....	....	17,261	2,668	6.47
Carter*........	....	....	....	....	....	8,142	4,190	1.94
Claiborne*......	....	....	....	....	....	16,876	4,798	3.52
Cocke*........	....	....	....	....	....	21,031	5,154	4.08
Franklin.......	36,253	....	764	27,735	64,752	39,447	5,730	6.88
Giles..........	50,404	....	....	26,646	77,050	43,717	4,546	9.62
Granger*......	....	....	....	....	....	41,455	6,397	6.48
Greene*.......	....	....	....	....	....	58,522	9,713	6.03
Hawkins*......	....	....	....	....	....	51,542	7,643	6.74
Hickman.......	35,170	....	345	5,820	41,335	19,913	2,583	7.71
Jackson........	55,125	....	....	....	55,125	17,563	5,401	3.25
Jefferson*......	....	....	....	....	....	46,406	7,309	6.36
Knox*.........	....	....	....	....	....	77,380	10,171	7.60
Lincoln........	61,350	....	460	5,587	67,397	34,198	6,104	5.60
Maury.........	193,328	....	1,303	212	194,843	97,422	10,359	9.40
Rhea*.........	....	....	....	....	....	17,014	2,504	6.79
Roane*........	....	....	....	....	....	36,212	5,581	6.49
Rutherford.....	247,936	....	....	....	247,936	123,968	10,265	12.08
Sevier*........	....	....	....	....	....	38,076	4,595	8.29
Smith..........	123,981	....	15,545	31,489	171,015	94,472	11,649	8.11
Sullivan*.......	....	....	....	....	....	33,956	6,847	4.96
Warren........	62,505	....	....	....	62,505	31,253	5,725	5.46
Washington*....	....	....	....	....	....	37,044	7,740	4.79
White..........	30,031	....	2,470	6,525	39,026	19,513	4,028	4.84
Ohio‡..............	56,072	1,093,031	93,074	701,156	1,943,333	1,032,235	216,164	4.77
Cos. on or§........	*43,444*	*748,942*	*60,569*	*472,083*	*1,325,038*	*695,149*	*163,493*	*4.25*
Adams.........	....	74,577	1,881	....	74,658	31,711	9,434	3.36
Athens.........	....	28,550	2,281	3,218	34,049	17,285	2,791	6.19
Butler.........	....	112,351	11,072	200	123,623	67,367	11,150	6.04
Belmont........	....	85,060	2,322	481	87,863	36,586	11,097	3.30
Clinton........	....	....	....	25,736	25,736	14,154	2,674	5.29
Columbiana.....	....	....	....	66,968	66,968	26,787	10,878	2.56

* Value only reported.

† Population of Bledsoe not reported separately.

‡ Nothing reported from Clermont and Gallia counties.

§ On or within about fifty miles of the Ohio River.

TABLE XII—*Continued*

States, Territories, and Counties	Yards of the Following Kinds of Goods					Value of All Kinds of Goods	Population, 1810	Per Capita Value
	Cotton	Flaxen	Woolen	Mixed and Unnamed	Total			
Ohio—*Continued*						Dollars		Dollars
Franklin	8,058	27,871	2,496	19,855	58,280	32,401	3,486	10.92
Fayette	90	16,995	176	5,133	22,394	12,589	1,854	6.78
Guernsey	2,282	19,652	....	1,207	23,141	10,174	3,051	3.33
Hamilton	18,888	89,093	11,856	23,910	143,747	85,519	15,258	5.74
Highland	9,000	22,680	5,000	....	36,680	25,590	5,766	4.44
Jefferson	25	57,714	5,170	44,785	107,694	58,656	17,260	3.40
Montgomery	....	....	....	55,744	55,744	27,872	7,722	3.61
Muskingum	....	....	....	39,685	39,685	21,826	10,036	2.17
Preble	....	....	....	10,024	10,024	10,024	3,304	3.03
Ross	2,805	104,006	1,809	47,060	155,680	82,050	15,514	5.29
Scioto	....	10,923	787	7,218	18,928	11,661	3,399	3.24
Stark	....	....	584	15,698	16,282	8,433	2,734	3.08
Tuskarawas	1,860	13,091	2,273	....	17,224	8,800	3,045	2.89
Warren	....	54,046	2,509	38,095	94,650	43,153	9,925	4.35
Washington	....	....	7,435	55,300	62,735	35,085	5,991	5.86
Pickaway	436	32,333	2,918	11,766	47,453	27,426	7,124	3.85
All other Cos	*12,628*	*344,089*	*32,505*	*220,073*	*618,205*	*337,086*	*52,671*	*6.40*
Champaign	....	37,568	1,148	104,416	143,132	68,927	6,303	10.94
Cuyahoga	....	3,000	1,200	6,432	10,632	7,075	1,459	4.85
Delaware	....	....	....	15,935	15,935	7,967	2,000	3.98
Fairfield	....	80,250	....	....	80,250	32,100	11,361	2.82
Geauga	374	20,199	11,021	19,645	51,239	46,649	2,917	15.99
Greene	803	57,824	3,075	20,217	81,919	43,603	5,870	7.43
Knox	1,215	5,283	....	1,838	8,336	4,929	2,149	2.29
Licking	359	29,678	445	7,931	38,413	21,591	3,852	5.61
Madison	3,044	10,275	3,522	....	16,841	10,061	1,603	6.28
Miami	6,833	24,262	507	10,205	41,807	24,398	3,491	6.99
Portage	....	....	....	29,699	29,699	15,819	2,995	5.28
Trumbull	....	75,750	11,587	12,755	100,092	53,967	8,671	6.22
Dist. of Columbia	26,000	....	....	20,000	46,000	39,500	24,023	1.64
Washington	....	....	....	20,000	20,000	20,000	15,471	1.22
Alexandria	26,000	....	....	....	26,000	19,500	8,552	2.28
Mississippi Ter.	342,472	450	7,898	....	350,820	266,493	40,352	6.63
Adams	58,794	....	6,818	....	65,612	52,936	10,002	5.29
Amite	51,216	....	....	....	51,216	38,412	4,750	8.07
Claiborne	28,375	150	580	....	29,105	22,167	3,102	7.37
Franklin	16,650	....	....	....	16,650	12,488	2,016	6.14
Jefferson	33,747	....	....	....	33,747	25,310	4,001	6.24
Madison	42,805	....	....	....	42,805	32,103	4,699	6.85
Baldwin	11,950	....	....	....	11,950	8,963	1,427	6.28
Warren	8,060	....	....	....	8,060	6,045	1,114	5.43
Washington	29,330	....	....	....	29,330	21,998	2,920	7.53
Wayne	16,685	....	....	....	16,685	12,513	1,253	9.98
Wilkinson	44,860	300	500	....	45,660	33,558	5,068	6.53

TABLE XII—*Continued*

States, Territories, and Counties	Yards of the Following Kinds of Goods: Cotton	Flaxen	Woolen	Mixed and Unnamed	Total	Value of All Kinds of Goods	Population, 1810	Per Capita Value
						Dollars		Dollars
Orleans Ter.*	133,180	....	....	....	133,180	106,941	43,154	2.48
Concordia	15,000	....	....	....	15,000	12,000	2,895	4.15
Iberville	13,188	....	....	....	13,188	10,550	4,142	2.55
LaFourche	14,907	....	....	....	14,907	11,926	4,467	2.67
Natchitoches	1,625	....	....	....	1,625	1,300	2,870	0.45
Ouachita	2,305	....	....	....	2,305	1,844	1,077	1.71
Point Coupe	2,500	....	....	....	2,500	2,000	4,539	0.44
Rapide	22,311	....	....	....	22,311	18,249	4,573	3.99
Opelousas	28,125	....	....	....	28,125	22,500	5,048	4.46
Attakapas	20,250	....	....	....	20,250	16,200	7,369	2.20
Acadia	12,969	....	....	....	12,969	10,372	6,174	1.68
Illinois Ter.	....	....	....	90,039	90,039	54,023	12,282	4.39
Randolph	....	....	....	53,443	53,443	32,066	7,275	4.41
St. Clair	....	....	....	36,596	36,596	21,957	5,007	4.38
Indiana Ter.	54,977	92,740	19,378	77,171	244,266	166,813	24,520 Population returned by counties	6.80
First Division	11,699	4,066	....	1,550	17,315	11,670		
Second Division	17,600	52,445	19,378	....	89,423	71,690		
Third Division	....	....	....	20,103	20,103	15,077		
Fourth Division	19,665	27,117	....	13,775	60,557	28,944		
Fifth Division	....	....	....	41,400	41,400	31,671		
Sixth Division	6,013	9,112	....	343	15,468	7,761		
Michigan Ter.†	....	1,216	2,405	....	3,621	3,470	4,147	0.83
Detroit district	....	421	1,300	....	1,721	1,616	2,227	0.73
Erie district	....	795	1,015	....	1,810	1,764	1,340	1.31
Huron district	....	....	90	....	90	90	580	0.16

* The outer districts of Louisiana reported 1,777 spinning-wheels and 601 looms, but no cloth There were no data for Orleans and the German Coast districts.

† Nothing reported from Michilimackinac district.

the fact that, relatively speaking, one county was doing about what every other county was. When one takes into consideration the simple life that many of the people lived at that time, it seems safe to conclude that many families must have supplied all their needs of goods exhibited in the table.

Another important fact revealed by the table is the influence of location with regard to transportation facilities on the output of the family factory. Except in the Maine district and in Vermont, where the output was rather uniform in all counties, this factor seems to have had the effect of increasing the amount. For example, the back-country counties in Massachusetts made a per capita value of $6.60, while the coast and island counties made but $3.05; the inland communities of Connecticut made $9.25 per capita and those on Long Island Sound but $8.14. In New York the inland and frontier counties made $5.64 and $5.99, while the river and coast counties made but $4.82. Similar conditions existed in Pennsylvania, the inland counties making $6.08 and the river and older ones but $4.71. Passing south of the Mason and Dixon line, one finds the counties above the Fall Line in Maryland making $4.47 per capita and those below but $2.22; in Virginia in the corresponding regions, $6.04 and $4.26; the people in the Valley and west of the mountains making $4.13 and $5.31. The back-country in South Carolina made a per capita value of $7.03 and the low-country $3.87. In Georgia the values were about equal, $8.75 and $8.45; while in North Carolina they were reversed, low-country $5.87, back $4.92.[1] In all three of the states west of the mountains the per capita value was higher in the counties some distance from the rivers. Since the territories were still in such frontier conditions, no attempt was made to classify the counties. Those in Mississippi and Indiana made about the same per capita values as inland counties everywhere.

[1] This reverse was probably due to the fact that there were few counties in the low-country where the slave outnumbered the free population. Table XIII shows that the slaves had no influence on the output of the family factory in this state.

Two other facts revealed by the table are: (1) counties in which the larger towns were situated had a relatively small per capita value, showing that the family system was peculiar to the rural communities; (2) in general, the material was raised in the county producing the goods, woolen goods predominating in the districts where sheep-raising was common and cotton cloth where cotton was grown. Since flax could be grown in all sections of the country, linen cloth was more generally produced than any other kind. It seems a little surprising that the homes in New Hampshire, Vermont, Rhode Island, and Maine were making so much cotton cloth at this date, those in Maine fabricating more than those in Pennsylvania, and those in each of the states of Rhode Island and New Hampshire more than those in New York. This means that the South was supplying New England with cotton for some time before the coming of the factory system into this section.

The table does not show the probable influence of one important factor in the southern states, viz., slave population. In order to determine the effects of this factor on the output of the plantation factory and the probable amount done by slave labor, three groups of counties were selected from the chief slave-holding states as follows: (1) counties with a slave population of less than 26 per cent of the total; (2) counties in which the slave and free population was about equal; and (3) counties in which the slaves largely predominated. The facts exhibited by such a selection are revealed in Table XIII.

This table reveals the following facts as to the relation which existed between slave population and household

TABLE XIII

SLAVE POPULATION AND HOUSEHOLD TEXTILE MANUFACTURES IN 1810

County and State	Population of Counties in 1810			Percentage of Total Population		Value of Manufactures	
	Slave	Free	Total	Slave	Free	Total	Per Capita
Alleghany, Md.	620	6,289	6,909	8.9	91.1	$23,109	$ 3.34
Harrison, Va.	459	9,499	9,958	4.6	95.4	44,270	4.44
Hardy, Va.	749	4,776	5,525	13.4	86.6	18,850	3.41
Berkley, Va.	1,529	9,950	11,479	13.3	86.7	21,739	1.89
Bulloch, Ga.	426	1,879	2,305	15.5	81.5	216,750	9.40
Montgomery, Ga.	747	2,207	2,954	25.2	74.8	49,500	16.54
Jackson, Ga.	1,816	8,753	10,569	17.1	82.9	97,359	9.21
Spartanburgh, S.C.	2,391	11,868	14,259	16.7	83.3	213,720	14.99
Laurens, S.C.	3,308	11,674	14,982	22.0	78.0	84,618	5.65
Moore, N.C.	944	5,423	6,367	14.8	85.2	39,550	4.22
Randolph, N.C.	798	9,314	10,112	7.9	92.1	34,600	3.42
Lincoln, N.C.	2,489	13,870	16,359	15.2	84.8	53,700	3.28
St. Marys, Md.	6,000	6,974	12,794	46.8	53.2	45,000	3.52
Albermarle, Va.	9,226	9,042	18,268	50.5	49.5	95,564	5.23
Elizabeth City, Va.	1,734	1,864	3,608	48.0	52.0	17,700	4.91
Henrico, Va.	4,856	5,109	9,945	48.8	51.2	33,500	3.36
Hertford, N.C.	2,805	3,247	6,052	46.3	53.7	44,823	7.41
Brunswick, N.C.	2,254	2,524	4,778	47.0	53.0	14.300	2.99
Orangeburgh, S.C.	6,564	6,665	13,229	49.6	50.4	10,031	0.76
Kershaw, S.C.	4.847	5,040	9,867	50.1	49.9	36,859	3.74
Wilkes, Ga.	7,284	7,603	14,887	48.9	51.1	104,255	7.00
Lincoln, Ga.	2,212	2,345	4,555	48.5	51.5	32,726	7.18
Columbia, Ga.	5,980	5,242	11,242	53.2	46.8	103,140	9.02
Greenville, N.C.	7,746	7,830	15,576	49.8	50.2	120,000	7.70
Charles, Md.	12,435	7,810	20,245	61.4	38.6	81,524	4.03
Amelia, Va.	7,186	3,408	10,594	67.8	32.2	75,709	7.15
Cumberland, Va.	6,102	3,890	9,992	61.0	39.0	56,172	5.62
Chesterfield, Va.	6,015	3,964	9,979	60.2	39.8	31,255	3.13
Beaufort, S.C.	20,914	4,973	25,887	80.7	19.3	27,736	1.07
Sumter, S.C.	11,638	7,416	19,054	61.0	39.0	89,388	4.36
Richland, S.C.	5,238	3,789	9,027	58.0	42.0	22,993	2.55
Liberty, Ga.	4,508	1,420	6,228	77.2	22.8	5,662	0.91
Mackintosh, Ga.	2,957	782	3,739	79.0	21.0	1,500	0.40
Chatham, Ga.	9,748	3,792	13,540	72.0	28.0	4,038	0.29
Warwick, Va.	1,120	715	1,835	60.0	40.0	7,347	4.00
Nottaway, Va.	6,368	2,910	9,278	68.6	31.4	48,543	5.23

manufactures: (1) In Virginia and Maryland the presence of slaves in a county seems to have had little effect upon the output of the family factory, the per capita values being very much the same regardless of whether the number of slaves was smaller, larger, or equal to the free population. This fact suggests the extent to which the slaves must have been employed in such manufacturing. (2) In Georgia the presence of a large number of slaves lessened the per capita value, while an equal number had little or no effect. (3) The presence of both a large and an equal number in South Carolina tended to decrease the amount of homemade goods. (4) This factor seems to have had no effect at all in North Carolina.

It should be said in concluding this chapter that the census of household manufactures taken in the autumn of 1810 came at a time when the demands on the system were very heavy. The operations of the Embargo and Non-Intercourse acts forced upon the people an industrial self-sufficiency which they could not have sustained without the assistance of the home factory. The material in Tables XI and XII demonstrates the fact that the people quite generally accepted the conditions forced upon them by the foregoing measures. Until a general system of factory manufacturing could be established to supplement their agricultural and commercial activities and to make real a dreamed-of industrial independence from European countries, the people in all sections of the country had to maintain the family system of manufacturing. The year 1808 is a rather important one in the economic history of this country. It may be thought of as marking the beginning of an industrial revolution which by 1860, along with other changes, had transferred the textile manufacturing business from homes to factories, thus putting an end to a system that so long had been such an important factor in the life and prosperity of the entire country. Since the story of the transition from family- to factory-made goods forms the subject of a succeeding chapter, no further consideration will be given it here.

CHAPTER VI

THE PRODUCTS OF THE FAMILY FACTORY

The fact that the products, materials, and processes relative to the output of the family factory varied so little, both as to locality and as to chronology, makes it possible and desirable to treat these three phases of the subject in one chapter. In order to facilitate this treatment, the discussion centers on the products made in the family, these being grouped into the following three main divisions: (1) wearing apparel and household textile supplies; (2) household implements, utensils, furniture, necessities, and comforts; (3) farming implements, building materials, and general supplies. Every product of the household factory can be classified under these headings except pot and pearl ashes, the manufacture of which will be discussed in connection with soap-making because of the similarity of the material from which each was made.

In order to call attention to the great variety of family-made goods and at the same time formulate an appropriate introduction to the chapter, the following list of articles is presented. It comprises the domestic staples which the Moravian Brethren proposed to contribute to a store which they opened in 1753 for the benefit of the "Family." This was one of the few stores on the forks of the Delaware at this time. The articles included in the list were:

Apron-skins, powder-horns, glue, shoes, slippers, shoe-lasts, wooden and horn heel pieces, saddle-trees, saddles, horse-collars, bridles, halters, saddle-bags, girths, pocket-books, martingales, straps, stockings, caps, gloves, socks, hats, felt caps and felt slippers, spinning-wheels, reels, boxes, guns, tea-caddies, writing-desks, deer and calf skins dressed for breeches, buckwheat groats, oat-groats, malt, millet, dried peaches, dried apples, dried cherries, rusks, ginger-bread, cakes, iron bands for chests, nails, plows, axes, hatchets, grubbing hoes, corn-hoes, grind-stones, whet-stones, punk, flint and steel, pipe-stems, pipe-heads, shirt studs, pewter plates, tea pots, lanterns, tallow candles, soap, starch, hair-powder, sealing-wax, wafers, tobacco boxes, buttons, buckles, spoons, bowls, shovels, brooms, baskets, wheat, flour, butter, cheese, handkerchiefs, neck-cloths, garters, knee-straps, linen, white, blue and checked woolens, currant-wine, beer, whiskey, tar, potash, turpentine, pitch, lamp-black, sulphur-matches, vinegar, flaxseed, linseed oil, rape seed and oil, nut oil, oil of sassafras, ammonia, rasped deer's-horn, bush-tea, medicine chests, brushes, shovels and tongs, chafing-dishes, combs, currycombs, glove-leather, leather-breeches, ropes, blank-books, soft-soap, rakes, knives, drawing-knives, guitars, violins, tobacco and tobacco-pouches, snuff, oil of turpentine, hemp, flax, buckets, milk pails, tubs, pottery, cotton yarn, cord, hatchels, oven-forks, linen nets, augers, hammers, pincers, candlesticks, tinware, chisels, mill-saws, homespun, boots, whips, harness, wheelbarrows, wagons, coffee-pots, chains, canoes, boards, bricks, roofing-tiles, lime, preserves and pickles, quills and slate pencils.[1]

This list includes more than 160 different articles—a wonderful example of how quickly a group of people living as one family could become economically independent when forced to do so by the exigencies of time and place. While many of the commodities, such as tobacco, millet, dried peaches, apples, and cherries, rape seed, hemp, flax, butter, and the like, cannot be classed as manufactured products in the sense in which they are used in this

[1] Reichel (editor), *Memorials of the Moravian Church*, I, 234 f., note.

discussion, yet, when all of these have been eliminated, the list is a long one and full of meaning.[1]

WEARING APPAREL AND HOUSEHOLD TEXTILE SUPPLIES

It has probably occurred again and again to the reader, before reaching this phase of the discussion, that wearing apparel was the most important as well as the most consistent product of the family factory. Most of the legislation in the colonies bearing on the subject of household manufactures had to do with providing raw material for clothing and manufacturing it into some kind of cloth; most of the reports on what was made in the homes dealt chiefly with articles of clothing. In fact, so much has been said in the foregoing discussion concerning the making of this one commodity in the homes that one is likely to forget that anything else was really made.

To explain why wearing apparel and household textile supplies composed such a large portion of the output of the family factory is not at all difficult. Soon after a new settlement was made, a sawmill, a gristmill, a distillery, and a brewery would appear; so the period of the grater, mortar, handmill, sawpit, private still, and brewery was usually short. A blacksmith, carpenter, cooper, shoemaker, hat-maker, and other handicraftsmen would

[1] It would be a little misleading to convey the idea that the articles in the foregoing list were ordinarily made in the average Moravian home. The fact that these people lived as one big family gave opportunity for specialization that was uncommon in ordinary communities. This possibility of specialization explains some of the articles appearing in the list, which should not, in the strict sense of the term, be considered as family manufactures.

also be plying their trades in a short time after the settlement was established.[1] While the professional weaver was also on the ground quite early, yet there was so much competition by the women who chose to do their own work that he did not get on in his trade as his brother-handicraftsmen did in theirs. After the spinning and weaving industries had become established in the home, it was difficult to crowd them out. In fact, even after the factory came to do the work of the handicraft system, its development along the line of textile industries was retarded by the tenacity with which the women held on to their spinning-wheels and looms.

The chief raw materials used in the manufacture of textile fabrics were wool, hemp, flax, and cotton. When the settlers arrived at Plymouth, they found an abundance of hemp and flax growing wild.[2] Since the cultivation of these plants was not entirely new to them, they had little difficulty in producing a sufficient quantity of such material for their household necessities. In order to safeguard the supply, regulations were early established and encouragements offered for their cultivation.[3] This

[1] For example, in the towns of Washington, Pittsburgh, Bedford, and Huntingdon, Pennsylvania, in 1790 there were respectively 32, 40, 15, and 23 artisans plying their trades. Among these there were but 6 weavers. Similar conditions existed even in the older communities. Lancaster, in the same state, had, in 1786, but 25 weavers out of a total of 234 artisans (Coxe, *A View of the U.S.*, pp. 311 f.).

[2] "Journal of a Plantation Settled at Plymouth in New England; First printed in 1622," reprint from Purchas' *Pilgrims*, Book X, chap. iv, in *Mass. Hist. Soc. Colls.*, 1st ser., VIII, 221 ff. Original was probably written by one of the company.

[3] See chap. ii, pp. 29 ff., for these early laws.

was more especially true in New England, where there was so much dependence on the products of these staples for ship supplies. In the course of time their growth became common throughout the country except in certain sections of the South. Conditions remained thus until about 1810, at which time the manufacture of linen in the household began to decline, owing to the rapid growth of cotton culture and manufacture and the introduction of merino sheep. The regular establishments for the manufacture of both cotton and wool which had grown up by this date also contributed to the diminution of household spinning and weaving into which flax and hemp entered so largely as materials.[1]

Wool was an important as well as a necessary commodity in a region where suitable clothing was so scarce. Whether for the fleeces or for other purposes, sheep were brought to the colonies quite early in their history. One writer says that they were introduced into Jamestown in 1609,[2] and another that by 1649 there were 3,000 head in Virginia.[3] Massachusetts had 1,000 in 1642.[4] The Dutch sent sheep to New Netherlands in 1625 and 1630; and in 1683 the Delaware colony had eighty.[5] All the legislation cited in chap. ii regarding the pasturing, protecting, and exporting of sheep is evidence of their importance to the New England and middle colonies. As the population

[1] Eighth Census of U.S., *Manufactures*, Introd., p. cvii.

[2] *Ibid.*, p. xxvi.

[3] "A Perfect Description of Virginia," Force, *Tracts*, II, sec. 8, p. 3.

[4] "New England's First Fruits," *Mass. Hist. Soc. Colls.*, 1st ser., I, 247.

[5] Eighth Census of U.S., *Manufactures*, Introd., p. xxvi.

increased in these regions, the number of sheep increased accordingly. In time practically every farmer owned a small flock, which was in reality a necessity forced upon him by the economic conditions under which he lived. The inventories examined in both Rhode Island and New York contained sheep as one of the most common entries.[1]

Both Massachusetts and Connecticut obtained cotton from the West Indies before 1643. In the latter colony the governor ordered the supply, which was apportioned to the towns when it arrived.[2] At this date flax and wool were scarce, and until they became more plentiful much cotton was used. Most of the supply came from the West Indies until about 1800. During the seventeenth century from about 1659 to 1678 it sold in the shops for from 1*s.* to 1*s.* 4*d.* a pound.[3]

The returns of the marshals in the fall of 1810 indicated how extensively and in what localities wool, flax, hemp, and cotton were used in the manufacture of textiles in the family.[4] Homemade woolen goods were common in all the counties of the New England and middle states, in the majority of those in the western country, and in many in the South; linen goods were quite generally made in families in all sections of the country; cotton fabrics were common in the South and at the same time were

[1] *Early Rec. of Providence, R.I.*, XVI; and *Ulster County, N.Y., Probate Records*, "Wills," II.

[2] Winthrop, *Hist. of N. Eng.* ("Orig. Nar. Early Am. Hist." ed.), II, 122, and *Col. Rec. of Conn.*, I, 59.

[3] Judd, *Hist. of Hadley* (ed. 1863), p. 389, note.

[4] See Tables XI and XII.

found in great abundance north of Maryland—a statement also true of mixed cloths of all kinds.

Besides the materials discussed above, a few others were used in cases of sheer necessity. These were buffalo wool, lint of the wild nettle, and cattle's hair. The pioneers west of the Alleghanies had to resort to such materials to supply their needs for clothing. George Wiley, speaking of early times in Natchez, Mississippi, said: "I have often heard my mother say that when it was impossible to procure cloth, she clothed herself and the children with a very nice linen from the large nettles that grew near the fort. . . . ."[1] The early settlers in Tennessee, Kentucky, Indiana, and Ohio were also obliged to resort to the same kind of material. Until these people had time to raise a crop of flax they used the lint from the bark of dead nettles. This was collected in the spring by all people of a station acting together, a portion of the men standing guard while the rest with the help of the women and children gathered the dead stalks. From the lint of these many dozen cuts of linen as fine as flax but not so strong were spun.[2] It was said of a part of Indiana about 1820: "The nettles grew very plentiful in Cicero bottoms, and during the winter it was found that they had as good lint as flax or hemp, and in the spring they were in good condition for working up. We all had shirts, pants, towels, sheets, and under-bed ticks made of these nettles."[3]

[1] "Recollections," Claiborne, *Miss. as Prov., Ter., and State*, App., p. 532.

[2] Roosevelt, *Winning of the West*, I, 317.

[3] Finch, "Recollections," *Ind. Mag. Hist.*, VI, 78.

When sheep's wool could not be secured, cattle's hair and buffalo wool were occasionally used instead, the former mainly east, and the latter west, of the Alleghanies. While the inhabitants of New Hampshire were yet living under pioneer conditions, they seem to have resorted to cattle's hair to take the place of sheep's wool. A supply of this material could be obtained from the tannery. It was spun into yarn, which was later made into bedcovers and other necessary articles.[1] The very first settlers in northern Ohio had to resort to the same sort of material for requisite supplies. In his account of early conditions near Cleveland, Ohio, Badger says: "Mr. Burke's family in Euclid had been in this lone situation over three years. The woman had been obliged to spin and weave cattle's hair to make covering for her children's bed."[2] It was quite common in New York as late as 1808 to mix wool with the hair from the tannery in variable proportions.[3] It was also customary for the people west of the mountains to spin buffalo wool into yarn. In fact, until it was possible to protect the sheep from the wolves and other wild animals, buffalo wool was their chief reliance. Speaking of the early conditions at Bryant's Station, Kentucky, Durrett remarked: "After the clothes with which they came from the mother-country were reduced to rags that could no longer be patched, the men wore buckskin

[1] Norton, *The Hist. of Fitzwilliam, N.H.*, p. 111.

[2] Quoted by Whittlesey, *Early Hist. of Cleveland, Ohio*, p. 384. Badger came to the Reserve in 1800 as a missionary from the Connecticut Missionary Society.

[3] *Trans. of Albany Inst.*, IV, 116.

breeches, hunting-shirts, and moccasins, with raccoon or fox skin caps; and the women, such coarse linsey gowns as they could make by spinning on the little wheel and weaving on the hand loom the lint of the wild nettle and the wool of the buffalo."[1] The use of these unusual materials by the pioneers is a capital illustration of the power of a people to adapt themselves to trying situations and in a large measure overcome them.

Materials for textile manufactures were by no means the only ones used by the family to supply wearing apparel and household supplies. Buffalo hides, cowhides, buckskins, squirrel, raccoon, rabbit, bear, wolf, fox, cat, woodchuck, and beaver skins furnished stuff from which to make coverings for the head and feet, as well as body clothing. Buffalo skins were used for robes, blankets, and wraps of all sorts. From them moccasins were also made. Deerskins were made into hunting-shirts, pantaloons, coats, waistcoats, leggings, moccasins, and petticoats.[2] Gloves and mittens were made from the skins of squirrels and beavers; caps, from the skins of raccoons, bears, foxes, cats, rabbits, and woodchucks.[3] Bearskins were

[1] "How They Lived at Bryant's Station," *Filson Club Pubs.*, No. 12, p. 27; also Roosevelt, *op. cit.*, III, 204.

[2] Strickland, *Autobiography of Rev. James F. Finley*, p. 74. Finley's father was a missionary in the Carolinas and Georgia until about 1785, at which time he moved to Kentucky, where he lived till the end of the century. The subject of the *Autobiography* tells of life as he saw it in Ohio and Kentucky about 1800.

[3] Hats for summer wear were often made out of oat straw, rye straw, flags, or the inside bark of the mulberry root (Vogel, "Homelife in Early Indiana," *Ind. Mag. of Hist.*, X, 13).

made into beds and bedding; and from the deerskins and cowhides, moccasins, shoepacks, and shoes were made.[1]

The preparation of the foregoing leather materials and their manufacture into useful articles was largely the work of the men and boys. Since this was true, the trades producing articles from them were among the first to gain a substantial foothold in a new settlement. The shoemaker, saddle-maker, and harness-maker soon appeared in the community and were shortly able to depend entirely upon their trade for a living. These tradesmen relieved the farmers of the difficult task of working up their own leather, since it could be exchanged at their shops for the finished products. An early independence in leather resulted from these conditions. Such an independence was common in practically all isolated communities—a situation not at all surprising. The high cost of freight from the interior towns almost prohibited the transportation of rawhides, one of the commonest products of the farm. This made the tannery a necessary adjunct to every village in order to save this very important product. With an abundant supply of hides, a number of tanneries, shoemakers, and harness-makers in a community, there was little need of outside aid to supply commodities made of leather.[2]

[1] References on the use of such materials as are discussed in this paragraph could be given in great numbers. The following are sufficient to sustain all facts in the paragraph: Parker, "Pioneer Life," *Ind. Mag. of Hist.*, III, 183 f.; Little, *Hist. of Weare, N.H.*, pp. 181 f.; King, *Ohio*, p. 299; Levering, *Historic Ind.*, chap. vi; and Roosevelt, *op. cit.*, III, 204 f.

[2] Bishop, *op. cit.*, I, chap. xvi, discusses the whole subject of leather manufactures.

It should not be inferred from the foregoing paragraph that the farmer never had to tan his own hides and make his own leather clothing, boots, and shoes. All this he certainly had to do, sometimes for only a brief period, but quite often for a long one if he persisted in living on the extreme frontier, where the number of settlers was too small to justify a tannery, shoemaker, etc. It was the custom under such conditions for each man to tan his own leather, unless he could secure it already tanned from the Indians, and to work it up into indispensable articles. To be tanned, the skins were thrown into a vat of strong lye after they had been well dried. The lye caused the hair to loosen and fall off. They were then placed in another vat of liquid made from black-oak bark and allowed to remain several months. When taken out of this they were scraped, and softened with bear's oil. They were then ready to be made into suits, boots, shoes, and harness.[1]

As suggested in a preceding paragraph, the tailoring of the leather suits usually fell to the male portion of the family, since the hard material was rather difficult for the women to handle. For the men it was a simple process. Large needles or shoemakers' awls were used in the sewing process. The thread was made either of the sinews from the legs of the deer, or by cutting a long strip from the deerskin. The latter was called "whang." It was cut as small as possible, so that it could be used in the awls or needles as thread. While the product of this crude tailoring was often rough and uncomfortable, especially after getting wet and stiff, it was certainly the best that

[1] Vogel, *op. cit.*, X, 17; also Cockrum, *A Pioneer Hist. of Ind.*, p. 194.

could have been devised for the wild country in which it was used. It protected the men and boys from nettles, briars, snakes, and the cold winter winds. Its greatest asset, however, was its cheapness, since it could be had by anyone with sufficient energy to secure the skins, and dress, tan, and make them into the requisite articles of wearing apparel.[1]

Some idea of the prevalence of leather wearing apparel among slaves and servants during much of the colonial period can be obtained from the newspaper extracts of advertisements of runaways in New Jersey. For example, from 1704 to 1739, out of a total of 97 cases, 32 had on apparel made of leather, buckskin, or bearskin; from 1740 to 1750, 36 out of 135; from 1751 to 1755, 64 out of 151; from 1756 to 1761, 20 out of 50, and similarly for the remainder of the period to 1779.[2] While these figures present conditions in respect to servants and slaves in but one colony, yet there is abundant evidence that such

[1] Duncan, "Old Settlers' Papers," *Ind. Hist. Soc. Pubs.*, II, 391 ff. It should be noted that as soon as a store appeared within reach, the settler could take his skins and exchange them for merchandise, and thus save himself and his wife the work of making the leather garments and the laborious task of spinning and weaving the cloth used by the family. The price he received for his hides depended on the ease and safety of the transportation facilities to the settlement. In the early Indiana settlements the prices were as follows: for a good deerskin taken in season, 50 cents in trade; for a raccoon, 37½ cents; and for a muskrat, 25 cents. The proper season for the deer was from the first of May to the middle of November, and for the raccoon, muskrat, and similar skins, from the first of December to the first of April. Thus the hunter could follow his trade almost the year around and from the exchange of his wares furnish himself and his family with whatever could be bought at the few stores (*ibid.*, p. 393).

[2] See Table VI.

apparel was common for a time among all classes in frontier settlements.[1]

The shoemaking business in New England had attained enormous proportions some time before the Revolution. In the year 1767, 80,000 pairs of shoes were made in Lynn, Massachusetts.[2] In fact, as early as 1650 this colony was manufacturing shoes for sale in the other colonies.[3] There seems to be no way to determine just how much of this work was done in the homes by members of the family, how much by the itinerant shoemaker, and how much in the shoemakers' shops. It is probable that in New England and the middle colonies during the seventeenth century the making of the majority of leather goods was done by the men and boys as a household industry. The abundance of material made the manufacture of shoes, boots, moccasins, shoe packs, leather coats, vests, breeches, and leggings a profitable household industry in both of these regions. To insure a sufficient supply of raw material in Massachusetts the General Court in 1640 enjoined upon the population the preservation of hides. A fine of five shillings was imposed for each hide not sent to the tannery. Leather searchers whose duty was to see that the law was enforced were appointed by each town.[4] Such care in the preservation of hides augmented the supply of leather

[1] Levering, *op. cit.*, chap. vi; Baird, *op. cit.*, p. 128; Wilkeson, "Recollections of the West," *Pubs. Buffalo Hist. Soc.*, V, 154; same in *Am. Pioneer*, II, 160; Duncan, *op. cit.*, II, 377 ff.

[2] *Essex Antiquarian*, V, 55.

[3] Coman, *Indust. Hist. of U.S.*, p. 66.

[4] *Rec. of Gov. and Co. Mass. Bay*, I, 305, 356.

and made possible a surplus of leather goods, which found a ready market in the other colonies.

The shoemaking industry seems to have been among the first to pass into the shop stage. The occasional appearance of shoemakers' tools in the Providence inventories covering the period from 1716 to 1726 indicates that shoes were then made in the homes either by resident or by itinerant shoemakers, while the total absence of these tools in the New York inventories covering the period from 1787 to 1792 suggests that the industry in Ulster County had migrated to the shops.[1] It should be noted, however, that among the farmers some distance from a market for their hides, and in frontier communities, the business remained in the household long after it had passed into the shops in the towns and villages and in districts favorably situated in respect to trade and transportation. Even as late as the middle of the eighteenth century many of the farmers and their families in Essex County, Massachusetts, spent long winter evenings in making shoes from the sides of leather tanned from their own animals and from those they had purchased. The wives and daughters did the binding and closing, and the sons helped with the sewing and pegging, after pegs began to be used. Some worked by the fireplace, but generally a small building was built near the house, in which the men worked. When the winter's work was done, or the leather was all made up, the farmers carried their shoes to some trade center and sold or bartered them.[2] Furthermore, negro shoemakers were common on the plantations, where

[1] See pp. 81 ff., 136 f. [2] *Essex Antiquarian*, V, 54.

they made shoes for themselves and sometimes for sale.[1] On the whole, it was a business that neither the plantation owners nor the ordinary farmers the country over were hasty about relinquishing. They were justified in their tardiness both by the convenience and the profitableness of the industry.

As suggested above, the spinning and weaving industries remained in the homes long after others had passed into shops or factories. Because of their continued importance in the economic life and prosperity of the people in all sections of the country, a somewhat extended discussion of the processes and products of these operations seems desirable, both of which are very important in this consideration, since they exemplify so well the persistence and ingenuity of the chief operators of the family factory.

The variety of homemade textile products was very great, especially when they were colored and in their final form. Some notion of this variety is obtained from the descriptions of the homespun clothing worn by runaway servants and slaves. The following articles of apparel are typical ones from a large number mentioned and described as homespun in advertisements of fugitive slaves and servants in New Jersey from 1707 to 1776:

"homespun olive colored coat," "homespun white shirt," "brown colored homespun drugget coat," "homespun coarse shirt," "homespun striped breeches," "brown or black homespun jacket," "homespun coat lined with blue," "homespun coat of black and white worsted and wool," "homespun gray coat lined with orange stuff," "dark colored homespun coat and jacket," "homespun gray

[1] Scott, *Hist. of Orange Co., Va.*, p. 121.

stockings," "suit of dark gray homespun cloth," "suit of light gray homespun drugget cloth," "new homespun blue striped trousers," "dark brown homespun kersey coat," "homespun worsted knit stockings," "gray woolen homespun coat," "cinnamon homespun kersey coat lined with broad striped homespun," "brown homespun jacket," "olive colored homespun breeches and jacket," "brown homespun breeches," "homespun gown of green woolen yarn," "dark colored homespun broadcloth jacket," "short homespun gown and petticoat with red, blue, green, and black stripes . . . . ," "homespun black jacket," "white homespun jacket," "homespun striped woolen jacket," "homespun coat of woolen and cotton lined," "moss colored homespun coat lined with brown homespun," "homespun blue and white striped linen jacket and breeches," "blue gray homespun drugget coat," "striped homespun waistcoat and breeches."[3]

Such a list is by no means exhaustive, but long enough to show the great variation in the simple articles of clothing made from the homespun cloth. All these variations were largely due to the ingenuity of the women in diversifying the products of their labors by means of combining and coloring them.

The chief textile products of the home factory were plain linen, woolen, and cotton cloth; mixtures of wool and flax, cotton and flax, cotton and wool, known as linsey-woolsey, fustian, and jeans; tow cloth, made from the coarsest fiber of the flax; ducking, chiefly from hemp and used for sailcloth; ordinary cotton, linen, and woolen yarn; linen, cotton, woolen, and worsted stockings; mittens, leggings, lace, and edging; white and colored thread; coverlets and counterpanes in which much ingenuity was displayed in the weaving of the various ornamental

[1] *Ante*, p. 91, for the reference to where these advertisements are found.

figures and colors; and carpets, most of which were made after the Revolution. The plain linen and woolen cloth and linsey-woolsey were most common in New England and in the middle colonies; fustian in the South; and jeans, fustian, and linsey-woolsey in the country west of the Alleghanies. Lace, edging, thread, and sailcloth were made chiefly in New England; while stockings, mittens, leggings, carpets, coverlets, and counterpanes were more or less common in all parts of the country. It should be added, in concluding this list, that silk thread was occasionally spun and woven into cloth, and a kind of cloth called "taurino" was made of sheep's wool and cattle's hair, the former chiefly in Connecticut and the latter in New York.

The existence of many combinations and variations in the cloth made of cotton, wool, and flax has been mentioned in a preceding paragraph. Some of these were due to the coloring of the yarn before it was woven into cloth, others to the fineness or coarseness of the threads, and still others to the color of the wool. For example, "sheep's gray" was made by mixing white and black wool, the universal material from which, in some sections of the country, men's clothing was made.[1] Besides the ordinary tow cloth, there was the coarse linen, used chiefly for ordinary summer shirts, frocks, underclothing, trousers, towels, tablecloths, sheets, and pillowcases; fine linen, from which undergarments were made, as well as towels, tablecloths, and sheets; the fine striped and checked linen, used for aprons, gowns, handkerchiefs, shirts for the men, and the coarser

[1] Musgrove, *Hist. of Bristol, N.H.*, I, 99.

sort for bedticks; diaper, diamond linen, and fine crash, all used mainly for towels and table covers.[1] Woolen cloth varied all the way from the coarse plain cloth to the fine worsted. The two kinds most in use were the pressed and fulled. The former was simply dyed and dressed, while the latter was dyed, fulled, sheared, and pressed. There was also a kind known as baize, woven for women's use and without fulling or napping. The dressed cloth was the most common, since the fulling process was difficult when no fulling-mill was in the neighborhood.

Besides clothing for the men, women, and children, heavy blankets were woven from woolen yarn; and a comfortable sort of coverlet, used for a sheet in winter and a light blanket in summer, was made of a cotton warp filled with wool. Checked woolens used for shawls, underskirts, dresses, and bedcovers were also common, as were fine, coarse, striped, and checked cotton cloths, used for bedticking, coverlids, shirts for the men and boys, and gowns for the women and girls. While all these

[1] The price charged by professional weavers furnishes some information as to the fineness of the different kinds of woven cloth. The following is from an old account book covering the period between 1745 and 1772: "Tow Cloth and Tow Linen, woven at 5 and 6 pence a yard, fine Linen, 9*d*. Cotton and Linen, 8*d*. and 10*d*. Sacking, 3*d*. and 4*d*. Linsey-Woolsey, 8*d*., plain Woolen Cloth 6⅗*d*. and fine, 8*d*. Checked Linen and Checked Woolen, 8*d*., fine check, 10*d*. Checked Cotton, 9*d*. Bed-tick, 9*d*. and 10*d*., fine Cotton Bed tick, 1*s*. 1*d*. Diaper, 10*d*. and 11*d*. Diamond Table Linen, 8*d*. and 9*d*. Birdseye, 8*d*., fine Wale, 7*d*. Striped or Streaked Cloth, 8*d*., Crape, 8*d*. Blanketing, 8*d*., fine Crash, 9*d*. Coverlids, 6*s*. 8*d*. each" (from Samuel Gaylord's *Account Book;* quoted by Judd, *Hist. of Hadley*, p. 395).

combinations and variations were more or less common, yet the fact should be kept in mind that the cloths most commonly made in the homes were linsey-woolsey, jeans, and tow linen. The ordinary clothing of the women and girls was usually made of the first; that of the men and boys, of the second; and that of the slaves in the South, of the third—much of which was sent down from New England.[1]

In order to appreciate the textile products of the household factory discussed above, it is necessary to know something of the labor connected with the turning of the raw materials into the useful articles of clothing and textile supplies. Those of us who have no recollection of the era of domestic spinning-wheels and handlooms can hardly appreciate the labor of manufacturing cloth from wool, flax, or cotton by hand. The operations connected with the fabrication of linen, woolen, and cotton cloth were both numerous and laborious. For linen, they were braking, swingling, combing or hatcheling, spinning, reeling, weaving, bleaching, and coloring; for woolen, carding or braking, spinning, weaving, fulling, "teaseling," dyeing, and dressing; and for cotton, much the same processes as for wool, omitting fulling and dressing. A brief description of these processes seems desirable, so

[1] To avoid duplications, references on the foregoing products of the home factory and their combinations and variations are all given here. The main ones are: Brown, *Hist. of Hampton Falls, N.H.*, p. 506; Moore, *Hist. of Candia, N.H.*, p. 265; Hayes, *Hist. of Rockingham, Vt.*, pp. 93 f.; Street, *Hist. of Mount Desert, Me.*, p. 290; Tucker, *Hist. of Hartford, Vt.*, p. 100; *Trans. Albany Inst.*, IV, 116; Doddridge, *Notes* (ed. 1912), p. 113; Duncan, *op. cit.*, p. 390; *Hamilton Papers* (1790–91), No. 1764.

that the reader may realize just what it cost in time and labor to produce sufficient clothing and household textiles for a family in the days of homespun industries.

In order to insure a supply of flax it was necessary for the farmer to have a patch in the garden or elsewhere. This patch was small even though the family was large, since a good yield on half an acre would have furnished enough for the whole state of Connecticut at the time the greatest amount was used.[1] When the flax was ripe in the fall it was usually pulled and placed upon the ground, where it remained for some time, to rot.[2] If the season was damp, the woody portion rotted and the fiber became pliable in a few weeks. If the farmer wished to save the seed, he pulled it carefully by the roots and tied it into small bundles which he left on the ground a day or so to dry. He then set it up in small shocks, and after it had become well dried it was stacked in the field a fortnight or more, when the seeds were threshed out. The stocks were then placed in water for a week or more when they were spread out upon the grass to be rotted, just as was the custom when the seed was not saved. After the woody portion was well rotted the flax was gathered up and packed away for the winter, unless the family was in need of a fresh supply of linen. During the winter or early spring it was dressed. The first operation in this process

[1] *Hamilton Papers* (1790–91), No. 1841.

[2] For accounts of the preparation of flax for spinning, see Duncan, *op. cit.*, p. 389; Bouton, *Hist. of Concord, N.H.*, p. 527; Brown, *op. cit.*, p. 506; Kingman, *Hist. of North Bridgewater, Mass.*, p. 367; Weston, *Hist. of Middleboro, Mass.*, p. 212.

was braking, which was done by means of a clumsy home-made arrangement called a flax brake, used to bruise the woody part in order to separate it from the fiber. After the fiber was separated, it was swingled, which was done by beating it with a wooden paddle called a swingling-knife. In this operation all the woody portion was removed, after which it was ready to be turned over to the women, as all the work up to the carding or hatcheling process was usually done by the men and the boys.

When the flax came into the hands of women and girls, the first process was to hatchel it. One writer has described this process as follows: ". . . . first, the hatchel was brought and fastened into a chair with a string or stick, and the mother, with her checked apron, and a handkerchief pinned about her neck, and another handkerchief tied about her head to keep off the dust, sat in another chair. Winding one end of the flax tightly around the fingers of the right hand, and holding it, she drew the flax through the hatchel,[1] till it was thoroughly combed; changing, she combed in a similar manner the other end."[2] Hatcheling took out the short and broken portions, called tow, which was used for making the coarser cloth, wrapping-twine, and ropes. When the flax had been combed sufficiently, which was often many times, since the quality of the cloth depended upon the fineness of the fibers, it was put upon the distaff and spun upon the little wheel,

[1] An instrument made of nail rods with pointed teeth about six inches in length, seven rows with twelve in a row (Brown, *op. cit.*, p. 506). Since the combs or hatchels were homemade, no doubt the variations were about as numerous as the makers.

[2] Kingman, *op. cit.*, p. 367.

an implement about twenty inches in diameter and operated by the foot resting upon a treadle. It usually had two grooves in the circumference, one to receive the band to drive the fliers, the other to drive the spool with quicker motion to receive the thread.[1]

Except the fulling, shearing, and pressing of the woolen cloth after it was woven, the process of converting the raw wool into the finished product was very similar to that of flax and needs no elaborate description. In brief, the steps were as follows: first, the fleeces were torn to pieces, and all the dirt and burrs carefully picked out, as well as the tarred locks, draglocks, brands, and feltings. Occasionally the white locks that had been carefully separated were dyed at this stage of the process. After breaking, came carding, then combing. Before the wool was carded it was greased, occasionally with rape oil, but more often with melted swine grease, which had to be thoroughly

[1] The spinning process has been admirably described by Bolles as follows: "In the household manufacture of our forefathers the spinning apparatus was a wheel, which drove a single horizontal spindle mounted on a standard at about the height of the elbow. A cord, passing around the circumference of the big fly-wheel, drove the spindle at a great velocity. The end of the roll of wool, flax, or cotton, was attached to the spindle by simply tying it around, and the big wheel was started. Simultaneously with the starting of the wheel, the spinner brought back her hand holding the roll of fibre, so as to stretch it at the same time that the spindle, on its longitudinal axis was giving the roll the twist; then, without stopping the wheel, the spinner suddenly relaxed the strain on the yarn, and let her hand come quickly up to the end of the spindle, by which means the yarn wound itself up on the spindle instantaneously instead of continuing to twist. As soon as this process had been repeated enough times to secure a spindle full of yarn, the wheel was stopped and the yarn reeled off upon a wooden reel into hanks for knitting, weaving, or sewing" (*Indust. Hist. of U.S.* [3d ed., 1881], p. 421).

worked in. The carder simply drew a tuft of wool across the card several times until a considerable quantity had been caught in the wire teeth; then a second card was drawn across the first several times until the fibers ran parallel. The carded wool was then made into small rolls ready for ordinary spinning. For hard-twisted spinning it had to be combed, which was a more skilful operation than carding. Two hot T-shaped combs were used. The wool was placed on one and with the other combed into a long staple. The part combed out was spun into coarse yarn. If a close thread was desired, the yarn was spun twice. The single-spun yarn was used for knitting; the double was woven into a stiff, wiry cloth.[1]

Because the woolen cloth as it came from the loom was stiff, wiry, and very uncomfortable to wear, it was subjected to what was termed fulling, in order to soften it. In the fulling-mill this process consisted of wetting it thoroughly with warm soap and water, after which it was vigorously pounded with great oaken mallets. Before the advent of a fulling-mill into a community the cloth was fulled by beating it with sticks, or if the young folks wished to have a party, it was kicked instead of beaten. An old-fashioned fulling-party has been described as follows:

> When the cloth of the season was woven, the young people were invited to the house, the kitchen floor was cleared for action, and in the middle were placed stout splint bottom chairs in a circle, connected by a cord to prevent recoil. On these the young men sat

[1] For fuller descriptions than the one given above, see Weston, *op. cit.*, p. 214; Smith, *Hist. of Peterborough, N.H.*, pp. 75 ff.; Sibley, *Hist. of Union, Lincoln Co., Mass.*, pp. 108 ff.; McClellan, *Hist. of Gorham, Me.*, pp. 329 ff.; Earle, *op. cit.*, chap. ix.

with shoes and stockings off and trousers rolled to the knee. In the center were placed the cloths, wetted with warm soap suds, and then the kicking commenced by measured steps, driving the bundles of goods round and round the circle, until they were shrunk to the desired size. Then the girls, bare to the elbows, rinsed and wrung out the flannels and blankets, and hung them on the fence to dry.[1]

Coloring, dyeing, and bleaching were very important processes in the manufacture of textile commodities in the home.[2] Sometimes the raw materials were colored before they were spun, but usually it was the thread, yarn, or cloth on which the women exercised their inherent sense of color. The highest handicraft of the women's work was most frequently seen in selecting, manufacturing, and using the various colors. Before the advent of the ill-smelling dyepot into New England the woods furnished the materials for coloring. Sumach and the bark of the black oak, chestnut, and other trees were much used. Hickory bark or peach leaves furnished the yellows; black and white walnut bark or hulls, the browns, or rusty black when mixed with sumach berries; sumach berries alone, the deep, warm reds; oak and maple, the shades of purple; and cedar berries, the delicate dove or lead colors. When it was possible to secure indigo, green vitriol, alum, copperas, cochineal, or madder, the process

[1] "New England Wool Manufactures," *N. Eng. States*, I, 191.

[2] On coloring and dyeing, see Judd., *op. cit.*, p. 388; Griffin, *Hist. of Keene, N.H.*, p. 323; Williams, "The Home-Spun Age," *Mag. Am. Hist.*, XXX, 241; Drake, *Pioneer Life in Ky.*, p. 100; Parker, *op. cit.*, p. 183; Little, *Hist. of Weare, N.H.*, p. 182; Wayland, *Hist. of Rockingham Co., Va.*, p. 382; Clute, *Annals of Staten Island*, pp. 77 f., and Brown, *op. cit.*, p. 506.

was much simplified. With these prepared coloring materials were combined the products of the forest and the field. Indigo was mixed with the flowers of the goldenrod and alum to make green. Sassafras was used instead of the goldenrod if yellow or orange was desired. Pokeberry was boiled with alum to make crimson; sorrel with logwood and copperas made black; and oak bark with indigo gave a brownish red. In the South a good yellow was made of the horse-laurel, and an excellent black from the leaves and berries of the gallberry bush. The root of the barberry and the leaves of the devil's-bit gave a beautiful yellow, as did the petals of the Jerusalem artichoke and St. John's wort. While all these combinations, and indeed many others, were made, yet the standard dye was indigo. It was either bought of peddlers going about the country or of neighborhood traders, or the plants were grown and the dye manufactured in the home. The dye pot or tub filled with its malodorous mixture of indigo and urine had an important place near the kitchen fire in most New England homes. Judd thinks that our foremothers began to dye blue with indigo before 1700, in order to make stripes and checks, and that it became a common practice before the end of the first quarter of the eighteenth century.[1] It was from these checks and stripes of wool, flax, and cotton, made possible by the presence of the dyetub in the chimney corner, that most of the shirts, trousers, aprons, gowns, and bedticks were made.

To bring the linen to the desired "degree of showiness" required many bleachings, both of the yarn and of the

[1] *Op. cit.*, p. 380.

cloth. One writer, speaking of her mother in connection with bleaching linen cloth, remarks: "I have heard her say that to bring the fine linen for shirts to the required degree of showiness no less than thirty and sometimes forty bleachings were necessary."[1] These forty bleachings refer to the cloth only. It should be remembered that the skeins of thread no doubt had gone through an equal number before they were woven. For bleaching, these were first placed in warm water for three or four days, which was frequently changed, the skeins being continually wrung out. After this treatment they were washed in clear pure water from the spring or brook. Then they were treated with ashes and hot water over and over again, and finally placed in clear water for another week or so. On being taken out of this they were seethed, rinsed, beaten, washed, and dried, and finally wound on bobbins ready for the loom. The bleaching was sometimes done with slaked lime or buttermilk instead of ashes.[2]

If the mother desired a whiter cloth than was produced from the carefully bleached thread, she spread the rolls out on the green grass and fastened the corners down with loops and sticks. Pure water was then carried and sprinkled over the outspread linen. This process was repeated hour after hour and from day to day until the sun had whitened the cloth to the mother's satisfaction.[3] It often took weeks to bring it to the desired shade. To make the cloth pure white, it was sometimes soaked in buttermilk.

[1] Smith, *Colonial Days and Ways*, p. 70.

[2] Earle, *op. cit.*, p. 175. [3] Drake, *op. cit.*, p. 103.

Reeling, spinning, and even weaving silk became household pursuits in some parts of New England after the Revolution. The principal center of the industry was in eastern Connecticut.[1] Sewing-silk, from which lace, ribbons, and handkerchiefs were made, was the commonest product. Occasionally dress goods were also made. These compared with the machine-made silk about as favorably as the homespun linen or woolen did with the fine linen or broadcloth. In his report to Hamilton in 1791,[2] Constant Southworth stated that the product was really of a good quality, and that by force of genius and application some people had wrought it into most useful and elegant silk fabrics, particularly handkerchiefs, buttons, and ribbons. The ribbons were flexible enough to tie up the hair, "for which purpose they were worn by the Honourable Mr. Wadsworth, Representative in Congress, and by the Honble. Mr. Chester, and other gentlemen in this State." The report concluded thus:

> The culture of the Mulberry tree is increasing, and I believe it would be very easy in a few years for most families in this State to produce annually each, one pound weight of raw silk without injury to other domestic business, *this* with the larger quantities that would naturally be raised by many, whose situation was favorable in a particular degree, would find employment for some and amusement for others, and supersede the necessity of importing an Article which has long drained this State of her Money and richest Commodities. . . . .

[1] The value of the sewing-silk made in Tolland, Windham, and New London counties in 1810 amounted to $28,503 (Coxe, "Digest of Manufactures," *Am. State Papers*, "Finance," II, 736).

[2] For the report, see *Hamilton Papers* (1790–91), Nos. 1828, 1829.

Another household industry that grew up in some sections of New England after the Revolution was the manufacture of lace and edging. Fessenden asserts that in 1790 no less than 4,197 yards of silk and thread lace were made in the town of Ipswich, Massachusetts, by the women and children and sold in Boston and other mercantile towns.[1] This statement is corroborated by reports to the Secretary of the Treasury in 1791, which stated that in various parts of Massachusetts the women made lace and edging for their own use and some for sale, and that in Ipswich no less than 600 persons did more or less of it—some devoting most of their time to the business, others only at intervals, all independent of each other.[2] The machinery used was very simple, consisting only of a round, or perhaps elliptical pillow, from eight to twelve inches in diameter, encircled by a strip of parchment or pasteboard, upon which the pattern of lace was printed. A few rows of pins and bobbins, from a dozen to 120, according to the width and figure of the pattern, completed the outfit needed by each individual engaged in the work.[3] The returns of the marshals in the autumn of 1810 indicated that this feminine industry was still carried on in some of the New England homes.[4]

In concluding this section brief mention will be made of carpet-making in the home, an industry appearing rather late, but remaining for some time after it did arrive.

[1] *Register of Arts*, p. 295.

[2] *Hamilton Papers* (1790–91), No. 1616.

[3] *Ibid.* (Joseph Dana's report).

[4] Coxe, "Digest of Manufactures," *op. cit.*, p. 736.

Throughout the colonial period carpets were rather uncommon everywhere. They were also slow in appearing in the frontier settlements. Those made in the colonies prior to 1776 were chiefly of rags. They were woven with a stout yarn warp and a woof composed of strips cut from the cast-off clothing of the people. At first the yarn for the warp was homespun; later it was purchased in the form of carpet chain from the merchants or peddlers. Since carpets were woven entirely by hand, even in the factories, up to 1845,[1] they remained somewhat of a luxury prior to this date. In the meantime, however, it was possible for those who desired to do so to weave them on the ordinary loom which many families kept for weaving common cloth. After this loom went out of general use, carpets for a neighborhood were woven by some member of the community. It was in this form that the business remained in a few homes long after the people in general had substituted factory- for home-made wearing apparel and the major portion of the household textile supplies.

HOUSEHOLD IMPLEMENTS, UTENSILS, FURNITURE, NECESSITIES, AND COMFORTS

While the home manufacture of the articles included in this portion of the discussion did not continue so long as those considered in the foregoing section, yet all of them were important products of the home factory at some time or other, and in some locality or other, during the entire period covered in this treatise. Practically all of the implements connected with the fabrication of linen, woolen,

[1] Bolles, *op. cit.*, p. 394.

and cotton cloth were occasionally made in the homes. The same was true of such common utensils as brooms, brushes, all kinds of table furniture, cooper and earthen wares, as well as such necessities and comforts as hominy, meal, maple syrup and sugar, candles, soap, cider, beer, and whiskey. It is with products such as these that this section deals.

The chief implements used in the manufacture of the various kinds of cloth were looms, little foot-wheels for spinning linen, large wheels and wheel heads for wool and cotton, and reels, quill winders, spools, warping-bars, reeds, shifts, harness, flax brakes, swingling blocks and knives, hatchels, cards, combs, and shuttles. All these were occasionally made in the home. Most any ordinary carpenter could make looms. Concerning his father, Doddridge remarked, "After making his loom, he often used it as a weaver."[1] It often happened that someone in the community would devote himself entirely to the business of making them, thus relieving the farmer of the work.[2] The making of spinning-wheels likewise soon became a specialty in any given community. They were peddled through the country by the makers. The foot-wheel usually sold at about two dollars, and the great wheel, the clock reel, and quill wheel at one dollar each.[3] In the absence of these peddlers on the frontier, it was often very difficult to secure the wheels. Joseph True, one of the pioneers of Dover Township, Ohio, in 1803, walked forty miles to Zanesville, carrying a few bear and

[1] *Op. cit.*, p. 114.

[2] Wayland, *op. cit.*, p. 385.

[3] Smith, *op. cit.*, p. 75.

deer skins, and purchased a wheel with the proceeds, bringing it home on his back, having made the round trip in two days.[1]

To obviate the many difficulties connected with the making of cards and combs and at the same time to meet the great demand for them, machinery for cutting the wire teeth and piercing the leather backs was perfected and brought into general use about 1789. Before this date cards were laboriously made at home by many persons. The wire for the teeth was secured at the nearest store.[2] Even after the invention of machinery for cutting the teeth and piercing the backs, the women and children spent many hours around the open fire setting the wire teeth in the leather backs.[3] Reeds, shuttles, small looms, swingling blocks and knives, flax brakes, and other implements used in making cloth in the home were made by the husbands or sons with little difficulty, if no one in the community chose to make them. The smaller looms, like the belt-loom, the tape-loom, the braid-loom, and the garter-loom, were rather simple implements and easily constructed at home.

Until a mill for grinding grain was set up in a neighborhood, the people were obliged to make their own hominy and meal. The length of time that these primitive operations had to be kept up depended upon many factors. If a rather large number of people settled simultaneously in a place, a mill for grinding grain would be set up very soon after the settlement was established; while, on the

[1] Walker, *Hist. of Athens Co., Ohio*, II, 469.

[2] Bagnall, *op. cit.*, I, 154.

[3] Earle, *op. cit.*, p. 205.

other hand, if one persisted in living on the extreme frontier some distance from a community group, he would either have to go some thirty or forty miles to the nearest mill, or grate, crush, or grind his corn at home. As a matter of fact, the pioneer, even when a mill was set up within his reach, was forced to keep the primitive implements for making meal in his home for fear of some accident to the mill or his inability to get to it in certain seasons.[1]

The implements used in the home manufacture of meal and hominy were the grater, the hominy block, and the handmill. All these were made in the home and were in constant use in frontier communities. Since they have been so admirably described by one who really made them, it seems most appropriate to quote his description in full. It runs as follows:

> The hominy block and hand mill were in use in most of our houses. The first was made of a large block of wood about three feet long, with an excavation burned in one end, wide at the top and narrow at the bottom, so that the action of the pestle on the bottom threw the corn up on the sides toward the top of it, from whence it continually fell down into the center. In consequence of this movement the whole mass of grain was pretty equally subjected to the stroke of the pestle. In the fall of the year, while the Indian corn was soft, the block and pestle did very well for making meal for johnny cake and mush, but were rather slow when the corn became hard.
>
> The sweep was sometimes used to lessen the toil of pounding grain for meal. This was a pole of some springy elastic wood, thirty feet long or more; the butt end was placed under the side of the house, or a large stump; this pole was supported by two forks, placed about one-third its length from the butt and so as to elevate

[1] Drake, *op. cit.*, p. 58.

the small end about fifteen feet from the ground; to this was attached, by a large mortise, a piece of a sapling about five or six inches in diameter and eight or ten feet long. The lower end of this was shaped so as to answer for a pestle. A pin of wood was put through it at a proper height, so that two persons could work the sweep at once. This simple machine very much lessened the labor, and expedited the work. I remember that when a boy I put up an excellent sweep at my father's. It was made of a sugar tree sapling. It was kept going almost constantly from morning till night by our neighbors for several weeks.

A machine, still more simple than the mortar and pestle, was used for making meal while the corn was too soft to be beaten. It was called a grater. This was a half-circular piece of tin, perforated with a punch from the concave side, and nailed by its edge to a block of wood. The ears of corn were rubbed on the rough edges of the holes, while the meal fell through them to the board or block to which the grater was nailed, which being in a slanting direction, discharged the meal into a cloth, or bowl placed for its reception. This to be sure was a slow way of making meal; but necessity has no law.

The hand mill was better than the mortar or grater. It was made of two circular stones, the lowest of which was called the bed stone, the upper one the runner. These were placed in a hoop, with a spout for discharging the meal. A staff was let into a hole in the upper surface of the runner, near the outer edge, and its upper end through a hole in a board fastened to a joist above, so that two persons could be employed in turning the mill at the same time. The grain was put into the opening in the runner by hand.[1]

The conditions described above were quite common in practically all sections of the country in certain periods of their history. The early settlers were glad to copy the Indian way of making meal by crushing the grain with a hand pestle in a mortar made of a hollow stump. The

[1] Doddridge, *op. cit.*, pp. 111 ff.

sweep that Doddridge describes was the invention of the white man to lessen the labor of crushing the grain. Yet this was only a makeshift until a better way could be found. This came first in the form of the handmill, then the horsemill, then the windmill, and finally the gristmill, run at first by water power and later by steam. However, with all of these inventions, except the last, it was necessary to keep some of the primitive instruments around, because the streams would sometimes go dry or the wind would fail to blow.[1]

The common household utensils of home manufacture were brooms, brushes, wooden trays, trenchers, bowls, platters, noggins, lamps, buckets, dyetubs, churns, firkins, doormats, baskets, wooden breadtroughs, cheese-ladders, cheese-hoops, butter-paddles, washboards, and similar serviceable articles used by all housekeepers. The art of manufacturing many of these was learned from the Indians. The making of brooms and brushes lingered longer in any one section than many of the others. Even in New England the Indian or peeled brooms continued in common use until about 1820.[2]

The winter evening's work of many farmers throughout the country was the making of brooms. In New England they were made principally of birch and ash; in other parts of the country hickory answered the purpose as well. To make an ordinary Indian or splint broom a birch or

[1] Other references besides Doddridge on this subject are Cartmell, *Hist. of Frederick Co., Va.*, chap. xiii; Bolles, *op. cit.*, p. 352; Drake, *op. cit.*, pp. 57 f.; Parker, "Pioneer Life," *op. cit.*, pp. 128 ff.; Callahan, *Hist. of W. Va.*, p. 51; Levering, *op. cit.*, p. 69.

[2] Temple, *Hist. of Whately, Mass.*, p. 177.

other tree, about five inches in diameter where it was cut off, was used. A stick about six feet long was cut from this tree. Twelve or fourteen inches from the big end of the stick a ring was cut and the bark removed from this end. The maker then began to sliver with a sharp jackknife little flat slivers up to the ring. This was continued until the heart was reached, or until the wood was too brittle to sliver or strip. After the brittle part was cut off, the slivers were tied down with a tow string. When all this was done, there only remained to whittle off the part above to the size of a handle. Besides this type of broom, there were the parlor, oven, scrub, and hemlock brooms. The first was made of bristles; the second, of husks; and the third, like the Indian or splint broom, except with a shorter handle. The last was simply a bunch of "full-foliaged hemlock branches tied tightly together and wound around with hempen twine," into which a handle was driven. All these were kept on sale at most of the stores, the ordinary Indian brooms selling during the colonial times in Massachusetts for 8*d.* or 9*d.* each. They were also peddled throughout the country by Indian squaws, who were glad to exchange them for cider and other articles.[1]

But brief note need be made of the making of the remainder of the utensils in common use in the home. Trenchers and bowls were hewn from sections of maple or other kinds of logs and burned or scraped smooth;

[1] On broom-making, see Judd, *op. cit.*, p. 368, note; Temple, *op. cit.*, p. 177; Drake, *op. cit.*, p. 94; Earle, *op. cit.*, p. 302; Bigelow, *Hist. of Cohasset, Mass.*, p. 235.

crude pots and lamps were made of clay, the latter in the form of cups;[1] and noggins were either hollowed out of the knots of trees or made of small staves and hoops.[2] Cheese-ladders, cheese-hoops, butter-paddles, and many parts of the churn-presses were whittled out of red cherry or similar timber by the boys. Much ingenuity was often displayed in making many of these articles. Concerning his father's skill along these lines Doddridge said: "His cooper-ware was made by himself. I have seen him make a small neat kind of woodenware called set work, in which the staves were all attached to the bottom of the vessel by means of a groove cut in them by a strong claspknife and a small chisel before a single hoop was put on."[3] The sailors, in their many hours of leisure which their long cruises afforded them, often executed cooperwise, with much neatness and elegance, a variety of little bowls and other utensils which they presented to their wives, children, or sweethearts upon their return.[4]

Until the cabinetmaker permanently established himself in a town or settlement, much or even all of the furniture had to be made by members of the household. This was especially true in pioneer settlements and even older communities devoid of transportation facilities, since furniture was too cumbersome to move any great distance. In such communities tables, cupboards, benches, chairs, bedsteads, cradles, and in fact every piece of rude furniture

[1] Levering, *op. cit.*, p. 69; and Parker, "Pioneer Life," *op. cit.*, III, 130.

[2] Roosevelt, *op. cit.*, II, 100.

[3] *Op. cit.*, p. 114.

[4] Crèvecœur, *Letters from an Am. Farmer* (Philadelphia, 1793), p. 152.

in the household were homemade. We learn how some of these articles were devised on the frontier from the following description of the making of bedsteads, given by Duncan in his *Old Settlers' Papers:*

For bedsteads, an oak tree that would split well was selected, cut down, and a log about eight feet long taken from the butt and split into such pieces as could be readily shaped into posts and rails. Another log not so long was split into such pieces as, with a slight dressing, made slats. Holes were bored with a tolerably large auger in suitable places in the posts for inserting the rails; two rails were used for each side and about three for each end, the end rails answering for head and foot boards. Like auger holes were made in the lower side rails at suitable points for inserting the slats. When properly prepared this bedstead was put together by pressing the rails and slats in the holes prepared for each, thus making a rough but strong high-post bedstead, the posts at the top being tightly held together by rods prepared for the purpose, upon which curtains were to be hung. Thus was created a bedstead.[1]

According to the same writer, tables were made in the manner described as follows:

A large tree was cut down, and a log, the length desired for the table, was cut off and split into pieces (slabs) as thin as possible. These slabs were generally two feet in width and six feet in length; when dressed and made as thin and smooth as possible, two were put together with strong cross pieces, tightly pinned with wood pins, the whole set upon four strong legs, thus making a strong but rough table four feet in width and six feet in length, the size of the table being governed by the size of the family.[2]

[1] *Op. cit.*, p. 398. See also Atkinson, *Hist. of Kanawha Co., Va.*, p. 101, for a description of primitive furniture.

[2] Duncan, *op. cit.*, pp. 399 f.

Three-legged stools were constructed in the same way as tables.[1] Cradles were made of poplar troughs and peeled hickory bark.[2] It should be said that as the frontier life became more and more settled the furniture became less and less crude, and finally, when the settlement was sufficiently large to support a cabinetmaker, the industry passed largely into his hands, when remarkably artistic and durable articles were supplied to his customers in exchange for such commodities as food and clothing.

Certain household necessities and comforts were regularly made at home by members of the family. Among these were articles of food, drink, light, and general household supplies. The first included hominy, meal, maple syrup and sugar, and cheese; the second, beer, cider, whiskey, and more than two score of other drinks; the third, candlewood and candles of various kinds; and the last, chiefly soft soap and potash. Because of the importance of all these in the daily life of the people, a brief account of the processes involved in their manufacture follows.

Since the making of hominy and meal in the home has been sufficiently considered in a preceding paragraph, the discussion may pass directly to the manufacture of maple syrup and sugar, which was one of the most extensive of all family industries. The business was carried on quite extensively as household labor in New England, the middle states, and sections of the South and West until about 1830,

[1] Durrett, "How the Pioneer Lived," *Filson Club Pubs.*, No. 7, p. 43.

[2] Roosevelt, *op. cit.*, I, 120; and Levering, *op. cit.*, p. 69.

largely because substitutes for these articles were expensive and consequently could not be secured when desired. It was a matter of great economy when with a few weeks' work in the spring enough syrup and sugar could be supplied for a year's store and often a surplus for a ready market. Indeed, some felt about 1791 that the entire country could be supplied from this source. Dr. Benjamin Rush estimated at this date that, allowing three persons capable of labor to a family, each person attending to 150 trees, each tree yielding five pounds of sugar in a season, 60,000 families living in the sugar-maple districts would produce 135,000,000 pounds annually. He further estimated that on the basis of 600,000 families in the United States at the taking of the first census, and 200 pounds to a family, a total of 120,000,000 pounds would be sufficient for the entire country, leaving 15,000,000 pounds for exportation.[1] While no dream like this ever came true, yet a very great deal of syrup and sugar was made in various sections of the country, both for home consumption and for sale.

Two-thirds of the families in Vermont were engaged in the business of making maple sugar in 1794. Much was sold to shopkeepers. It was common for a family to make 200 or 300 pounds in three weeks. Large trees yielded five gallons of sap a day and from twelve to fifteen pounds of sugar in a season. In the town of Cavendish, in the spring of 1794, eighty-three families made 80,000 pounds.[2] Similar conditions existed in other states. Great quantities were made in the outer districts of New

[1] *Essays, Literary, Moral, and Philosophical*, p. 287.

[2] Williams, *op. cit.*, pp. 318 f.

Hampshire as early as 1784.[1] New Jersey, in 1789, was giving considerable attention to maple-sugar making.[2] It was an important business in the western country before 1790.[3] The vicinity of Asylum, Pennsylvania, produced great quantities in 1796.[4] It was said of Genesee County, New York, in 1803, that "maple sugar is manufactured in such quantities that some of the inhabitants make from five hundred to upwards of a thousand pounds of it in a season."[5] The census of manufactures taken in the autumn of 1810 indicated that much maple sugar was annually made in the homes. Five counties in Vermont returned 352,532 pounds; twenty-two in Pennsylvania, 1,046,268; fifty-four in Kentucky, 2,471,647; and eight in Ohio, 667,660. The total amount in Ohio was estimated by the marshals at 3,023,806 pounds.[6]

The sugar-making season was a busy one for all members of the household. Fortunately it came at a time when there was little farm work to do, thus making it possible for the male portion of the family to assist in the work. Baily's description of the season as he saw it in 1796 in western Pennsylvania and southern Ohio shows how it employed every member of a family.

[1] "Belknap Papers," in *Mass. Hist. Soc. Colls.*, 5th ser., III, 181.

[2] "Letters of Phineas Bond," *Am. Hist. Ass'n Rept.*, 1896, I, 652.

[3] Imlay, *Topographical Description of the Western Country* (3d ed., 1797), p. 61.

[4] Weld and Liancourt, *Travels in U.S. of N.A.* (London, 1801), p. 153.

[5] Munro, "A Description of Genesee County, in the State of New York," *Doc. Hist. of N.Y.*, II, 1174.

[6] Coxe, "Digest of Manufactures," *op. cit.*, pp. 731, 762, 789, 797.

The season of sugar-making is a very busy time in those parts where trees are plenty; it furnishes employment for every branch of a family; and that, happily, at a season when they are not otherwise employed on their plantations. It employs them night and day; for in the day they are busily employed in collecting the sap as it runs from the trees, and during the greater part of the night in boiling this sap down to its proper consistency. The children are equally useful in this office with the men; for whilst the latter are doing the laborious part of the undertaking, the children are employed in graining the sugar and watching the kettle.[1]

Cheese-making long remained a household industry throughout many sections of the country. Besides its value as food, cheese utilized a large supply of milk that otherwise would have been cast aside. With a few rude utensils and a little care ten gallons of milk could be made into cheese in a short time. How this was done has been described or rather related as follows:

Pour about ten gallons of milk into a cheese tub. Pour into the milk a pint of liquid from a calf's rennet which has been soaking in a bowl. In about half an hour this acid turns the milk into curd floating upon whey. Cut the curd into small square blocks by running a wooden sword through it repeatedly. Spread a cheese cloth over the tub, pressing it down upon the curds so that they will flow up through the cloth. Then empty the remaining curd into a basket lined with a sheet of cheese cloth so that the rest of the whey shall drain off into a tub underneath the basket. Turn the corners of the cloth over upon the curd and put on stones to press all day. The dry curd is then to be salted to taste, and if sage cheese is to be made, some sage leaves and corn leaves to color it and to give flavor are mashed and soaked until enough liquid is

[1] *Journal of a Tour, 1796 and 1797*, p. 182. For sugar-making in Kentucky, see Drake, *op. cit.*, p. 86; and for an excellent general article on the same subject, *Am. Museum*, VI, 98 ff. and 209 ff.

obtained to mix into the curd. Then for the press! A stout frame with pulleys on each side is used to press down the curd into a wooden cylinder, squeezing out the piece until it can be made no harder. After several days of continuous pressure the cheese is taken out of its hoop. The cheese is done and needs only time to ripen and strengthen it.[1]

Cider was the only drink of any consequence that was made in the household way for any considerable time. While beer was brewed and whiskey distilled in private homes, yet their manufacture passed quite early in any given community into the hands of professionals. As early as 1649 there were six public brew-houses in Virginia.[2] In the western country distilleries made their appearance soon after the farmers had raised a crop of corn and rye.[3] While it is true that many families in New England had beer apparatus with which they brewed their common beverage,[4] and that the planters of Virginia often "brewed their own beer, strong and good,"[5] yet such conditions were temporary and passed away as public and private breweries were set up and orchards increased and came to maturity, from which a supply of cider could be secured.

Cider, cider-brandy, cider-wine, and water-cider were for many generations the common beverage of the people of New England as well as many of those in other sections

[1] A description by Robert T. Burbank; quoted by Bigelow, *op. cit.*, p. 232.

[2] "A Perfect Description of Virginia," Force, *Tracts*, II, No. 8, p. 3.

[3] Hunter, "The Pathfinders of Jefferson Co., Ohio," *Ohio Arch. and Hist. Soc. Pubs.*, VI, 232.

[4] Felt, *Hist. of Ipswich, Essex, and Hamilton, Mass.*, p. 27.

[5] "A Perfect Description of Virginia," *op. cit.*

of the country. Well-to-do farmers put away from twenty to seventy barrels of cider in the cellar each year to drink. It was on the table three times a day. The farmer commonly took a jug of it into the field in the fore- and afternoons and into the woods for drink in winter.[1] Until a cider-mill was set up in a town or community, the cider for the family's use was made in the home, by a very crude process at first, but later by one more elaborate. A log hollowed out to hold three or four barrels and a maul hung upon a spring pole for a press were the essentials of the first crude cider-mills.[2] These, however, were soon supplanted by regular homemade ones, somewhat more serviceable and expedient, but on the whole almost as crude. Fortunately, a careful description of an old New England cider-mill has been preserved in the words of one who when a boy "scraped the nuts" of his father's mill many a day during the cider-making season. His description follows:

> These mills were very rude affairs. They consisted of two cuts of hardwood logs about twenty-two inches in diameter, and about two feet long, set upright and made to revolve, or roll against each other, cavities being morticed into one, and projections which they called "nuts" being set in the other to fit these cavities, and draw in the apples. The apples were poured into a "hopper" so arranged that their weight would press them against the revolving surfaces. From the top of one of these vertical rollers, extended a wooden crank twenty feet long, ten inches square at the wheel and tapering

[1] Cochrane and Wood, *Hist. of Franceston, N.H.*, pp. 364 f.; also Brown, *op. cit.*, p. 507. It was estimated in 1728 that a Boston family of nine persons of the "middle figure" consumed in a year twelve barrels of beer, four barrels of cider, and six gallons of wine (Judd, *op. cit.*, p. 372, note).

[2] Blood, *Hist. of Temple, N.H.*, p. 165.

to five, and so crooked as to reach nearly to the ground at the outer extremity. To this small end a horse was hitched and supplied the motive power by walking round and round in a circle. It required a man and two small boys to run the thing to an advantage. One small boy was to follow the horse and keep him from stopping, and the other was to "scrape the nuts" while the man poured in the apples, bringing them a bushel at a time upon his shoulder, and dodging under the crank as it swept slowly around. . . . . The process was slow, a cart load of apples going through in about three hours. Then the "trough" must stand over night, and then it [the pomace] was put into a press and the juice squeezed out. Afterwards it was cut up, soaked with water and pressed again. The last result was "water cider" and was considered strong enough for boys and women to drink.[1]

Good substitutes for cider, cider-brandy, and cider-wine before the orchards matured in new settlements were "metheglin," maple-beer, and maple-wine. The first was made of steeped honeycomb and fermented honey and was very common on the frontier where wild honey was plentiful. It was preferred in the place of cider by some people.[2] Maple-beer and maple-wine were made in the home with little difficulty. To make the former, one mixed with about four gallons of boiling sap a quart of syrup. On cooling to blood heat enough yeast was added to cause fermentation and malt or bran to strengthen it. A little essence of spruce gave it a most excellent flavor. Maple-wine was made by boiling four or five gallons of sap down to make one, to which yeast was added in proportion to the quantity made. After fermentation had

[1] Cochrane and Wood, *op. cit.*, p. 364; also Donovan and Woodward, *op. cit.*, pp. 476 f.

[2] Anderson, *Counties of Warren, Benton, Jasper, Ind.*, p. 444.

taken place it was set aside in a cool place for two or three years, when it became pleasant and sweet. Good vinegar was made by simply leaving the sap in the sun for a short time.[1]

Supplying material to light the home was largely an individual household problem, not only during the colonial period, but even throughout the eighteenth century, and in some sections of the country far into the nineteenth. Before the advent of tallow candles into a neighborhood various materials were used. Candles were made from the tallow of the berries of the bayberry bush found in all the colonies and from whale oil and from honeycomb wax. Other materials much used were candle-wood found in all the colonies; rushes, after the bark had been removed and dipped into tallow or grease; and fish, bear, whale, and moose oil. All these did good service when there were no tallow or other candles, or to save the precious home-made ones carefully packed away in candle-boxes.[2]

Candle-wood, bayberry, and tallow candles were the chief sources for light in the homes prior to the appearance of kerosene in the first half of the nineteenth century. Since candle-wood was nothing more than the knots and hearts of the resinous pine trees, it requires no description; but, owing to their vast importance, a brief account of the making of bayberry and tallow candles seems apropos here. Such an account of the bayberries and the process

[1] *Am. Museum*, IV, 350.

[2] Anburey, *Travels through the Interior of Am.*, II, 269; Felt, *op. cit.*, p. 26; Weeden, *Early R.I.*, p. 100; Wells and Wells, *Hist. of Hatfield, Mass.*, p. 145; Judd, *op. cit.*, p. 302.

of extracting the fat from them for tallow has come down to us from the pen of the Swedish naturalist, Peter Kalm, who came to America in 1748 and wrote of what he saw. His description follows:

> There is a plant here, from the berries of which they make a kind of wax or tallow, and for that reason the Swedes call it Tallow-schrub. The English call the same tree the Candle-berry-tree or Bayberry-bush; . . . . It grows abundantly in wet soil, and seems to thrive particularly well in the neighborhood of the sea. . . . . The berries grow abundantly on the female schrub, and look as if flour had been strewed upon them. They are gathered late in autumn, being ripe about that time, and are then thrown into a kettle or pot full of boiling water; by this means their fat melts out, floats at the top of the water, and may be skimmed off into a vessel; with the skimming they go on until there is no tallow left. The tallow, as soon as it is congealed, looks like common tallow or wax, but has a dirty green color; it is for that reason melted over again, and refined; by which means it acquires a fine and pretty transparent green color. This tallow is dearer than common tallow, but cheaper than wax. Candles of this kind do not easily bend, nor melt in summer as common candles do; they burn better and slower, nor do they cause any smoke, but yield rather an agreeable smell when they are extinguished. . . . . In Carolina, they not only make candles out of the wax of the berries, but likewise sealing-wax.[3]

Since the farmers killed their beeves on the farm, they usually had a supply of material to make tallow candles. When enough of the carefully saved tallow had been accumulated, it was placed in a large kettle and melted to make candles, most of which in the early days were "dips." In time, however, molds became common.

[3] *Travels into N. A.* (2d ed., 1772), I, 150.

Some families owned them, others depended upon itinerant candle-makers. The process of making dipped candles was rather laborious. It has been described by one writer as follows:

> When enough [tallow] had been accumulated it was placed in a large kettle and melted. The candle wicking was made of cotton, and was bought.[1] It came in balls. The wicking was cut twice the length of the candle and doubled over a stick made for the purpose and then twisted together. These sticks were two feet in length and an inch in diameter. Six wicks were placed upon each stick, and as many used as would hold all the candles to be made at one time. Two sticks, six or eight feet in length, often old rake handles, were used for support. These were placed upon two chairs about eighteen inches apart. On these the sticks were placed with the wicks hanging down. By taking a couple of the sticks in the hand the wicks were placed in the hot tallow until they were soaked. When all had been thus treated dipping began. Each time a little tallow adhered, which was allowed to cool. Care was taken not to allow them to remain in the hot tallow long enough to melt off what had already cooled. While the dipping was going on candles were suspended where a draft of air would pass over and cause them to cool quickly. Care was taken not to have the candles touch each other. The dipping continued until the candles were large enough for use. If the tallow in the kettle became too cool to work well, some boiling water was put in the kettle which went to the bottom and kept the tallow above warm enough to work.[2]

In a country where money was scarce and transportation facilities meager, it was necessary for the inhabitants

[1] It was also made in the home of loosely spun hemp or from tow and from the silk down of milkweeds which grew in the fields (Earle, *op. cit.*, p. 35).

[2] Brown, *op. cit.*, pp. 507 f.; also Bigelow, *op. cit.*, p. 234.

to seek a product that would bear the expense of transportation to a market some distance from where it was produced. Such was found in the salts of lye, or black salts. The manufacture of these was one of the main sources of income among the early settlers from New England to Ohio. To secure the lye from which to make them, ashes were collected from the clearings, saved from the wood burned in the dwellings and from log heaps made and burned especially for this purpose. While this last method was wasteful, yet necessity often forced it upon the frontiersman. After the ashes were collected, they were placed either in rude conical boxes, made of staves and flaring at the top, in leaches constructed of hollow logs, or in what was known as a mesh tub or ashhopper, made much like the conical boxes. When water was poured in at the top of any of these receptacles, the lye would leach through into a kettle or some similar vessel. If salts were to be made, it was boiled until evaporation left the matter held in the solution in soluble form. In this form it was usually sold to persons who made a business of converting it into potash; or the farmer himself might finish the process, which consisted of placing the salts in a kettle, subjecting them to red heat for one or two hours, when most of the combustible matter was consumed. The residuum, when cold, was broken up, packed into tight casks, and sent to market. Sometimes the settlers bartered their ashes to traders for eight or ten cents a bushel instead of making salts themselves. These traders made them into potash, which they sent to the nearest refinery for sale. The black salts were sometimes sold for three or four dollars a hundred to those who made it a business of converting them into potash.[1]

The lye from the ashes was also used for making soft soap, one of the commonest products of the home factory. It was a very simple matter to mix the old grease, which had accumulated during the year, with some lye, boil it until the mixture did not separate when cooled, and secure a product known as soft soap, the making of which was one of the spring chores in many country districts long after they had passed out of the frontier stage of their development. Many years after the manufacture of other household necessities and comforts had passed to the shop or factory, soap-making remained an important part of the spring work of the women.[2]

FARMING IMPLEMENTS, BUILDING MATERIALS, AND GENERAL SUPPLIES

Since the making of the articles included in this section passed so quickly to handicraftsmen, no extended treatment of them seems necessary here. The fact must be kept in mind, however, that until the blacksmith, carpenter, harness-maker, and sawmill became permanently established in a community the farmers had to make their wagons, plows, harrows, pitchforks, hand rakes, flails,

[1] On the uses made of ashes by the early settlers, see Williams, *Hist. of the Fire Lands*, p. 44; Wadleigh and Worthen, *Hist. of Sutton, N.H.*, I, 452; Lapham, *Hist. of Bethel, Me.*, p. 388; Winterbotham, *View of U.S.*, II, 118; Abbot, *Hist. of Concord, N.H.*, II, 1064; Brown, *op. cit.*, p. 509; Williams, *op. cit.*, p. 318.

[2] Bigelow, *op. cit.*, p. 233.

shovels, ox-yokes, sleds, ax handles, hoe handles, scythe-snaths, single- and double-trees, horse traces, collars, hames, bridles, clips, clevises, laprings, lumber, shingles, and nails, as well as many other articles of less importance yet much used on the farm. All manner of makeshifts were necessary to supply these when it was impossible to secure them already made. For example, horse collars were made of corn husks; hames, of crooked roots; clips, clevises, and laprings, of hickory withes; ox-yokes, of bent hickory wood; traces and bridles, of twisted deer hide; and pitchforks, from forked bows or antler horns.[1]

Vehicles for transportation, harrows, and plows were in great demand in a country where the majority of the people made their living by agriculture. All these were often very crude, being made by the farmer himself prior to the advent of the blacksmith and the carpenter into the village or community. The first vehicles were nothing more than log boats and sleds, the former consisting of a forked tree shaped with the ax to slide over the ground; the latter much like the first, except that the forks of the triangle were longer and the main stem was left long enough to form a tongue to which the oxen were hitched.[2] In communities where the sled was not so well adapted to the farmer's use wooden-wheel wagons took its place. These wagons were very common in many sections of the country, especially throughout the German settlements

[1] Scharf and Westcott, *op. cit.*, I, 136; Vogel, *op. cit.*, p. 21; Wilkinson, *Annals of Ia.*, 3d ser., VI, 452; Wheeler, "Inventors and Inventions of Cayuga Co., N.Y.," *Cayuga Co. Hist. Colls.*, II, 103; Donovan and Woodward, *op. cit.*, p. 465.

[2] Wheeler, *op. cit.*, pp. 103 ff.

of Pennsylvania and elsewhere. The wheels, sawed from the trunks of trees, axles made from hickory or white oak, and a coupling pole to connect them, were the essentials of these crude but serviceable wagons.[1]

If circumstances demanded it, the farmer made plows and harrows needed in his farming operations. These were made entirely of wood at first. In the course of time in any community it became possible to get iron teeth for the A-shaped harrow and iron for the point, share, and wing of the plow. As soon as the blacksmith and carpenter appeared, these implements were supplied by their joint labor, the former making the iron parts and the latter the wooden beam, handles, and moldboard of the plow and the beams of the harrow. The "bar share" plows were in general use on the frontier until about 1815, when they were replaced in the older communities by the "Carey" plow, which in turn was superseded in about 1835 by one known as the "Daniel Webster."[2]

Unless there was a sawmill very near, the farmer had to make all the lumber he used on his farm; and since these mills were slow to make their appearance in sparsely settled and out-of-the-way districts because of the difficulties connected with getting the lumber to market, the farmers in such districts often had to depend upon the "sawpit" for several years for their supply of lumber. This structure usually consisted of a platform and a pit, set in a hillside, where two men, one above and the other

[1] Schultz, *First Settlements of the Germans in Md.*, p. 18.

[2] Donovan and Woodward, *op. cit.*, 465; Vogel, *op. cit.*, p. 21; Stevens, *Ind. Mag. Hist.*, X, 401.

below, were able to saw about one hundred feet of boards in a day when the logs were squared and brought to the pit. While sawmills made their appearance in the colonies before 1700, yet they could not always follow the sturdy frontiersmen into the new settlements; hence the "sawpit," as well as many other crude implements, remained practically as long as the frontier itself.[1]

Other building materials commonly made by the farmer and his sons were shingles of various lengths, wooden hinges, and doorlatches. Since there was a great demand for them in the West Indies, many of the New England farmers spent much of their spare time in making shingles for this market. In the new settlements everywhere during the first few years it was necessary to make all the shingles and boards needed to cover the dwellings and other buildings. The shingles were often shaved after they were rived. A man could shave about 1,000 in a day. The wooden hinges and doorlatches were among the many products of the New England "jackknife" industries.[2]

Before and even after the invention of the nail-cutting machine in 1790 by Jacob Perkins[3] the manufacture of nails was one of the common household industries of New England, as well as of some other sections of the country. In 1789 Fisher Ames said in a speech which he made in Congress that it was quite common for the country people of Massachusetts to erect small forges in their chimney

[1] Judd, *op. cit.*, p. 49; Temple, *Hist. of North Brookfield, Mass.*, p. 60; Stevens, *op. cit.*, X, 402.

[2] Earle, *op. cit.*, p. 318.

[3] Perley, "The Manufacture of Nails in Essex Co., Mass.," *Essex Antiquarian*, II, 70.

corners and in winter, and on evenings when little other work could be done, to make great quantities of nails.[1] Nehemiah Bennett, in his description of the town of Middleboro, Massachusetts, written in 1793, said: "Nailing, or the business of making nails, is carried on largely in winters by the farmers and young men, who have but little other business during that season of the year."[2] The manufacture of nails was also one of the plantation industries in Virginia. Thomas Jefferson required about a dozen of his younger slaves to make nails. They made about a ton a month at a considerable profit.[3]

Besides nails tacks were also made in the household way in New England during the eighteenth century. A writer in the *Furniture Trade Journal*, speaking of this industry, said:

> In the queer-shaped, homely farm houses, or the little, contracted shops of certain New England villages, the industrious and frugal descendants of the Pilgrims toiled providently through the long winter months at beating into shape little nails which play so useful a part in modern industry. A small anvil served to beat the wire or strip of iron into shape and point it; a vise, worked by the foot, clutched it between jaws furnished with a gauge to regulate the length, leaving a certain portion projecting, which, when beaten flat by a hammer, formed the head. By this process a man might make, toilsomely, perhaps 2,000 tacks per day.[4]

[1] *Annals of Cong.*, 1st Cong., 1789–91, I, 156 f.

[2] Quoted by Swank, *Hist. of the Manufacture of Iron in All Ages* (2d ed., 1892), p. 133.

[3] *Ibid.*, p. 269.

[4] *Ibid.*, p. 134. Other references on nail- and tack-making are Coxe, *View of the U.S.*, p. 269; Hayes, *op. cit.*, p. 89; and Perley, "The Manufacture of Nails in Essex County, Mass.," *op. cit.*, II, 70.

The making of such useful articles as pitchforks, scythe-snaths, wooden shovels, flails, ax handles, hoe handles, hand rakes, sleds, single- and double-trees, gave the farmer little difficulty, since wood was the only material entering into their construction. After the manufacture of all other of these articles had long passed to the shop or factory, a farmer ax-handle maker was not uncommon in many communities. This individual would search the woods in the fall for the best hickory or other suitable material from which he would supply the neighborhood with ax handles made during his leisure winter hours.

Briefly summarizing the trend of the chapter as a whole, it should be said that, judged by both the quantity made and the length of time their manufacture remained in the home, the relative importance of the three general classes of homemade products has been indicated by the space given to each division. Wearing apparel and household textile supplies were, during the entire existence of the family system of manufacturing, the most important and most generally produced articles. Of the articles included in the second section, maple syrup and sugar, cider, and soap were the ones that remained along with those in the first section when others had passed to the shop or factory. Most of the articles included in the last section were made by the farmer only in cases of sheer necessity. It was only on the plantations that they were regularly manufactured for any considerable time.

CHAPTER VII

THE TRANSITION FROM FAMILY- TO SHOP- AND FACTORY-MADE GOODS

The title of this chapter might well have been chosen as a fitting one for the entire discussion. Indeed, the history of household manufactures in the United States from 1640 to 1860 is mainly concerned with that slow transfer from goods made entirely in the home by the members of a family and from materials largely grown on the farm to goods made wholly in shop or factory. This transfer was gradually going on during all the years between the foregoing dates. Its story would be a simple one if it had been marked with uniformity either in time or in place. Since this was not the case, such a story becomes a very complex one. While one section of the country was in one stage of the transfer, another section would be in quite a different stage, and another would have passed through it entirely, while still another had not begun it. The purpose of this chapter is to present in as clear and logical a manner as the data at hand warrant the history of this complex problem from its beginning to about 1830. It will be unnecessary to go into detail before 1810, since the preceding discussion has exhibited the status of the subject prior to this date. The general plan of procedure is, first, to give a brief statement of certain steps in and phases of the transition; secondly, to present a résumé of its progress down to 1810; and, thirdly, to portray the actual status of the family factory and the factors influencing the transfer, from 1810 to 1830, under the caption "The Transfer Completed, in Whole or in Part."

STAGES IN, AND PHASES OF, THE TRANSITION

The fact that the United States had a large frontier population during its entire history to 1860 made the transfer from household- to shop- and factory-made goods something that was always taking place but never quite completed when the country as a whole is considered; so, for this reason, in discussing the stages in this transfer the fact that they were both geographical and temporal must be kept in mind. In general the older the community the more complete the transfer at any given date; but when adequate transportation facilities paralleled the establishment of a new settlement this general rule was violated. In this case shop- and factory-made goods were accessible from the outset, making the transfer an omitted phase of such a community's economic history. Nevertheless, in spite of the many exceptions to the general rule, especially when one considers individual homes and communities before transportation facilities preceded their establishment, there existed certain well-marked stages in the evolution of the simple household industry into the present-day highly organized and intricate factory system. The first stage in this evolution was what might be termed the family stage, in which household manufacturing was supreme. Practically all of the family's needs were supplied by its members. The producer and consumer were virtually identical. The family was the economic unit, and the whole system of production was based upon it. Before 1810 this stage was common throughout many sections of the country; after this date it became more or less localized.

Closely related to the first stage was the second, the itinerant-supplementary stage, which involved either the hiring by the family of some outsider—a dressmaker, a tailor, a weaver, or shoemaker—to come in and perform a part of the work in the process of manufacturing or the sending of both raw materials and semi-finished products to regular establishments, the business of which was to supplement the household operations. The appearance of the foregoing itinerants along with fulling-mills, carding-machines, dyeing and bleaching establishments, and tanneries in a community meant that the homes were sooner or later to be relieved of many of the operations relative to the making of a multitude of articles. Thus, as the years passed by, it became more and more common for the itinerant workmen to go their rounds each season, spinning the yarn from wool carded at the neighborhood machine, working up the cloth that had been fulled, pressed, and dyed at the fulling-mill and shop, or making up the leather tanned at the nearest tannery.

The shop stage both followed and paralleled the itinerant-supplementary, following the itinerant phase and paralleling the supplementary. But few communities escaped some phase of this stage. In fact, prior to 1840 few cared to escape it and fewer still desired to give it up after it had once been established therein. New Hampshire, one of the oldest states in the Union, was still in this stage as late as 1832, at which date it was the rule for most of the manufacturing in the several towns for the supply of the immediate community to be done by handicraftsmen in permanently established shops. Occasionally work was sent out from the shops to families. Tanning, blacksmithing, shoemaking, coopering, cabinetmaking, chaise- and wagon-making, hatting, harness-making, tailoring, and fulling were all done in shops, the output being consumed by the inhabitants of the neighborhood. For example, in Lancaster in the year 1831 shoes and boots to the value of $3,116 were made, all of which were sold to the local inhabitants.[1] These shops accepted for pay raw wool, hides, lard, feathers, pork, bacon, or in fact almost anything the farmers had to offer. Generally the shopkeeper owned his place of business and furnished the raw materials and tools as well as the labor. The variations, however, were as numerous in this stage as in some of the preceding ones. Often a shop grew into a real manufactory. This was especially true in the line of textile manufactures. An ambitious weaver would furnish his place of business with several looms, for which the mothers and daughters of the neighborhood often spun yarn, either selling it outright or taking in exchange the finished product. Some of these so-called manufactories kept several women busy. In 1764 there was one in Philadelphia which employed 100 persons in both the spinning and the weaving operations. A company in New York during the year 1767 employed some 300 poor

[1] *Documents Relative to Manufactures in the U.S.* (1832), I, 669.

and needy persons; one in Philadelphia in 1775 employed 400 women, and a Rhode Island gentleman in 1777 was receiving work from 500 spinners.[1] These facts are cited to call attention to the multiple variations in the handicraft system and at the same time to show how easy and natural, when the factory system finally came, was the transfer of the girls from the spinning and weaving operations done in their homes to the same work done in factories.

The foregoing variations in the handicraft system foreshadowed another system or stage, namely, the mill-small-factory stage. The gristmills, flour-mills, sawmills, cotton- and woolen-mills which became so common in the various sections of the country prior to 1860 were the means through which the people were supplied with products once made in their homes. Corn, wheat, sawlogs, raw cotton, and raw wool were brought to these mills and exchanged for the corresponding manufactured articles. The sail-duck factory established in Boston[2] in 1788 or 1789 is an example of the small-factory phase of this stage; and the mills set up in the South just after the War of 1812 and those in the West between 1830 and 1860 are good examples of the strictly mill phase. Between 1812 and 1830 northern mill-builders went into certain sections of the South and built many yarn-mills in which both cotton and woolen yarn were spun and given out to the settlers for raw materials or the finished products. At first these mills, often situated on a plantation, merely

[1] Abbott, *Women in Industry*, p. 38.

[2] Bishop, *op. cit.*, I, 419.

supplied the plantation and neighborhood demands. Later, however, they were able to enter the northern markets.[1]

The mill-small-factory stage was followed in any given community by the large factory, which was made possible by the invention of machinery. Along the line of textile manufactures this machinery was the carding-machine, the spinning-jenny, and the power-loom. Up to 1813 the cotton-mills throughout the country were principally for spinning, the weaving being done elsewhere in handlooms. In this year the power-loom and all the operations for converting raw cotton into finished cloth were for the first time introduced into this country at Waltham, Massachusetts. It was soon seen after this successful application of power spinning- and weaving-machines to the manufacture of textiles that the household system of manufacturing could not long contend against the economy and efficiency of the factory system. Yet the transition was not so rapid as some supposed it would be. The first textile-mills had many ups and downs, especially after the close of the War of 1812. Springing up mushroom-like during this war, they met with disastrous reverses upon its close on account of the large influx of foreign goods. But after the hard times of 1819 had passed the factories regained their prestige, and by 1830 much of the family spinning and weaving, especially in the older sections of the country, had been transferred to them. The unprecedented growth in the number of factories during the twenty years following the War of 1812 was

[1] Clark, "Manufactures," *op. cit.*, V, 321.

chiefly due to the factory and the power-loom taking the place of home manufacturing and the handloom. The growth between 1830 and 1860 was due to the increase in population in the United States in both numbers and wealth. While the family system of manufacturing had by no means disappeared in the country at large in 1830, yet at the same time there were sections where it had ceased to be an important factor in the economic life and prosperity of the people. In such sections combers, spinners, and weavers as individuals, whether in homes or shops, by this date had become a part of the great monster, the mill machine.

PROGRESS OF THE TRANSITION TO 1810

The foregoing résumé of the phases of, and the stages in, the evolution of simple household industry into the complicated factory system furnishes an excellent background upon which to throw the discussion in the remaining sections of this chapter. There is no thought of presenting in detail the history of the phases and stages mentioned above; for, as stated in the Introduction, each as it once existed in this country is worthy of a separate history. The discussion in the present section is concerned with showing, first, how certain operations connected with textile manufacturing in the home passed into regular establishments; secondly, the availability in any given community of certain supplies with which the home had little or nothing to do in their manufacture; thirdly, how the handicraft system gradually evolved through the "jack of all trades" into the itinerant weavers, shoemakers, and tailors; and, finally, how the transition was accelerated by the system which was established to distribute the shop- and factory-made goods. All these were actualities before 1810 in many sections of the country, and it was through them that the greater part of whatever transition took place during the period under consideration was effected. Their consideration follows in the order enumerated.

Connected with the manufacture of wearing apparel and household textile supplies were certain operations difficult to perform in the home. For this reason it was quite natural that they should be transferred to regular establishments rather early in a community's history. Fulling, pressing, shearing, dyeing, bleaching, and carding were operations which sooner or later the women and girls of a neighborhood turned over to professionals. Among the first to be professionalized was fulling, a phase of the manufacture of woolen cloth requiring appliances not convenient to have or easy to manipulate in the home. One of the first establishments set up in a New England town was the fulling-mill. Rowley, Massachusetts, seems to have had one as early as 1643; others were established as the need for them arose. Watertown had one in 1662; Andover, in 1673; Salem and Ipswich, in 1675; Dedham, in 1681; Barnstable and Byfield, in 1687; Ballards, in 1689; New London and Sewall, in 1693; Stanford, in 1700; Guilford, in 1706; and Dorchester, in 1709.[1] As early as 1784 there were as many as 41 of these mills

[1] North, "New England Wool Manufacture," *N. Eng. States*, I, 192; Weeden, *Soc. and Econ. Hist. of N. Eng.*, I, 306.

in New Jersey;[1] and in 1810 Maine reported 59; Massachusetts, 221; New Hampshire, 135; Vermont, 166; Rhode Island, 24; Connecticut, 218; New York, 427; New Jersey, 52; Pennsylvania, 213; Delaware, 8; Maryland, 28; Virginia, 55; Ohio, 21; Kentucky, 33; North Carolina, 20; and Tennessee, 2—a total of 1,682.[2] While these figures by no means represent all the fulling-mills in the various states and territories at this date, yet they do serve to show in some degree at least the prevalence of the demand for this one process in the manufacture of woolen cloth to be done outside the home; and, judging from the advertisements in the newspapers, one is led to conclude that even before 1810 the fulling business was no longer a monopoly, as it had been in some of the early New England towns, but had passed into the competitive stage, in the older communities at least. One such newspaper notice will illustrate the sort of a campaign carried on by the fullers to maintain their business. The following appeared in the November 24, 1810, issue of *The Western Citizen*, published in Paris, Kentucky.

Look Here!
☞ Call all you good wives that know how to spin
To turn round your wheels we would have you begin
The subscribers intend carrying on the, *Fulling* Business this season where they did last, where business will be done with neatness and dispatch. They will attend on the first day of each month Court to receive cloth, at Geo. Slaughter's Tavern in Paris opposite the court-house door, at Z. Moore's, Cynthiana, at Saml. Paston's Store, Winchester, and at Doct. Haydon's Shop in Mountsterling:

[1] Bishop, *op. cit.*, I, 414.
[2] *Am. State Papers*, "Finance," II, 693.

and on the 2d Saturday in each month at John Rules in Millersburg; and on the 4th Saturday in each month, at Theo Mather's near Concord meeting house. Cloth left at any of the above mentioned places, with directions for us, will be punctually attended to and accounted for. We hope from the general satisfaction we gave last season in dressing 319 pieces that we shall merit the Patronage of the People.

SAMUEL J. DAWSON
and
JOHN G. CAMPBULL.

October 9th, 1810.

The fact that this firm dressed 319 pieces of woolen cloth in one season shows that the people were ready to transfer this operation to these mills. The owners would accept almost anything the farmers had to offer them in exchange for this work.

The appearance of the carding-machine near the close of the eighteenth century was the forerunner of what finally came to be another important phase of the evolution of the textile manufactures away from the family household. At first the housewives were rather slow to patronize this important invention; but in due time they saw its utility and economy, since they could spin twice as much from a machine-carded roll as they could from a hand-carded one. The number of carding-machines in operation in 1810 evidences how enthusiastically the mothers and daughters accepted the innovation as soon as its usefulness had been demonstrated. The incomplete census returns for this year showed that in Maine there were 75 machines; in Massachusetts, 180; in New Hampshire, 109; in Vermont, 139; in Rhode Island, 23; in Connecticut, 184; in New York, 413; in New Jersey, 128;

in Pennsylvania, 340; in Delaware, 11; in Maryland, 32; in Virginia, 96; in Ohio, 18; in Kentucky, 21; in South Carolina, 4; in Mississippi Territory, 1; and in the District of Columbia, 2—a total of 1,776.[1] These returns and those in a preceding paragraph relative to fulling-mills give some notion at least of the progress of the fulling and carding phases of the transition under consideration. The large number of both fulling-mills and carding-machines in some of the older and more densely populated sections and the extremely small number in the newer and less densely populated ones demonstrate the fact that until the arrival of adequate transportation facilities the stage of the process in a community at any given time was determined largely by its age and the density of its population; the large number of mills in New York and Pennsylvania and the small number in Virginia and South Carolina and the West disclose this fact.

In the course of time pressing, shearing, dyeing, and bleaching were done in connection with the processes of fulling and carding, or in separate establishments. These businesses were as extensively advertised in the newspapers as the fulling. The following, which appeared in the *Tennessee Gazette and Mero District Advertiser*, October 24, 1804, shows how the community's attention was called to the work these establishments did.

> Blue, Red, Green, Black, and Yellow Dying. I will color cotton and linen thread, a deep blue, at four shillings and six pence per pound; and a light blue at two shillings and six pence per pound;

[1] *Am. State Papers*, "Finance," II, 693.

and the other colors mentioned I will dye upon woolen at 2 shillings per pound, and will warrant them to stand equal to eny ever dyed in America, for I dye with warm dye.

ADRIAN MAGUIRE.[1]

Maguire ran a weaving establishment also. In conjunction with the foregoing advertisement he notified the public that he was ready to furnish to anyone desiring them diaper carpets, double coverlids, and summer counterpanes. For pay he accepted cotton thread or woolen yarn, provided each was spun according to directions sent out by him. Furthermore, he not only promised to do dyeing and weaving, but also agreed to teach all who came how to spin cotton thread and woolen yarn. From this and many similar notices it seems that, in the more settled communities, it was customary to make the yarn and the thread in the homes and exchange them for the finished cloth at the shops of the weavers. These supplementary establishments were evidently patronized by the people, even though they were miles away from them. One Norton assured his customers in advertising his wool-carding business that the rolls would be so packed as to carry on horseback fifty miles.[2] While no statement can be made which would be true of the country at large in 1810, yet it seems to be a safe generalization to say that more cloth was fulled, dyed, and pressed in regular establishments than outside of them, and that a very great deal of the wool was machine- and not hand-carded. It should also be said that the influence of the small factory,

[1] Quoted by Phillips, *Plantation and Frontier*, II, 328.

[2] *Ibid.*, p. 329.

which had been in operation in certain sections of the country[1] for almost two decades before 1810, was being felt more and more as the demand for domestic manufactures increased, owing to the threatened war with England.

Paralleling the foregoing so-called supplementary operations to the family factory was a kind of manufacturing which was carried on entirely independently of the home, namely, that done by the gristmills, flour-mills, and sawmills. In all except the most recently established communities, one or all of these mills had existed long before 1810. Their presence relieved the people of serious anxiety concerning some most important articles relative to their daily existence—articles which were gladly accepted to supplant what individual homes had supplied by means of the mortar and pestle, handmill, and sawpit before the advent of the foregoing conveniences into a community. If necessary, severe hardships were undergone to secure the products of some of these mills, farmers often journeying twenty, thirty, or even forty miles to a gristmill and waiting days or even weeks for their turn.[2] However, such hardships were by no means endured indefinitely; for in due time after the beginning of a new settlement mills of various kinds were set up, a systematic account of the first and subsequent appearance of which in the various sections of the country is a story too long for this discussion. In fact, such a narrative would

[1] Woodward, "Manufacturing Interests of Hartford," *N. Eng. States*, II, 815.

[2] Drake, *Pioneer Life in Ky.*, p. 60.

throw little light on the transfer in question. It does seem necessary, however, to call attention to the early existence of the various kinds of mills in certain sections of the country in order to show the availability of their output.

It is a well-known fact that mills for grinding grain were among the first conveniences set up by the colonists, since they wished to escape as soon as possible the task of making meal Indian-fashion one day for the next; so, very soon after the beginning of a new community some sort of a mill for grinding corn into coarse meal was erected. This mill was either a handmill, a horsemill, a windmill, or a water-mill. In New England it was the custom for a town either to subsidize the mill or to assume the entire expense of its establishment. For example, at a town meeting in Hartford, Connecticut, April 6, 1657, the inhabitants decided to build a mill to grind their corn, the cost of erecting it to be borne by all.[1] The general custom, however, was to encourage some citizen to set up a sawmill or gristmill by granting him a monopoly on the business as well as land and other inducements.[2] Wallingford, Connecticut, is an example of the early consideration of this important matter by the people of a new community. This town was incorporated in 1670. At a town meeting on January 30, 1673, steps were taken which led to the

[1] *Conn. Hist. Soc. Colls.*, XIV, 484.

[2] Sheldon, *Hist. of Deerfield*, I, 609. For an elaborate discussion of this subject, see Bishop, *op. cit.*, I, chap. vi. The first and subsequent appearance of mills in each colony is discussed at some length in this chapter.

construction of a mill to grind the corn of the community. This mill was completed on December 12, 1674.[1]

Horsemills, windmills, and water-mills were as common in the early history of the middle colonies as they were in New England, while quite the contrary was true in the region farther south. On account of the nature of the settlements and the presence of slaves and other servants the southern colonies did not establish such mills as early and as rapidly as did their northern neighbors, handmills serving instead. The presence of the handmill on a plantation made possible the profitable employment of slaves and indentured servants in seasons when other work was slack; and, furthermore, no toll was exacted for the grinding. Largely for these reasons it became necessary to subsidize the establishment of other kinds of mills in this region. Maryland, in 1669, passed a law to encourage the setting up of water-mills. This law gave to every man who would set up such a mill twenty acres of land on either side of the stream and fixed the toll at one-eighth of a bushel of wheat and one-sixth of a bushel of corn. However, few mills seem to have been built in this colony before 1760.[2] According to Hugh Jones, Virginia was supplied with mills in 1724. In discussing this point he says: "As for grinding Corn etc. they have good Mills upon the Runs and Creeks."[3] The reliance upon these

[1] Hubbard, "Manufacturing Interests of Wallingford," *N. Eng. States*, II, 940.

[2] Tyson, "A Brief Account of the Settlement of Ellicott's Mills," *Md. Hist. Soc. Pubs.*, I–VI, No. 4, pp. 31 f.

[3] *Present State of Va.* (Sabin's Reprints, No. 5, 1865), p. 53.

neighborhood gristmills and flour-mills was by no means as absolute in the tide-water region before 1790 as it was in the region north of Maryland. The certainty of securing a supply from either their northern neighbors or from the handmills operated by servants or slaves on the plantations relieved the seaboard people of quite a bit of that anxiety concerning one important phase of their economic life, found among the northern colonies.

The southern back-country and the trans-Alleghany settlements were supplied with both gristmills and sawmills early in their history, the former usually appearing soon after the arrival of the first settlers,[1] who were always glad to exchange the old hominy block and wooden pestle for stone handmills, which in the course of time they exchanged for the water-propelled tubmill. Nor did the evolution stop here, for as soon as a settlement took on the appearance of permanence, the tubmills were superseded by the water gristmills, which appeared in the trans-Alleghany country before the close of the eighteenth century.

While the mill period proper did not begin in the Ohio Valley before 1810,[2] yet at the same time there were many sawmills, gristmills, and flour-mills in this region before this date. Floating mills appeared on the Ohio River as early as 1796. Windmills and water-mills had appeared before this date.[3] The floating mills were more dependable

[1] See Cartmell, "Mills and Other Developments," *Hist. of Frederick Co., Va.*, chap. xiii; also Callahan, *Hist. of W. Va.*, p. 51.

[2] Lippincott, *Hist. of Manufactures in the Ohio Valley to the Year 1860*, chap. iv.

[3] Ellicott, *Journal*, p. 11.

than either of the other two. They were of most service during the fall and summer, when the water in the river was low and there was not enough water for the water-mills along the shores.[1] A gristmill was in operation at Eaton's Station, one of the settlements on the Cumberland River near the present site of Nashville, Tennessee, as early as 1783.[2] Other stations along the river were also supplied with mills quite early in their history. Horse and water gristmills as well as sawmills were in operation in Illinois before the close of the eighteenth century.[3] All these facts are briefly mentioned in this connection

[1] Hildreth gives the following description of one of these mills: "The mill was erected on two boats: one of them five, the other ten feet wide and forty-five feet long. The smaller one was made of the trunk of a large hollow sycamore tree, and the larger, of timber and plank, like a flat boat. They were placed eight feet apart, and fastened firmly together by beams running across the boats. The smaller boat on the outside supported one end of the shaft of the water-wheel, and the larger boat the other, in which was placed the mill stones and running gear, covered with a tight frame building or mill house, for the protection of the grain and meal and the comfort of the miller. The space between the boats was covered with planks, forming a deck, fore and aft of the water wheel. It was turned by the natural current of water, and was put into motion, or checked, by pulling up or pushing down a set of boards, similar to a gate, in front of the wheel. It could grind from twenty-five to fifty bushels of grain in twenty-four hours, according to the strength of the current. The larger boat was fastened by a chain cable to an anchor made of timbers and filled with stones, and the smaller one by a grape vine to the same anchor. The mill was placed in a rapid portion of the Ohio, about the middle of Backus's island, a few rods from the shore, and in sight of the castle. The current here was strong and the position safe from the Indians"—(*Pioneer History*, p. 376).

[2] Putnam, *Hist. of Middle Tenn.*, p. 177.

[3] Reynolds, *My Own Times*, p. 23.

to make the point that among the first homemade products to be supplanted by mill- or factory-made goods were meal, flour, and lumber. In all sections of the country except the most recently settled regions and possibly some sections of the southern seaboard this transfer had taken place before 1810. There were indeed few sections of the country at this date that did not have access to the output of these mills. The fact that meal or flour could be secured in exchange for two of the commonest farm products placed these pioneer luxuries in the reach of all.

While the gristmills, flour-mills, and sawmills were supplying the people of a neighborhood with meal, flour, and lumber, the handicraft system was providing them with a multitude of other necessities. This system evolved out of what has been denominated the itinerant-supplementary stage of the transfer under consideration. Before a shoemaker, a tailor, or a weaver could eke out a living in a stationary shop it was often necessary for him to serve some time as an itinerant. At first he had to go to the houses of his customers and do his work there; later he supplemented his shop activities with occasional trips through the community, and finally it was possible for him to do all his work in his own shop. How this evolution actually took place may be seen by following one of its phases through. For example, the shoemaker at first went from house to house to make up the leather. Sometimes he farmed in the summer and did the shoemaking for the whole neighborhood in the winter. This "village cobbler," as he was commonly designated, gradually came to carry a little stock of leather and to exchange shoes with the farmers, tanners, and traders for leather, foreign goods, and foodstuffs. After a while this same cobbler employed many helpers and manufactured shoes for the shopkeepers in the town to keep in stock and to export to other towns. The system of barter which was so common made it possible for the neighborhood to receive its supply of shoes from either the shoeshop or store in exchange for all kinds of farm produce. The store would take the leather as willingly as the shoemaker, since it could be exchanged for more ready-made shoes at the shop of the shoemaker. Thus in a generation or so after its settlement, even though it were isolated from the rest of the world, a community could secure a supply of shoes made by professionals in regularly established shops.

What came to pass in the shoe business happened in the weaving and tailoring businesses as well. In fact, the itinerant-supplementary system as it existed, especially in these three lines of endeavor, was the direct forerunner of the handicraft system, the latter being the logical outcome of the former, and both being essential in the early development of communities devoid of the transportation facilities necessary to exchange the results of the farm labor for manufactured commodities brought from distant centers. The part that the handicraft system played in the economic history of this country down to 1810 and in some sections much later than this date would be difficult to overestimate. There is no idea of giving the system adequate treatment here, the purpose simply being to show the part it played in the transfer herein considered.

The early appearance in a community of handicraftsmen and establishments to relieve the settlers of the arduous task of manufacturing the necessities of life within their homes is well illustrated in the history of Ipswich, Massachusetts. This town, according to Felt,[1] had carpenters in 1633; a tannery in 1634; a gunsmith and a gristmill in 1635; a currier in 1638; a basket-maker and a cooper in 1639; malt works in 1641; a weaver in 1647; a ropemaker in 1648; salt works in 1652; a sawmill in 1656; a hempmill in 1657; a brewery in 1663; cordwainers and glaziers in 1664; smiths in 1667; a fulling-mill in 1675; soapmakers in 1678; a brickyard in 1683; and a clothier in 1727. All these were considered beneficial accessories to a town and in many cases they were subsidized in order to make their existence both possible and permanent.

Other New England towns settled during the seventeenth and eighteenth centuries duplicated what Felt has recorded of Ipswich. The interior towns were almost entirely economically independent and had all the elements of prosperity within their own limits. The tanner tanned the hides and sent what leather the neighborhood did not use to Boston or some other coast town; the hatter sheared the lambs and made hats for the people and sent felt shapes for hats to market; the clothier carded the wool and dressed the cloth woven either by the professional weaver or by the women in their homes; the blacksmith

[1] *Hist. of Ipswich, Essex, and Hamilton*, pp. 95 ff.

made all manner of useful implements; and so on, with the remaining handicraftsmen. All these usually took farm produce in exchange for their wares, making it possible for a community to exist on a minimum amount of household manufacturing.

The handicraft system flourished in the middle states as well as in New England. The following examples give an idea of its extensiveness in both the older and the newer sections in one of the states of this group. In the borough of Lancaster, Pennsylvania, in 1786, there were 234 manufacturers out of a total of 700 families. Among this number there were 14 hatters, 36 shoemakers, 4 tanners, 17 saddlers, 25 tailors, 25 weavers of woolen, cotton, and linen cloth, 3 stocking-weavers, 25 white- and blacksmiths, 6 wheelwrights, 11 coopers, 6 clock- and watchmakers, 6 tobacco and snuff manufacturers, 4 dyers, 7 gunsmiths, 5 ropemakers, 4 tinners, 2 brass founders, 3 skin-dressers, 1 brushmaker, 7 turners, 7 nail-makers, 5 silversmiths, 3 potters, 3 brewers, 3 copper-smiths, and 2 printers.[1] While one has no records of the output of these workmen, yet at the same time their very presence shows that the people had ample opportunities to provide themselves with what would seem to be a sufficient supply of most all the necessities of life.

While the foregoing enumeration shows that one of the older communities in Pennsylvania had an abundance of handicraftsmen, yet at about the same time there were practically the same proportion of these desirable citizens to the whole population in the western portion of this

[1] Coxe, *View of the U.S.*, p. 313.

state as in the older section. The distance from the coast towns and the lack of transportation facilities made it a safe venture for the professional workmen in the back-country districts. In the towns of Washington, Bedford, Pittsburgh, and Huntingdon in 1790 there were clockmakers and watchmakers, silversmiths, coopers, skin dressers, breeches-makers, tanners, curriers, tailors, cabinetmakers, blacksmiths, shoemakers, hatters, dyers, weavers, reedmakers, saddlers, saddletree-makers, spinning-wheel makers, maltsters, brewers, tinners, wheelwrights, stocking-weavers, gunsmiths, ropemakers, and whitesmiths. The total number of manufacturers in these towns in the order named above was 32, 15, 40, and 23. At the same date there were but 130 families in Pittsburgh, 40 in Bedford, and 85 in Huntingdon.[1]

The people in the Northwest, in Kentucky, and in Tennessee were by no means deprived of the wares manufactured in the shops of the handicraftsmen. Imlay, a commissioner for laying out land in this region, left, in a series of letters to a friend in England, an excellent description of industrial conditions here between 1783 and 1790. He says:

> Linen and woollen cloths, leather, and hats for home consumption, are manufactured with considerable success. The first two articles are only made in families for their own use; but the latter are made by men of profession in that business, and are of a quality

[1] *Ibid.*, p. 311. On account of the nature of the tidewater settlements the handicraft system did not thrive here as it did in the region north of Maryland. Conditions in the back-country districts of the South were so similar to those in Pennsylvania that they need not be treated separately.

that would not disgrace the mechanics of Europe. Blacksmiths' work of all sorts, even to making of firearms, is done there; as is also cabinet work, wheel-wright, mill-wright, house carpentry, joinery, shoe-making, etc., etc., in short, all trades immediately necessary to the promotion of the comforts of new settlements, are to be found there.[1]

This statement is good evidence of what really happened wherever the population was sufficiently dense to support the tradesmen. It also shows that the weaving business was kept in the home after most of the others had been transferred to the shops. In other words, the transfer from family- to shop- and factory-made fabrics was the last to take place in this and the other sections of the country as well.

One great problem in the transition, down to 1810 and for years after, for that matter, was the distribution of the shop- and factory-made products to the people in remote districts. There were of course stores established quite early in the history of any community.[2] After the purchase of Louisiana many supplies came to the trans-Alleghany country by way of New Orleans on keelboats; previous to this event the region had been supplied by the great Pennsylvania wagons from Pittsburgh and the ports along the Ohio. In spite of these facts the stores were by no means able to reach all the people. Some scheme had to be devised to get the goods from the producer to the consumer, who was usually a willing customer provided ways and means of both exchange and distribution were

[1] *Topographical Description of the Western Territory* (3d ed., 1797), p. 62.

[2] Phelan, *Hist. of Tenn.*, p. 177.

discovered. The handicraftsmen and the small-factory operators solved these two problems by establishing a system of peddling their wares through the country and at the same time accepting almost anything the people had to give in exchange for them. This was the beginning in this country of the huckster system which subsequently became so general, and in fact has not been entirely abolished to this day.

All manner of articles, from spinning-wheels to wooden cups, were peddled through the country, usually by the tradesmen themselves.[1] Quite an elaborate plan of huckster distribution was worked out by some manufacturers. An example of one such scheme was the distribution of the output of the tinware industry at Berlin, New Hampshire. Dwight, in his *Travels in New England and New York*, gives an excellent description of this system as it existed in 1797 when he visited this town. He says:

> For many years, after tinned plates were manufactured in this place [Berlin] into culinary vessels, the only method used by the pedlars for conveying them to distant towns, for sale, was by means of horse and two baskets, balanced on his back. After the war [Revolutionary], carts and wagons were used for this purpose, and have, from that time to the present, been the only means of conveyance which have been adopted.
>
> The manner in which this ware is disposed of, puts to flight all calculations. A young man is furnished by the proprietor with a horse, and a cart covered with a box, containing as many tin vessels, as the horse can conveniently draw. This vehicle within a few years has, indeed, been frequently exchanged for a wagon; and then

[1] Cogswell, *Hist. of Henneker, N.H.*, p. 397.

the load is doubled. Thus prepared, he sets out on an expedition for the winter. A multitude of these young men direct themselves to the Southern States; and in their excursions travel wherever they can find settlements. Each of them walks, and rides, alternately, through this vast distance, till he reaches Richmond, Newbern, Charleston, or Savannah; and usually carries with him to the place of his destination no small part of the gain, which he has acquired upon the road. Here he finds one or more workmen, who have been sent forward to cooperate with him, furnished with a sufficient quantity of tinned plates to supply him with all the ware, which he can sell during the season. With this he wanders into the interiour country; calls at every door on his way; and with an address, and pertinacity, not easily resisted, compels no small number of the inhabitants to buy. At the commencement of summer they return to New-York; and thence to New-Haven, by water; after selling their vehicles and their horses. . . . .

Every inhabited part of the United States is visited by these men. I have seen them on the peninsula of Cape Cod, and in the neighbourhood of Lake Erie; distant from each other more than six hundred miles. They make their way to Detroit, four hundred miles farther; to Canada; to Kentucky; and if I mistake not, to New-Orleans and St. Louis.[1]

By 1830 the business of these peddlers had extended to all sorts of merchandise. At first, pins, needles, scissors, combs, coat and vest buttons, trifling articles of hardware, children's books, and cotton stuffs, made in New England, were added to the tinware. Later, a number set out with large wagons loaded with dry goods, hats, boots, shoes, clocks, firearms, nails, and even furniture. Stores were also established in many of the interior towns throughout the South and West. As the stock of each peddler became exhausted, he repaired to these stores to replenish his

[1] Vol. II (1797), pp. 53 f.

supply. Great quantities of goods were thus sold by these hucksters during a season.[1]

There seems to be no way to definitely determine the contribution of the foregoing system of distribution to the complete transfer to factory-made goods. Even in the face of this difficulty, however, one must conclude that many families would certainly have waited much longer than they did for the wares the peddlers sold them had no such system been introduced. In the absence of other means of exchange, two things were made possible by this system, namely, the very existence of the factory itself and the opportunity for the farmer and his family to devote their spare time to pursuits other than those connected with household manufacturing. Thus in the course of time through the operations of the various agencies supplementing the manufacture of wearing apparel and household textile supplies in the home, from the output of the gristmills, flour-mills, and sawmills and the shops of the handicraftsmen, and by means of the scheme for distributing manufactured goods in conjunction with the barter system, many families were in a position to discontinue their manufacturing activities along all lines except the few operations which the fulling, dyeing, and carding establishment did not perform; and after 1790 it was even possible to discontinue much of the family spinning, for, with the establishment of spinning-mills came a supply of cotton thread and woolen yarn at a rate so low that the homes could no longer afford to spin them.

[1] *Ibid.*, p. 55, note; Callender, *Econ. Hist. of U.S.*, pp. 304 f., note.

THE TRANSFER COMPLETED IN WHOLE OR IN PART, 1810–30

Considering the country as a whole the transfer from home- to shop- and factory-made goods was rather generally completed before the close of the third decade of the nineteenth century. Even before this date ways and means to supply the people in most sections of the country with all the necessities of life except clothing and household textile supplies had been pretty generally provided. The home manufacture of these last-named articles was somewhat common for a number of years after 1830; for, until the factory system became firmly established, there was no escape from both spinning-wheels and looms for the women and girls of many sections of the country. Indeed, they did not seem to care to escape them. Female industries as old as spinning and weaving were not to be crowded out of their strongholds except by some powerful agency like the modern factory system.

During the period under discussion there were many forces tending either to hasten or to retard the transition, chief among the former being the improvements in the means of trade and transportation, the rise of the factory system, and the opportunities for exchanging farm produce and household manufactures for shop and factory goods; retarding agencies were inventions to aid family manufacturing, difficulties and restrictions thrown in the way of foreign trade and transportation following 1807, the War of 1812, and the flooding of the country with foreign goods at the close of this war. An extended treatment of each of these factors does not seem necessary in this connection. For the purpose of this discussion it will suffice simply to call attention to their existence and to show how they affected the subject under consideration.

Up to 1815 the inhabitants of Kentucky, Tennessee, the Northwest Territory, western New York, and northern New England were in the same relation to the seaboard regions as the New England and middle colonies were to the mother-country during the colonial period. Just as the people north of Maryland in colonial times were without products to exchange for the commodities of England, so were the pioneers of the regions mentioned above without products to exchange for commodities to satisfy their daily needs. While it is true that their furs would stand the expense of carriage to the seaboard, and that they could drive a few cattle to the eastern markets, and float some grain and provisions down the rivers, yet at the same time the income from these sources barely furnished the necessities which they were totally unable to supply themselves. This was the supreme age of the handicraft system and home manufacturing in these regions. Communities became practically self-supporting. The handicraftsmen could live on the products of the farm which they received in exchange for the output of their shops. Few factory-made goods reached many of these people. What they were obliged to have came mostly from Boston, Philadelphia, New York, and Baltimore. The cost of transporting goods from these towns was almost prohibitive during the early history of these sections. In 1805 it cost $4.50 a hundred to get goods from Baltimore to Pittsburgh, and $5.00 a hundred from Philadelphia to the same place.[1] After the goods reached Pittsburgh they were sent down the Ohio to be distributed to merchants in the river towns. Even though the merchants did take farm produce for pay, the price of the goods from the East was so outrageous that few could afford to exchange even farm products for commodities which could be made in the home.

The appearance of the steamboat on the western waters after 1811 revolutionized the commerce of this region. While the canoes, pirogues, bateaux, barges, keelboats, flatboats, arks, and sailing vessels had done good service before this date, yet the problem of upstream navigation was not solved until the application of steam to river transportation, the influence of which on the economic history of the interior would be difficult to overestimate. The numerous rivers upon which steamboats could be used made it possible to reach almost every section of the country settled before 1830. Even above the points of large steamboat navigation on the upper courses of the streams and their tributaries, small steamboats and keelboats were found; and a great deal of produce was floated down even out of the creeks on flatboats and canoes to the point of steamboat navigation. This system of natural waterway transportation made possible much of the transfer to factory-made goods that took place in the interior before 1830.[2]

[1] Harris, *Journal of a Tour into the Territory Northwest of the Allegheny Mountains*, p. 42.

[2] For an extended discussion of this interior commerce, see Gephart, *Transportation and Industrial Development in the Middle West*.

The rapid extension of the factory system between 1790 and 1830 was largely responsible for the revolution which occurred during these decades in the factory manufacture of cotton, woolen, and linen fabrics, the domestic production of which had lagged behind that of many other necessities. Outside of textiles a storekeeper as early as 1814 could stock his store almost wholly with articles manufactured in the United States,[1] the handicraftsmen, the factory, both small and large, supplying them. Because of this fact the discussion in the remainder of this chapter and all of the following one may be focused on the transfer of clothing and household textile supplies from those made wholly or in part in the home to those made wholly within the factory.

[1] Proof of this statement is found in a list of articles in a store at Wilmington, Delaware, in 1814, all of which were manufactured within the United States. Here is the list: "Andirons of brass and iron, shovels and tongs, brass and iron tops, bed-screws and wood screws of all descriptions; plane bitts and planes of all kinds; screw augers, hatchets and axes, tutania ladles and spoons, and iron ladles; box coffee mills; bellows, brass and iron pipes; wagon boxes and hollow ware of all kinds; shovels and spades; mill, cross cut and frame saws; girth and straining webbing; spikes, nails, tacks and springs of all descriptions; whitened and brass knobs and coach makers ware generally, plated and plain; shoe knives, stirrup and bridle bitts, plated and plain; window glass of all kinds; white and red lead; litharge; spirits turpentine; linseed oil; Spanish brown and yellow ochre, ground and dry; painting brushes and other brushes generally; trace chains and other chains, shoe maker's hammers; carpenter's rules; brass candlesticks; patent lamps; straw knives and window bolts; glass; paper; drawing knives; iron squares; frying pans; currying combs; horn combs and whet stones; lamp black; stone jugs; iron and steel shovels and ditching shovels; nail and spike gimblets; grid irons, griddles and roasting pans; weights of all kinds; house, horse and sheep bells; sad irons; masons' trowels and stones of all kinds" (*Niles' Register*, VI, 173).

Except in certain out-of-the-way districts in the New England and middle states, both spinning and weaving in these regions passed into the factories, taking the women and girls with them, before 1830. The stages through which these operations passed in their transition from the homes to the factories were rather well marked. First, there was the stage in which the home was absolutely independent of the factory; secondly, the stage in which the factory was supplementary to the home; thirdly, the stage in which the factory was preparatory to the home; and, finally, the stage in which the factory was independent of the home. A brief consideration of these stages will show how each succeeding one trespassed on the one preceding it, serving to lessen more and more the amount of work which had to be done in the home.

But little needs to be said here concerning the first and second stages. The first simply means that for a time in each new community it was necessary to perform all the operations relative to the making of cotton, linen, and woolen cloth within the home. A community remained in this stage until some arrangement was made for the setting up of a fulling-mill, the first supplementary agency to the household factory. Other similar agencies were the pressing, shearing, coloring, dyeing, and carding establishments which were run either in conjunction with or separate from the fulling-mill. Since these have been discussed elsewhere,[1] they may be dismissed here with mere mention.

Besides the foregoing supplementary agencies to the family textile factory there were factories which wove

[1] Pp. 252 ff.

cloth from the yarn spun in the homes, and spinning-mills which furnished the women with yarn for their looms. The former were in operation before the close of the colonial period. The American Manufactory, located in Philadelphia, Pennsylvania, was an establishment to manufacture cotton, linen, and woolen cloth from yarn spun by the women in the vicinity.[1] More important, however, than the few similar establishments and even the professional weavers of the country were the mills for spinning yarn and thread. It was quite natural for improvements in spinning to precede those in weaving, since the weavers were always crowding the spinners for yarn. On account of the British government's policy of forbidding under penalty the exportation of the inventions of Hargreaves, Arkwright, and Crompton relative to spinning, America did not acquire the latest improvements along this line until some years after they were in successful

[1] Evidence of this is found in the following advertisement which appeared in the *Pa. Packet and Gen. Advertiser*, December 4, 1775: "To the good women of the province. As the spinning of yarn is a great part of the business in cloth manufactures in those countries where they are carried on extensively and to the best advantage, the women of the whole country are employed as much as possible. The managers of the American Manufactory in the city, wish to employ every good spinner that can apply however remote from the factory, and as many women in the country may supply themselves with the materials there, and may have leisure to spin considerable quantities, they are hereby informed that ready money will be given at the factory, up Market street, for any parcel, either great or small, of hemp, flax or woolen yarn. The managers return their thanks to all these industrious women who are now employed in spinning for the factory. The skill and diligence of many entitles them to public acknowledgement. We hope that, as you have begun, so you will go on, and never be weary in well doing" (quoted by Bagnall, *The Textile Industries in the U.S.*, pp. 70 f.).

operation in England. While spinning machinery was used in Philadelphia as early as 1775 and the common jenny and stock card were in operation in various parts of the country before 1790, yet this latter date is generally accepted as the birth year of the factory system in the United States. It was this year that Samuel Slater erected at Pawtucket, Rhode Island, a cotton factory, which was supplied with spinning machinery on the English plan.[1] Soon after the success of this mill had been demonstrated, others were erected in New England and throughout other sections of the country as well.[2] These mills spun yarn and thread for distribution to the families of the neighborhood to be woven into the cloth they needed for themselves or which they desired to sell.[3] If there chanced

[1] Wright, "The Factory System in the United States," *10th Census of U.S., Manufactures*, pp. 6 f.

[2] A second was erected in Rhode Island in 1795; two more in Massachusetts in the years 1803 and 1804; ten more were erected or begun in Rhode Island and one in Connecticut during the years 1805, 1806, and 1807, making a total of fifteen erected before 1808. At the beginning of 1811 there were eighty-seven mills, working 80,000 spindles, spinning 2,880,000 pounds of yarn worth $3,240,000, and employing 500 men and 3,500 women. All these were for spinning cotton. At the same date there were eleven for spinning wool, and a smaller number for spinning flax (Gallatin, "Report on Manufactures," *Am. State Papers*, "Finance," II, 427).

[3] An idea of the extent and value of this work can be secured from the following petition to the United States Congress in 1815 by the cotton manufactures in Providence, Rhode Island. These petitioners said: "But the benefits resulting from this vast amount of labor are much more extensively diffused than if the whole were done by people constantly engaged in the business, a considerable portion of it being done by persons who are partially occupied in other pursuits, particularly the weaving, which is almost wholly executed at the farmhouses throughout the country, few of which are to be found not supplied with looms" (*Niles' Register*, IX, 190).

to be no mill in the neighborhood, a supply could be secured at the store in exchange for cotton, wool, and other farm products.[1] The yarn was not expensive and it proved a great convenience to the housewives, since its use enormously diminished their labors. Spinning-mills became so common throughout the country that it is proper to speak of a mill stage in connection with the rise of textile manufactures in any given section. The New England and middle states passed through such a stage between 1790 and 1820, the southern states between 1812 and 1830,[2] and the Ohio Valley states between 1830 and 1860.[3]

The completion of the textile manufacturing system came with the introduction of the power-loom. This important event happened in 1815, at Waltham, Massachusetts,[4] thirty years after its invention by Cartwright. While there had been factories run entirely independently of the homes before this date,[5] yet the introduction of such a tremendous time- and labor-saver, in the matter of cloth-weaving, ushered in a period of independence never before known. The establishments could now individually employ all the various processes in the manufacture of cloth, from the receipt of the raw material to the production of the finished web. Thus the factory system proper came into existence in this country. While

[1] Somers, *Hist. of Lancaster, N.H.*, p. 370.

[2] Clark, "Manufactures," *op. cit.*, V, 318 ff.

[3] Lippincott, *op. cit.*, chap. iv.

[4] De Bow, *Indust. Resources of the S. and W.*, I, 222.

[5] See Bagnall, *op. cit.*, chaps. iv and v.

it had a hard time during the decade from 1815 to 1825 on account of foreign competition, lack of capital, inferior machinery, lack of skilled labor, and a coarse quality of raw materials, yet at the same time by 1830 the system was sufficiently established in the New England, the middle states, and certain centers in the West to assure a future independence of foreign manufactures for the various fabrics in domestic use, and to relieve the housewives of a great deal of the strenuous labor which their foremothers had been obliged to perform. For when the price of the ordinary brown shirting was reduced from 42 to 7½ cents a yard between 1815 and 1830,[1] there was little inducement for one to labor all day at the loom to weave four yards of such cloth. The housewives could no longer compete against a system which made it possible for one man tending three or four power-looms to turn out from 90 to 160 yards a day.[2]

In spite of the improvements in the means of trade and transportation, the rise of the factory system, and the presence of an army of handicraftsmen in the country during the first quarter of the nineteenth century, family manufactures were by no means given up; for all of these factors combined were not able continuously to furnish the country with a sufficient quantity of clothing and household textile supplies. So it was well that there

[1] The price of brown shirting three-fourths of a yard wide between 1808 and 1830 in New England was as follows: 1808 to 1815, 42 cents a yard; 1815, 36; 1816, 30; 1817 and 1818, 22; 1819, 18; 1820–23, 13; 1823 and 1824, 12½; 1825, 11½; 1826, 1827, and 1828, 11; 1829, 6½; 1830, 7½ (*Documents Relative to the Manufactures in the U.S.* [1832], I, 173).

[2] Bolles, *Indust. Hist. of the U.S.*, p. 414.

existed side by side with them others which tended to increase the amount of home manufacturing. Since these have already been listed,[1] the discussion may turn at once to a portrayal of their influence.

During the period from 1807 to 1816, when trade with England and France was so uncertain, irregular, and even dangerous, many inventions to aid family manufactures came into use. These included an improved carding-machine, spinning-jenny, loom with a flying shuttle, and in the early twenties a machine for dressing flax.[2] By the use of this inexpensive machinery the output of the home could be greatly increased.[3] With the spinning-jenny, invented by John Schofield, a woman could spin from twenty to thirty runs of fine yarn a day in the best of manner. Besides increasing the possible output of yarn from the work of one spinner, the jenny could be conveniently worked in a private family and bought for about $50. It was customary for families to join in buying one. The machine for which Burgiss Allison, of Philadelphia, secured a patent in 1812 drove from ten to fifteen spindles and occupied very little more space than the common

[1] P. 268.

[2] One Samuel Davidson, of Romulus, New York, put a machine on the market in 1822 for dressing flax. The cost of this machine was but $40. The saving in labor was about three-fourths and that of flax one-fifth compared with the common mode. The process of rotting could be dispensed with. A neighborhood usually had one of these machines (*Niles' Register*, XXIII, 1).

[3] The improved carding-machine could be purchased for about $60, the spinning-machine for from $10 to $50, and the machine for dressing flax for about $40 (*Niles' Register*, XXIII, 1; Jefferson, *Works* [Federal ed.], XI, 260, 272).

spinning-wheel. It spun wool and could be used for cotton if the cotton was previously carded into rolls.[1] That this machine and the other improvements mentioned above were in common use is evidenced by the following quotation from a letter of Jefferson's to Kosciusko, June 28, 1812:

> Our manufactures are now very nearly on a footing with those of England. . . . . We have reduced the large and expensive machinery for most things to the compass of a private family, and every family of any size is now getting machines on a small scale for their household processes. Quoting myself as an example, and I am much behind many others in this business, my household manufactures are just getting into operation on the scale of a carding machine costing $60 only, which may be worked by a girl of twelve years old, a spinning machine, which may be made for $10, carrying 6 spindles for wool, to be worked by a girl also, another which can be made for $25, carrying 12 spindles for cotton, and a loom, with a flying shuttle, weaving its twenty yards a day. I need 2000 yards of linen, cotton and woollen yearly, to clothe my family, which this machinery, costing $150 only, and worked by two women and two girls, will more than furnish.[2]

The difficulties and restrictions thrown in the way of foreign trade and transportation just after 1807, which in turn caused an advance in the price of foreign goods, forced a multitude of families to resort to their own labor to supply many of life's necessities. Both the territorial extent and the amount of manufacturing done in the homes in 1809 have already been shown by the elaborate table based on the returns of the marshals in the fall of

[1] Bishop, *op. cit.*, II, 188.

[2] Jefferson, *Works* (Federal ed.), XI, 260, 272.

1810.[1] While there are no statistics in existence to show for the country as a whole whether there was a per capita increase or decrease during the decade between 1810 and 1820, yet at the same time there is sufficient evidence to establish the fact that there was probably little decrease in the matter of clothing and household textile supplies made in the home during these years. The contents of a letter from a Delaware farmer quoted by Niles in the June 23, 1821, issue of the *Register* suggest both the amount and the value of the clothing made in one family. The writer said that in 1809 he began (since when he had bought only one coat) to clothe himself and family, ten in number, in homespun by the houseloom. At the rate of $30 a year for each member this farmer estimated that he had saved by such acts in his family $300 a year, which in the twelve years since 1809 amounted to $3,600.[2] Another family near Baltimore, consisting of about twenty persons, was spending in 1814 not over $60 a year for foreign manufactured textiles, the family factory supplying the needs and some to sell.[3] Commenting on this fact, Niles said: "Now this gentleman is a mere farmer—but while he and his males attend to the field, the females are equally busy in the house, and the long winter evenings are not wasted by the children and servants in doing mischief or wasting fire-wood, because they have nothing else to do. . . . . This is the case in thousands of families."[4] Jefferson said of Virginia in 1812: "Every family in the country is a manufactory within itself, and is very generally

[1] See chap. v.

[2] Vol. XX, 257.

[3] Niles, *Register*, XI, 178.

[4] *Ibid.*

able to make within itself all the stouter and middling stuff for its own clothing and household use."[1] In 1814 the families in Berkshire County, Massachusetts, were making great quantities of woolen goods for sale outside of the state.[2] It seems that the making and wearing of homespun became a fad about this date. Speaking of this fact in 1814, a well-informed editor said: "It is astonishing to be informed of the extent to which this industry is applied. Many of the most elegant belles that trip our streets are covered with superb shawls, and otherwise protected from the cold, by the labor of their own hands—hands that, heretofore, chiefly held a romance or touched a piano."[3] This same editor in summing up conditions relative to household manufactures in 1816 felt that their actual value was not less than $120,000,000 a year, and that four-fifths of the laboring classes in the country were generally clothed wholly in household manufactures.[4]

Before the War of 1812 came to a close small manufacturing establishments had been set up in almost every nook and corner of the more settled portions of the New England, the middle states, and certain sections of the West. These establishments offered a dependable market for the produce of the flocks and fields of the northern

[1] *Works* (Federal ed.), XI, 218. What Jefferson thought of the family industry in 1812 is shown in the following statement which he made to John Adams in a letter June 21 of this year: "The economy and thriftiness resulting from household manufactures are such that they will never again be laid aside" (*ibid.*, p. 219).

[2] *Niles' Register*, VII, 280.

[3] *Ibid.*, VII, 280.

[4] *Ibid.*, X, 323.

farmers and increased the demand for the staples of the southern planters. The country as a whole seemed well on the way toward an economic independence of foreign nations in all the common necessities of life. Progress toward this much-to-be-desired independence received a serious backset from the flood of foreign goods which poured into the country immediately following the Treaty of 1815. English merchants had accumulated during the duration of the war a large supply of woolens, cotton cloth, and iron ware that had to be disposed of even at a loss. They felt that the American trade must be recovered even if it had to be done by selling their wares at a much lower price than they were sold in London. Besides those from England, ships came from Holland and Russia, bringing sail duck and linen; from China and India, carrying nankeens and silks. These goods were hurried to the auction blocks and many of the more wealthy class of citizens, who were tiring of their homespun, seized the first chance to buy the finer stuffs.[1] The result of all this activity in transporting and marketing foreign goods was disastrous to the growing domestic manufactures. Table XIV shows the extent of the disaster in one county and city in the country.

What happened to the manufacturing establishments in the city and county of Philadelphia between 1814 and 1819 happened to similar establishments the country over; and, what is more, the disaster did not stop with

[1] For fuller treatments of this enormous surplus of foreign goods, see *Niles' Register*, X, 322 f.; Lee, *N. J. as Col. and State*, III, 139 ff.; and Coman, *Indust. Hist. of U.S.*, p. 138.

the factory owners and workers—it reached the farmers and planters as well. For when the market for the products

TABLE XIV

DIMINUTION OF MANUFACTURES IN THE CITY AND COUNTY OF PHILADELPHIA, 1814–19*

Branches of Manufacturing	Number of Hands Employed in		
	1814	1816	1819
Cotton	1,761	2,325	149
Hosiery	96	48	29
Thread	444	191	20
Silver-plating	114	210	30
Smithery	852	750	149
Coach-making	220	185	67
Chemicals	71	52	16
Hatting	134	172	60
Carving and gilding	62	121	24
Potteries	132	132	27
Tobacco pipes	33	33	0
Printing ink	5	5	1
Book-printing	198	241	170
Type foundry	74	90	42
Brass foundry	300	240	80
Wire factory	60	22	6
Floor-cloth manufactory	50	30	25
Woolen	1,310	1,226	260
Iron casting	1,093	1,152	52
Paper-making	950	950	175
Coppersmith and tinware	77	77	35
Gun-smithery	154	124	93
Cabinetmaking	180	250	70
Brush-making	65	112	50
Plaster and stucco	120	150	90
Bricklaying	250	300	150
Patent-lamp making	6	5	1
Morocco, leather, etc.	68	111	84
Ropemaking	110	200	100
Paper-hanging and playing cards	189	168	82
Total	9,188	9,672	2,137

* *Niles' Register*, XVII, 117.

of the flocks and fields was cut off, the country people found themselves without the necessary exchange to secure the foreign goods even at the low price for which they were selling. Hence, the only thing left for these people was to fall back upon the old stand-by, the family factory, just as their forefathers had done when faced with like conditions following the Revolutionary War. Some idea of the extent to which the family factory was brought back into operation is given in the following account from Hodgson, who toured the country during the three years following 1818. In speaking of family manufactures, he said:

> I am surprised to find to how great an extent this species of manufactures is carried, and how rapidly the events of the last two years have increased it. In some parts of the state of New York, I was told the little farmers could not make a living without it. In Pennsylvania, it is perhaps more general; some of the lower descriptions of East India goods having almost entirely given place to a domestic substitute actually made in the family; and the importation of Irish linen having been most seriously checked by the greatly increased cultivation and manufacture of flax in the immediate vicinity of Philadelphia. In Virginia and North Carolina, I had opportunities of seeing these domestic manufactures as I passed in the stage: and on my horseback route, it was a constant source of surprise—to *you*, I may add, without danger of being suspected to be a Radical, and of gratification; for this combination of agriculture and manufacture in the same family appears to me to form a state of society of all others best adapted to produce a happy, independent, and virtuous population.[1]

The foregoing was the observation of a foreigner. That his estimates were not exaggerated is shown by statements made at about the same date by editor Niles

[1] *Letters from N. A.*, II, 71.

and Henry Clay. In a debate in the House of Representatives, April 26, 1820, the latter spoke as follows:

If you want to find an example of order, of freedom from debt, of economy, of expenditure falling short of rather than exceeding income, you will go to a well regulated family of a farmer. You will go to the house of such a man as Isaac Shelby. You will not find him resorting to taverns, engaged in broils, prosecuting angry law suits. You will behold every member of his family clad with the product of their own hands, and usefully employed—the spinning wheel and the loom in motion by day-break. With what pleasure will his wife carry you into her neat dairy, lead you into her storehouse, and point to the table cloths, the sheets, the counterpanes, which lie on this shelf for her daughter Sally, or that for Nancy, all prepared in advance by their provident care, for the day of their respective marriages.[1]

Niles spoke no less enthusiastically in September, 1821, when he said:

We never reflect upon the progress and prospects of that portion of the national labor which is applied to household manufactures, without feeling our hearts warmed with a national pride; for all the virtues —moral, religious and political, are interested in it. Tens of thousands of amiable, respectable and lovely young women, (ladies, if the term pleases better), of those ranks and conditions in life which, a few years since, almost as much despised a distaff as they did a field-hoe, are now engaged to drive away the diseases and distresses of inanity, and keep themselves in health and cheerfulness, render themselves good wives, and estimable mothers, while they add to the comforts and conveniences of their parents, and make a "plentiful house" by a diligent attention to spinning, weaving, bleaching, dyeing, etc., by which all the real wants of the family, as to articles of clothing, are supplied, with something still left to furnish themselves with more delicate and luxurious articles for their own ornament or use.[2]

[1] *Annals of 16th Cong.*, I Sess., II, column 2041. [2] *Register*, XXI, 35.

Evidence is not lacking to show that these men were keen observers. An agricultural society in Pennsylvania in 1822 granted W. C. Terrel a premium for the greatest quantity of goods made by one family—the amount being 1,600 yards of different kinds of cloth besides many stockings and much yarn which were sold.[1] At a cattle show and fair in Pittsfield, Massachusetts, in 1822, a Mrs. Perkins exhibited ample proof that, since the last anniversary, she and four girls had manufactured 438 yards of fulled cloth, 171½ yards of raw flannel, 53 yards of carpeting, 142¾ yards of tablecloth and other linen goods, in all 805¼ yards.[2] At Cross Creek, Washington County, Pennsylvania, in this same year, about one hundred young men met and unanimously resolved that in paying their address to the young ladies they would give most marked preference to such as clothed themselves in homespun and made use of articles grown in their own country.[3] During the summer and fall of 1821 two daughters of a Virginia farmer, besides going two quarters to school, spun 160 pounds of wool. In the house of this farmer's father no thread was spun except a little for making shoes, dependence

[1] *Ibid.*, XXIII, 144.

[2] *Ibid.*, XXII, 266.

[3] *Ibid.*, XXII, 195. In commenting on this resolution Niles said: "'The deuce is in it'; provided these resolutions are maintained on both sides, if it does not become *fashionable* in this country to be clothed in homespun. But, indeed, there are many farmers in Pennsylvania and New York, etc., worth more than 50,000 dollars, who hardly expend 10 dollars a year for foreign articles of clothing; and by hundreds of others, their daughters are required to make as much homespun goods, beyond the family wants, as will furnish themselves with such imported things as they desire to have. The present pinching times are doing wonders for the good of our country."

being entirely upon European goods. The son found that when he depended on this same source his family was always bare of bedclothes, table linen, etc., but since he had been relying on the family factory there was not only plenty of these things, but piles of them in reserve.[1]

In summing up the conditions as he saw them the country over in about 1822, Holmes said:

> Before I quit the subject of manufactures, it is proper to state, that household, or domestic manufactures of woollen, linen &c. are carried on to a great extent: many thousands of families spin and make up their own clothing, sheets, table linen, &c. They purchase cotton yarn, and have it frequently mixed with their linen and woollen. Blankets, quilts, or coverlets, in short, nearly every article of domestic use, is made, or a great part made, in the family. It is supposed that nearly two-thirds of all the clothing, linen, blankets, &c. of those inhabitants who reside in the interior of the country, are of home or household manufacture. It is the same in the interior with soap and candles, for they have no excisemen to prevent their making those articles in the family.[2]

During the early twenties and even later it was very common to exhibit family manufactures at the agricultural fairs which were held throughout New York and other eastern states. Itemized statements of premiums awarded at these fairs show both the variety and amount of goods made in some homes. Four such statements of premiums given by the Ontario County, New York, Agricultural Society for the year 1822 follow:

> (1) In the family of Seth Jones, Bristol: 319 yards of linen cloth, 25 of kersey for bags, 42 of shirting, 35 of diaper, 52 of cotton and

[1] *Niles' Register*, XXI, 36.

[2] *An Account of the U.S. of Am.* (1823), p. 208.

linen, 199 of woolen cloth, 16 of kersey for blankets, 24 of plain flannel for blankets, 28 of cotton and wool, 34 of cotton, 22 of worsted, 30 pairs of socks, 7 pairs of stockings, 3 pairs of mittens, 5 bed quilts, 1 carpet, 27 pairs of pantaloons, 23 frocks, 2 surtouts, 4 coats, 4 sailor coats, 12 aprons, 1 bed tick, 7 blankets, 10 flannel sheets, 20 linen sheets, 30 shirts, 5 vests and 12 kersey bags.

(2) In the family of Nathaniel Allen, Richmond: 486½ yards of linen cloth, 193 yards of woolen cloth and enough yarn on hand to make 77 yards more, 5 bed quilts, 4 feather bed ticks, 20 pairs of woolen socks, 14 pairs of woolen stockings, 9 pairs of mittens for men and boys, 29 pairs of pantaloons, 9 coats and surtouts, 9 vests, 16 pairs of linen pillow cases, 21 linen sheets, 24 diaper towels, 3 diaper table cloths, 12 kersey towels, 12 kersey bags, 20 frocks, 1 mantle, 2 great coats for females, 15 runs of thread, 9 runs of worsted stocking yarn and 43 shirts.

(3) In the family of William Ottley, Phelps: 201 yards of linen cloth, 69 of diaper, 30 of linen check, 112 of fulled cloth, 89 of flannel, 28 of pressed flannel, 8 of linen handkerchiefs, 11 of cotton and woolen coverlets, 20 of double work blankets, 1 pair of rose blankets, 14 pairs of women's stockings, 10 pairs of socks, 3 pairs of mittens, 16 runs of worsted yarn for stockings, and 6 runs of linen thread.

(4) In the family of James Harland, Manchester: 61½ yards of fulled cloth, 16 of pressed flannel, 20 of mixed flannel, 46½ of plain flannel, 16 of diaper, 10½ of tow cloth, 3½ of kersey, 2 coverlets, 5 towels, 5 pairs of pillow cases, 3 pairs of tow and linen sheets, 1 feather bed, 1 under bed tick, 1 pair of horse blankets, 3 pairs of socks, 5 pairs of women's stockings, 5 meal bags, and 42 yards of worsted plaid, spun and partly woven not having time to finish.[1]

It should be kept in mind that the cases cited above were the extraordinary ones. It was for this reason that they received the premiums. Be this as it may, there is excellent evidence at hand to show that other families in New York state were by no means neglecting this

[1] *Niles' Register*, XXIII, 181.

TABLE XV

One Year's Output of Household Textile Manufactures in New York, 1820–21

Counties	No. Yards Fulled Cloth	No. Yards Flannel and Other Woolen Cloth Not Fulled	No. Yards Cotton, Linen, and Other Thin Cloth	Total Yards of All Kinds of Cloth	Population in 1820	Per Capita Yards
Albany	43,146	48,796	98,880	190,822	38,116	5.00
Alleghany	10,595	17,319	37,709	65,623	9,330	7.03
Broome	20,460	20,886	76,883	118,229	14,343	8.24
Cattaraugus	2,177	4,283	11,088	17,548	4,090	4.03
Cayuga	80,323	98,256	197,692	376,271	38,897	9.67
Chautauqua	15,758	18,647	49,145	83,550	12,568	6.65
Chenango	59,990	73,808	417,075	550,873	31,215	17.64
Clinton	20,249	19,729	32,290	72,268	12,070	6.07
Columbia	73,450	64,121	37,098	174,669	38,330	4.60
Cortland	32,465	38,671	88,872	160,008	16,507	9.70
Delaware	46,715	64,392	96,132	207,239	26,587	7.80
Dutchess	58,974	65,465	192,467	316,906	46,615	6.80
Erie	21,473	22,487	74,971	118,931	......	....
Essex	25,270	28,302	37,796	91,368	12,811	7.13
Franklin	6,179	7,450	18,645	32,274	4,439	7.26
Genesee	73,150	75,180	153,346	301,676	58,093	5.19
Green	32,464	32,129	77,341	141,934	22,996	6.17
Herkimer	60,785	67,133	307,913	435,831	31,017	14.05
Jefferson	54,470	77,082	144,758	276,310	32,952	8.39
King's	462	281	18,807	19,550	11,187	1.75
Lewis	16,890	20,888	41,422	79,200	9,227	8.47
Livingston	32,832	40,780	53,680	127,292	......	....
Madison	63,456	77,208	153,224	293,888	32,208	9.12
Monroe	41,358	46,957	97,650	185,965	......	....
Montgomery	71,225	99,064	131,306	301,595	37,569	8.03
Niagara	7,062	10,023	19,865	36,950	22,990	1.17
Oneida	87,951	107,134	201,553	396,638	50,997	7.77
Onondaga	74,346	81,157	174,872	330,375	41,467	7.96
Orange	44,995	38,563	314,330	397,888	41,213	9.65
Ontario	116,945	139,260	221,789	477,994	88,267	5.41
Oswego	16,061	20,583	58,610	95,254	12,374	7.70
Otsego	86,071	109,869	222,903	418,843	44,856	9.03
Putnam	14,914	14,973	47,434	77,321	11,268	6.86
Queen's	15,857	31,551	51,537	98,945	21,519	4.13
Rensselaer	65,012	73,116	179,586	317,714	40,153	7.94
Richmond	25	1,677	10,895	12,597	6,135	2.05

TABLE XV—*Continued*

Counties	No. Yards Fulled Cloth	No. Yards Flannel and Other Woolen Cloth Not Fulled	No. Yards Cotton, Linen, and Other Thin Cloth	Total Yards of All Kinds of Cloth	Population in 1820	Per Capita Yards
Rockland.......	5,159	3,426	255,539	264,124	8,837	29.89
Saratoga.......	68,615	73,460	144,871	286,946	36,052	7.96
Schenectady....	14,006	16,007	21,494	51,507	13,081	3.93
Schoharie.......	40,733	43,126	77,499	161,358	23,154	6.96
Seneca.........	40,442	45,218	109,880	195,540	23,619	8.27
St. Lawrence ...	25,238	33,626	62,339	121,203	16,037	7.55
Steuben........	31,168	39,729	80,265	151,162	21,989	6.89
Suffolk.........	32,705	24,256	97,105	154,066	24,272	6.43
Sullivan........	8,109	11,223	31,474	50,806	8,900	5.70
Tioga..........	25,934	29,927	91,525	147,386	16,971	8.67
Tompkins......	37,895	44,767	103,549	186,211	20,861	8.92
Ulster..........	37,362	30,814	119,992	188,168	30,934	6.08
Warren........	10,405	11,471	22,803	44,679	9,453	4.72
Washington	68,351	97,689	165,218	331,258	38,831	8.52
Westchester* ...	26,077	33,152	119,392	178,621	32,638	5.47
Total......	1,965,754	2,295,111	5,652,509	9,913,374	1,248,035	7.94

* *Jour. of the Assembly of N.Y.*, 45th Session, 1822, App. A, p. 60. The total population was not taken. The population statistics are from the United States census for 1820. Nothing was reported from the counties of Hamilton and New York. There were 993 fulling-mills and 1,235 carding-machines reported, which indicates that fulling and carding were largely done outside of the homes. Erie, Livingston, and Monroe counties were formed after the census reports for 1820 were in, hence there are no population statistics on which to base per capita yards. New York County had a population of 123,706, and Hamilton, 1,251.

important industry. In March, 1821, the state legislature authorized a census of the state to be taken. Fortunately for this discussion this census included data on household manufactures. Table XV exhibits the results along this line.

The discussion in this chapter thus far has dealt with the transfer from family- to shop- and factory-made goods without any special reference to locality. Since conditions were not uniform throughout the country at any particular date, it seems necessary before closing the chapter to summarize the movement and show its status in the New England and the middle states, in the South, and in the West and Northwest during the decade between 1820 and 1830. The discussion will now turn to this consideration, treating the sections in the order named.

That section of the country north of Maryland and east of the Alleghany Mountains far outstripped the South and the West in the transfer during the period under consideration. In reality, the new order of things began in this region with the beginning of the nineteenth century, especially in those parts along the rivers and near the coast. The sawmills, gristmills, and fulling-mills gradually ceased to be of prime importance, yielding their water rights to more extensive and profitable industries. The farms became less and less the chief means of support of the people, the farmers' children going into the factories and the one-time farming village becoming a thriving factory town. Indeed, the proprietor of a mill often employed the entire family. A case is on record where, in 1815, in the town of Clinton, Massachusetts, the father received $5.00 a week; his son, sixteen years old, $2.00; his daughter of thirteen, $1.50; his daughter of twelve, $1.25; his son of ten, $0.80; his sister, $2.33½; her son of thirteen, $1.50; and her daughter of eight, $0.75.[1] This opportunity to secure work in the factory coupled with the reduction in the price of mill-made goods brought an end to the weaving and spinning operations within the

[1] Ford, *Hist. of Clinton, Mass.*, p. 149.

home in many sections of this region before the end of the third decade of the nineteenth century.[1]

The foregoing conclusion is based on data contained in a report on manufactures made by the Secretary of the Treasury in 1832 in response to a resolution of the House of Representatives asking for material on which to base tariff legislation. While most of the material in the two large volumes deals with manufactures outside of the home, yet there were two questions relating to the status of those within the family between 1824 and 1832. They read as follows: "To what extent and what kinds of articles is household manufacture carried on in the county? Has it increased or decreased, and to what extent, since 1824?" These queries along with thirty-eight others were sent in most cases to persons in a position to have or to acquire reliable information relative to them as well as to the accompanying ones. While the answers were general and very incomplete, yet the fact that they were rather uniform indicates that they were more than mere guesses. A brief consideration of some of them will show the status of household manufactures at the time the reports were made and the decrease since 1824.

From Rhode Island there were nine reports in which the foregoing questions were answered, eight stating that

[1] It should be said here that in various sections of New England between 1820 and 1830 a new household industry sprang up, namely, the making of palm-leaf hats. Stores would give out the material and pay the women and girls in calicoes, ribbons, and laces at the rate of from 14 to 20 cents a hat. In some towns 20,000 hats a year were made. This no doubt helped to decrease the other household manufactures, since it was much easier to make hats than to weave cloth (*Documents Relative to the Manufactures in the U.S.*, I, 805).

there had been a great diminution in household manufactures since 1824. The following is the substance of the majority of the answers: Household manufacturing has been almost or wholly discontinued; female labor has been transferred to the factories; mill manufactures are substituted for household and are at a cheaper rate.[1] There was absolute unanimity of opinion among those answering from Vermont as to the decrease of household manufactures since 1824, the amount of the diminution varying from one-half to nine-tenths. The same reasons were given as in the case of Rhode Island, with the additional one that because of the increase in the price of wool farmers sold their fleeces and purchased cloth with which to clothe their families.[2] A general report based on the individual ones for the state of New Hampshire stated that there was not over four-fifths as much manufacturing done in the home then as formerly and that possibly one-half of the wearing apparel, carpeting, table linen, and bedding was made therein.[3] This estimate seems conservative enough when viewed in connection with some of the individual reports. For example, the reporter from Richmond, Cheshire County, said that there was not one yard woven in 1832 where 100 were woven in 1824; that the American system had killed household manufactures; and that women who formerly worked at

[1] *Documents Relative to the Manufactures in the U.S.*, I, 927 ff.

[2] *Ibid.*, I, 905 ff.

[3] *Ibid.*, I, 585. The returns from the various counties and towns of New Hampshire were very full on amounts and values of goods made in the home.

household manufacturing had gone into the large factories.[1] The reports from Massachusetts indicated that very little or no household manufacturing at all was done along the coast, while in the interior considerable was done, but not as much as formerly.[2] The returns from Connecticut and Maine were too incomplete to be of any value on the point under consideration. For the New England states as a whole this answer was somewhat common: "In New England household manufactures are very generally discontinued, and female labor has been transferred to factories, where it is more profitably employed, and the inhabitants are supplied by the manufacturers with cottons for their consumption, in lieu of their household manufactures, at a much cheaper rate."[3]

Household manufactures in the middle states did not decrease from 1824 to 1830 as they did in New England. The meager reports from this section to the Secretary of the Treasury in 1832 indicated that the industry had diminished in New Jersey, increased in Pennsylvania and Delaware, no data on the subject coming from New York. The report from Bergen County, New Jersey, said that cotton goods had mostly superseded linen, which formerly was the chief household manufacture, the farmers and the mechanics having a market for their produce or industry, which enabled them to purchase goods for less a yard than it formerly cost to have flax spun.[4] Conditions in Kent County, Delaware, were somewhat different. The low price of cotton yarn, occasioned by the improvement

[1] *Ibid.*, I, 810.

[2] *Ibid.*, I, 68, 87 f.

[3] *Ibid.*, I, 946, 962.

[4] *Ibid.*, II, 137.

in its manufacture, caused a considerable increase in household manufactures. In the opinion of the one making the report, fully one-half of the agricultural citizens in this county were clothed with the products of their own industry.[1] Eight of the nine accounts from western Pennsylvania said that family manufactures had increased since 1824, one placing the increase as high as 75 per cent.[2] That these statements presented the situation as it really existed in this section of the state is evidenced by the report of a special committee on an exhibit of household manufactures in Washington County in 1828. This report read as follows:

> The Cloths, Flannels, Baizes, Carpets, Linens, Bed Tickings, Coverlids, Hearth Rugs, Stockings etc. with several beautiful specimens of needle work, were such as to call forth the admiration of everyone who beheld them, and to furnish evidence (were evidence wanting) of the industry and taste of the ladies of Washington county. Amongst the great variety of household manufactures (about 150 in number) nothing appeared to excite greater attention than the sewing Silk, several pounds of which were exhibited, made by Mrs. Axtel, Riggs, Bombarger and Quail, and which we have no hesitation in pronouncing equal to any imported silk we have seen.[3]

Generally speaking, there had been as much progress made prior to 1830 in the matter of the transfer from family- to factory-made goods in that section of the country south of the Ohio River and Pennsylvania and

[1] *Documents Relative to the Manufactures in the U.S.*, II, 674.

[2] *Ibid.*, II, 274 ff.

[3] "Report to the President and Directors of the Washington County [Pa.] Society, for the Promotion of Agriculture and Domestic Manufacture," Hazard, *Register of Pa.*, II, 328.

east of the Mississippi River as in the regions considered above. The invention of the cotton gin, the market for cotton created by Arkwright's machinery, improved transportation facilities, and slavery all combined to throw the South, outside of certain sections of the back-country, once more upon her staple products of agriculture, just as had been the case with Virginia and Maryland during the colonial period. The great increase in the cultivation of cotton and rice between 1820 and 1830, the extension of the sugar industry in Louisiana, and the tobacco culture in Tennessee and Kentucky gave all of these regions staples which were in great demand; and because of this demand they were able to bear the expense of land transportation for a considerable distance, even over the poor roads of the new settlements. The many rivers in the South and the application of steam power to navigation made it possible to market the cotton and at the same time bring manufactured goods to the plantations.

The great profits which accrued to the plantation-owners in South Carolina and the Gulf States from their attention to rice and cotton caused them to give up mixed farming and devote all their industrial forces to the raising of these staples. The effects of this system were soon felt in the other sections of the country. For example, the plantation had to have large supplies of such important products as pork, bacon, lard, beef, butter, cheese, corn, flour, apples, cider, vinegar, soap, candles, and whiskey. These were furnished by the farmers of Tennessee, Kentucky, and the Northwest. The manufactured goods came from Europe or from the New England and the middle states; and many of the slaves for the plantations came from Maryland, Virginia, and North Carolina. Thus, by 1830, the agricultural system in South Carolina and the Gulf states was furnishing a means whereby thousands of people the country over could give up their former dependence upon their own labors for manufactured commodities. Cotton was indeed *king*. Through its production and sale the planters secured their manufactured supplies from the East or from Europe, their supply of labor from the Old South, their necessary raw products from Kentucky, Tennessee, and the Northwest, which in turn made it possible for the farmers of this latter region and the slave-breeders of the Old South to secure the means to supply themselves with manufactured goods either from the European mills or from the mills of New England and middle states; for the great army of workers in the industrial and commercial towns in the East to secure theirs from the product of their labor in mills and stores and on ships, which in turn gave the farmers east of the Alleghanies an opportunity to exchange their produce for manufactured commodities. This industrial revolution brought about by the few-staple farming system of the South made it possible for the country as a whole to discontinue to a considerable degree the old system of household manufacturing and supply itself either from the products of its own factories or from those of foreign countries. This transfer was by no means completed by 1830, yet it was well on the way, with every indication of ultimate success.

Even though the foregoing statement is true for the greater portion of the South and Southwest in 1830, it should be said that there were to be found at this date many communities in the back-country districts living under semi-pioneer conditions. It is to be noted, however, that many things modern had reached even these communities. By 1820 spinning-jennies were familiar here. In 1825 one Cincinnati factory was selling, mostly in this region, $20,000 worth annually of machines, which, by the operation of a single crank, ginned, carded, and spun simultaneously six threads of cotton.[1] Indeed, the two decades following 1812 mark the mill period in this region, mill-builders from the North coming in just after the War of 1812. The yarn spun in these mills was given out to the settlers for raw wool or woven cloth. Plantations even came to be supplied with spinning-mills, the local demand supporting them at first, and later their output finding its way to the northern markets.[2]

The true status of the spinning and weaving operation in the whole back-country region is reflected in what Kercheval saw and heard in a farmhouse in the south-eastern part of Shenandoah County, Virginia, in about 1830. While going through this region he called at the house of a farmer where he saw five spinning-wheels at work. The wife, three daughters, and a hired girl were engaged in spinning finely prepared hemp. The visitor inquired of the mother whether she sold any part of the

[1] Clark, "Manufactures during the Ante-Bellum and War Periods," *South in the Building of the Nation*, V, 318.

[2] *Ibid.*, p. 321.

domestic goods. Her answer was: "Yes; when de gals wants to puy some fine dings in de sthore, dey bay for it in linen and linsey; and I puy sugar and goffee and salt and many dings we wants, und bay for all of it in our own coods."[1]

It should be said in concluding the consideration of family or plantation manufactures in the South in about 1830 that whatever was done even by the slaves was rather unprofitable. Evidence of this fact is found in a letter from an overseer of a Georgia plantation to his employer, dated February 18, 1831. On this plantation both cotton and woolen cloth were manufactured by slaves. In calling his employer's attention to the unprofitableness of the work of the slaves engaged in spinning warp the overseer showed in his letter that the warp made by four slaves in a year could be bought at the factory for $120. Now, when $80 was subtracted for the cotton annually spun and an equal amount for boarding and clothing the slaves, there was a deficit. This deficit was avoided on some plantations by buying the warp and spinning wool only.[2]

In all those regions of the West and Northwest where the floating pioneer population of the earlier days had given way to the succeeding wave which was composed of people who desired to settle down and establish permanent homes, the transfer under consideration in this chapter had made remarkable progress before the close of the third decade of the nineteenth century. While the pioneer costumes and customs had undergone astounding changes even before 1820, yet it was between this

[1] Kercheval, *op. cit.*, p. 202. [2] Phillips, *op. cit.*, I, 334.

date and 1830 that the great revolution in most every phase of life in these sections occurred. Between 1790 and 1830 manufacturing establishments of almost every description grew up along the Ohio and other rivers. The appearance of the steamboat made the distribution of the output of these establishments possible, as well as overcame the disadvantages of the industrial isolation that was so marked during earlier days, when the western country was practically as far from the eastern markets as the Atlantic coast settlements were from the European during the colonial period. Since many of the immigrants who came west between 1820 and 1830 were from the older sections of the country where household industrial dependence had ceased to be necessary, they were unwilling, except in cases of sheer necessity, to revert to the primitive modes of life practiced by their ancestors; hence all that was needed were facilities to supply them with goods formerly made in the homes. Such facilities existed in the thriving manufacturing establishments, the army of handicraftsmen in the towns and villages, and the steamboats on the navigable rivers.

A rather minute and perhaps somewhat exaggerated portrayal of the change that took place in the wearing apparel of the people in the older sections of the West between 1818 and 1830 is on record from the pen of one who was a close observer of the manners and customs of his day. His account follows:

> A most remarkable change occurred during this period [1818 to 1830] and a little before, in the habits of dress and appearance of the people. Before the year 1830, a man dressed in the costume of the

territory, which was a raccoon-cap, linsey hunting-shirt, buckskin breeches and moccasins, with a belt around the waist, to which the butcher-knife and tomahawk on the side and back were appended, was rarely to be seen. The blue linsey hunting-shirt with red or white fringe, had given place to the cloth coat; the raccoon-cap with the tail of the animal dangling down behind, had been thrown aside for hats of wool or fur. Boots and shoes had supplanted the deer-skin moccasins, and the leather breeches, strapped tight around the ancle, had disappeared before unmentionables of modern material. The female sex had made a still greater progress in dress. The old sort of cotton or woolen frocks, spun, wove and made with their own fair hands, and striped and cross-barred with blue dye and turkey red, had given place to gowns of silk and calico. The feet, before in a state of nudity, now charmed in shoes of calfskin or slippers of kid; and the head formerly unbonnetted but covered with a cotton handkerchief, now displayed the charms of the female face, under many forms of bonnets of straw, silk, or leghorn. The young ladies, instead of walking a mile or two to church on Sunday, carrying their shoes and stockings in their hands to within a hundred yards of the place of worship as formerly, now came forth arrayed complete in all the pride of dress, mounted on fine horses, and attended by their male admirers.[1]

While the foregoing is interesting and at the same time contains much truth, yet the picture of farm life in central Ohio in about 1832, by another contemporary, probably portrays somewhat more accurately conditions as they generally existed throughout the older portions of the West and Northwest at this date. According to this writer the split broom was yet found in every household, as were also the big and little spinning-wheels, the weaving, however, being for the most part done by the neighborhood weaver. The village or crossroads blacksmith made most

[1] Ford, *A Hist. of Ill.*, p. 94.

of the farm implements; water-mills on the streams did all the grinding of the grain; the village tanner tanned the hides into leather on the halves; the itinerant shoemaker made the shoes for his neighborhood; small distilleries scattered throughout every county made whiskey from the corn, rye, or barley; maple sugar and syrup were made for the family's use; the everyday clothing was generally of the homespun variety, the men usually having a Sunday suit of broadcloth and the women and girls an extra one or two, for dress occasions, of alpaca, merino, or other fine goods, as well as fashionable bonnets, shawls, and wraps of various kinds. Each village had its store, which took, in exchange for goods, all sorts of farm produce, such as butter, eggs, cheese, rags, feathers, beeswax, tallow, lard, hops, corn, pork, cider, fur, and ginseng.[1]

It should be said in closing this section that while flax brakes, hackles, looms, spinning-wheels, handmills, and cider-mills were common implements in most rural households, and that straw hats, shoes, clothing, and household textile supplies were common articles of family production about 1830 and even after, yet, as the imported goods became more easily obtainable on account of their low price and the market for the output of the farm, the establishment of water-mills and horsemills for grinding corn, wheat, rye, and barley in each community, as well as tanneries and distilleries, it became possible, profitable, and desirable for the people to replace their pioneer food, furniture, implements, and dress with shop-, mill-, and

[1] Welker, "Farm Life in Central Ohio Sixty Years Ago," *Western Reserve Hist. Soc. Tracts*, IV, No. 86, pp. 43 ff.

factory-made products. This transfer from family- to factory-made goods, that had made so much headway by 1830 in all the older regions of the western country, gradually increased in territorial extent and the number of articles during the next few decades and by 1860 was practically completed in all its more important phases. The succeeding chapter shows statistically the progress and *final* general completion of this transfer.[1]

[1] For additional references on the change that occurred in social and industrial conditions in the West and Northwest between 1820 and 1830, see Patterson, "Early Society in Southern Illinois," *Fergus Hist. Series*, I, No. 14, pp. 109 ff.; Haines, "Social Life and Scenes in the Early Settlement of Southern Illinois," *Trans. Ill. State Hist. Soc.*, No. 10, pp. 36 f. and pp. 39 f.; Esarey, Logan, *Hist. of Ind.*, p. 424; McMath, "The Willow Run Settlement," *Mich. Pioneer and Hist. Soc. Colls.*, XIV, 491 f.; and Howells, *Recollections of Life in Ohio from 1813 to 1840*, chaps. xviii and xx.

CHAPTER VIII

THE PASSING OF THE FAMILY FACTORY

The industrial revolution which occurred in the United States during the three decades next following 1830 put an end to the family system of manufacturing as it had existed up to this date. During these thirty years the transfer from family- to factory-made goods made such rapid strides that the end of the period found family-made goods the exception rather than the general rule as formerly. While some of the new-made settlements and those absolutely devoid of transportation facilities were forced to maintain the primitive modes of life, yet the former escaped such conditions much earlier in their history than settlements established before 1830. Fortunately, statistics are at hand to show the gradual diminution of household manufactures between 1830 and 1860. These statistics relate to one state as to the decrease in quantity and to the country as a whole as to the decline in value, both gross and per capita. They are presented in some detail in the following pages.

WHAT HAPPENED IN ONE STATE (NEW YORK)

The slow but certain passing of the family factory is well illustrated by what happened in New York in the matter of household textile manufactures between 1825 and 1855. The constitutions of 1821 and of 1845 in this

TABLE XVI

Household Textile Manufactures in New York in 1825, 1835, 1845, and 1855*

Counties	When Formed	Total Yards of All Kinds of Textile Goods				Population				Per Capita Yards			
		1825	1835	1845	1855	1825	1835	1845	1855	1825	1835	1845	1855
Albany	1683	227,665	142,568	83,472	17,960	42,821	59,762	77,268	103,681	5.32	2.38	1.08	0.17
Alleghany	1806	170,415	220,047	213,982	30,963	18,164	35,214	40,084	42,910	9.38	6.25	5.34	0.72
Broome	1806	133,004	110,619	111,089	27,251	13,893	20,190	25,808	36,650	9.57	5.48	4.30	0.74
Cattaraugus	1808	74,028	140,341	164,153	35,073	8,643	24,986	30,169	39,530	8.57	5.62	5.44	0.89
Cayuga	1799	407,556	237,549	171,092	16,590	42,743	49,202	49,663	53,571	9.54	4.83	3.44	0.31
Chautauqua	1808	215,124	286,561	279,910	35,258	20,640	44,869	46,548	53,380	10.42	6.39	6.01	0.66
Chemung	1836	....	....	59,514	7,013	....	....	23,689	27,288	......	......	2.51	0.26
Chenango	1798	418,424	286,044	186,335	42,652	34,215	40,762	39,900	39,915	12.23	7.02	4.67	1.07
Clinton	1788	100,997	63,596	57,145	10,580	14,486	20,742	31,278	42,482	6.97	3.07	1.83	0.25
Columbia	1786	828,350	148,344	62,028	8,575	37,970	40,746	41,976	44,391	21.81	3.64	1.48	0.19
Cortland	1808	253,807	184,022	116,581	21,801	20,271	24,168	25,081	24,575	12.52	7.61	4.65	0.89
Delaware	1797	327,750	220,327	165,468	39,558	29,565	34,192	36,990	39,749	11.08	6.44	4.47	0.99
Dutchess	1683	390,143	116,086	37,909	3,193	46,698	50,704	55,124	60,635	8.35	2.29	0.69	0.05
Erie	1821	198,676	177,211	183,709	26,654	24,316	57,594	78,635	132,331	8.17	3.08	2.34	0.20
Essex	1799	125,902	90,236	56,975	6,460	15,993	20,699	25,102	28,539	7.87	4.36	2.27	0.23
Franklin	1808	48,410	59,897	83,309	23,214	7,978	12,501	18,692	25,477	6.07	4.79	4.46	0.91
Fulton	1838	....	....	69,007	7,477	....	....	18,579	23,284	......	......	3.71	0.32
Genesee	1802	372,033	307,039	90,989	4,135	40,905	58,588	28,845	31,034	9.09	5.24	3.15	0.13
Greene	1800	234,238	106,112	64,411	8,611	26,225	30,173	31,957	31,137	8.93	3.52	2.01	0.28
Hamilton	1816	....	....	6,709	1,463	....	....	1,882	2,543	......	......	3.56	0.57
Herkimer	1791	349,884	163,982	102,834	14,110	33,040	36,201	37,424	38,566	10.59	4.53	2.75	0.36
Jefferson	1805	307,175	269,536	263,543	45,956	41,650	53,088	64,999	65,420	7.37	5.08	4.05	0.70
Kings	1683	13,070	8,689	132	....	14,679	32,057	78,691	216,229	0.89	0.27	0.00	......
Lewis	1805	96,837	78,819	71,297	15,801	11,669	16,093	20,218	25,229	8.30	4.90	3.53	0.63
Livingston	1821	208,293	134,713	99,324	9,005	23,860	31,092	33,193	37,943	8.73	4.33	2.99	0.24
Madison	1806	380,748	211,640	128,745	17,164	35,646	41,741	40,987	43,687	10.68	5.07	3.14	0.39
Monroe	1821	291,865	155,090	101,692	7,348	39,108	58,085	70,899	96,324	7.46	2.67	1.43	0.08
Montgomery	1772	370,709	233,620	88,137	12,287	40,902	48,359	29,643	30,808	9.06	4.83	2.97	0.40
New York	1683	1,172,859	868,500	904,081	....	166,086	270,089	371,223	629,904	7.06	3.21	2.43	......
Niagara	1808	60,171	70,500	75,900	11,499	14,069	26,490	34,550	48,282	4.28	2.66	2.20	0.24
Oneida	1798	478,937	241,211	409,857	27,989	37,847	77,518	84,776	107,749	12.65	3.11	4.83	0.26

Onondaga	1794	391,237	230,810	159,992	15,589	48,435	60,908	70,175	86,575	8.08	3.79	2.28	0.18
Ontario	1789	376,681	178,998	88,093	4,885	37,422	40,870	42,592	42,672	10.06	4.38	2.07	0.11
Orange	1683	442,111	80,098	34,056	2,948	41,732	45,096	32,227	60,868	10.59	1.78	1.06	0.05
Orleans	1824	88,560	84,701	74,338	6,324	14,460	22,893	25,845	28,435	6.12	3.70	2.88	0.22
Oswego	1816	144,086	152,727	164,341	28,617	17,875	38,245	48,441	69,398	8.06	3.99	3.39	0.41
Otsego	1791	575,996	347,023	211,230	32,779	47,898	50,428	50,509	49,735	12.02	6.88	4.18	0.66
Putnam	1812	99,788	30,108	12,695	1,221	11,866	11,551	13,258	13,934	8.41	2.61	0.96	0.09
Queens	1683	99,099	13,193	80,219	……	20,331	25,130	31,849	46,266	4.87	0.52	2.52	……
Rensselaer	1791	402,864	229,140	95,688	4,949	44,065	55,515	62,338	79,234	9.14	4.13	1.53	0.06
Richmond	1683	6,524	165	……	……	5,932	7,691	13,673	21,389	1.10	0.02	……	……
Rockland	1798	49,319	8,924	2,456	……	8,016	9,696	13,741	19,511	6.15	0.92	0.18	……
St. Lawrence	1802	171,716	215,535	287,274	89,863	27,595	42,047	62,354	74,977	6.22	5.13	4.61	1.20
Saratoga	1791	338,516	164,092	84,710	7,753	36,295	38,012	41,477	49,379	9.33	4.32	2.04	0.16
Schenectady	1809	384,025	44,408	29,002	3,462	12,876	16,230	16,630	19,572	29.82	2.74	1.74	0.18
Schuyler	1854	……	……	……	11,346	……	……	……	18,777	……	……	……	0.60
Schoharie	1795	238,541	198,594	147,981	34,915	25,926	28,508	32,488	33,519	9.20	6.97	4.55	1.04
Seneca	1804	153,033	80,492	36,616	3,215	20,169	22,627	24,972	25,358	7.59	3.56	1.47	0.13
Steuben	1796	250,666	231,834	211,596	34,935	29,245	41,435	51,679	62,965	8.57	5.59	4.09	0.55
Suffolk	1683	166,067	53,799	24,396	870	23,695	28,274	34,579	40,906	7.01	1.90	0.70	0.02
Sullivan	1809	85,127	48,263	40,587	9,435	10,373	13,755	18,727	29,487	8.21	3.51	2.17	0.32
Tioga	1791	188,906	158,732	95,868	16,390	19,951	33,999	22,456	26,962	9.47	4.67	4.27	0.61
Tompkins	1817	293,342	201,168	126,321	14,847	32,908	38,008	38,168	31,516	8.91	5.29	3.31	0.47
Ulster	1683	275,445	135,971	94,357	16,647	32,015	39,960	48,907	67,936	8.60	3.40	1.93	0.25
Warren	1813	88,846	61,242	49,354	11,435	10,906	12,034	14,908	19,669	8.15	5.09	3.31	0.58
Washington	1772	403,155	195,054	86,631	6,298	39,280	39,326	40,554	44,405	10.26	4.96	2.14	0.14
Wayne	1823	213,317	163,190	147,555	13,064	26,761	37,788	42,515	46,760	7.97	4.32	3.47	0.28
Westchester	1683	169,484	36,414	14,856	847	33,131	38,790	47,578	80,678	5.11	0.94	0.31	0.01
Wyoming	1841	……	……	121,851	17,173	……	……	27,205	32,140	……	……	4.52	0.53
Yates	1823	115,901	96,239	58,582	3,793	13,214	19,796	20,777	19,812	8.77	4.86	2.82	0.19
Total		16,469,422	8,773,813	7,089,984	929,241	1,616,214	2,174,517	2,584,495	3,466,078	8.95	4.03	2.74	0.27

*This table is based on the following sources: "Census of the State of New York for the Year 1825," *New York Senate Journal*, 49th Sess., 1826, App.; *Censuses of the State of New York for 1835, 1845, and 1855*, Albany, 1836, 1846, and 1857. The dates for the organization of each county are in the Introduction to the *Census of 1855*, p. xxxiii.

state provided for a decennial census,[1] the first being taken in 1825. For each of the years 1825, 1835, 1845, and 1855 household textile manufactures were included. Table XVI, based on the returns for each of the four years included therein, shows exactly what took place in each county of the state during this period.[2]

Table XVI tells its story so well that little comment is necessary. However, for the sake of emphasis, mention should be made of some of the outstanding facts, the first and the most impressive one being the great decrease in both total and per capita yards of textiles made in the home between 1825 and 1855. A decrease from 16,469,422 to 929,241 total yards and from 8.95 to 0.27 per capita yards is conclusive evidence that a great industrial revolution was going on in this state during these years. That this revolution began in the towns and cities and finally spread to the country districts is evidenced by the fact that counties such as Kings, Queens, Orange, Westchester, Suffolk, Richmond, and Rockland gave up their household manufactures first. The enormous decrease, both in total and in per capita yards, between 1825 and 1835 was largely the result of the passing of the family factory from the urban districts. The tenacity with which the rural

[1] *Census of 1865, N. Y.*, Introd., p. v.

[2] The fact should be noted here that New York offered special encouragements to family manufactures. In 1819 the legislature appropriated $10,000 a year for two years for the promotion of agriculture and family manufactures. This money was distributed among the counties to assist them in organizing agricultural societies, which in turn offered premiums for family-made goods (*Laws of N. Y.*, 40th Sess., c. 107). In 1820 the foregoing act was extended for a period of four years after the expiration fixed by the first law (*ibid.*, 43d Sess., c. 97).

districts held on to the system is shown by the relatively small decrease in total yards between 1835 and 1845, the rather large per capita decrease during this decade being due to the increase in population. The all but total abandonment of the family factory even in the rural districts is demonstrated by what happened between 1845 and 1855. The great drop from 7,089,984 to 929,241 total yards demonstrates the fact that when the women decided to give up their time-honored home industry it did not take them long to do it.

The explanation of what happened to the family factory in New York during the period covered by Table XVI is found in the general economic and industrial revolution which occurred during these years. The two phases of this revolution which were most closely related to the diminution of the amount of household manufactures[1] were the increase in transportation facilities and establishments making articles from fibrous and textile substances, the latter creating a market for the output of the

[1] In 1831 there were in New York 314 establishments making articles from fibrous and textile substances. This number had increased to 345 in 1835; to 463 in 1845; and to 889 in 1855. The value of the output of such factories increased from $5,463,891 in 1835 to $19,643,028 in 1855 (*Census of N. Y.*, 1835, recapitulation table; *ibid.*, 1855, Introd., pp. 57, 60, 411). Along with this increase in fibrous and textile manufactures went a corresponding increase in transportation facilities. In 1832 there were but 17 miles of railroad in New York; in 1840 there were 394.50 miles; in 1850, 1,452.50 and in 1859, 2,643.75 (Dunbar, *Hist. of Travel in Am.*, IV, 1,391). To supplement these railroads there were 995.94 miles of canals in 1840 as well as the numerous natural navigable waterways. Hence by 1860 it was no longer a problem for the rural districts in New York to secure factory-made goods in exchange for the output of the farm, since the supply of goods was so adequate and the transportation facilities so ample.

TABLE XVII

TOTAL AND PER CAPITA VALUES BY STATES AND TERRITORIES OF HOUSEHOLD MANUFACTURES IN THE UNITED STATES IN 1840, 1850, AND 1860*

States and Territories	Total Valuation			Population			Per Capita Value		
	1840	1850	1860	1840	1850	1860	1840	1850	1860
Alabama	$1,656,119	$1,934,120	$1,817,520	590,756	771,623	964,201	$2.80	$2.51	$1.88
Arkansas	489,750	638,217	1,019,240	97,574	209,897	435,450	5.02	3.04	2.34
California	....	7,000	255,653	....	92,597	379,994	......	0.07	0.67
Connecticut	226,162	192,252	48,954	309,978	370,792	460,147	0.73	0.52	0.11
Delaware	62,116	38,121	17,591	78,085	91,532	112,216	0.79	0.42	0.16
Florida	20,205	75,582	63,259	54,477	87,445	140,424	0.37	0.86	0.45
Georgia	1,467,630	1,838,968	1,431,413	691,392	906,185	1,057,286	2.12	2.03	1.35
Illinois	993,567	1,155,902	923,220	476,183	851,470	1,711,951	2.09	1.36	0.53
Indiana	1,289,802	1,631,039	986,393	685,866	988,416	1,350,428	1.88	1.65	0.73
Iowa	25,966	221,292	317,690	43,112	192,214	674,913	0.60	1.15	0.47
Kansas	....	....	24,748	....	....	107,206	......	......	0.23
Kentucky	2,622,462	2,459,128	2,095,578	779,828	982,405	1,155,684	3.36	2.50	1.81
Louisiana	65,190	139,232	502,100	352,411	517,762	708,002	0.18	0.27	0.71
Maine	804,397	513,599	490,786	501,793	583,169	628,279	1.60	0.88	0.78
Maryland	176,050	111,828	67,003	470,019	583,034	687,049	0.37	0.19	0.10
Massachusetts	231,942	205,333	245,886	737,699	994,514	1,231,066	0.31	0.21	0.20
Michigan	113,955	340,947	142,756	212,267	397,654	749,113	0.54	0.86	0.19
Minnesota	....	....	7,981	....	6,077	172,023	......	0.00	0.05
Mississippi	682,945	1,164,020	1,382,144	375,651	606,526	791,305	1.82	1.92	1.75
Missouri	1,149,544	1,674,705	1,984,262	383,702	682,044	1,182,012	2.99	2.45	1.68
New Hampshire	538,303	393,455	251,052	284,574	317,976	326,073	1.89	1.24	0.78
New Jersey	201,625	112,781	27,588	373,306	489,555	672,035	0.54	0.23	0.04

New York	4,636,547	1,280,333	717,898	2,428,921	3,097,394	3,880,735	1.91	0.41	0.18
North Carolina	1,413,242	2,086,522	2,045,372	753,419	869,039	992,622	1.87	2.40	2.06
Ohio	1,853,937	1,712,196	596,197	1,519,467	1,980,329	2,339,511	1.22	0.86	0.25
Oregon	...	...	46,278	...	13,294	52,465	...	...	0.88
Pennsylvania	1,303,093	749,132	544,728	1,724,033	2,311,786	2,906,215	0.75	0.32	0.19
Rhode Island	51,180	26,495	7,824	108,830	147,545	174,620	0.47	0.18	0.04
South Carolina	930,703	909,525	815,117	594,398	668,507	703,708	1.56	1.36	1.16
Tennessee	2,886,661	3,137,790	3,174,977	829,210	1,002,717	1,109,801	3.48	3.13	2.86
Texas	...	266,984	584,217	...	212,592	604,215	...	1.25	0.97
Vermont	674,548	267,710	63,334	291,948	314,120	315,098	2.31	0.85	0.20
Virginia	2,441,672	2,156,312	1,576,627	1,239,797	1,421,661	1,596,318	1.97	1.52	0.99
Wisconsin	12,567	43,624	127,992	30,945	305,391	775,881	0.41	0.14	0.16
Colorado	...	...	...	...	...	34,277	...	...	...
Dakota	...	...	...	...	...	4,837	...	...	...
Nebraska	...	...	15,995	...	...	28,841	...	...	0.55
Nevada	...	...	300	...	...	6,857	...	...	0.04
New Mexico	...	6,033	26,406	...	61,547	93,516	...	0.10	0.28
Utah	...	1,392	66,851	...	11,380	40,273	...	0.12	1.66
Washington	...	...	33,506	...	...	11,594	...	...	2.89
Dist. of Columbia	1,500	2,075	440	43,712	51,687	75,080	0.03	0.04	0.00
Total	$29,023,380	$27,493,644	$24,546,876	17,069,453	23,191,876	31,443,321	$1.70	$1.18	$0.78

* For the value of home- or family-made goods, see *Compendium of the Sixth Census* (1840), p. 359; *Eighth Census of the U.S.*, "Agriculture" (1860), pp. 187, 191. For the population statistics, see *Eighth Census of the U.S.*, "Population," pp. 599, 603, and 604. (Six thousand one hundred persons are included in the total population for 1840 for individuals on ships at sea.)

farms as well as furnishing articles formerly made in the family, and the former furnishing both the agriculturalist and the manufacturer a system for marketing the products of their labor, thus making it possible for the farmer and his family to devote their entire time to the ordinary farm and home work.

WHAT HAPPENED IN THE COUNTRY AS A WHOLE

There is no reason to believe that the diminution in the amount of manufacturing done in the households in New York during the period covered by Table XVI was not duplicated in the country as a whole. While the per capita value of such manufactures in 1860 was one dollar or more in Alabama, Arkansas, Georgia, Kentucky, Mississippi, North Carolina, South Carolina, Tennessee, Utah, and Washington, yet, at the same time, there was a drop in the per capita value for the country as a whole from $1.70 in 1840 to $0.78 in 1860. What happened in each state during the period under consideration is shown by Table XVII.

While this table proves the thesis defended in this chapter, namely, that between 1830 and 1860 household manufactures ceased to be an important factor in the industrial life and prosperity of the people as a whole, yet one needs a closer approach to the individual homes than is furnished by it in order to learn the details of the passing of the family factory. Fortunately for this discussion these details are at hand; for, in collecting data for each of the censuses of 1840, 1850, and 1860, statistics on the value of home- or family-made goods were included.

Among the numerous questions the enumerators asked was one concerning the value of goods made in the family during the year ending with the date of the taking of the census. The accompanying elaborate table (XVIII) is based on the return from each county in existence at the taking of each of the foregoing censuses. It shows better than words can describe what happened to household manufactures in each county in the Union during the three decades just prior to 1860.

Before commenting on the significant facts exhibited in Tables XVII and XVIII something should be said of the states and territories not included in the latter. In 1860 population statistics were returned from 19 counties in Oregon, 34 in Nebraska, 44 in California, 64 in Minnesota, 11 in New Mexico, 19 in Washington, 41 in Kansas, 17 in Utah, and 3 in Nevada. The number of counties reporting household manufactures in these states and territories in the order named was as follows: 10, 7, 11, 18, 6, 7, 18, 13, and 1. Table XIX shows the per capita value of goods made in the families in these counties in 1860.

TABLE XVIII

TOTAL AND PER CAPITA VALUE BY COUNTIES OF HOUSEHOLD MANUFACTURES IN THE UNITED STATES IN 1840, 1850, AND 1860*

Counties	Total Valuation			Population			Per Capita Value		
	1840	1850	1860	1840	1850	1860	1840	1850	1860
MAINE									
Aroostook	$24,486	$21,734	$45,879	9,413	12,529	22,479	$2.60	$1.73	$2.04
Cumberland	65,863	52,222	26,926	68,658	79,538	75,591	0.96	0.66	0.36
Franklin	26,346	51,205	26,639	20,801	20,027	20,403	1.27	2.56	1.31
Hancock	30,356	18,780	64,346	28,605	34,372	37,757	1.06	0.55	1.70
Kennebec	80,672	37,907	26,491	55,823	62,521	55,655	1.45	0.61	0.48
Lincoln	93,761	50,843	22,796	63,517	74,875	27,860	1.48	0.68	0.82
Oxford	45,518	31,037	44,907	38,351	39,763	36,698	1.19	0.78	1.22
Penobscot	48,126	36,991	44,667	45,705	63,089	72,731	1.05	0.59	0.61
Piscataquis	21,232	16,335	16,037	13,138	14,735	15,032	1.62	1.11	1.07
Somerset	106,942	64,276	33,346	33,912	35,581	21,790	3.15	1.81	0.91
Waldo	113,661	75,042	26,969	41,509	47,230	38,447	2.74	1.59	0.70
Washington	46,825	31,287	31,327	28,327	38,811	42,534	1.65	0.81	0.74
York	100,609	25,940	25,162	54,034	60,098	62,107	1.86	0.41	0.41
NEW HAMPSHIRE									
Cheshire	46,384	56,630	26,062	26,429	30,144	27,434	1.76	1.88	0.95
Coos	42,108	36,772	11,475	9,849	11,853	13,161	4.28	3.10	0.87
Grafton	123,540	139,305	127,320	42,311	42,343	42,260	2.92	3.29	3.01
Hillsborough	41,681	5,356	4,977	42,494	57,478	62,140	0.99	0.09	0.08

Merrimack	95,122	30,012	3,054	30,253	40,337	41,400	2.02	0.74	0.07
Rockingham	26,621	36,330	54,757	45,771	49,194	50,122	0.58	0.74	1.09
Strafford	124,922	9,157	3,527	61,127	29,374	31,493	2.04	0.31	0.11
Sullivan†	37,925	27,468	8,213	20,340	19,375	19,041	1.86	1.42	0.43
VERMONT									
Addison	30,795	9,648	1,563	23,583	26,549	24,010	1.31	0.36	0.07
Bennington	18,569	6,450	11,145	16,872	18,589	19,436	1.10	0.35	0.57
Caledonia	85,324	40,343	4,357	21,891	23,595	21,708	3.90	1.71	0.20
Chittenden	34,351	13,359	734	22,977	29,036	28,171	1.50	0.46	0.03
Essex	15,983	22,044	6,667	4,226	4,650	5,786	3.78	4.74	1.15
Franklin	88,277	26,247	1,312	24,531	28,586	27,231	3.60	0.92	0.05
Grand Isle	11,626	3,449	150	3,883	4,145	4,276	2.99	0.83	0.04
Lamoille	24,850	6,584	3,414	10,475	10,872	12,311	2.37	0.61	0.28
Orange	88,977	27,346	6,982	27,873	27,296	25,455	3.19	1.00	0.27
Orleans	35,553	16,422	8,686	13,634	15,707	18,981	2.61	0.94	0.46
Rutland	45,291	12,620	1,590	30,699	33,059	35,946	1.48	0.38	0.04
Washington	68,153	17,269	6,054	23,506	24,654	27,612	2.05	0.70	0.20
Windham	61,573	13,321	7,620	27,442	29,062	26,982	2.24	0.46	0.28
Windsor	65,226	52,608	3,060	40,356	38,320	37,193	1.62	1.37	0.08

* This table is based on the sixth, seventh, and eighth United States censuses. For 1850 the material is all in one volume; for 1840 and 1860 the population and the agricultural statistics were published in separate volumes. See bibliography. Because of the space consumed, out of proportion to the value of the data, no county is included in the table which was not in existence at the taking of the census in 1840. Counties in existence in 1860 and not in 1840 are included in the footnotes. To facilitate the matter of checking the spelling for the counties in the Census of 1860, "Agriculture" is used.

The writer fully realizes the character of the data on which this table is based. The fact that there was a feeling in 1840 when the census enumerators for the first time gathered agricultural statistics, in which were included the value of household or family-made goods, that the government wished to tax each product, caused the returns in many instances to fall below their actual amount. On the other hand, there is little danger of overestimating the household industry as it existed during the three decades included in the table by the use of these returns; if they err it is in the matter of omissions rather than exaggerations. The chief fact shown by the combined returns is the gradual diminishing of the per capita output of the family factory. If one grants that the returns in one decade were about as accurate as in another, the decline in the output of the family factory is certainly demonstrated by the table.

† Counties in Maine and New Hampshire not in existence in 1840: *Maine:* Androscoggin, Knox, and Sagadahoc, with a per capita value in 1860, in the order named, of $0.43, $0.91, and $0.58; *New Hampshire:* Belknap and Carroll, with a per capita value in 1850 of $1.00 and $1.73; in 1860 of $0.11 and $0.47.

TABLE XVIII—*Continued*

Counties	Total Valuation			Population			Per Capita Value		
	1840	1850	1860	1840	1850	1860	1840	1850	1860
MASSACHUSETTS									
Barnstable	$13,010	$ 3,682	........*	32,548	35,276	35,990	$0.40	$0.10	......
Berkshire	36,476	8,557	$11,094	41,745	49,591	55,120	0.87	0.17	$0.20
Bristol	12,673	6,990	35,065	60,164	76,192	93,794	0.22	0.09	0.37
Dukes	2,575	853	1,445	3,958	4,540	4,403	0.65	0.19	0.33
Essex	3,666	14,580	65	94,987	131,300	165,611	0.04	0.11	......
Franklin	59,524	56,929	13,713	28,812	30,870	31,434	2.07	1.84	0.44
Hampden	8,225	11,482	3,326	37,366	51,283	57,366	0.22	0.22	0.06
Hampshire	39,626	26,697	32,514	30,897	35,732	37,823	1.28	0.75	0.86
Middlesex	4,094	17,908	40,200	106,611	161,383	216,354	0.04	0.11	0.19
Nantucket	....	....	....	9,012	8,452	6,094	......	......	......
Norfolk	7,475	25,702	33,165	53,140	78,892	109,950	0.15	0.33	0.30
Plymouth	21,018	953	4,988	47,373	55,697	64,768	0.44	0.02	0.08
Suffolk	....	....	....	95,773	144,517	192,700	......	......	......
Worcester	23,580	31,000	70,311	95,313	130,789	159,659	0.25	0.24	0.44
CONNECTICUT									
Fairfield	19,139	984	2,754	49,917	59,775	77,476	0.38	0.02	0.04
Hartford	26,836	25,156	9,361	55,629	69,967	89,962	0.48	0.36	0.10
Litchfield	56,314	18,819	4,700	40,448	45,253	47,318	1.39	0.42	0.10
Middlesex	10,006	54,152	8,660	24,879	27,216	30,859	0.40	1.99	0.28
New Haven	42,603	73,439	8,104	48,619	65,588	97,345	0.88	1.12	0.08
New London	15,934	1,780	2,889	44,463	51,821	61,731	0.36	0.03	0.05
Tolland	26,289	5,200	7,647	17,980	20,091	20,709	1.46	0.26	0.37
Windham	29,041	12,722	4,839	28,080	31,081	34,747	1.03	0.41	0.14

RHODE ISLAND

Bristol	56	56	....	6,476	8,514	8,907	0.01	0.01	......
Kent	4,850	2,465	....	13,083	15,068	17,303	0.37	0.16	......
Newport	10,931	5,100	2,755	16,874	20,007	21,896	0.65	0.25	0.13
Providence	19,831	12,245	4,476	58,073	87,526	107,799	0.34	0.14	0.04
Washington	15,512	6,629	593	14,324	16,430	18,715	1.08	0.40	0.03

NEW YORK

Albany	60,386	22,112	9,182	68,593	93,279	113,917	0.88	0.24	0.08
Alleghany	87,581	64,924	14,817	40,975	37,808	41,881	2.14	1.72	0.35
Broome	36,354	17,947	8,965	22,338	30,660	35,906	1.63	0.59	0.25
Cattaraugus	101,851	48,455	19,548	28,872	38,950	43,886	3.53	1.24	0.45
Cayuga	103,430	23,117	11,439	50,338	55,458	55,767	2.05	0.42	0.21
Chautauqua	1,313,522	45,962	18,258	47,975	50,493	58,422	27.38	0.91	0.31
Chemung	32,876	11,120	3,719	20,732	28,821	26,917	1.59	0.39	0.14
Chenango	77,297	30,798	20,303	40,785	40,311	40,934	1.90	1.76	0.50
Clinton	49,327	36,978	10,222	28,157	40,047	45,735	1.75	0.92	0.22
Columbia	31,282	17,054	5,057	43,252	43,073	47,172	0.72	0.40	0.11
Cortland	87,945	21,173	11,182	24,607	25,140	26,294	3.57	0.84	0.43
Delaware	68,146	46,671	22,833	35,396	39,834	42,465	1.93	1.17	0.54
Dutchess	43,204	8,183	2,241	52,398	58,992	64,941	0.82	0.14	0.03
Erie	75,878	44,776	23,627	62,465	100,993	141,971	1.21	0.44	0.17
Essex	55,155	5,396	21,832	23,634	31,148	28,214	2.33	0.17	0.75
Franklin	48,528	18,781	23,007	16,518	25,102	30,837	2.91	0.75	0.75
Fulton	25,821	6,811	1,517	18,049	20,171	24,162	1.43	0.34	0.06
Genesee	105,215	17,749	13,375	59,587	28,488	32,189	1.77	0.62	0.42
Greene	26,419	8,525	3,910	30,446	33,126	31,930	0.87	0.26	0.12
Hamilton	4,972	6,969	1,638	1,907	2,188	3,024	2.61	3.19	0.54

* Blank spaces indicate that the census returns do not give this information. In most cases it is probable that there was nothing to report.

TABLE XVIII—*Continued*

Counties	Total Valuation			Population			Per Capita Value		
	1840	1850	1860	1840	1850	1860	1840	1850	1860
NEW YORK—*Continued*									
Herkimer	$ 67,271	$16,417	$19,630	37,477	38,244	40,561	$1.79	$0.43	$0.48
Jefferson	123,528	80,110	34,072	60,984	68,153	69,825	2.03	1.18	0.49
Kings	1,699	....	....	47,613	138,882	279,122	0.04	.....	.....
Lewis	25,253	15,971	10,606	17,830	24,564	28,580	1.42	0.65	0.37
Livingston	58,842	14,158	23,345	35,140	40,875	39,546	1.67	0.35	0.59
Madison	55,279	25,013	14,826	40,008	43,072	43,545	1.38	0.59	0.34
Monroe	79,688	15,764	7,134	64,902	87,650	100,648	1.23	0.18	0.07
Montgomery	39,435	17,841	4,616	35,818	31,992	30,866	1.10	0.56	0.15
New York	....	....	....	312,710	515,547	813,669	.....	.....	.....
Niagara	41,741	25,234	15,867	31,132	42,276	50,399	1.34	0.60	0.31
Oneida	124,162	37,696	18,160	85,310	99,566	105,202	1.46	0.38	0.17
Onandaga	97,236	24,430	10,394	67,911	85,890	90,686	1.43	0.28	0.11
Ontario	62,064	13,013	3,734	43,501	43,929	44,563	1.43	0.30	0.08
Orange	36,188	3,901	530	50,739	57,145	63,812	0.71	0.07	0.01
Orleans	68,126	13,234	3,036	25,127	28,501	28,717	2.71	0.46	0.11
Oswego	81,745	50,132	40,310	43,619	62,198	75,958	1.87	0.81	0.53
Otsego	119,507	32,271	14,771	49,628	48,638	50,157	2.41	0.66	0.29
Putnam	8,654	2,064	1,731	12,825	14,138	14,002	0.67	0.15	0.12
Queens	2,857	767	....	30,324	36,833	57,391	0.09	0.02	.....
Rensselaer	69,942	9,458	3,962	60,259	73,363	86,328	1.16	0.12	0.05
Richmond	1,279	....	....	10,965	15,061	25,492	0.12	.....	.....
Rockland	2,400	204	22	11,975	16,962	22,492	0.20	0.01	0.00

St. Lawrence	136,635	82,812	47,483	56,706	68,617	83,689	2.41	1.21	0.57
Saratoga	95,926	20,721	5,453	40,553	45,646	51,729	2.37	0.45	0.11
Schenectady	17,781	1,971	2,609	17,387	20,054	20,002	1.02	0.10	0.13
Schoharie	60,260	26,093	13,525	32,358	33,548	34,469	1.86	0.78	0.39
Seneca	19,735	3,904	1,015	24,874	25,441	28,138	0.79	0.15	0.04
Steuben	92,387	76,287	89,300	46,138	63,771	66,690	2.00	1.20	1.34
Suffolk	49,488	5,677	1,050	32,469	36,922	43,275	1.52	0.15	0.02
Sullivan	22,925	10,546	6,076	15,629	25,088	32,385	1.47	0.42	0.19
Tioga	37,370	13,158	7,892	20,527	24,880	28,748	1.82	0.53	0.27
Tompkins	52,037	20,942	4,724	37,948	38,746	31,409	1.37	0.54	0.15
Ulster	90,669	21,689	7,503	45,822	59,384	76,381	1.98	0.37	0.10
Warren	29,939	10,330	8,943	13,422	17,199	21,434	2.23	0.61	0.42
Washington	41,041	9,870	4,873	41,080	44,750	45,904	1.00	0.22	0.11
Wayne	88,051	31,287	11,686	42,057	44,953	47,762	2.09	0.70	0.24
Westchester	45,770	8,555	323	48,686	58,263	99,497	0.94	0.15	0.00
Yates	154,448	6,283	4,592	20,444	20,590	20,290	7.55	0.31	0.23
PENNSYLVANIA									
Adams	7,313	3,068	3,178	23,044	25,981	28,006	0.32	0.12	0.11
Allegheny	11,431	11,514	4,307	81,235	138,290	178,831	0.14	0.08	0.02
Armstrong	51,152	15,520	7,379	28,365	29,560	35,797	1.80	0.53	0.21
Beaver	36,301	14,517	5,893	29,368	26,689	29,140	1.24	0.54	0.20
Bedford	10,544	5,621	12,193	29,335	23,052	26,736	0.36	0.24	0.46
Berks	12,515	21,175	5,377	64,569	77,129	93,818	0.19	0.27	0.06
Bradford	55,652	39,858	17,271	32,769	42,831	48,734	1.70	0.93	0.35
Bucks	23,587	14,862	3,436	48,107	56,091	63,578	0.49	0.26	0.05
Butler	78,016	31,166	16,092	22,378	30,346	35,594	3.49	1.03	0.45
Cambria	6,173	9,970	6,884	11,256	17,773	29,155	0.55	0.56	0.24
Center	8,690	5,472	635	20,492	23,355	27,000	0.42	0.23	0.02

TABLE XVIII—*Continued*

Counties	Total Valuation			Population			Per Capita Value		
	1840	1850	1860	1840	1850	1860	1840	1850	1860
PENNSYLVANIA—*Continued*									
Chester	$11,224	$ 4,013	$ 3,706	57,515	66,438	74,578	$0.20	$0.06	$0.05
Clearfield	642	7,701	2,149	7,834	12,586	18,759	0.08	0.61	0.11
Clinton	3,046	693	....	8,323	11,207	17,723	2.73	0.06	.....
Columbia	18,710	14,202	5,453	24,267	17,710	25,065	0.77	0.80	0.22
Crawford	38,695	32,802	31,692	31,724	37,849	48,755	1.22	0.87	0.65
Cumberland	24,666	5,416	8,597	30,953	34,327	40,098	0.80	0.16	0.21
Dauphin	13,330	3,793	54,234	30,118	35,754	46,756	0.44	0.11	1.16
Delaware	283	2,226	92	19,791	24,679	30,597	0.01	0.09	0.00
Erie	74,459	28,581	7,807	31,344	38,742	49,432	2.38	0.74	0.16
Fayette	37,378	24,374	10,028	33,574	39,112	39,909	1.11	0.62	0.25
Franklin	21,766	4,245	18,222	37,793	39,904	42,126	0.58	0.11	0.44
Greene	43,689	27,340	15,286	19,147	22,136	24,343	2.28	1.24	0.63
Huntingdon	9,652	10,582	673	35,484	24,786	28,100	0.27	0.43	0.02
Indiana	30,053	31,182	22,315	20,782	27,170	33,687	1.45	1.15	0.66
Jefferson	8,382	5,126	8,363	7,253	13,518	18,270	1.16	0.38	0.46
Juniata	10,664	....	2,163	11,080	13,029	16,986	0.96	.....	0.13
Lancaster	14,360	14,056	6,413	84,203	98,944	116,314	0.17	0.14	0.06
Lebanon	9,722	3,267	3,217	21,872	26,071	31,831	0.44	0.13	0.10
Lehigh	18,007	9,316	7,311	25,787	32,479	43,753	0.70	0.29	0.17
Luzerne	64,672	17,883	11,411	44,006	56,072	90,244	1.47	0.32	0.13
Lycoming	19,333	2,260	1,653	22,649	26,257	37,399	0.85	0.09	0.04
McKean	4,382	1,759	3,879	2,975	5,254	8,859	1.47	0.34	0.44

Mercer	41,403	19,712	13,297	32,873	33,172	36,856	1.26	0.59	0.36
Mifflin	2,641	742	....	13,092	14,980	16,340	0.22	0.05	......
Monroe	5,716	6,057	3,088	9,879	13,270	16,758	0.58	0.46	0.18
Montgomery	13,643	8,360	6,662	47,241	58,291	70,500	0.29	0.14	0.09
Northampton	32,199	252	1,810	40,996	40,235	47,904	0.79	0.01	0.04
Northumberland	14,213	8,280	1,112	20,027	23,272	28,922	0.71	0.36	0.04
Perry	20,934	11,518	7,332	17,096	20,088	22,793	1.22	0.57	0.32
Philadelphia	169	156	764	258,037	408,762	565,529	0.00	0.00	0.00
Pike	4,475	175	30	3,832	5,881	7,155	1.17	0.03	0.00
Potter	6,509	9,829	10,811	3,371	6,048	11,470	1.93	1.63	0.94
Schuylkill	9,311	2,976	8,486	29,053	60,713	89,510	0.32	0.05	0.09
Somerset	71,070	26,887	37,927	19,650	24,416	26,778	3.62	1.10	1.42
Susquehanna	53,680	39,084	17,378	21,195	28,688	36,267	2.53	1.36	0.48
Tioga	32,140	13,462	8,146	15,498	23,987	31,044	2.07	0.56	0.26
Union	15,364	4,362	237	22,787	26,083	14,145	0.67	0.17	0.02
Venango	28,112	14,045	12,746	17,900	18,310	25,043	1.57	0.77	0.51
Warren	13,344	10,758	3,297	9,278	13,671	19,190	1.44	0.79	0.17
Washington	43,844	24,724	36,711	41,279	44,939	46,805	1.06	0.55	0.78
Wayne	5,792	10,051	2,910	11,848	21,890	32,239	0.49	0.46	0.09
Westmoreland	79,159	51,616	30,006	42,699	51,726	53,736	1.85	1.00	0.56
York	30,946	7,463	12,819	47,010	57,450	68,200	0.66	0.13	0.19

NEW JERSEY

Atlantic	4,131	9,411	511	8,726	8,960	11,786	0.47	1.05	0.04
Bergen	9,259	213	....	13,223	14,684	21,618	0.70	0.02	......
Burlington	8,201	433	375	32,831	43,203	49,730	0.25	0.01	0.01
Cape May	3,344	1,425	1,340	5,324	6,433	7,130	0.63	0.22	0.19
Cumberland	7,810	3,172	602	14,374	17,189	22,605	0.54	0.18	0.03

TABLE XVIII—*Continued*

Counties	Total Valuation			Population			Per Capita Value		
	1840	1850	1860	1840	1850	1860	1840	1850	1860
NEW JERSEY—*Continued*									
Essex	$ 6,471	$ 864	$ 120	44,621	73,944	98,877	$0.15	$0.01	$0.00
Gloucester	5,971	624	......	25,438	14,655	18,444	0.23	0.04	......
Hudson	377	......	345	9,843	21,819	62,717	0.04	......	0.01
Hunterdon	29,835	5,428	2,994	24,789	28,981	33,650	1.20	0.19	0.09
Mercer	3,003	471	......	21,502	27,986	37,419	0.14	0.02	......
Middlesex	2,823	763	3,079	21,893	28,624	34,811	0.13	0.03	0.09
Monmouth	7,617	17,375	250	32,909	30,238	39,346	0.23	0.57	0.01
Morris	29,695	16,302	3,777	25,844	30,139	34,676	1.15	0.54	0.11
Passaic	6,230	1,116	20	16,734	22,538	29,011	0.37	0.05	0.00
Salem	6,643	427	2,166	16,024	19,467	22,458	0.41	0.02	0.10
Somerset	18,125	29,860	990	17,455	19,661	22,048	1.04	1.52	0.04
Sussex	32,667	9,647	1,220	21,770	22,988	23,846	1.50	0.42	0.05
Warren	19,423	13,174	4,437	20,366	22,356	28,432	0.95	0.59	0.16
DELAWARE									
Kent	28,171	8,443	3,021	19,872	22,816	27,804	1.42	0.37	0.11
New Castle	1,380	50	59	33,120	42,780	54,797	0.04	0.00	0.00
Sussex	32,565	29,628	14,511	25,093	25,936	29,615	1.30	1.14	0.49

MARYLAND

Alleghany	13,098	9,397	9,178	15,690	22,769	28,348	0.83	0.41	0.32
Anne Arundel	25,895	2,885	....	29,532	32,393	23,900	0.88	0.09	......
Baltimore	3,408	10	190	134,379	210,646	266,553	0.03	0.00	0.00
Calvert	8,446	5,941	1,717	9,229	9,646	10,447	0.92	0.62	0.16
Caroline	4,348	593	10	7,806	9,692	11,129	0.56	0.06	0.00
Carroll	8,723	3,303	1,066	17,241	20,616	24,533	0.50	0.16	0.04
Cecil	4,186	634	258	17,232	18,939	23,862	0.24	0.03	0.01
Charles	4,483	13,408	10,108	16,023	16,162	16,517	0.28	0.83	0.61
Dorchester	9,104	3,287	1,846	18,843	18,877	20,461	0.48	0.17	0.09
Frederick	21,460	2,384	1,478	36,405	40,987	46,591	0.59	0.06	0.03
Harford	7,817	5,051	1,174	17,120	19,356	23,415	0.46	0.26	0.05
Kent	9,013	400	112	10,842	11,386	13,267	0.83	0.04	0.01
Montgomery	8,274	9,802	12,455	15,456	15,860	18,322	0.55	0.62	0.68
Prince George	4,861	3,331	....	19,539	21,549	23,327	0.25	0.15	......
Queen Anne	2,574	1,820	....	12,633	14,484	15,961	0.20	0.13	......
Saint Mary	8,434	14,095	5,989	13,224	13,698	15,213	0.64	1.03	0.39
Somerset	14,458	11,115	7,084	19,508	22,456	24,992	0.74	0.49	0.28
Talbot	5,551	2,154	153	12,090	13,811	14,795	0.46	0.16	0.01
Washington	5,446	....	140	28,850	30,848	31,417	0.19	......	0.04
Worcester*	6,471	22,218	13,338	18,377	18,859	20,661	0.35	1.18	0.65

* Counties in the Middle States and Maryland not in existence in 1840: *New York:* Schuyler and Wyoming with a per capita value of $0.95 in 1860 for the former and $0.91 in 1850 and $0.30 in 1860 for the latter; *Pennsylvania:* the following counties with per capita values in 1850 and 1860—Blair, $0.08, $0.03; Carbon, $0.01, $0.02; Clarion, $0.71, $0.07; Elk, $3.01, $0.00; Fulton, $0.47, $0.26; Lawrence, $0.12, $0.05; Montour, $0.61, $0.06; Sullivan, $1.56, $0.82; Wyoming, $0.57, $0.57; and Forest and Snyder with per capita values in 1860 only of $0.21 and $0.16; *New Jersey:* Camden and Ocean with per capita values in 1850 of $0.01 and $0.19; in 1860 of $0.01 and $0.46; Union, 1860 only of $....; *Maryland:* Howard, with a per capita value in 1860 of $0.05.

TABLE XVIII—*Continued*

Counties	Total Valuation			Population			Per Capita Value		
	1840	1850	1860	1840	1850	1860	1840	1850	1860
VIRGINIA									
Accomack	$38,937	$23,712	$ 2,169	17,096	17,890	18,586	$2.28	$1.33	$0.12
Albermarle	55,251	33,200	19,490	22,924	25,800	26,625	2.41	1.29	0.73
Alleghany	5,823	6,586	4,550	2,749	3,515	6,765	2.12	1.87	0.67
Amelia	15,167	13,856	5,193	10,320	9,770	10,741	1.47	1.42	0.48
Amherst	31,405	14,982	5,736	12,576	12,699	13,742	2.50	1.18	0.42
Augusta	5,411	13,314	16,024	19,628	24,610	27,749	0.28	0.54	0.58
Bath	23,597	10,360	7,523	4,300	3,426	3,676	5.49	3.02	2.05
Bedford	24,257	55,450	29,226	20,203	24,080	25,068	1.10	2.30	1.17
Berkeley	7,540	512	....	10,972	11,771	12,525	0.69	0.04	.....
Botetourt	14,745	15,870	5,236	11,679	14,908	11,516	1.26	1.07	0.45
Braxton	5,929	17,560	7,652	2,575	4,212	4,992	2.30	4.17	1.53
Brooke	6,085	819	....	7,948	5,054	5,494	0.77	0.16	.....
Brunswick	13,213	35,241	12,745	14,346	13,894	14,809	0.92	2.54	0.86
Buckingham	46,081	21,559	12,534	18,786	13,837	15,212	2.45	1.56	0.82
Cabell	28,621	11,083	4,518	8,163	6,299	8,020	3.26	1.76	0.56
Campbell	32,389	21,122	28,451	21,030	23,245	26,197	1.54	0.91	1.09
Caroline	28,419	36,292	12,291	17,813	18,456	18,464	1.60	1.97	0.67
Charles City	3,414	3,509	100	4,774	5,200	5,609	0.72	0.67	0.02
Charlotte	57,958	40,463	12,919	14,595	13,955	14,471	3.97	2.90	0.89
Chesterfield	5,586	8,214	4,277	17,148	17,489	19,016	0.33	0.47	0.22
Clarke	9,308	2,369	....	6,353	7,352	7,146	1.47	0.32	.....
Culpeper	30,911	21,306	5,071	11,393	12,282	12,063	2.71	1.73	0.42

Cumberland	24,608	20,955	8,586	10,399	9,751	9,961	2.37	2.15	0.86
Dinwiddie	11,938	25,000	5,123	22,558	25,118	30,198	0.53	1.00	0.17
Elizabeth City	1,700	......	......	3,706	4,586	5,798	0.46	......	......
Essex	35,167	15,541	12,554	11,309	10,206	10,469	3.11	1.52	1.20
Fairfax	5,127	4,676	834	9,370	10,682	11,834	0.55	0.44	0.07
Fauquier	60,458	23,147	9,311	21,897	20,868	21,706	2.76	1.11	0.43
Fayette	9,846	14,705	13,787	3,924	3,955	5,997	2.51	3.72	2.30
Floyd	9,977	13,085	16,505	4,453	6,458	8,236	2.24	2.03	2.00
Fluvanna	12,506	10,851	5,370	8,812	9,487	10,353	1.42	1.14	0.52
Franklin	23,737	30,430	30,736	15,832	17,430	20,098	1.50	1.75	1.53
Frederick	7,077	7,376	4,203	14,242	15,975	16,546	0.50	0.46	0.25
Giles	18,442	21,274	11,961	5,307	6,570	6,883	3.48	3.24	1.74
Gloucester	18,988	29,104	5,695	10,715	10,527	10,956	1.77	2.76	0.52
Goochland	13,946	15,164	3,678	9,760	10,352	10,656	1.43	1.46	0.35
Grayson	12,480	20,324	28,492	9,087	6,677	8,252	1.37	3.04	3.45
Greenbrier	27,283	22,526	25,643	8,695	10,022	12,211	3.14	2.25	2.10
Greene	25,296	8,033	6,129	4,232	4,400	5,022	5.98	1.83	1.22
Greenville	11,059	7,641	6,433	6,366	5,639	6,374	1.74	1.36	1.01
Halifax	97,799	104,946	57,970	25,936	25,962	26,520	3.77	4.04	2.19
Hampshire	21,468	31,839	22,756	12,295	14,036	13,913	1.75	2.27	1.64
Hanover	12,015	15,675	5,684	14,968	15,153	17,222	0.80	1.03	0.33
Hardy	19,030	24,993	10,256	7,622	9,543	9,864	2.50	2.62	1.04
Harrison	44,230	27,243	7,889	17,669	11,728	13,790	2.50	2.32	0.57
Henrico	3,184	1,463	1,042	33,076	43,572	61,616	0.10	0.03	0.02
Henry	18,702	15,743	15,537	7,335	8,872	12,105	2.55	1.77	1.28
Isle of Wight	13,305	8,882	6,378	9,972	9,353	9,977	1.33	0.95	0.64
James City	2,301	544	1,196	3,779	4,020	5,798	0.61	0.14	0.21
Jefferson	5,672	546	7,825	14,082	15,357	14,535	0.40	0.04	0.54
Kanawha	8,846	12,673	1,382	13,567	15,353	16,150	0.65	0.83	0.09
King and Queen	30,986	14,541	12,658	10,862	10,319	10,328	2.85	1.41	1.23
King George	1,290	5,432	2,350	5,927	5,971	6,571	0.22	0.91	0.36

TABLE XVIII—*Continued*

Counties	Total Valuation			Population			Per Capita Value		
	1840	1850	1860	1840	1850	1860	1840	1850	1860
				VIRGINIA—*Continued*					
King William	$32,111	$ 6,671	$11,700	9,258	8,779	8,530	$3.47	$0.76	$1.37
Lancaster	4,064	3,265	10,714	4,628	4,708	5,151	0.88	0.69	2.08
Lee	37,697	28,060	17,986	8,441	10,267	11,032	4.47	2.73	1.63
Lewis	28,411	18,700	10,142	8,151	10,031	7,999	4.89	1.86	1.27
Logan	8,344	13,301	12,474	4,309	3,620	4,938	1.94	3.67	2.53
Louisa	55,426	28,093	10,176	15,433	16,691	16,701	3.59	1.68	0.61
Jackson	....	17,900	8,908	4,890	6,544	8,306	.....	2.74	1.07
Loudon	33,310	4,171	4,258	20,431	22,079	21,774	1.63	0.19	0.20
Lunenburg	17,650	18,347	20,168	11,055	11,692	11,983	1.60	1.57	1.02
Madison	27,755	31,079	12,122	8,107	9,331	8,854	3.42	3.33	1.37
Marshall	6,779	8,171	7,602	6,937	10,138	12,997	0.98	0.81	0.58
Mason	14,519	11,136	3,670	6,777	7,539	9,173	2.14	1.48	0.40
Matthews	10,205	5,097	5,350	7,442	6,714	7,091	1.37	0.76	0.75
Mecklenburg	31,633	35,423	24,427	20,724	20,630	20,096	1.53	1.72	1.22
Mercer	9,214	14,204	30,885	2,233	4,222	6,819	4.13	3.36	4.53
Middlesex	7,722	7,092	3,212	4,392	4,394	4,364	1.74	1.61	0.74
Monongalia	34,054	17,946	13,290	17,368	12,387	13,048	1.96	1.45	1.02
Monroe	26,668	33,408	20,335	8,422	10,204	10,757	3.17	3.27	1.89
Montgomery	25,143	13,871	8,248	7,405	8,359	10,617	3.39	1.66	0.78
Morgan	4,858	2,226	2,190	4,253	3,557	3,732	1.14	0.63	0.59
Nansemond	5,536	15,941	5,853	10,795	12,283	13,693	0.51	1.30	0.43
Nelson	14,964	13,981	6,016	12,287	12,758	13,015	1.22	1.10	0.46

New Kent	5,353	6,330	1,875	6,230	6,064	5,884	0.86	1.04	0.32
Nicholas	11,673	11,533	24,543	2,515	3,963	4,627	4.64	2.91	5.30
Norfolk	8,620	2,837	1,315	27,569	33,036	36,227	0.31	0.09	0.04
Northampton	11,150	13,067	1,798	7,715	7,498	7,832	1.45	1.74	0.23
Northumberland	7,750	7,802	5,264	7,924	7,346	7,531	0.98	1.06	0.70
Nottoway	12,874	10,005	5,241	9,719	8,437	8,836	1.32	1.19	0.59
Ohio	2,646	1,120	....	13,357	18,006	22,422	0.20	0.06	.....
Orange	33,852	12,766	6,122	9,125	10,067	10,851	3.71	1.27	0.56
Page	13,792	13,200	9,828	6,194	7,600	8,109	2.23	1.74	1.21
Patrick	23,030	20,802	13,644	8,032	9,609	9,359	2.87	2.16	1.46
Pendleton	18,769	17,598	14,614	6,940	5,795	6,164	2.70	3.04	2.37
Pittsylvania	97,090	51,251	32,137	26,398	28,796	32,104	3.68	1.78	1.00
Pocahontas	15,856	17,941	14,846	2,922	3,598	3,958	5.43	4.99	3.75
Powhatan	8,826	8,065	8,426	7,924	8,178	8,392	1.11	0.99	1.00
Preston	21,544	20,813	20,088	6,866	11,708	13,312	3.14	1.78	1.51
Prince Edward	59,456	3,794	11,452	14,069	11,857	11,844	4.23	0.32	0.97
Prince George	6,125	5,067	2,560	7,175	7,596	8,411	0.85	0.67	0.30
Prince William	6,106	5,213	2,863	8,144	8,129	8,565	0.75	0.64	0.33
Princess Anne	13,119	9,987	4,535	7,285	7,669	7,714	1.80	1.36	0.59
Pulaski	18,878	17,202	12,372	3,739	5,118	5,416	5.05	3.36	2.28
Randolph	18,585	13,872	10,594	6,208	5,243	4,990	2.99	2.65	2.12
Rappahannock	36,603	16,890	7,109	9,257	9,782	8,850	3.95	1.73	0.80
Richmond	7,064	6,688	3,443	5,965	6,448	6,856	1.18	1.04	0.50
Roanoke	11,324	10,451	1,900	5,499	8,447	8,048	2.06	1.24	0.24
Rockbridge	61,682	22,018	53,617	14,284	16,045	17,248	4.32	1.37	3.11
Rockingham	67,901	26,584	13,973	17,344	20,294	23,408	3.91	1.31	0.60
Russell	20,118	37,676	29,937	7,878	11,919	10,280	2.55	3.16	2.91
Scott	20,625	20,115	30,386	7,303	9,829	12,072	2.79	2.05	2.52
Shenandoah	27,917	7,689	6,676	11,618	13,768	13,896	2.40	0.56	0.48
Smyth	18,753	21,029	12,560	6,522	8,162	8,952	3.88	2.58	1.40
Southampton	20,619	22,325	8,084	14,525	13,521	12,915	1.42	1.65	0.63

TABLE XVIII—*Continued*

Counties	Total Valuation			Population			Per Capita Value		
	1840	1850	1860	1840	1850	1860	1840	1850	1860
VIRGINIA—*Continued*									
Spottsylvania	$22,508	$12,204	$ 5,439	15,161	14,911	16,076	$1.48	$0.82	$0.34
Stafford	12,614	7,081	2,286	8,454	8,044	8,555	1.49	0.88	0.27
Surry	8,431	5,048	1,177	6,480	5,679	6,133	1.30	0.89	0.19
Sussex	18,681	15,803	17,816	11,229	9,820	10,175	1.66	1.61	1.75
Tazewell	....	32,969	26,003	6,290	9,942	9,920	.....	3.32	2.62
Tyler	15,387	8,866	10,354	6,954	5,498	6,517	2.21	1.61	1.59
Warren	14,423	7,895	4,552	5,627	6,607	6,442	2.56	1.19	0.71
Warwick	8,720	1,032	700	1,456	1,546	1,740	5.99	0.67	0.40
Washington	33,905	31,545	27,341	13,001	14,612	16,891	2.61	2.16	1.62
Westmoreland	9,921	7,843	....	8,019	8,080	8,282	1.24	0.97	.....
Wood	17,909	13,077	6,366	7,923	9,450	11,046	2.26	1.38	0.58
Wythe	36,900	28,804	20,038	9,375	12,024	12,305	3.94	2.40	1.63
York*	....	3,981	1,890	4,720	4,460	4,949	.....	0.89	0.38
NORTH CAROLINA									
Anson	34,231	45,787	21,479	15,077	13,489	13,664	2.27	3.39	1.57
Ashe	20,310	58,302	38,461	7,467	8,777	7,956	2.72	6.64	5.00
Beaufort	29,078	18,351	15,784	12,225	13,816	14,766	2.38	1.33	1.07
Bertie	20,957	15,880	25,378	12,175	12,851	14,310	1.72	1.24	1.77

Bladen	12,726	45,123	56,028	8,022	9,767	11,995	1.59	4.62	4.67
Brunswick	2,118	12,920	8,799	5,265	7,272	8,406	0.40	1.78	1.05
Buncombe	63,373	93,312	51,004	10,084	13,425	12,654	6.28	6.95	4.03
Burke	51,054	14,591	12,179	15,799	7,772	9,237	3.23	1.88	1.32
Cabarras	41,462	14,698	11,898	9,259	9,747	10,546	4.48	1.51	1.13
Camden	....	10,586	6,010	5,663	6,049	5,343	......	1.75	1.12
Carteret	2,986	4,159	1,735	6,591	6,939	8,186	0.45	0.60	0.21
Caswell	31,833	39,849	17,643	14,693	15,269	16,215	2.17	2.61	1.09
Chatham	39,594	48,425	88,983	16,242	18,449	19,101	2.44	2.62	4.66
Cherokee	12,706	18,306	32,907	3,427	3,385	9,166	3.71	5.41	3.59
Chowan	11,863	7,884	6,044	6,690	10,174	6,842	1.77	0.77	0.88
Columbus	7,244	11,365	57,032	3,941	5,909	8,597	1.84	1.92	6.63
Craven	12,725	8,986	17,148	13,438	14,709	16,268	0.95	0.61	1.05
Cumberland	7,120	31,671	9,590	15,284	20,616	16,369	0.46	1.54	0.59
Currituck	13,305	13,630	10,068	6,703	7,236	7,415	1.98	1.88	1.36
Davidson	38,433	53,044	23,190	14,606	15,320	16,601	2.63	3.46	1.40
Davie	16,613	24,348	14,043	7,574	7,866	8,494	2.19	3.10	1.65
Duplin	13,035	36,435	67,019	11,182	13,514	15,784	1.17	2.70	4.25
Edgecomb	13,699	25,495	80,997	15,708	17,189	17,376	0.87	1.48	4.66
Franklin	23,963	17,839	23,855	10,980	11,713	14,107	2.18	1.52	1.69
Gates	7,361	12,045	6,522	8,161	8,426	8,443	0.90	1.43	0.77
Granville	28,912	28,213	23,755	18,817	21,249	23,396	1.54	1.33	1.02
Greene	20,920	14,361	14,400	6,595	6,619	7,925	3.17	2.17	1.82
Guilford	7,497	53,594	25,306	19,175	19,754	20,056	0.39	2.71	1.26
Halifax	23,346	18,206	23,339	16,865	16,589	19,442	1.38	1.10	1.20
Haywood	8,605	30,027	28,590	4,975	7,074	5,801	1.73	4.24	4.93

* Counties not in existence in 1840 with per capita values in each in 1850 and 1860: Alexandria, \$...., \$....; Appomattox, \$2.00, \$5.19; Barbour, \$2.90, \$1.82; Boone, \$4.25, \$1.73; Carroll, \$3.11, \$2.12; Doddridge, \$1.63, \$0.96; Gilmer, \$2.55, \$2.32; Hancock, \$0.32, \$....; Highland, \$2.85, \$1.99; Marion, \$2.27, \$1.11; Putnam, \$2.37, \$5.82; Raleigh, \$2.84, \$2.10; Ritchie, \$2.06, \$1.39; Taylor, \$2.96, \$0.74; Wayne, \$3.27, \$1.73; Wetzel, \$2.55, \$1.13; Wirt, \$2.07, \$1.61; Wyoming, \$3.84, \$2.19; and Buchanan, Calhoun, Clay, Craig, McDowell, Pleasants, Roane, Tucker, Upshur, Webster, and Wise with per capita values in 1860 only, in order named, of \$1.84, \$2.42, \$2.98, \$2.96, \$1.86, \$0.88, \$1.17, \$2.25, \$2.41, \$2.09, and \$2.22.

TABLE XVIII—*Continued*

Counties	Total Valuation			Population			Per Capita Value		
	1840	1850	1860	1840	1850	1860	1840	1850	1860
NORTH CAROLINA—*Continued*									
Henderson	$ 6,765	$17,941	$22,157	5,129	6,853	10,448	$1.32	$2.62	$2.11
Hertford	....	17,678	20,932	7,484	8,142	9,504	......	2.17	2.20
Hyde	24,803	3,734	....	6,458	7,636	7,732	3.84	0.49	......
Iredell	56,552	55,433	29,408	15,685	14,719	15,347	3.61	3.77	1.92
Johnson	35,221	61,465	28,756	10,599	13,726	15,656	3.32	4.48	1.84
Jones	11,076	8,058	6,889	4,945	5,038	5,730	2.24	1.60	1.20
Lenoir	15,870	14,979	10,767	7,605	7,828	10,220	2.09	1.91	1.05
Lincoln	54,925	18,062	18,493	25,160	7,746	8,195	2.18	2.33	2.26
Macon	17,972	33,187	51,870	4,869	6,389	6,004	3.67	5.19	8.64
Martin	8,568	14,005	6,770	7,637	8,307	10,195	1.12	1.69	0.66
Mecklenburg	32,768	17,624	10,927	18,273	13,914	17,374	1.79	1.27	0.63
Montgomery	22,938	15,741	35,102	10,780	6,872	7,649	2.13	2.29	4.59
Moore	9,350	20,956	34,135	7,988	9,342	11,427	1.17	2.24	2.99
Nash	1,295	30,244	19,682	9,047	10,651	11,687	0.14	2.84	1.68
New Hanover	19,472	137	8,619	13,312	17,668	15,429	1.46	0.01	0.56
Northampton	25,825	14,183	15,993	13,369	13,335	13,372	1.93	1.06	1.20
Onslow	17,209	11,264	24,682	7,527	8,283	8,856	2.29	1.36	2.78
Orange	2,785	44,202	19,367	24,356	17,055	16,947	0.11	1.14	1.14
Pasquotank	6,718	10,715	5,544	8,514	8,950	8,940	0.79	1.20	0.62
Perquimans	17,970	12,617	7,744	7,346	7,332	7,238	2.45	1.72	1.07
Person	12,823	24,309	18,392	9,790	10,781	11,221	1.31	2.25	1.64
Pitt	9,330	33,454	22,945	11,806	13,397	16,080	0.79	2.50	1.43

Randolf	24,883	27,366	47,299	12,875	15,832	16,793	1.93	1.73	2.83
Richmond	20,211	16,048	13,187	8,909	9,818	11,009	2.27	1.63	1.20
Robeson	19,329	37,348	38,017	10,370	12,826	15,489	1.86	2.91	2.45
Rockingham	12,102	23,224	16,262	13,442	14,495	16,746	0.90	1.60	0.97
Rowan	....	37,658	10,827	12,109	13,870	14,589	......	2.72	0.74
Rutherford	22,105	33,486	21,158	19,202	13,550	11,573	1.15	2.47	1.83
Sampson	14,433	26,925	46,265	12,157	14,585	16,624	1.19	1.85	2.78
Stokes	32,687	16,226	19,577	16,265	9,206	10,402	2.01	1.76	1.88
Surry	63,510	40,037	24,717	15,079	18,443	10,380	4.21	2.17	2.35
Tyrrel	12,969	6,381	5,882	4,657	5,133	4,944	2.78	1.24	1.19
Wake	28,733	57,218	38,942	21,118	24,888	28,627	1.36	1.56	1.36
Warren	22,664	27,925	22,585	12,919	13,912	15,726	1.75	2.01	1.44
Washington	39,842	21,129	7,605	4,525	5,664	6,357	8.80	3.73	1.20
Wayne	29,036	26,893	18,957	10,891	13,486	14,905	2.67	1.99	1.28
Wilkes	38,746	69,148	35,804	12,577	12,099	14,749	3.08	5.72	2.43
Yancey*	4,688	64,279	43,316	5,962	8,205	8,655	0.79	7.83	5.00

SOUTH CAROLINA

Abbeville	21,248	71,774	37,186	29,351	32,318	32,385	0.72	2.22	1.15
Anderson	80,444	86,795	86,688	18,493	21,475	22,873	4.35	4.06	3.79
Barnwell	44,684	14,643	20,036	21,471	26,608	30,743	2.08	0.55	0.65
Beaufort	11,760	10,690	17,071	35,794	38,805	40,053	0.33	0.28	0.43
Charleston	1,220	17,799	1,376	82,661	72,805	70,100	0.01	0.24	0.02
Chester	52,565	22,405	10,455	17,747	18,038	18,122	2.96	1.24	0.58

* Counties not in existence in 1840 with the per capita values in each in 1850 and 1860: Alamance, $2.63, $1.07; Alexander, $2.45, $4.33; Caldwell, $2.12, $2.93; Catawba, $3.31, $2.30; Cleveland, $2.80, $2.18; Forsyth, $1.94, $1.43; Gaston, $3.47, $1.34; McDowell, $2.48, $2.51; Stanly, $3.11, $2.55; Union, $2.89, $2.89; Watauga, $5.12, $8.47; and Alleghany, Harnett, Jackson, Lillington, Madison, Polk, Wilson, and Yadkin, with per capita values in 1860 only, in the order named, $4.53, $2.01, $4.93, $...., $4.70, $3.85, $1.05, and $2.63.

TABLE XVIII—*Continued*

Counties	Total Valuation			Population			Per Capita Value		
	1840	1850	1860	1840	1850	1860	1840	1850	1860
SOUTH CAROLINA—*Continued*									
Chesterfield	$ 4,845	$45,080	$10,815	8,574	10,790	11,834	$0.57	$4.18	$0.91
Colleton	14,486	19,240	22,203	25,548	39,505	41,916	0.57	0.49	0.53
Darlington	28,293	12,070	535	14,822	16,830	20,361	1.91	0.72	0.03
Edgefield	124,877	94,468	36,269	32,852	39,262	39,887	3.80	2.41	0.91
Fairfield	16,528	16,360	11,789	20,165	21,404	22,111	0.82	0.76	0.53
Georgetown	550	....	25,120	18,274	20,647	21,305	0.03	.....	1.18
Greenville	30,554	28,625	35,663	17,839	20,156	21,892	1.71	1.42	1.63
Horry	13,493	24,555	27,401	5,755	7,646	7,962	2.34	3.21	3.44
Kershaw	8,255	7,686	19,091	12,281	14,473	13,086	0.67	0.53	1.46
Lancaster	26,370	19,590	22,435	9,907	10,988	11,797	2.66	1.78	1.90
Laurens	57,600	54,670	37,965	21,584	23,407	23,858	2.67	2.34	1.59
Lexington	29,031	17,458	24,341	12,111	12,930	15,579	2.40	1.35	1.56
Marion	35,483	40,634	69,267	13,932	17,407	21,190	2.55	2.33	3.27
Marlborough	20,078	32,674	10,280	8,408	10,789	12,434	2.39	3.03	0.83
Newberry	28,453	35,343	25,894	18,350	20,143	20,879	1.55	1.75	1.24
Orangeburgh	8,833	27,597	10,026	18,519	23,582	24,896	0.48	1.17	0.40
Pickens	50,647	68,599	49,879	14,356	16,904	19,639	3.53	4.06	2.54
Richland	6,172	4,442	1,425	16,397	20,243	18,307	0.38	0.22	0.08
Spartanburgh	76,197	39,078	49,823	23,669	26,400	26,919	3.22	1.48	1.85
Sumter	52,145	24,248	99,750	27,892	33,220	23,859	1.87	0.73	4.18
Union	41,851	41,897	17,391	18,936	19,852	19,635	2.21	2.11	0.89
Williamsburgh	17,648	12,825	205	10,327	12,447	15,489	1.71	1.03	0.01
York	26,393	18,290	32,412	18,383	19,433	21,502	1.44	0.94	1.51

GEORGIA

Appling	7,845	10,785	12,490	2,052	2,949	4,190	3.82	3.66	2.98
Baker	3,449	14,051	324	4,226	8,120	4,985	0.82	1.73	0.06
Baldwin	10,377	947	7,228	7,250	8,148	9,078	1.43	0.12	0.80
Bibb	2,950	7,456	1,383	9,802	12,699	16,291	0.30	0.59	0.08
Bryan	*	3,811	1,450	3,182	3,424	4,015	*	1.11	0.36
Bullock	4,213	8,441	11,854	3,102	4,300	5,668	0.14	1.96	2.09
Burke	9,214	5,673	2,479	13,176	16,100	17,165	0.70	0.35	0.14
Butts	32,190	9,715	9,866	5,308	6,488	6,455	6.06	1.50	1.53
Camden	752	....	....	6,075	6,319	5,420	0.12	......	......
Campbell	15,635	16,570	13,771	5,370	7,232	8,301	2.91	2.29	1.66
Carroll	17,448	27,316	12,923	5,252	9,357	11,991	3.32	2.92	1.08
Cass	33,075	19,070	15,025	9,390	13,300	15,724	3.52	1.43	0.96
Chattooga	10,824	17,872	11,601	3,438	6,815	7,165	3.15	2.62	1.62
Chatham	40	1,217	4,175	18,801	23,901	31,043	0.00	0.05	0.13
Cherokee	16,271	20,120	21,613	5,895	12,800	11,291	2.76	1.57	1.92
Clark	23,565	13,621	5,747	10,522	11,119	11,218	2.24	1.23	0.51
Cobb	20,432	55,438	22,351	7,539	13,843	14,242	2.71	4.00	1.57
Columbia	20,991	11,293	3,133	11,356	11,961	11,860	1.85	0.94	2.64
Coweta	19,733	25,477	13,770	10,364	13,635	14,703	1.90	1.87	0.94
Crawford	12,665	19,729	6,512	7,981	8,984	7,693	1.59	2.20	0.85
Dade	6,433	14,761	7,409	1,364	2,680	3,069	4.72	5.51	2.41
Decatur	18,762	13,720	8,989	5,872	8,262	11,922	3.20	1.66	0.75
De Kalb	14,727	32,284	9,869	10,467	14,328	7,806	1.41	2.25	1.26
Dooly	42,400	33,502	10,963	4,427	8,361	8,917	9.58	4.01	1.23
Early	13,805	....	3,494	5,444	7,246	6,149	2.54	......	0.57
Effingham	1,586	3,553	450	3,075	3,864	4,755	0.52	0.96	0.09
Elbert	23,244	27,062	14,050	11,125	12,959	10,433	2.09	2.09	1.35
Emmanuel	9,774	21,436	11,896	3,129	4,577	5,081	3.12	4.68	2.14
Fayette	15,473	30,367	654	6,191	8,709	7,047	2.50	3.49	0.09
Floyd	11,493	8,093	20,304	4,441	8,205	15,195	2.59	0.99	1.34

* No returns.

TABLE XVIII—*Continued*

Counties	Total Valuation			Population			Per Capita Value		
	1840	1850	1860	1840	1850	1860	1840	1850	1860
				GEORGIA—*Continued*					
Forsyth	$21,735	$ 57,162	$29,217	5,619	8,850	7,749	$3.87	$6.46	$3.77
Franklin	59,325	105,066	6,751	9,886	11,513	7,393	6.00	9.13	0.91
Gilmer	7,619	19,997	23,281	2,536	8,440	6,724	3.00	2.37	3.46
Glynn	....	1,032	50	5,302	4,933	3,889	......	0.21	0.01
Greene	16,411	15,712	41,619	11,690	13,068	12,652	1.40	1.20	3.29
Gwinnett	2,389	27,374	33,227	10,804	11,257	12,940	0.22	2.43	2.57
Habersham	25,528	31,275	34,178	7,961	8,895	5,966	3.21	3.52	5.73
Hall	22,778	31,556	39,321	7,875	8,713	9,366	2.89	3.62	4.20
Hancock	12,802	17,809	1,648	9,659	11,578	12,044	1.33	1.54	0.14
Harris*	350	25,901	2,805	13,933	14,721	13,736	0.03	1.76	0.20
Heard	10,200	34,734	11,150	5,329	6,923	7,805	1.91	5.02	1.42
Henry	13,208	70,944	24,477	11,756	14,726	10,702	1.12	4.82	2.29
Houston	†	23,439	1,310	9,711	16,450	15,611	†	1.42	0.08
Irwin	....	12,134	6,897	2,038	3,334	1,699	......	3.64	4.06
Jackson	22,006	27,145	14,670	8,522	9,768	10,605	2.58	2.78	1.38
Jasper	22,372	17,322	20,364	11,111	11,486	10,743	2.01	1.51	1.90
Jefferson	5,408	12,782	2,297	7,254	9,131	10,219	0.75	1.40	0.22
Jones	21,601	16,455	6,134	10,065	10,224	9,107	2.15	1.61	0.67
Laurens	15,494	12,168	10,654	5,585	6,442	6,998	2.77	1.89	1.52
Lee	10,488	32,962	24,514	4,520	6,660	7,196	2.32	4.95	3.41
Liberty	1,680	4,737	85	7,241	7,926	8,367	0.23	0.60	0.01
Lincoln	6,176	8,064	5,530	5,895	5,998	5,466	1.05	1.34	1.01

Lowndes	45,801	21,721	11,298	5,574	7,714	5,249	8.22	2.82	2.15
Lumpkin	12,717	21,050	9,146	5,671	8,955	4,626	2.24	2.35	1.98
McIntosh	....	....	....	5,360	6,027	5,546	......	......	......
Macon	45,505	25,210	8,491	5,045	7,052	8,449	9.00	3.57	1.00
Madison	5,316	21,276	96,281	4,510	5,703	5,933	1.18	3.73	16.23
Marion	7,866	13,637	5,390	4,812	10,280	7,390	1.63	1.33	0.73
Meriwether	5,393	26,571	30,133	14,132	16,476	15,330	0.38	1.61	1.97
Monroe	18,240	35,556	16,718	16,275	16,985	15,953	1.12	2.09	1.05
Montgomery	2,675	6,293	18,763	1,616	2,154	2,997	1.66	2.92	6.26
Morgan	....	5,625	1,880	9,121	10,744	9,997	......	0.52	0.19
Murray	16,154	47,556	40,959	4,695	14,433	7,083	3.46	3.29	5.78
Muscogee	8,238	9,441	563	11,699	18,578	16,584	0.70	0.51	0.03
Newton	19,307	15,615	30,030	11,628	13,296	14,320	1.66	1.17	2.10
Oglethorpe	23,768	18,963	10,510	10,868	12,259	11,549	2.19	1.55	0.91
Paulding	7,193	16,247	14,118	2,556	7,039	7,038	2.81	2.31	2.01
Pike	28,945	41,934	11,250	9,176	14,306	10,078	3.15	2.93	1.12
Pulaski	20,383	7,263	4,037	5,389	6,627	8,744	3.78	1.10	0.46
Putnam	14,400	9,469	3,995	10,260	10,794	10,125	1.40	0.88	0.39
Rabun	8,288	19,363	7,511	1,912	2,448	3,271	4.33	7.91	2.30
Randolph	3,862	31,270	2,034	8,276	12,868	9,571	0.47	2.43	0.21
Richmond	....	2,351	404	11,932	16,246	21,284	......	0.14	0.02
Scriven	4,296	12,762	5,765	4,794	6,847	8,274	0.90	1.86	0.70
Stewart	18,124	15,247	4,890	12,933	16,027	13,422	1.40	0.95	0.36
Sumter	24,700	20,855	8,732	5,759	10,322	9,428	4.29	2.02	0.93
Talbot	47,736	29,698	6,877	15,627	16,534	13,616	3.05	1.80	0.51
Taliaferro	8,257	7,819	4,042	5,190	5,146	4,583	1.59	1.52	0.88
Tattnall	830	6,283	10,800	2,724	3,227	4,352	0.30	1.95	2.48
Telfair	11,734	7,800	7,241	2,763	3,026	2,713	4.25	2.58	2.67
Thomas	11,753	23,561	32,875	6,766	10,103	10,766	1.74	2.33	3.05

* Returns imperfect. † No returns.

TABLE XVIII—*Continued*

Counties	Total Valuation			Population			Per Capita Value		
	1840	1850	1860	1840	1850	1860	1840	1850	1860
GEORGIA—*Continued*									
Troup	$ 33,146	$23,702	$ 2,742	15,733	16,879	16,262	$2.11	$1.40	$0.17
Twiggs	31,048	15,256	4,882	8,422	8,179	8,320	3.69	1.87	0.59
Union	15,593	24,665	14,794	3,152	7,234	4,413	4.95	3.41	3.35
Upson	9,877	10,477	12,403	9,408	9,424	9,910	1.05	1.11	1.25
Walker	157,225	11,513	14,200	6,572	13,109	10,082	23.92	0.88	1.41
Walton	7,563	59,812	20,376	10,209	10,821	11,074	0.74	5.53	1.84
Warren	4,245	3,818	7,979	9,789	12,425	9,820	0.43	0.31	0.81
Ware	9,682	9,526	3,757	2,323	3,888	2,200	4.17	2.45	1.71
Washington	19,880	24,116	26,461	10,565	11,766	12,698	1.88	2.05	2.08
Wayne	4,327	2,336	1,421	1,258	1,499	2,268	3.44	1.56	0.63
Wilkes	9,149	16,422	5,184	10,148	12,107	11,420	0.90	1.36	0.45
Wilkinson*	27,478	19,875	11,915	6,842	8,296	9,376	4.02	2.40	1.27
TENNESSEE									
Anderson	7,982	24,285	25,500	5,658	6,938	7,068	1.41	3.50	3.61
Bedford	50,503	59,070	24,157	20,546	21,511	21,584	2.46	2.75	1.12
Benton	17,691	16,964	29,415	4,772	6,315	8,463	3.71	2.69	3.48
Bledsoe	13,394	18,508	16,663	5,676	5,959	4,459	2.36	3.11	3.74
Blount	145,625	38,416	42,117	11,745	12,424	13,270	12.40	3.09	3.17
Bradley	21,138	27,309	29,096	7,385	12,259	11,710	2.68	2.23	2.48

Campbell	19,254	20,637	20,332	6,149	6,068	6,712	3.13	3.40	3.03
Cannon	32,385	51,516	68,432	7,193	8,982	9,509	4.50	5.74	7.20
Carroll	28,273	76,756	39,477	12,362	15,967	17,437	2.29	4.81	2.26
Carter	5,156	53,350	30,848	5,372	6,296	7,124	0.96	8.47	4.33
Claiborne	37,366	28,692	33,858	9,474	9,369	9,643	3.94	3.06	3.51
Cocke	3,095	28,120	39,104	6,992	8,300	10,408	0.44	3.39	3.76
Coffee	33,705	21,529	28,430	8,184	8,351	9,689	4.12	2.58	2.93
Davidson	80,890	40,695	17,825	30,509	38,882	47,055	2.65	1.05	0.38
De Kalb	18,351	31,214	92,287	5,868	8,016	10,573	3.13	3.89	8.73
Dickson	32,442	19,098	31,752	7,074	8,404	9,982	4.59	2.27	3.18
Dyer	37,930	13,563	18,257	4,484	6,361	10,536	8.46	2.13	1.73
Fayette	35,206	35,785	22,228	21,501	26,719	24,327	1.64	1.34	0.91
Fentress	10,995	14,073	19,461	3,550	4,454	5,054	3.10	3.16	3.85
Franklin	43,061	45,009	34,988	12,033	13,768	13,848	3.58	3.27	2.53
Gibson	50,594	113,345	92,081	13,689	19,548	21,777	3.70	5.80	4.23
Giles	52,027	77,977	120,030	21,494	25,949	26,166	2.42	3.01	4.59
Grainger	32,276	32,310	25,402	10,572	12,370	10,962	3.05	2.61	2.32
Greene	43,979	60,035	38,333	16,076	17,824	19,004	2.74	3.36	2.02
Hamilton	28,116	21,964	21,069	8,175	10,075	13,258	3.44	2.18	1.59
Hardeman	67,202	36,023	30,152	14,563	17,456	17,769	4.61	2.06	1.70
Hardin	46,677	27,037	47,758	8,245	10,328	11,214	5.66	2.62	4.26
Hawkins	67,560	35,603	56,819	15,035	13,370	16,162	4.49	2.66	3.52
Haywood	55,000	26,565	30,935	13,870	17,259	19,232	3.97	1.54	1.61
Henderson	40,301	63,186	122,477	11,875	13,164	14,491	3.39	4.80	8.45
Henry	43,016	36,347	38,718	14,906	18,233	19,133	2.89	1.99	2.02

* Counties not in existence in 1840 with per capita values in each in 1850 and 1860: Clinch, \$2.22, \$2.16; Gordon, \$2.75, \$1.69; and the following for 1860 only—Banks, \$3.72; Berrien, \$2.38; Brooke, \$1.55; Calhoun, \$0.74; Catoosa, \$0.72; Chattahoochee, \$0.16; Charlton, \$0.36; Clay, \$0.97; Clayton, \$2.27; Colquitt, \$2.36; Coffee, \$2.95; Dawson, \$3.61; Dougherty, \$0.003; Eckols, \$1.63; Fannin, \$0.73; Fulton, \$0.32; Glasscock, \$1.63; Haralson, \$5.54; Hart, \$5.57; Johnson, \$4.09; Miller, \$1.70; Milton, \$3.23; Mitchell, \$0.83; Pickins, \$3.43; Pierce, \$2.05; Polk, \$1.71; Quitman, \$0.35; Schley, \$0.67; Spalding, \$0.52; Taylor, \$1.44; Terrel, \$3.85; Towns, \$5.43; Webster, \$0.48; White, \$3.36; Whitfield, \$1.04; Wilcox, \$4.73; and Worth \$3.06.

Clarendon County, South Carolina, in 1860, had a per capita value of \$0.18.

TABLE XVIII—*Continued*

Counties	Total Valuation			Population			Per Capita Value		
	1840	1850	1860	1840	1850	1860	1840	1850	1860
TENNESSEE—*Continued*									
Hickman	$ 65,804	$ 57,233	$ 24,700	8,618	9,397	9,312	$7.64	$6.09	$2.65
Humphreys	26,789	31,976	21,594	5,195	6,422	9,096	5.15	4.98	2.37
Jackson	41,373	98,012	32,614	12,872	15,673	11,725	3.21	6.25	2.78
Jefferson	36,599	31,825	82,580	12,076	13,204	16,043	3.03	2.41	5.15
Johnson	3,853	15,814	19,320	2,658	3,705	5,018	1.45	4.27	3.85
Knox	39,088	58,203	33,537	15,485	18,807	22,813	2.52	3.09	1.47
Lauderdale	10,962	15,233	6,550	3,435	5,169	7,559	3.19	2.95	0.87
Lawrence	18,434	36,473	27,295	7,121	9,280	9,320	2.59	3.93	2.93
Lincoln	140,964	111,174	60,443	21,493	23,492	22,828	6.52	4.73	2.65
McMinn	27,608	50,906	33,515	12,719	13,906	13,555	2.17	3.66	2.47
McNairy	55,071	49,821	41,384	9,385	12,864	14,732	5.87	3.87	2.81
Madison	56,184	41,727	35,160	16,530	21,470	21,535	3.40	1.94	1.63
Marion	49,060	496	22,143	6,070	6,314	6,190	8.08	0.08	3.58
Marshall	53,083	74,549	65,316	14,555	15,616	14,592	3.65	4.77	4.40
Maury	57,884	69,982	63,477	28,186	29,520	32,498	2.05	2.37	1.95
Meigs	20,122	23,343	12,749	4,794	4,879	4,667	4.20	4.80	3.73
Monroe	23,154	36,437	46,490	12,056	11,874	12,607	1.92	3.07	3.69
Montgomery	52,138	49,299	10,719	16,927	21,045	20,895	3.08	2.34	0.51
Morgan	5,006	10,826	10,213	2,660	3,430	3,353	1.88	3.16	3.05
Obion	26,405	13,999	17,705	4,814	7,633	12,817	5.49	1.83	1.38
Overton	38,599	41,733	41,403	9,279	11,211	12,637	4.16	3.72	3.28
Perry	2,626	28,014	22,845	7,419	5,821	6,042	0.35	4.81	3.78

Polk	16,677	23,456	14,393	3,570	6,338	8,726	4.67	3.70	1.65
Rhea	10,855	12,791	10,437	3,985	4,415	4,991	2.72	2.90	2.09
Roane	29,286	48,259	155,707	10,948	12,185	13,583	2.68	3.96	11.46
Robertson	....	69,592	27,137	13,801	16,145	15,265	......	4.31	1.78
Rutherford	210,000	75,257	63,754	24,280	29,122	27,918	8.65	2.58	2.28
Sevier	18,162	43,806	31,584	6,442	6,920	9,122	2.82	6.33	3.46
Shelby	25,333	24,503	10,421	14,721	31,157	48,092	1.72	0.79	0.22
Smith	102,526	63,646	45,710	21,179	18,412	16,357	4.85	3.46	2.79
Stewart	....	30,711	17,529	8,587	9,719	9,896	......	3.16	1.77
Sullivan	48,200	36,537	37,294	10,736	11,742	13,552	4.49	3.11	2.75
Sumner	89,504	83,130	83,599	22,445	22,717	22,030	3.99	3.66	3.79
Tipton	13,360	18,252	26,461	6,800	8,887	10,705	1.96	2.05	2.47
Warren	20,778	27,998	29,026	10,803	10,179	11,147	1.92	2.75	2.60
Washington	12,207	56,792	30,086	11,751	13,861	14,829	1.04	4.10	2.03
Wayne	35,087	28,902	76,881	7,705	8,170	9,115	4.57	3.54	8.43
Weakley	31,837	31,273	36,299	9,870	14,608	18,216	3.23	2.14	1.99
White	44,722	42,734	18,007	10,747	11,444	9,381	4.16	3.73	1.92
Williamson	101,181	81,831	18,829	27,006	27,201	23,827	3.75	3.01	0.79
Wilson	24,950	77,501	222,236	24,460	27,443	26,072	1.02	2.84	8.52
KENTUCKY									
Adair	54,485	26,844	20,721	8,466	9,898	9,509	6.43	2.71	2.19
Allen	26,715	33,432	25,906	7,329	8,742	9,187	3.64	3.82	2.82
Anderson	10,663	12,879	15,076	5,442	6,260	7,404	1.96	2.05	2.04
Barren	86,767	56,349	43,455	17,288	20,240	16,665	5.01	2.78	2.61
Bath	41,058	34,565	24,141	9,763	12,115	12,113	4.20	2.85	1.99
Boone	26,802	22,855	13,447	10,034	11,185	11,196	2.67	2.04	1.20
Bourbon	60,346	27,597	23,713	14,478	14,466	14,860	4.16	1.91	1.60
Bracken	16,723	14,711	9,415	7,053	8,903	11,021	2.37	1.65	0.85

TABLE XVIII—*Continued*

Counties	Total Valuation			Population			Per Capita Value		
	1840	1850	1860	1840	1850	1860	1840	1850	1860
KENTUCKY—*Continued*									
Breathitt	$ 7,024	$ 9,176	$ 16,334	2,195	3,785	4,980	$3.20	$2.42	$3.28
Breckinridge	25,999	20,786	16,717	8,944	10,593	13,236	2.90	1.95	1.26
Bullitt	20,652	7,120	8,717	6,334	6,774	7,289	3.26	1.05	1.20
Butler	21,094	28,890	27,968	3,898	5,755	7,927	5.41	5.02	3.64
Caldwell	39,114	25,029	15,174	10,365	13,048	9,318	3.77	1.92	1.63
Calloway	28,749	29,633	28,891	9,794	8,096	9,915	2.94	3.66	2.91
Campbell	3,323	1,560	1,380	5,214	13,127	20,909	0.64	0.12	0.07
Carroll	9,135	8,504	7,988	3,966	5,526	6,579	2.30	1.54	1.21
Carter	33,460	19,933	34,106	2,905	6,241	8,516	11.52	3.19	4.00
Casey	87,270	45,069	52,988	4,939	6,556	6,466	17.67	6.87	8.19
Christian	63,403	51,412	28,994	15,587	19,580	21,627	4.07	2.12	1.34
Clark	128,950	28,440	20,483	10,802	12,683	11,484	11.99	2.24	1.78
Clay	14,607	10,492	11,613	4,607	5,421	6,652	3.17	1.94	1.75
Clinton	13,814	16,440	23,249	3,863	4,889	5,781	3.58	3.36	4.02
Cumberland	33,000	37,640	37,435	6,090	7,005	7,340	5.42	5.37	5.10
Daviess	22,499	14,350	16,421	8,331	12,362	15,549	2.70	1.16	1.06
Edmondson	5,139	15,084	15,179	2,914	4,088	4,645	1.76	3.22	3.27
Estill	15,997	13,153	11,882	5,535	5,985	6,886	2.20	2.52	1.73
Fayette	40,702	38,296	7,007	21,194	22,735	22,599	1.92	1.68	0.31
Fleming	50,828	30,454	23,614	13,268	13,914	12,489	3.83	2.19	1.98
Floyd	7,851	10,317	18,804	6,302	5,714	6,388	1.24	1.80	2.94
Franklin	12,585	17,958	7,437	9,420	12,462	12,694	1.34	1.44	0.59

Gallatin	8,410	7,805	6,326	4,003	5,137	5,056	2.10	1.52	1.25
Garrard	71,035	30,611	19,662	10,480	10,237	10,531	6.77	2.99	1.87
Grant	14,747	13,770	9,807	4,192	6,531	8,356	3.52	2.11	1.17
Graves	40,593	59,824	52,174	7,465	11,397	16,233	5.44	5.25	3.21
Grayson	22,792	30,560	26,718	4,461	6,837	7,982	5.11	4.47	3.35
Greene	56,968	26,985	19,270	14,212	9,060	8,086	4.01	2.98	2.19
Greenup	5,665	6,232	3,950	6,297	9,654	8,760	0.89	0.69	0.45
Hancock	12,418	9,644	10,708	2,581	3,853	6,213	4.81	2.55	1.72
Hardin	52,333	47,463	25,368	16,357	14,525	15,189	3.81	3.26	1.67
Harlan	10,939	12,846	19,027	3,015	4,268	5,494	3.63	3.01	3.46
Harrison	85,667	33,680	23,508	12,472	13,064	13,779	6.88	2.58	1.71
Hart	22,481	21,656	19,067	7,031	9,093	10,348	3.19	2.38	1.84
Henderson	12,023	19,930	9,584	9,548	12,171	14,262	1.26	1.64	0.67
Henry	31,896	19,608	21,602	10,015	11,442	11,949	3.18	1.71	1.81
Hickman	46,879	17,462	8,352	8,968	4,791	7,008	5.34	3.65	1.18
Hopkins	52,695	35,822	17,938	9,171	12,441	11,875	5.75	2.88	1.51
Jefferson	26,356	8,806	6,086	36,346	59,831	89,404	0.73	0.15	0.07
Jessamine	15,299	24,188	7,240	9,396	10,249	9,465	1.63	2.36	0.76
Kenton	18,578	11,025	9,456	7,816	17,038	25,467	2.38	0.64	0.36
Knox	29,050	20,676	40,002	5,722	7,050	7,707	5.08	2.93	5.19
Laurel	9,430	10,892	17,931	3,079	4,145	5,488	3.06	2.63	3.27
Lawrence	2,869	15,004	26,193	4,730	6,281	7,601	0.61	2.39	3.45
Lewis	8,539	12,225	8,667	6,306	7,202	8,361	1.35	1.69	1.04
Lincoln	22,029	22,987	19,677	10,187	10,093	10,647	2.16	2.28	1.85
Livingston	22,226	10,962	13,467	9,025	6,578	7,213	2.46	1.67	1.87
Logan	15,388	35,646	38,221	13,615	16,581	19,021	1.13	2.18	2.01
McCracken	16,282	5,618	5,309	4,745	6,067	10,360	3.43	0.82	0.51
Madison	42,350	44,672	35,120	16,355	15,727	17,207	2.58	2.84	2.04
Marion	37,188	46,981	26,547	11,032	11,765	12,593	3.37	3.99	2.11
Mason	36,862	24,973	20,208	15,719	18,344	18,222	2.35	1.36	1.11
Meade	72,845	8,405	13,410	5,780	7,393	8,898	12.60	1.14	1.51

TABLE XVIII—*Continued*

Counties	Total Valuation			Population			Per Capita Value		
	1840	1850	1860	1840	1850	1860	1840	1850	1860
KENTUCKY—*Continued*									
Mercer	$30,004	$51,852	$18,140	18,720	14,067	13,701	$1.61	$3.66	$1.32
Monroe	30,235	27,522	28,226	6,526	7,756	8,551	4.63	3.55	3.30
Montgomery	41,449	33,145	14,342	9,332	9,903	7,859	4.44	3.35	1.82
Morgan	22,384	18,792	26,836	4,603	7,620	9,237	4.86	2.46	2.91
Muhlenburg	27,564	23,640	23,346	6,964	9,809	10,725	3.96	2.41	2.18
Nelson	26,437	31,735	23,481	13,637	14,789	15,799	1.94	2.14	1.49
Nicholas	34,253	22,468	16,639	8,745	10,361	11,030	3.92	2.17	1.51
Ohio	19,307	41,937	24,780	6,592	9,749	12,209	2.93	4.30	2.03
Oldham	29,930	8,180	7,215	7,380	7,629	7,283	4.06	1.07	0.99
Owen	49,670	31,086	23,924	8,232	10,444	12,719	6.03	2.97	1.88
Pendleton	10,849	18,711	13,832	4,455	6,774	10,443	2.44	2.76	1.32
Perry	10,282	17,164	14,993	3,089	3,092	3,950	3.33	5.55	3.80
Pike	15,138	16,539	26,904	3,507	5,365	7,384	4.32	3.08	3.66
Pulaski	....	50,912	49,675	9,620	14,195	17,201	.....	3.59	3.34
Rock Castle	4,104	11,910	18,489	3,409	4,697	5,343	1.20	2.54	3.46
Russel	12,498	30,896	18,927	4,238	5,349	6,024	2.95	5.77	3.14
Scott	33,958	20,044	16,669	13,668	14,946	14,417	2.48	1.34	1.16
Shelby	71,126	42,092	32,506	17,768	17,095	16,433	4.00	2.46	1.98
Simpson	35,138	33,468	24,061	6,537	7,733	8,146	5.37	4.47	2.86
Spencer	....	19,775	11,152	6,581	6,842	6,188	.....	2.89	1.80
Todd	38,678	30,489	20,435	9,991	12,268	11,575	3.87	2.48	1.77
Trigg	26,073	28,233	15,631	7,716	10,129	11,051	3.38	2.78	1.41

Trimble	15,156	11,622	6,983	4,480	5,963	5,880	3.38	1.95	1.19
Union	22,278	22,212	25,075	6,673	9,012	12,791	3.34	2.46	1.96
Warren	....	107,276	50,350	15,446	15,123	17,320	......	7.09	2.91
Washington	7,131	27,319	25,980	10,596	12,194	11,575	0.61	2.24	2.24
Wayne	17,040	38,766	40,014	7,399	8,692	10,259	2.30	4.46	3.90
Whitley	16,852	40,081	36,478	4,673	7,447	7,762	3.61	5.38	4.70
Woodford*	43,342	15,637	16,241	11,740	12,423	11,219	3.69	1.26	1.45
OHIO									
Adams	17,832	30,097	9,476	13,183	18,883	20,309	1.35	1.59	0.47
Allen	8,463	14,703	13,732	9,079	12,109	19,185	0.93	1.21	0.72
Ashtabula	35,082	22,784	26,708	23,724	28,767	31,814	1.48	0.79	0.84
Athens	35,638	28,325	15,978	19,109	18,215	21,364	1.86	1.56	0.75
Belmont	21,283	25,482	4,396	30,901	34,600	36,398	0.69	0.74	0.12
Brown	46,350	28,531	14,316	22,715	27,332	29,958	2.04	1.04	0.48
Butler	19,230	15,320	3,555	28,173	30,789	35,840	0.68	0.50	0.10
Carroll	19,500	12,441	2,451	18,108	17,685	15,738	1.08	0.70	0.16
Champaign	14,106	12,192	2,718	16,721	19,782	22,698	0.84	0.62	0.12
Clark	21,007	7,781	2,557	16,882	22,178	25,300	1.24	0.35	0.10
Clermont	42,716	22,300	8,558	23,106	30,455	33,034	1.84	0.73	0.26
Clinton	41,504	20,913	1,094	15,719	18,838	21,461	2.64	1.11	0.05
Columbiana	5,712	14,914	4,535	40,378	33,621	32,836	0.14	0.44	0.14
Coshocton	24,284	43,251	6,422	21,590	25,674	25,032	1.12	1.68	0.26

* Counties in Tennessee and Kentucky not in existence in 1840 with per capita values in each in 1850 and 1860: *Tennessee:* Decatur, $3.10, $7.96; Grundy, $4.07, $3.17; Hancock, $5.82, $2.71; Lewis, $3.10, $3.40; Macon, $8.10, $1.07; Scott, $6.92, $4.77; Van Buren, $4.74, $3.77; in 1860 only—Cheatham, $1.13; Cumberland, $2.09; Putnam, $4.58; Sequatchie, $4.35; and Union, $2.47; *Kentucky:* Ballard, $1.54, $1.18; Boyce, $2.46, $1.94; Crittenden, $4.73, $1.49; Fulton, $1.84, $2.09; Johnson, $3.95, $2.93; Larue, $2.18, $2.10; Letcher, $6.29, $5.28; Marshall, $8.87, $2.38; Owsley, $2.95, $2.85; Taylor, $4.22, $2.45; in 1860 only—Boyd, $0.51; Jackson, $2.30; Lyon, $1.13; McLean, $3.10; Magoffin, $5.46; Metcalfe, $1.53; Powell, $3.09; Rowan, $3.35; Webster, $1.83.

TABLE XVIII—*Continued*

Counties	Total Valuation			Population			Per Capita Value		
	1840	1850	1860	1840	1850	1860	1840	1850	1860
				OHIO—*Continued*					
Crawford	$ 16,647	$16,187	$ 5,694	13,152	18,177	23,881	$1.27	$0.89	$0.24
Cuyahoga	24,200	12,279	3,065	26,506	48,099	78,033	0.91	0.26	0.04
Darke	....	42,577	7,152	13,282	20,276	26,009	......	2.10	0.27
Delaware	27,211	21,895	20,077	22,060	21,817	23,902	1.23	1.00	0.84
Erie	4,151	4,600	2,837	12,599	18,568	24,474	0.33	0.25	0.12
Fairfield	41,628	30,352	10,232	31,924	30,264	30,538	1.30	1.00	0.34
Fayette	29,880	18,594	1,905	10,984	12,726	15,935	2.72	1.46	0.12
Franklin	14,642	28,943	9,325	25,049	42,909	50,361	0.58	0.67	0.19
Gallia	27,647	19,512	21,374	13,444	17,063	22,043	2.06	1.14	0.97
Geauga	24,681	9,556	6,453	16,297	17,827	15,817	1.51	0.54	0.41
Greene	6,805	10,973	453	17,528	21,946	26,197	0.39	0.50	0.02
Guernsey	52,446	37,659	7,027	27,748	30,438	24,474	1.89	1.24	0.29
Hamilton	11,064	30,994	10,593	80,145	156,844	216,410	0.14	0.20	0.05
Hancock	8,704	28,970	6,866	9,986	16,751	22,886	0.87	1.73	0.30
Hardin	6,776	10,815	3,434	4,598	8,251	13,570	1.47	1.31	0.25
Harrison	12,589	20,223	1,371	20,099	20,157	19,110	0.63	1.00	0.07
Henry	375	2,209	2,813	2,503	3,434	8,901	0.15	0.64	0.32
Highland	66,487	33,726	5,857	22,269	25,781	27,773	2.99	1.31	0.21
Hocking	19,615	22,717	19,868	9,741	14,119	17,057	2.01	1.61	1.16
Holmes	48,294	35,359	4,863	18,088	20,452	20,589	2.67	1.73	0.24
Huron	14,755	28,864	4,623	23,933	26,203	29,616	0.62	1.10	0.16
Jackson	18,731	20,289	16,140	9,744	12,719	17,941	1.92	1.60	0.90

Jefferson	7,220	16,693	23	25,030	29,133	26,115	0.29	0.57	0.00
Knox	28,932	15,151	5,435	29,579	28,872	27,735	0.98	0.52	0.20
Lake	17,553	35,648	2,470	13,719	14,654	15,576	1.28	2.43	0.16
Lawrence	....	4,786	11,464	9,738	15,246	23,249	......	0.31	0.49
Licking	114,111	35,659	9,198	35,096	38,846	37,011	3.25	0.92	0.25
Logan	....	25,990	1,650	14,015	19,162	20,996	......	1.36	0.08
Lorain	26,061	11,764	2,752	18,467	26,086	29,744	1.41	0.45	0.09
Lucas	584	2,715	166	9,382	12,363	25,831	0.06	0.22	0.01
Madison	10,425	12,171	480	9,025	10,015	13,015	1.10	1.22	0.04
Marion	33,093	10,869	5,985	14,765	12,618	15,490	2.12	0.86	0.39
Medina	45,884	26,699	6,850	18,352	24,441	22,517	2.50	1.09	0.30
Meigs	29,357	21,046	10,681	11,452	17,971	26,534	2.56	1.17	0.40
Mercer	1,288	4,620	6,682	8,277	7,712	14,104	0.16	0.60	0.47
Miami	15,585	15,934	3,136	19,688	24,999	29,959	0.79	0.64	0.10
Monroe	27,096	33,759	16,275	18,521	28,351	25,741	1.46	1.19	0.63
Montgomery	22,228	2,146	3,196	31,938	38,218	52,230	0 70	0.06	0.06
Morgan	31,160	36,838	4,919	20,852	28,585	22,119	1.49	1.29	0.22
Muskingum	56,265	49,229	8,631	38,749	45,049	44,416	1.45	1.09	0.19
Ottawa	2,030	2,611	225	2,248	3,308	7,016	0.90	0.79	0.03
Paulding	....	596	920	1,034	1,766	4,945	......	0.34	0.19
Perry	27,358	22,771	16,389	19,344	20,775	19,678	1.41	1.10	0.83
Pickaway	20,534	18,568	5,601	19,725	21,006	23,469	1.04	0.88	0.24
Pike	....	14,824	11,875	7,626	10,953	13,643	......	1.35	0.87
Portage	34,914	15,101	9,147	22,965	24,419	24,208	1.52	0.62	0.38
Preble	34,176	26,983	3,961	19,482	21,736	21,820	1.75	1.24	0.18
Putnam	2,250	8,602	4,599	5,189	7,221	12,808	0.43	1.19	0.36
Richland	8,070	29,221	6,454	44,532	30,879	31,158	0.18	0.95	0.21
Ross	17,980	22,994	10,255	27,460	32,074	35,071	0.65	c.72	0.29
Sandusky	12,121	15,866	....	10,182	14,305	21,429	1.19	1.11	......
Scioto	16,295	15,424	4,969	11,192	18,428	24,297	1.46	0.84	0.20
Seneca	20,891	41,711	12,643	18,128	27,104	30,868	1.15	1.54	0.41

TABLE XVIII—*Continued*

Counties	Total Valuation			Population			Per Capita Value		
	1840	1850	1860	1840	1850	1860	1840	1850	1860
OHIO—*Continued*									
Shelby	$ 15,200	$ 3,741	$ 3,991	12,154	13,958	17,493	$1.25	$0.27	$0.23
Stark	34,114	13,107	2,281	34,603	39,878	42,978	0.99	0.33	0.05
Summit	27,415	15,977	1,312	22,560	27,485	27,344	1.22	0.58	0.05
Trumbull	129,771	23,669	2,035	38,107	30,490	30,656	3.41	0.78	0.07
Tuscarawas	21,387	26,910	9,760	25,631	31,761	32,463	0.83	0.85	0.30
Union	10,633	20,378	9,317	8,422	12,204	16,507	1.26	1.67	0.56
Van Wert	345	2,928	5,791	1,577	4,793	10,238	0.22	0.61	0.57
Warren	36,965	33,415	3,410	23,141	25,560	26,902	1.60	1.31	0.13
Washington	27,986	34,960	13,153	20,823	29,540	36,268	1.34	1.18	0.36
Wayne	50,460	25,025	8,978	35,808	32,981	32,483	1.41	0.76	0.28
Williams	1,383	7,226	1,784	4,465	8,018	16,633	0.31	0.90	0.11
Wood*	3,220	5,779	2,890	5,357	9,157	17,886	0.60	0.63	0.16
INDIANA									
Adams	372	5,628	7,785	2,264	5,797	9,252	0.16	0.97	0.84
Allen	357	6,341	6,113	5,942	16,919	29,328	0.06	0.37	0.21
Bartholomew	16,418	28,675	9,684	10,042	12,428	17,865	1.63	2.31	0.45
Blackford	693	4,675	6,663	1,226	2,860	4,122	0.57	1.63	1.62

* Counties not in existence in 1840 and the per capita value in each in 1850 and 1860: Ashland, $1.01, $0.12; Auglaize, $0.79; $0.41; Defiance, $0.33, $0.44; Fulton, $1.17, $0.31; Mahoning, $0.83, $0.01; Morrow, $1.07, $0.14; Vinton, $2.14, $1.04; Wyandott, $0.90, $0.51; and Noble (1860), $0.55.

Boone	12,765	30,566	20,850	8,121	11,631	16,753	1.57	2.63	1.24
Brown	4,416	7,993	7,493	2,364	4,846	6,507	1.87	1.66	1.15
Carroll	14,641	18,848	10,616	7,819	11,015	13,489	1.87	1.71	0.79
Cass	1,894	11,433	6,350	5,480	11,021	16,843	0.35	1.04	0.38
Clark	48,428	14,713	10,895	14,595	15,828	20,502	3.32	0.93	0.53
Clay	14,970	15,239	12,501	5,567	7,944	12,161	2.69	1.92	1.03
Clinton	13,012	19,446	12,890	7,508	11,869	14,505	1.73	1.64	0.89
Crawford	....	9,251	9,086	5,282	6,524	8,226	.....	1.42	1.10
Daviess	20,671	30,274	19,127	6,720	10,352	13,323	3.08	2.92	1.44
Dearborn	32,502	13,605	1,523	19,327	20,166	24,406	1.68	0.67	0.06
Decatur	34,107	32,076	10,789	12,171	15,107	17,294	2.80	2.12	0.62
DeKalb	886	7,942	6,787	1,968	8,251	13,880	0.45	0.96	0.49
Delaware	6,606	20,291	14,581	8,843	10,843	15,753	0.75	1.87	0.93
Dubois	4,831	7,125	3,795	3,632	6,321	10,394	1.33	1.13	0.37
Elkhart	5,614	12,563	3,835	6,660	12,690	20,986	0.84	0.99	0.18
Fayette	11,843	10,428	998	9,837	10,217	10,225	1.20	1.02	0.10
Floyd	6,933	4,178	1,833	9,454	14,875	20,183	0.73	0.28	0.10
Fountain	25,262	25,450	8,326	11,218	13,253	15,566	2.25	1.92	0.53
Franklin	11,735	17,540	2,913	13,349	17,968	19,549	0.88	0.98	0.15
Fulton	2,174	7,764	5,087	1,993	5,982	9,422	1.09	1.30	0.54
Gibson	17,105	24,039	27,912	8,977	10,771	14,532	1.91	2.23	1.92
Grant	11,714	16,105	12,539	4,875	11,092	15,797	2.40	1.45	0.79
Greene	21,279	30,725	19,478	8,321	12,313	16,041	2.56	2.49	1.21
Hamilton	20,020	16,734	13,706	9,855	12,684	17,310	2.03	1.32	0.79
Hancock	9,239	18,586	10,175	7,535	9,698	12,802	1.23	1.92	0.79
Harrison	13,938	23,375	13,874	12,459	15,286	18,521	1.12	1.53	0.75
Hendricks	29,075	45,695	16,808	11,264	14,083	16,953	2.58	3.24	0.99
Henry	16,383	28,905	6,214	15,128	17,605	20,119	1.08	1.64	0.31
Huntington	13,405	6,562	8,838	1,579	7,850	14,867	8.49	0.84	0.59

TABLE XVIII—*Continued*

Counties	Total Valuation			Population			Per Capita Value		
	1840	1850	1860	1840	1850	1860	1840	1850	1860
				INDIANA—*Continued*					
Jackson	$15,983	$13,389	$ 15,314	8,961	11,047	16,286	$1.78	$1.21	$0.94
Jasper	3,884	5,891	2,516	1,267	3,540	4,291	3.07	1.66	0.59
Jay	998	16,529	15,334	3,863	7,047	11,399	0.26	2.35	1.35
Jefferson	24,906	20,590	12,736	16,614	23,916	25,036	1.50	0.87	0.51
Jennings	....	26,078	12,109	8,829	12,096	14,749	......	2.16	0.82
Johnson	25,050	29,824	14,187	9,352	12,101	14,854	2.68	2.46	0.96
Knox	24,595	8,048	8,894	10,657	11,084	16,056	2.31	0.73	0.55
Kosciusko	6,916	14,186	11,429	4,170	10,243	17,418	1.66	1.39	0.66
La Grange	4,226	10,252	2,330	3,663	8,387	11,366	1.15	1.22	0.21
Lake	548	1,450	623	1,468	3,991	9,145	0.37	0.36	0.07
Laporte	8,519	11,796	601	8,184	12,145	22,919	1.04	0.97	0.03
Lawrence	70,186	25,975	16,897	11,782	12,097	13,692	5.96	2.15	1.23
Madison	12,988	29,573	13,908	8,874	12,375	16,518	1.46	2.39	0.84
Marion	30,280	22,060	6,449	16,080	24,103	39,855	1.88	0.92	0.16
Marshall	919	8,400	4,419	1,651	5,348	12,722	0.56	1.57	0.35
Martin	8,766	13,221	11,073	3,875	5,941	8,975	2.26	2.23	1.23
Miami	3,413	13,482	11,047	3,048	11,304	16,851	1.12	1.19	0.66
Monroe	10,464	46,379	16,291	10,143	11,286	12,847	1.03	4.11	1.27
Montgomery	22,367	43,378	15,511	14,438	18,084	20,888	1.05	3.40	0.74
Morgan	....	34,565	23,459	10,741	14,576	16,110	......	2.37	1.46
Noble	2,263	11,563	5,575	2,702	7,946	14,915	0.84	1.46	0.37
Orange	34,268	25,540	18,398	9,602	10,809	12,076	3.57	2.36	1.52

Owen	20,124	32,523	17,049	8,359	12,106	14,376	2.41	2.69	1.19
Parke	59,155	29,858	6,921	13,499	14,968	15,538	4.38	1.99	0.45
Perry	7,966	4,880	4,779	4,655	7,268	11,847	1.71	0.67	0.40
Pike	21,654	12,952	15,338	4,769	7,720	10,078	4.54	1.68	1.52
Porter	2,426	6,652	480	2,162	5,234	10,313	1.12	1.27	0.05
Posey	....	12,605	3,547	9,683	12,549	16,167	......	1.00	0.22
Pulaski	427	2,102	2,929	561	2,595	5,711	0.76	0.81	0.51
Putnam	49,102	46,740	19,184	16,483	18,615	20,681	2.91	2.51	0.93
Randolph	25,801	23,013	17,554	10,684	14,725	18,997	2.41	1.57	0.92
Ripley	8,253	26,706	12,270	10,392	14,820	19,054	0.79	1.80	0.64
Rush	35,158	31,215	6,319	16,456	16,445	16,193	2.14	1.90	0.39
St. Joseph	5,069	9,884	1,848	6,425	10,954	18,455	0.79	0.90	0.10
Scott	8,184	27,504	14,829	4,242	5,885	7,303	1.93	4.67	2.03
Shelby	25,303	24,246	118,906	12,005	15,502	19,569	2.11	1.56	6.08
Spencer	11,282	47,931	9,453	6,305	8,616	14,556	1.79	5.56	0.65
Stark	50	371	669	149	557	2,195	0.34	0.67	0.30
Steuben	1,616	5,161	6,656	2,578	6,104	10,374	0.63	0.85	0.60
Sullivan	26,567	27,454	20,853	8,315	10,141	15,064	3.20	2.71	1.38
Switzerland	13,550	22,112	12,096	9,920	12,932	12,698	1.37	1.71	0.95
Tippecanoe	29,202	12,273	1,886	13,724	19,377	25,726	2.13	0.63	0.07
Union	17,757	15,549	20	8,017	6,944	7,109	2.21	2.24	0.00
Vanderburgh	798	2,986	1,703	6,250	11,414	20,552	0.13	0.26	0.08
Vermillion	18,528	15,926	8,884	8,274	8,661	9,422	2.24	1.84	0.94
Vigo	27,018	16,498	6,847	12,076	15,289	22,517	2.24	1.08	0.30
Wabash	4,861	10,572	18,225	2,756	12,138	17,547	1.76	0.88	1.04
Warren	21,361	15,317	2,965	5,656	7,387	10,057	3.78	2.07	0.29
Warrick	....	20,347	17,353	6,321	8,811	13,261	......	2.31	1.31
Washington	27,509	52,384	18,709	15,269	17,040	17,909	1.80	3.07	1.04
Wayne	60,043	30,490	6,487	23,290	25,320	29,558	2.58	1.10	0.22
Wells	1,056	8,653	9,635	1,822	6,152	10,844	0.58	1.41	0.89
White	4,470	6,868	3,470	1,832	4,761	8,258	2.44	1.44	0.42
Whitley	685	5,958	7,307	1,237	5,190	10,730	0.55	1.15	0.68

TABLE XVIII—*Continued*

Counties	Total Valuation			Population			Per Capita Value		
	1840	1850	1860	1840	1850	1860	1840	1850	1860
ILLINOIS									
Adams	$ 5,604	$34,749	$ 4,296	14,476	26,508	41,323	$0.39	$1.31	$0.10
Alexander	1,205	1,614	....	3,313	2,484	4,707	0.36	0.65	......
Bond	8,751	11,169	5,971	5,060	6,144	9,815	1.73	1.82	0.61
Boone	563	6,691	55	1,705	7,624	11,678	0.33	0.88	0.00
Brown	9,560	28,198	21,687	4,183	7,198	9,938	2.29	3.92	2.18
Bureau	....	4,259	125	3,067	8,841	26,426	......	0.48	0.00
Calhoun	1,702	934	1,590	1,741	3,231	5,144	0.98	0.29	0.31
Carroll	....	3,194	628	1,023	4,586	11,733	......	0.69	0.05
Cass	5,416	6,068	3,568	2,981	7,253	11,325	1.82	0.84	0.32
Champaign	3,162	3,439	3,624	1,475	2,649	14,629	2.14	1.30	0.25
Christian	9,601	8,407	2,823	1,878	3,203	10,492	5.11	2.62	0.27
Clark	26,208	13,050	17,839	7,453	9,532	14,987	3.52	1.37	1.19
Clay	6,633	7,794	16,344	3,228	4,289	9,336	2.05	1.82	1.75
Clinton	4,646	4,509	75	3,718	5,139	10,941	1.25	0.88	0.00
Coles	29,519	28,558	7,355	9,616	9,335	14,203	3.07	3.06	0.52
Cook	....	4,131	1,112	10,201	43,385	144,954	......	0.10	0.00
Crawford	9,075	17,406	23,376	4,422	7,135	11,551	2.05	2.44	2.02
DeKalb	921	2,683	1,448	1,697	7,540	19,086	0.54	0.36	0.08
DeWitt	12,107	12,956	3,583	3,247	5,002	10,820	3.73	2.59	0.33
DuPage	900	2,568	628	3,535	9,290	14,701	0.25	0.28	0.04
Edgar	32,546	28,217	15,040	8,225	10,692	16,925	3.96	2.64	0.89
Edwards	2,403	7,549	6,392	3,070	3,524	5,454	0.78	2.14	1.17

Effingham	2,500	6,311	6,681	1,675	3,799	7,816	1.49	1.66	0.85
Fayette	6,873	22,164	13,820	6,328	8,075	11,189	1.09	2.74	1.23
Franklin	10,190	20,288	22,693	3,682	5,681	9,393	2.77	3.57	2.42
Fulton	15,581	35,587	26,266	13,142	22,508	33,338	1.19	1.58	0.79
Gallatin	12,894	6,398	5,342	10,760	5,448	8,055	1.20	1.17	0.66
Greene	9,347	21,163	16,409	11,951	12,429	16,093	0.78	1.70	1.02
Hamilton	21,979	18,080	25,538	3,945	6,362	9,915	5.70	2.84	2.60
Hancock	11,170	16,451	9,061	9,946	14,652	29,061	1.12	1.12	0.31
Hardin	5,319	5,044	3,126	1,378	2,887	3,759	3.86	1.75	0.83
Henry	215	....	6,040	1,260	3,807	20,660	0.17	......	0.29
Iroquois	5,805	3,686	2,568	1,695	4,149	12,325	3.42	0.89	0.21
Jackson	8,979	11,537	8,875	3,566	5,862	9,589	2.52	1.97	0.93
Jasper	1,878	6,656	18,716	1,472	3,220	8,364	1.28	2.07	2.24
Jefferson	40,986	18,648	28,518	5,762	8,109	12,965	7.11	2.40	2.20
Jersey	48,968	5,450	705	4,535	7,354	12,051	1.08	0.74	0.06
Jo Daviess	....	4,542	61,812	6,180	18,604	27,325	......	0.24	2.26
Johnson	8,698	9,996	27,260	3,626	4,114	9,342	2.50	2.43	2.92
Kane	1,359	4,180	5,942	6,501	16,703	30,062	0.21	0.25	0.20
Knox	104,234	18,745	5,202	7,060	13,279	28,663	14.76	1.41	0.18
Lake	187	3,383	2,068	2,634	14,226	18,257	0.07	0.24	0.11
La Salle	983	1,792	10	9,348	17,815	48,332	0.11	0.10	0.00
Lawrence	12,805	12,274	12,003	7,092	6,121	9,214	1.82	2.01	1.30
Lee	....	2,785	40	2,035	5,292	17,651	......	1.90	0.00
Livingston	2,581	200	1,784	759	1,552	11,637	3.40	0.13	0.15
Logan	8,837	11,372	3,036	2,333	5,128	14,272	3.79	2.22	0.21
McDonough	54,746	25,279	6,452	5,308	7,616	20,069	10.31	3.32	0.32
McHenry	1,029	5,741	2,827	2,578	14,978	22,089	0.40	0.38	0.13
McLean	5,300	15,363	544	6,565	10,163	28,772	0.81	1.51	0.02
Macon	8,527	9,914	265	3,039	3,988	13,738	2.81	2.49	0.02
Macoupin	16,875	57,665	13,151	7,826	12,355	24,602	2.16	4.67	0.53
Madison	33,460	28,960	2,106	14,433	20,441	31,251	2.32	1.42	0.07

TABLE XVIII—*Continued*

Counties	Total Valuation			Population			Per Capita Value		
	1840	1850	1860	1840	1850	1860	1840	1850	1860
ILLINOIS—*Continued*									
Marion	$11,725	$17,636	$ 2,002	4,742	6,720	12,739	$2.47	$2.62	$0.16
Marshall	3,382	732	244	1,849	5,180	13,437	1.83	0.14	0.02
Menard	16,161	15,758	27,100	4,431	6,349	9,584	2.65	2.48	2.83
Mercer	3,294	7,723	16,512	2,352	5,246	15,042	1.40	1.47	1.01
Monroe	5,781	1,595	....	4,481	7,679	12,832	1.29	0.21	......
Montgomery	16,630	10,868	9,753	4,490	6,277	13,979	3.70	1.73	0.70
Morgan	14,238	30,155	4,733	19,547	16,064	22,112	0.73	1.88	0.21
Ogle	485	6,856	1,319	3,479	10,020	22,888	0.14	0.68	0.06
Peoria	4,242	8,603	1,260	6,153	17,547	36,601	0.69	0.49	0.03
Perry	285	16,878	4,405	3,222	5,278	9,552	0.09	3.20	0.46
Pike	23,679	18,748	10,408	11,728	18,819	27,249	2.02	1.00	0.38
Pope	820	6,409	9,998	4,094	3,975	6,742	0.20	1.61	1.48
Putnam	3,122	2,083	124	2,131	3,924	5,587	1.47	0.53	0.02
Randolph	6,961	1,167	4,148	7,944	11,079	17,205	0.88	0.11	0.24
Rock Island	948	3,999	2,349	2,610	6,937	21,005	0.36	0.58	0.11
St. Clair	3,201	10,242	21,103	13,631	20,180	37,694	0.23	0.51	0.56
Sangamon	34,691	33,143	5,115	14,716	19,228	32,274	2.36	1.72	0.16
Schuyler	14,315	8,346	6,004	6,972	10,573	14,684	2.05	0.79	0.41
Scott	16,414	16,829	890	6,215	7,914	9,069	2.64	2.13	0.10
Shelby	25,552	25,827	19,650	6,659	7,807	14,613	3.84	3.31	1.34
Stark	1,298	5,249	653	1,573	3,710	9,004	0.83	1.41	0.07
Stephenson	....	6,313	1,277	2,800	11,666	25,112	......	0.54	0.05

Tazewell	10,571	6,561	3,042	7,221	12,052	21,470	1.46	0.54	0.14
Union	20,535	12,698	15,262	5,524	7,615	11,181	3.70	1.67	1.36
Vermillion	42,962	21,461	16,052	9,303	11,492	19,800	4.62	1.87	0.81
Wabash	7,533	8,590	8,229	4,240	4,690	7,313	1.78	1.83	1.13
Warren	18,008	23,278	4,252	6,739	8,176	18,336	2.67	2.85	0.23
Washington	9,678	14,234	7,884	4,810	6,953	13,731	2.01	2.05	0.57
Wayne	13,832	18,318	22,000	5,133	6,825	12,223	2.69	2.68	1.80
White	9,262	26,558	21,910	7,919	8,925	12,403	1.17	2.98	1.77
Whiteside	660	4,715	3,313	2,514	5,361	18,737	0.26	0.88	0.18
Will	4,710	4,742	679	10,167	16,703	29,321	0.46	0.28	0.02
Williamson*	15,774	31,563	76,043	4,457	7,216	12,205	3.54	4.37	6.23
Winnebago	....	3,651	1,082	4,609	11,773	24,491	......	0.31	0.04

MICHIGAN

Allegan	....	2,515	3,322	1,783	5,125	16,087	......	0.49	0.21
Barry	....	5,634	2,568	1,078	5,072	13,858	......	1.11	0.19
Berrien	2,651	5,235	3,845	5,011	11,417	22,378	0.53	0.46	0.17
Branch	750	14,818	1,025	5,715	12,472	20,981	0.13	1.19	0.05
Calhoun	2,780	7,471	6,738	10,599	19,162	29,564	0.26	0.39	0.23
Cass	8,760	7,492	2,425	5,710	10,907	17,721	1.53	0.69	0.13
Clinton	....	7,718	1,982	1,614	5,102	13,916	......	1.51	0.14
Eaton	160	7,357	9,388	2,379	7,058	16,476	0.07	1.04	0.57
Genesee	2,958	9,404	2,227	4,268	12,031	22,498	0.69	0.78	0.10
Hillsdale	2,216	17,645	9,246	7,240	16,159	25,675	0.31	1.09	0.36
Ingham	525	9,626	15,603	2,498	8,631	17,435	0.21	1.12	0.89

* Counties in Indiana and Illinois not in existence in 1840 and the per capita values in each in 1850 and 1860: *Indiana:* Benton, \$1.71, \$....; Howard, \$0.91, \$0.81; Ohio, \$0.92, \$0.49; and Tipton, \$1.55, \$1.13; *Illinois:* Cumberland, \$2.60, \$0.88; Grundy, \$0.06, \$....; Henderson, \$2.95, \$0.20; Kendall, \$0.41, \$....; Mason, \$0.52, \$0.14; Massac, \$1.14, \$3.86; Moultrie, \$2.66, \$1.40; Piatt, \$2.09, \$0.05; Pulaski, \$1.46, \$0.09; Richland, \$1.14, \$0.98; Saline \$2.64, \$4.79; Woodford, \$1.76, \$1.25; Douglas (1860), \$0.17; Ford (1860), \$0.03; and Kankakee (1860), \$0.10.

TABLE XVIII—*Continued*

Counties	Total Valuation			Population			Per Capita Value		
	1840	1850	1860	1840	1850	1860	1840	1850	1860
MICHIGAN—*Continued*									
Ionia	....	$ 7,216	$ 6,590	1,923	7,597	16,682	......	$0.95	$0.40
Jackson	$ 2,931	19,278	6,551	13,130	19,431	26,671	$0.22	0.95	0.25
Kalamazoo	621	4,534	3,253	7,380	13,179	24,646	0.08	0.34	0.13
Kent	....	8,637	13,507	2,587	12,016	30,716	......	0.72	0.44
Lapeer	945	11,503	6,915	4,265	7,029	14,754	0.22	1.64	0.45
Lenawee	5,827	23,547	2,300	17,889	26,372	38,112	0.33	0.89	0.06
Livingston	1,247	21,677	3,845	7,430	13,485	16,851	0.17	1.61	0.23
Macomb	6,920	35,487	6,789	9,716	15,530	22,843	0.71	2.29	0.30
Michilimackinac*	570	....	....	923	3,598	1,938	0.62	......	......
Monroe	4,953	9,915	1,887	9,922	14,698	21,593	0.50	0.67	0.09
Oakland	29,031	30,988	7,359	23,646	31,270	38,261	1.24	0.99	0.19
Ottawa	....	1,256	2,147	208	5,587	13,215	......	0.22	0.16
Saginaw	....	418	400	892	2,609	12,693	......	0.16	0.03
St. Clair	779	12,861	1,248	4,606	10,420	26,604	0.17	0.12	0.05
Shiawasse	1,000	9,144	3,643	2,103	5,230	12,349	0.48	1.73	0.29
St. Joseph's	2,336	9,568	6,273	7,068	12,725	21,262	0.33	0.75	0.30
Van Buren	1,079	8,950	980	1,910	5,800	15,224	0.56	1.54	0.06
Washtenaw	26,541	25,960	5,316	23,571	28,567	35,686	1.13	0.91	0.15
Wayne†	8,375	15,345	4,138	24,173	42,756	75,547	0.35	0.36	0.05

WISCONSIN

Brown	648	100	195	2,107	6,215	11,795	0.31	0.02	0.02
Calumet	......	423	278	275	1,743	7,895	......	0.24	0.04
Crawford	......	......	600	1,502	2,498	8,068	......	......	0.07
Dane	......	4,479	2,452	314	16,639	43,922	......	0.27	0.06
Dodge	......	2,432	8,238	67	19,138	42,818	......	0.13	0.19
Fond du Lac	300	339	3,123	139	14,510	34,154	2.16	0.02	0.09
Grant	8,858	4,635	6,964	3,926	16,169	31,189	2.26	0.29	0.22
Green	484	9,039	9,181	933	9,566	19,808	0.52	1.06	0.46
Iowa	90	119	312	3,978	9,525	18,967	0.02	0.01	0.02
Jefferson	162	2,522	1,163	914	15,317	30,438	0.18	0.17	0.04
Manitowoc	......	894	100	235	3,702	22,416	......	0.24	0.00
Marquette	......	......	526	18	8,641	8,233	......	......	0.06
Milwaukee	15	......	677	5,605	31,077	62,518	0.00	......	0.01
Portage	......	1,240	1,473	1,623	1,250	7,507	......	0.99	0.20
Racine	127	75	9,382	3,475	14,973	21,360	0.04	0.15	0.44
Rock	1,058	......	19,567	1,701	20,750	36,690	0.62	......	0.53
St. Croix	......	......	333	809	624	5,392	......	......	0.06
Sauk	......	......	312	102	4,371	18,963	......	......	0.02
Sheboygan	......	......	1,056	133	8,379	26,875	......	......	0.04
Walworth	825	5,099	5,369	2,611	17,862	26,496	0.32	0.29	0.20
Washington	......	......	4,966	343	19,485	23,622	......	......	0.21
Winnebago‡	......	343	407	135	10,167	23,770	......	0.03	0.02

* And 21 unorganized counties.

† Counties not in existence in 1840 and the per capita value in each in 1850 and 1860: Montcalm, $0.28, $0.21; Newaygo, $0.04, $....; Sanilac, $0.50, $....; Tuscola, $...., $0.06; Alcona (1860), $0.18; Muskegon, $0.02. In the following counties there was nothing reported in the way of household manufactures in either of the foregoing years: Alpena, Antrim, Bay, Cheboygan, Emmet, Gladwin, Grand Traverse, Gratiot, Houghton, Huron, Iosco, Isabella, Leelenau, Manitou, Manistee, Marquette, Mason, Mecosta, Midland, Ontonagon, Osceola, Presque Isle, Schoolcraft, Delta, Oceana, and Chippewa.

‡ Counties not in existence in 1840 and the per capita value in each in 1850 and 1860: Adams, $0.28, $0.04; Columbia, $0.12, $0.05; Lafayette, $0.26, $0.10; Kenosha, $0.24, $1.13; La Pointe, $1.92, $....; Richland, $2.53, $0.22; Waukesha, $0.10, $0.09. In 1860 only: Bad Ax, $0.23; Buffalo, $0.05; Greenlake, $0.02; Juneau, $0.13; Monroe, $0.02; Outagamie, $1.81; Ozaukee, $0.07; Pepin, $0.01; Pierce, $0.66; Waupacca, $0.06; Waushara, $0.11. In the following counties nothing was reported in either of the foregoing years: Ashland, Burnette, Chippewa, Clark, Dallas, Door, Douglas, Dunn, Eau Claire, Jackson, Kewaunee, La Crosse, Marathon, Oconto, Polk, Shawano, Trempeleau, and Wood.

TABLE XVIII—*Continued*

Counties	Total Valuation			Population			Per Capita Value		
	1840	1850	1860	1840	1850	1860	1840	1850	1860
				LOUISIANA					
Ascension	....	$19,300	$52,073	6,951	10,752	11,484	......	$1.80	$4.55
Assumption	....	5,318	34,203	7,141	10,538	15,379	......	0.50	2.22
Avoyelles	....	8,522	42,486	6,616	9,326	13,167	......	0.91	3.23
Baton Rouge, E.	$ 223	....	....	8,138	11,977	16,046	$0.03	......	......
Baton Rouge, W.	452	337	....	4,638	6,270	7,312	0.10	0.05	......
Caddo	1,957	1,113	2,840	5,282	8,884	12,140	0.37	0.13	0.23
Calcasieu	890	4,943	16,285	2,057	3,914	5,928	0.43	1.26	2.75
Caldwell	*	2,103	190	2,017	2,815	4,833	*	0.75	0.04
Carroll	....	125	16,464	4,237	8,789	18,052	......	0.01	0.91
Catahoula	7,868	25	....	4,955	7,132	11,651	1.59	0.00	......
Claiborne	*	3,416	9,202	6,185	7,471	16,848	*	0.46	0.55
Concordia	....	....	600	9,414	7,758	13,805	......	......	0.04
Feliciana, E.	3,883	5,343	....	11,893	13,598	14,697	0.33	0.39	......
Feliciana, W.	4,865	995	....	10,910	13,245	11,671	0.45	0.08	......
Iberville	....	....	200	8,495	12,278	14,661	......	......	0.01
Lafayette	....	12,586	20,667	7,841	6,720	9,003	......	1.87	2.30
Livingston	....	954	....	2,315	3,385	4,431	......	0.28	......
Madison	....	554	....	5,142	8,773	14,133	......	0.06	......
Natchitoches	10,674	6,089	....	14,350	14,228	16,699	0.74	0.43	......
Ouachita	19,495	5,505	....	4,640	5,008	4,727	4.20	1.10	......
Point Coupee	108	1,950	....	7,898	11,339	17,718	0.01	0.17	......
Rapides	2,815	6,795	3,336	14,132	16,561	25,360	0.20	0.41	0.13

St. Charles	....	....	225,600	4,700	5,120	5,297	......	......	42.59
St. Helena	4,639	5,335	2,941	3,525	4,561	7,130	1.32	1.17	0.41
St. Landry	3,000	11,280	17,916	15,233	22,253	23,104	0.20	0.51	0.78
St. Mary's	321	....	....	8,950	13,697	16,816	0.04	......	......
St. Tammany	1,500	229	500	4,598	6,364	5,406	0.33	0.04	0.09
Union	*	5,794	12,720	1,838	8,203	10,389	*	0.71	1.22
Washington†	2,500	....	6,924	2,649	3,408	4,708	0.94	......	1.47

MISSISSIPPI

Adams	2,160	6,945	6,980	19,434	18,601	20,165	0.11	0.37	0.35
Amite	27,228	10,588	9,586	9,511	9,694	12,336	2.86	1.09	0.78
Attala	15,893	28,802	18,405	4,303	10,991	14,169	3.69	2.62	1.30
Bolivar	....	150	....	1,356	2,577	10,471	......	0.06	......
Carroll	4,555	22,558	3,949	10,481	18,491	22,035	0.43	3.84	0.18
Chickasaw	12,179	37,892	45,996	2,955	16,369	16,426	4.12	2.31	2.80
Choctaw	22,320	44,546	136,848	6,010	11,402	15,722	3.71	3.91	8.70
Claiborne	10,585	13,030	128,245	13,078	14,941	15,679	0.81	0.87	8.18
Clark	....	18,720	2,393	2,986	5,477	10,771	......	3.42	0.22
Coahoma	....	8,676	....	1,290	2,780	6,606	......	3.12	......
Copiah	24,198	32,768	1,668	8,954	11,794	15,398	2.70	2.78	0.11
Covington	11,707	29,124	75,190	2,717	3,338	4,408	4.31	8.72	17.06
De Soto	8,000	35,496	7,521	7,002	19,042	23,336	1.14	1.86	0.32
Franklin	6,713	6,696	2,358	4,775	5,904	8,265	1.41	1.13	0.29
Greene	5,527	1,581	4,351	1,636	2,018	2,232	3.38	0.78	1.95

* No returns.

† No household manufactures reported in any of the census returns for the parishes of Jefferson, Plaquemines, St. Bernard, St. James, and St. John Baptist. The following parishes were not in existence in 1840; the per capita value in each in 1850 and 1860 is also given: Bienville, $0.49, $....; Bossier, $0.05, $....; De Soto, $0.14, $0.24; Franklin, $0.11, $....; Jackson, $2.36, $2.04; Morehouse, $1.03, $0.00; Sabine, $0.97, $0.58; Tensas, $0.10, $0.01; Vermilion, $1.03, $1.57; and Winn (1860 only), $0.53. Orleans, La Fourche, St. Martin's, and Terre Bonne reported small amounts in 1860, but none at all in 1840 and 1850.

TABLE XVIII—*Continued*

Counties	Total Valuation			Population			Per Capita Value		
	1840	1850	1860	1840	1850	1860	1840	1850	1860
MISSISSIPPI—*Continued*									
Hancock	$ 1,170	$ 1,441	....	3,367	3,672	3,139	$0.35	$0.39	.....
Hinds	6,220	14,018	$ 1,016	19,098	25,340	31,339	0.33	0.55	$0.03
Holmes	12,564	11,949	9,417	9,452	13,928	17,791	1.33	0.86	0.53
Itawamba	107,879	48,424	86,699	5,375	13,528	17,695	20.07	3.58	4.90
Jackson	....	2,474	6,355	1,965	3,196	4,122	.....	0.77	1.54
Jasper	12,559	20,382	20,820	3,958	6,184	11,007	3.17	3.30	1.89
Jefferson	6,394	5,589	40,782	11,650	13,193	15,349	0.55	0.42	0.53
Jones	3,622	8,903	19,782	1,258	2,164	3,323	2.88	4.11	5.95
Kemper	12,453	41,648	17,684	7,663	12,517	11,682	1.63	3.33	1.51
Lafayette	25,099	129,944	27,490	6,531	14,069	16,125	3.84	9.24	1.70
Lauderdale	....	28,234	19,063	5,358	8,717	13,313	.....	3.24	1.43
Lawrence	27,079	21,217	10,367	5,920	6,478	9,213	4.57	3.28	1.13
Leake	3,310	10,976	14,278	2,162	5,533	9,324	1.53	1.98	1.53
Lowndes	17,018	28,342	9,596	14,513	19,544	23,635	1.17	1.45	0.41
Madison	....	11,560	18,628	15,530	18,173	23,382	.....	0.64	0.80
Marion	10,824	10,402	10,773	3,830	4,410	4,686	2.84	2.36	2.30
Marshall	25,647	42,435	49,656	17,526	29,689	28,823	1.46	1.43	1.72
Monroe	20,741	31,329	22,944	9,250	21,172	21,283	2.24	1.48	1.08
Neshoba	11,002	10,631	19,985	2,437	4,728	8,343	4.51	2.25	2.40
Newton	9,150	20,686	11,299	2,527	4,465	9,661	3.62	4.63	1.17
Noxubee	1,664	16,958	9,513	9,975	16,299	20,667	0.17	1.04	0.46
Oktibbeha	6,668	14,254	28,896	4,276	9,171	12,977	1.56	1.55	2.23

Panola	4,930	80	6,313	4,657	11,444	13,794	1.06	0.01	0.46
Perry	....	16,595	7,186	1,889	2,438	2,606	......	6.81	2.76
Pike	51,095	21,375	17,644	6,151	7,360	11,135	8.31	2.90	1.58
Pontotoc	12,272	32,362	57,320	4,491	17,112	22,113	2.73	1.89	2.59
Rankin	....	14,742	11,457	4,631	7,227	13,635	......	2.04	0.84
Scott	8,452	7,988	14,733	1,653	3,961	8,139	5.11	2.02	1.81
Simpson	11,266	38,063	13,275	3,380	4,734	6,080	3.33	8.04	2.18
Smith	6,949	21,637	31,263	1,961	4,071	7,638	3.54	5.31	4.09
Tallahatchie	7,652	4,637	2,308	2,985	4,643	7,890	2.56	1.00	0.29
Tippah	33,957	53,648	144,269	9,444	20,741	22,550	3.60	2.59	6.40
Tishomingo	15,459	39,703	83,990	6,681	15,490	24,149	2.31	2.56	3.48
Tunica	395	1,055	....	821	1,314	4,366	0.48	0.80	......
Warren	3,783	2,787	51,798	15,820	18,120	20,696	0.24	0.15	2.50
Wayne	4,428	....	1,285	2,120	2,892	3,691	3.95	......	0.35
Wilkinson	5,182	1,081	428	14,193	16,914	15,933	0.37	0.06	0.03
Winston	17,301	21,698	14,820	4,650	7,956	9,811	3.72	2.73	1.51
Yalabusha	18,937	49,966	220	12,248	17,258	16,952	1.55	2.90	0.01
Yazoo	8,759	6,763	....	10,480	14,418	22,373	0.84	0.47	......

ALABAMA

Autauga	19,215	98,348	47,784	14,342	15,023	16,739	1.34	6.55	2.85
Baldwin	295	1,744	1,537	2,951	4,414	7,530	0.10	0.40	0.20
Barbour	10,698	31,839	18,415	12,024	23,632	30,812	0.89	1.35	0.60
Benton	329,096	65,308	....	14,260	17,163	....	19.17	3.80	......
Bibb	25,269	22,431	35,618	8,284	9,969	11,894	3.05	2.25	2.99
Blount	8,036	21,480	30,280	5,570	7,367	10,865	1.44	2.92	2.79
Butler	13,131	16,855	21,214	8,685	10,836	18,122	1.51	1.56	1.17
Chambers	26,229	40,714	9,204	17,333	23,960	23,214	1.51	1.70	0.40
Cherokee	31,984	76,111	65,596	8,773	13,884	18,360	3.65	5.48	3.57

TABLE XVIII—*Continued*

Counties	Total Valuation			Population			Per Capita Value		
	1840	1850	1860	1840	1850	1860	1840	1850	1860
ALABAMA—*Continued*									
Clarke	$ 23,808	$28,301	$26,362	8,640	9,786	15,049	$2.76	$2.89	$1.75
Conecuh	....	21,281	59,085	8,197	9,322	11,311	......	2.59	6.34
Coosa	16,187	98,118	62,884	6,995	14,543	19,273	2.31	6.75	3.26
Covington	7,542	14,890	35,458	2,435	3,645	6,469	3.10	4.09	5.48
Dale	3,305	26,045	70,824	7,397	6,382	12,195	0.45	4.08	5.81
Dallas	45,908	24,799	8,372	25,199	29,727	33,625	1.82	0.83	0.25
DeKalb	62,283	27,573	85,433	5,929	8,245	10,705	10.50	3.34	7.98
Fayette	101,324	80,687	93,100	6,942	9,681	12,850	14.60	8.33	7.25
Franklin	48,932	42,333	76,502	14,270	19,610	18,627	3.43	2.16	4.11
Greene	6,942	66,016	12,894	24,024	31,441	30,859	0.28	2.10	0.42
Henry	7,679	43,178	24,892	5,787	9,019	14,918	1.33	4.79	1.67
Jackson	67,492	42,600	85,995	15,715	14,088	18,283	4.29	3.02	4.70
Jefferson	20,725	37,692	51,155	7,131	8,989	11,746	2.90	4.19	4.36
Lauderdale	72,171	47,844	22,833	14,485	17,172	17,420	4.98	2.79	1.05
Lawrence	31,082	58,970	18,263	13,313	15,258	13,975	2.33	3.86	1.63
Limestone	58,142	44,905	16,551	14,374	16,483	15,306	4.04	2.72	1.08
Lowndes	5,372	20,041	6,709	19,539	21,915	27,716	0.75	0.91	0.27
Macon	7,022	35,962	11,333	11,247	26,898	26,802	0.62	1.34	2.44
Madison	56,558	43,449	65,305	25,706	26,427	26,451	2.20	1.64	2.47
Marengo	8,486	25,115	42,251	17,264	27,831	31,171	0.49	1.01	1.35
Marion	51,275	38,084	45,862	5,847	7,833	11,182	8.77	4.86	4.10
Marshall	30,061	22,655	44,297	7,553	8,846	11,472	3.98	2.56	3.86

Mobile	50	240	....	18,741	27,600	41,131	0.00	0.01	......
Monroe	32,678	48,513	28,483	10,680	12,013	15,667	3.06	4.04	1.82
Montgomery	36,614	31,869	9,997	24,574	29,711	35,904	1.49	1.07	0.25
Morgan	37,282	28,569	25,923	9,841	10,125	11,335	3.79	2.82	2.29
Perry	64,727	20,211	6,845	19,086	22,285	27,724	3.39	0.91	0.25
Pickens	*	51,743	18,391	17,118	21,512	22,316	*	2.41	0.82
Pike	36,580	52,300	71,320	10,108	15,920	24,435	3.62	3.29	2.92
Randolph	51,613	61,225	86,339	4,973	11,581	20,059	10.38	5.29	4.30
Russell	19,653	25,000	4,754	13,513	19,548	26,592	1.45	1.28	0.18
St. Clair	44,555	48,651	37,912	5,638	6,829	11,013	7.90	7.12	3.44
Shelby	14,392	63,091	36,293	6,112	9,536	12,618	2.35	6.62	2.87
Sumter	*	24,524	13,265	29,937	22,250	24,035	*	1.10	0.55
Talladega	32,590	42,489	23,327	12,587	18,624	23,520	2.59	2.28	2.19
Tallapoosa	13,469	46,739	51,621	6,444	15,584	23,827	2.12	3.00	0.98
Tuscaloosa	8,008	23,947	37,706	16,583	18,056	23,200	0.48	1.33	1.63
Walker	47,328	27,532	32,983	4,032	5,124	7,980	11.74	5.37	4.13
Washington	7,619	3,208	....	5,300	2,713	4,669	1.44	1.18	......
Wilcox	12,532	20,002	25,344	15,278	17,352	24,618	0.82	1.15	1.03

FLORIDA

Alachua	....	5,198	5,182	2,282	2,524	8,232	......	2.06	0.63
Calhoun	1,070	1,253	....	1,142	1,377	1,446	0.94	0.91	......
Columbia	....	9,624	2,362	2,102	4,808	4,646	......	2.00	0.51
Duval	....	7,995	1	4,156	4,539	5,074	......	1.76	0.00
Escambia	20	595	....	3,993	4,351	5,768	0.01	0.14	......
Gadsden	3,450	....	5	5,992	8,784	9,396	0.58	......	0.00
Hamilton	1,691	4,483	2,698	1,464	2,511	4,154	1.16	1.79	0.65
Jackson	....	2,125	2,672	4,681	6,639	10,209	......	0.32	0.26

* No returns.

TABLE XVIII—*Continued*

Counties	Total Valuation			Population			Per Capita Value		
	1840	1850	1860	1840	1850	1860	1840	1850	1860
				FLORIDA—*Continued*					
Jefferson	$ 4,330	$10,652	$ 3,858	5,713	7,718	9,876	$0.76	$1.38	$0.39
Leon	1,931	3,995	888	10,713	11,442	12,343	0.18	0.35	0.07
Madison	1,435	9,405	5,132	2,644	5,490	7,779	0.54	1.71	0.66
Nassau	....	6,071	88	1,892	2,164	3,644	......	2.81	0.02
Walton	4,908	2,998	12,232	1,461	1,817	3,037	3.36	1.65	4.03
Washington*	1,370	2,298	6,981	859	1,950	2,154	1.59	1.18	3.24
				MISSOURI					
Audrain	5,885	12,924	20,522	1,949	3,506	8,075	3.02	3.69	2.54
Barry	47,767	11,447	20,985	4,795	3,467	7,995	9.96	3.30	2.62
Benton	8,754	12,259	10,886	4,205	5,015	9,072	2.08	2.44	1.20
Boone	49,631	36,588	33,817	13,561	14,979	19,486	3.66	2.46	1.74
Buchanan	13,426	38,923	20,346	6,237	12,975	23,861	2.15	3.00	0.85
Caldwell	....	6,790	17,493	1,458	2,310	5,034	......	?	3.47
Callaway	35,241	39,758	46,876	11,765	13,827	17,449	3.00	2.88	2.69
Cape Girardeau	49,487	29,582	29,619	9,359	13,912	15,547	5.29	2.13	1.91
Carrol	13,652	21,262	16,690	2,423	5,441	9,763	5.62	3.91	1.71
Chariton	15,129	11,290	16,563	4,746	7,514	12,562	2.19	1.50	1.32
Clark	5,369	13,429	6,898	2,846	5,527	11,684	1.89	2.43	0.59

Clay	28,702	31,947	21,227	8,282	10,332	13,023	3.47	3.09	1.71
Clinton	8,890	19,366	16,519	2,724	3,786	7,848	3.27	5.12	2.10
Cole	25,032	10,479	4,649	9,286	6,696	9,697	2.70	1.56	0.48
Cooper	45,533	19,938	17,612	10,484	12,950	17,356	4.34	1.54	1.01
Crawford	13,098	18,346	13,296	3,561	6,397	5,823	3.68	2.87	2.12
Daviess	1,383	8,919	11,304	2,736	5,298	9,606	0.51	1.68	1.18
Franklin	23,401	12,342	5,606	7,515	11,021	18,085	3.11	1.12	0.31
Gasconade	10,956	6,764	16,518	5,330	4,996	8,727	2.06	1.35	1.89
Greene	19,849	108,797	50,721	5,372	12,785	13,186	3.69	8.51	3.85
Howard	19,102	100,088	43,263	13,108	13,969	15,946	1.46	7.17	2.71
Jackson	24,802	21,869	21,837	7,612	14,000	22,896	3.26	1.56	0.95
Jefferson	3,742	5,131	2,732	4,296	6,928	10,344	0.87	0.74	0.26
Johnson	19,286	21,369	33,690	4,471	7,464	14,644	4.31	2.86	2.30
Lafayette	13,960	25,429	13,629	6,815	13,690	20,098	2.05	1.86	0.68
Lewis	18,258	14,578	19,944	6,040	6,578	12,286	3.02	2.22	1.54
Lincoln	29,672	14,775	29,369	7,449	9,421	14,210	3.98	1.57	2.07
Linn	4,192	9,399	20,354	2,245	4,058	9,112	1.87	2.32	2.23
Livingston	5,897	13,659	17,155	4,325	4,247	7,417	1.34	3.22	2.31
Macon	8,279	17,156	37,411	6,034	6,565	14,346	1.37	2.61	2.61
Madison	9,276	11,744	7,544	3,395	6,003	5,664	2.73	1.96	1.33
Marion	35,134	29,516	20,925	9,623	12,230	18,838	3.65	2.41	1.11
Miller	10,487	11,689	17,131	2,282	3,834	6,812	4.60	3.05	2.51
Monroe	34,666	33,287	33,271	9,505	10,541	14,785	3.65	3.16	2.25
Montgomery	18,887	16,236	13,570	4,371	5,489	9,718	4.32	2.96	1.40

* Counties in Mississippi, Alabama, and Florida not in existence in 1840 and per capita value in each in 1850 and 1860: *Mississippi:* Harrison, \$0.08, \$0.35; Issaquena, \$0.02, \$....; Calhoun (1860 only), \$2.42; Sunflower and Washington reported nothing for any of the foregoing years; *Alabama:* Choctaw, \$1.60, \$0.77; Coffee, \$4.45, \$2.73; Calhoun (1860 only), \$2.75; Winston, \$4.19; Hancock and Benton had a per capita value in 1850 of \$5.85 and \$3.80, respectively; they were not in the list of counties for 1860; *Florida:* Benton, \$3.80, \$0.00; Levy, \$1.71, \$0.36; Marion, \$0.81, \$0.06; Orange, \$0.30, \$0.38; Putnam, \$0.17, \$0.03; Santa Rosa, \$0.42, \$....; Wakulla, \$0.89, \$0.48; Clay (1860 only), \$0.01; Lafayette, \$1.81; Liberty, \$1.45; New River, \$0.96; Suwannee, \$0.27; Taylor, \$1.82; Volusia, \$0.05. Nothing reported from the following for any of the foregoing years: Mosquito, St. Lucie, Brevard, Dade, Franklin, Hernando, Manatee, Monroe, St. John's, Sumter. Hillsborough reported a small amount in 1860, but nothing at all in 1840 and 1850.

TABLE XVIII—*Continued*

Counties	Total Valuation			Population			Per Capita Value		
	1840	1850	1860	1840	1850	1860	1840	1850	1860
				MISSOURI—*Continued*					
Morgan	$13,157	$17,958	$ 13,230	4,407	4,650	8,202	$2.99	$3.86	$1.61
New Madrid	6,484	....	....	4,554	5,541	5,654	1.42	......	......
Newton	12,640	10,956	12,131	3,790	4,268	9,319	3.34	2.57	1.30
Perry	12,300	12,147	15,033	5,760	7,215	9,128	2.14	1.68	1.65
Pettis	8,589	14,623	13,359	2,930	5,150	9,392	2.93	2.84	1.42
Pike	34,690	38,122	46,157	10,646	13,609	18,417	3.26	2.80	2.51
Platte	31,301	54,179	24,702	8,913	16,845	18,350	3.51	3.22	1.35
Polk	8,650	21,852	35,335	8,449	6,186	9,995	1.02	3.53	3.54
Pulaski	28,482	11,459	5,187	6,529	3,998	3,835	4.36	2.87	1.35
Ralls	12,986	16,846	26,224	5,670	6,151	8,592	2.29	2.74	3.05
Randolph	31,112	39,176	21,494	7,198	9,439	11,407	4.32	4.15	1.88
Ray	31,300	30,159	110,115	6,553	10,373	14,092	4.78	2.91	7.81
Ripley	9,980	16,733	9,276	2,856	2,830	3,747	3.50	5.91	2.48
St. Charles	13,000	8,443	3,666	7,911	11,454	16,523	1.64	0.74	0.22
St. Francois	6,851	10,187	14,123	3,211	4,964	7,249	2.13	2.05	1.95
St. Genevieve	3,804	3,714	6,917	3,148	5,313	8,029	1.21	0.70	0.86
St. Louis	13,495	6,898	180	35,979	104,978	190,524	0.38	0.07	0.00
Saline	16,801	14,854	15,276	5,258	8,843	14,699	3.20	1.68	1.04
Scott	8,132	2,930	2,323	5,974	3,182	5,247	1.36	0.92	0.44
Shelby	4,881	13,670	52,025	3,056	4,253	7,301	1.60	3.21	7.13
Stoddard	81,688	11,285	11,486	3,153	4,277	7,877	25.91	2.64	1.46
Taney	16,178	20,880	9,266	3,264	4,373	3,576	4.96	4.77	2.59

Warren	15,012	11,311	7,317	4,253	5,860	8,839	3.53	1.93	0.83
Washington	11,995	19,986	10,930	7,213	8,811	9,723	1.66	2.27	1.12
Wayne*	23,790	14,103	23,639	3,403	4,518	5,629	6.99	3.12	4.20

ARKANSAS

Arkansas	585	395	283	1,346	3,245	8,844	0.43	0.12	0.03
Benton	8,785	9,608	18,761	2,228	3,710	9,306	3.94	2.59	2.02
Carroll	63,950	19,983	51,119	2,844	4,614	9,383	2.25	4.33	5.45
Chicot	1,580	230	....	3,806	5,115	9,234	0.42	0.04	......
Clark	34,651	12,253	11,408	2,309	4,070	9,735	14.57	3.01	1.17
Conway	5,021	20,361	13,117	2,892	3,583	6,697	1.74	5.68	1.96
Crawford	5,468	19,885	6,541	4,266	7,960	7,850	1.28	2.50	0.83
Crittenden	231	130	70	1,561	2,648	4,920	0.15	0.05	0.01
Desha	1,220	30	....	1,598	2,911	6,459	0.76	0.01	......
Franklin	10,675	16,848	21,231	2,665	3,972	7,298	4.01	4.24	2.91
Greene	1,930	41,515	26,257	1,586	2,593	5,843	1.22	16.01	4.49
Hempstead	52,295	17,972	67,848	4,921	7,672	13,989	10.63	2.34	4.85
Hot Springs	40	7,198	64,569	1,907	3,609	5,635	0.02	1.99	11.46
Independence	11,054	25,729	51,110	3,669	7,767	14,307	3.01	3.31	3.57
Izard	9,328	24,281	32,163	2,240	3,213	7,215	4.16	7.56	4.46
Jackson	7,940	3,717	326	1,540	3,086	10,493	5.16	1.20	0.03

* Counties not in existence in 1840 and the per capita value in each in 1850 and 1860: Adair, \$3.89, \$2.41; Andrew, \$2.91, \$1.69; Atchison, \$2.04, \$1.51; Bates, \$3.84, \$1.39; Butler, \$3.00, \$1.60; Camden, \$7.71, \$1.63; Cass, \$3.19, \$2.61; Cedar, \$5.94, \$3.11; Dade, \$6.43, \$4.06; Dallas, \$2.92, \$3.89; DeKalb, \$4.24, \$1.82; Dunklin, \$2.61, \$1.29; Gentry, \$2.61, \$2.19; Grundy \$2.45, \$3.35; Harrison, \$2.06, \$1.42; Henry, \$3.50, \$2.49; Hickory, \$2.13, \$2.39; Holt, \$1.73, \$1.32; Jasper, \$3.91, \$2.78; Knox, \$2.36, \$1.71; Laclede, \$3.55, \$1.81; Lawrence, \$4.01, \$2.18; McDonald, \$7.41, \$3.71; Mercer, \$3.70, \$3.33; Mississippi, \$0.54, \$0.37; Moniteau, \$3.81, \$1.71; Nodaway, \$3.18, \$2.51; Oregon, \$3.14, \$2.27; Osage, \$1.48, \$2.98; Ozark, \$3.09, \$2.39; Putnam, \$1.44, \$2.84; Reynolds, \$2.47, \$2.09; St. Clair, \$3.92, \$0.97; Schuyler, \$2.88, \$2.77; Scotland, \$2.24, \$1.75; Shannon, \$3.53, \$4.60; Sullivan, \$5.50, \$4.11; Texas, \$3.63, \$2.13; and Wright, \$4.61, \$2.28; the following for 1860 only: Barton, \$1.01; Bollinger, \$2.15; Carter, \$2.12; Christian, \$4.15; Dent, \$1.28; Douglas, \$3.03; Howell, \$2.85; Iron, \$0.84; Maries, \$2.85; Phelps, \$2.07; Stone, \$2.33; Vernon, \$5.35; Webster, \$2.21; Pemiscot, \$0.64.

TABLE XVIII—*Continued*

Counties	Total Valuation			Population			Per Capita Value		
	1840	1850	1860	1840	1850	1860	1840	1850	1860
ARKANSAS—*Continued*									
Jefferson	$ 1,101	....	$ 2,043	2,566	5,834	14,971	$0.43	......	$0.14
Johnson	15,269	$15,278	32,334	3,433	5,227	7,612	4.45	$2.92	4.25
Lafayette	581	10,810	3,242	2,200	5,220	8,464	0.46	2.07	0.38
Lawrence	13,469	50,291	37,827	2,835	5,274	9,372	4.75	9.53	4.04
Madison	9,745	28,041	38,644	2,775	4,823	7,740	3.51	5.81	4.99
Marion	10,811	9,824	23,284	1,325	2,308	6,192	8.16	4.26	3.76
Mississippi	401	1,384	2,386	1,410	2,368	3,895	0.28	0.58	0.61
Monroe	603	1,982	959	936	2,049	5,657	0.64	0.97	0.17
Phillips	2,082	4,168	65	3,547	6,935	14,876	0.59	0.60	0.00
Pike	2,726	4,820	15,931	969	1,861	4,025	2.81	2.59	3.96
Poinsett	4,491	8,695	4,750	1,320	2,308	3,621	3.40	3.77	1.31
Pope	28,275	14,352	77,427	2,850	4,710	7,883	9.92	3.05	9.82
Pulaski	2,479	5,614	4,025	5,350	5,657	11,699	0.46	0.99	0.34
Randolph	10,206	14,133	7,980	2,196	3,275	6,261	4.57	4.32	1.27
St. Francis	8,472	5,916	8,335	2,499	4,479	8,672	3.39	1.32	0.96
Saline	1,375	12,705	13,237	2,061	3,903	6,649	6.67	3.26	1.99
Scott	6,774	12,426	14,266	1,694	3,083	5,145	4.00	4.03	2.77
Searcy	15,690	22,330	22,692	936	1,979	5,271	1.68	11.28	4.31
Sevier	76,790	14,463	19,795	2,810	4,240	10,516	2.73	3.41	1.88
Union	19,582	15,456	19,204	2,889	10,298	12,288	6.78	1.50	1.56
Van Buren	5,170	18,024	19,204	1,518	2,864	5,357	3.41	6.29	3.58
Washington	37,257	52,411	36,314	7,148	9,970	14,673	5.21	5.26	2.47
White*	1,648	5,684	9,112	929	2,619	8,316	1.77	2.17	1.10

IOWA

Appanoose	....	1,602	21,253	....	3,131	11,931	......	0.51	1.78
Benton	....	1,195	3,554	....	672	8,496	......	1.78	0.42
Black Hawk	....	76	842	....	135	8,244	......	0.56	0.10
Buchanan	....	371	1,577	....	517	7,906	......	0.72	0.20
Cedar	....	5,768	6,295	....	3,941	12,949	......	1.47	0.49
Clarke	....	....	4,697	....	79	5,427	......	......	0.87
Clayton	....	414	1,029	....	3,873	20,728	......	0.10	0.05
Clinton	....	4,734	157	....	2,822	18,938	......	1.68	0.01
Davis	....	16,162	19,383	....	7,264	13,764	......	2.22	1.41
Decatur	....	1,207	10,981	....	965	8,677	......	1.25	1.27
Delaware	....	1,371	2,053	....	1,759	11,024	......	0.78	0.19
Des Moines	....	7,098	3,396	....	12,988	19,611	......	0.55	0.17
Dubuque	....	2,178	2,013	....	10,841	31,164	......	0.20	0.06
Fayette	....	48	1,073	....	825	12,073	......	0.06	0.09
Fremont	....	1,585	5,210	....	1,244	5,074	......	1.27	1.03
Henry	....	14,978	7,315	....	8,707	18,701	......	1.72	0.39
Iowa	....	1,108	10,190	....	822	8,029	......	1.35	1.27
Jackson	....	4,942	2,328	....	7,210	18,493	......	0.69	0.13
Jasper	....	1,900	5,964	....	1,280	9,883	......	1.02	0.60
Jefferson	....	22,263	14,301	....	9,904	15,038	......	2.25	0.95
Johnson	....	5,762	139	....	4,472	17,573	......	1.29	0.01
Jones	....	2,783	2,083	....	3,007	13,306	......	0.93	0.16
Keokuk	....	9,221	8,392	....	4,822	13,271	......	1.91	0.63
Lee	....	12,941	4,489	....	18,861	29,232	......	0.69	0.15
Linn	....	8,618	8,522	....	5,444	18,947	......	1.58	0.45
Louisa	....	6,720	1,906	....	4,939	10,370	......	1.36	0.18

* Counties not in existence in 1840 and the per capita value in each in 1850 and 1860: Ashley, \$1.18, \$1.42; Bradley, \$1.73, \$7.67; Dallas, \$0.87, \$1.44; Drew, \$1.60, \$0.78; Fulton, \$4.58, \$5.66; Montgomery, \$3.63, \$7.50; Newton, \$7.38, \$4.37; Ouachita, \$1.64, \$0.28; Perry, \$2.06, \$1.60; Polk, \$5.95, \$4.31; Prairie, \$1.69, \$0.49; Yell, \$3.53, \$3.53; for 1860 only: Calhoun, \$1.36; Columbia, \$0.80; Craighead, \$1.23; Sebastian, \$0.97.

TABLE XVIII—*Continued*

Counties	Total Valuation			Population			Per Capita Value		
	1840	1850	1860	1840	1850	1860	1840	1850	1860
IOWA—*Continued*									
Lucas	....	$ 302	$ 6,344	....	471	5,766	......	$0.64	$1.10
Madison	....	1,055	7,768	....	1,179	7,339	......	0.89	1.05
Mahaska	....	7,818	10,088	....	5,989	14,816	......	1.30	0.68
Marion	....	5,252	15,383	....	5,482	16,813	......	0.96	0.92
Marshall	....	419	1,552	....	338	6,015	......	1.21	0.26
Monroe	....	6,062	14,145	....	2,884	8,612	......	2.10	1.64
Muscatine	....	3,400	2,677	....	5,731	16,444	......	0.59	0.16
Page	....	1,181	7,188	....	551	4,419	......	2.14	1.63
Polk	....	4,994	5,041	....	4,513	11,625	......	1.11	0.43
Pottawatamie	....	444	690	....	7,828	4,968	......	0.06	0.14
Poweshiek	....	943	1,268	....	615	5,668	......	1.53	0.22
Scott	....	1,417	1,470	....	5,986	25,959	......	0.24	0.06
Taylor	....	932	3,507	....	204	3,590	......	4.57	0.98
Van Buren	....	23,589	12,454	....	12,270	17,081	......	1.92	0.73
Wapello	....	19,519	12,618	....	8,471	14,518	......	2.30	0.87
Warren	....	849	8,489	....	961	10,281	......	0.88	0.83
Washington	....	7,676	7,688	....	4,957	14,235	......	1.55	0.54
Wayne	....	395	8,527	....	340	6,409	......	1.16	1.33
Winneshiek*	....	....	2,008	....	546	13,942	......	......	0.14

TEXAS

Anderson	......	4,340	15,594	......	2,884	10,398	......	1.50	1.50
Angelina	......	1,930	17,617	......	1,665	4,271	......	1.66	4.12
Austin	......	710	930	......	3,841	10,139	......	0.18	0.09
Bastrop	......	812	800	......	3,099	7,006	......	0.26	0.11
Bowie	......	......	5,302	......	2,912	5,052	......	......	1.49
Brazos	......	100	......	......	614	2,776	......	0.16	......
Burleson	......	427	90	......	1,713	5,683	......	0.25	0.02
Caldwell	......	29,534	12,836	......	1,329	4,481	......	22.22	2.86
Cass	......	20,099	11,733	......	4,991	8,411	......	4.03	1.39
Cherokee	......	12,936	10,429	......	6,673	12,098	......	1.94	0.86
Collin	......	6,516	14,265	......	1,950	9,264	......	3.34	1.54
Comal	......	379	......	......	1,723	4,030	......	0.22	......
Cook	......	854	5,286	......	220	3,760	......	3.88	1.41
Dallas	......	3,058	15,191	......	2,743	8,665	......	1.11	1.82
Denton	......	2,493	6,843	......	641	5,031	......	3.89	1.36
DeWitt	......	100	150	......	1,716	5,108	......	0.58	0.03
Ellis	......	1,711	11,312	......	989	5,246	......	1.73	2.16
Fannin	......	11,464	12,713	......	3,788	9,217	......	3.03	1.38
Fayette	......	2,516	8	......	3,756	11,604	......	0.67	0.00
Gillespie	......	30	199	......	1,240	2,736	......	0.02	0.07
Goliad	......	......	18,010	......	648	3,384	......	......	5.32
Gonzales	......	10,553	2,945	......	1,492	8,059	......	7.07	0.37
Grayson	......	5,260	15,909	......	2,008	8,184	......	2.62	1.94
Grimes	......	5,848	......	......	4,008	10,307	......	1.46	......

* All of the 18 counties from which returns were received in 1840 have not been included in the tabulation. But nine of these reported anything at all on household manufactures. For purposes of comparison these follow with the per capita value in each in 1840: Cedar, \$5.06; Clinton, \$3.23; Des Moines, \$0.82; Dubuque, \$0.02; Henry, \$1.41; Lee, \$0.36; Linn, \$1.93; Van Buren, \$0.28; and Washington, \$0.26.

It does not seem worth while to enumerate the 53 counties which were in existence in 1860 and not in 1850. Twenty-six of these reported no household manufactures in 1860, while the remaining 28 reported per capita values ranging from \$0.05 to \$1.11, most of them running between \$0.20 and \$0.30. These facts are rather significant, since they show that the new communities in this state between 1850 and 1860 did not rely upon household manufactures as did the new communities in the early history of other states.

TABLE XVIII—*Continued*

Counties	Total Valuation			Population			Per Capita Value		
	1840	1850	1860	1840	1850	1860	1840	1850	1860
TEXAS—*Continued*									
Guadalupe	....	$ 110	$ 1,778	....	1,511	5,444	......	$0.07	$0.33
Harrison	....	2,610	7,127	....	11,822	15,001	......	0.22	0.48
Hays	....	240	....	....	387	2,126	......	0.63	......
Henderson	....	9,788	8,432	....	1,237	4,595	......	7.91	1.84
Hopkins	....	6,774	14,334	....	2,623	7,745	......	2.58	1.85
Houston	....	1,717	26,260	....	2,721	8,058	......	0.63	3.26
Hunt	....	2,485	14,828	....	1,520	6,630	......	1.64	2.23
Jackson	....	3,635	1,436	....	996	2,612	......	3.65	0.55
Jasper	....	2,241	275	....	1,767	4,037	......	1.27	0.07
Jefferson	....	1,984	623	....	1,836	1,995	......	1.08	0.31
Kaufman	....	7,622	6,043	....	1,047	3,936	......	7.28	1.54
Lamar	....	21,698	16,797	....	3,978	10,136	......	5.45	1.66
Leon	....	940	1,343	....	1,946	6,781	......	0.48	0.20
Liberty	....	40	....	....	2,522	3,189	......	0.02	......
Limestone	....	1,714	4,765	....	2,608	4,537	......	0.66	1.05
Milam	....	698	1,445	....	2,907	5,175	......	0.24	0.28
Montgomery	....	1,130	....	....	2,384	5,479	......	0.47	......
Nacogdoches	....	6,194	18,239	....	5,193	8,292	......	1.19	2.20
Navarro	....	3,211	4,750	....	2,190	5,996	......	1.47	0.79
Newton	....	2,730	60	....	1,689	3,119	......	1.62	0.02
Panola	....	6,096	21,376	....	3,871	8,475	......	1.57	2.52
Polk	....	....	290	....	2,348	8,300	......	......	0.03

Red River	....	6,566	16,693	....	3,906	8,535	......	1.68	1.96
Robertson	....	387	....	....	934	4,997	......	0.41	......
Rusk	....	7,643	22,185	....	8,148	15,803	......	0.94	1.40
Sabine	....	2,646	3,428	....	2,498	2,750	......	1.06	1.25
San Augustine	....	3,061	4,483	....	3,648	4,094	......	0.84	1.10
Shelby	....	7,929	19,051	....	4,239	5,362	......	1.87	3.55
Smith	....	4,112	31,619	....	4,292	13,392	......	0.96	2.36
Tarrant	....	1,112	....	....	664	6,020	......	1.67	......
Titus	....	6,507	30,820	....	3,636	9,648	......	1.79	3.19
Travis	....	140	813	....	3,138	8,080	......	0.04	0.10
Tyler	....	1,046	5,286	....	1,894	4,525	......	0.55	1.17
Upshur	....	2,840	3,780	....	3,394	10,645	......	0.84	0.36
Van Zandt	....	2,872	14,024	....	1,348	3,777	......	2.13	3.71
Victoria	....	....	4,630	....	2,019	4,171	......	......	1.11
Walker	....	....	300	....	3,964	8,191	......	......	0.04
Washington	....	150	100	....	5,983	15,215	......	0.03	0.01
Wharton	....	200	3,159	....	1,752	3,380	......	0.11	0.93
Williamson*	....	3,186	958	....	1,568	4,529	......	2.03	0.21

* In 1860 there were 151 counties in Texas. Eighty of these were in existence in 1850, 16 of which returned no household manufactures in 1850 and 1860. These have not been included in the table. The returns from the 71 organized between 1850 and 1860 were too meager to justify listing them here. There was nothing in the line of household manufactures reported from 43 of them. The per capita values in the remaining 28 ranged from $0.04 to $6.92, the majority running less than $1.00.

TABLE XIX

PER CAPITA VALUE FOR THE YEAR 1860 OF HOUSEHOLD MANUFACTURES IN COUNTIES NOT INCLUDED IN TABLE XVIII

PER CAPITA VALUE	NUMBER OF COUNTIES IN									
	Ore.	Neb.	Cal.	Minn.	Wash.	Kan.	Utah	Nev.	N.M.	Total
Less than $0.26	4	3	4	17	2	11	0	1	4	46
From $0.26 to $1.00	5	2	1	1	0	6	4	0	1	20
From $1.01 to $2.00	0	0	3	0	1	1	6	0	1	12
From $2.01 to $3.00	0	1	0	0	1	0	1	0	0	3
From $3.01 to $4.00	0	1	0	0	0	0	1	0	0	2
From $4.01 to $5.00	0	0	0	0	0	0	1	0	0	1
Above $5.00	1	0	3	0	3	0	0	0	0	7
Total	10	7	11	18	7	18	13	1	6	91

GENERALIZATIONS AND CONCLUSIONS

A casual examination of the three foregoing tables reveals certain large generalizations relative to the diminution of household manufactures after 1840. The important ones are: (1) the wholesale discontinuance of the system by 1860 in the New England, the Middle States, and Maryland, and the Northwest Territory, there being but 8 counties out of 62 in New England with a per capita value of $1.00 or more, 3 out of 149 in the second group, and 49 out of 398 in the third. Thus it becomes evident that in the 609 counties in these sections household manufactures were almost wholly superseded between 1840 and 1860 by factory-made goods, there being at the latter date but 221, or more than one-third of all the counties, in which the per capita value did not exceed ten cents. (2) In Virginia, South Carolina, Georgia, Kentucky, and Missouri there was a heavy proportional decrease, but not the practical discontinuance, as in the three foregoing sections. For example, out of the 376 counties in these states in 1840, 228 had a per capita value of $2.00 or more; and in 1860 there were but 105 of these same counties with a like value. While there were more states in this group with a per capita value of $2.00 or more than in those in the foregoing groups, yet, since there were so many counties here with a rather high per capita value in 1840, the proportional decrease was greater than in the former. (3) In North Carolina, Tennessee, Alabama, Arkansas, and Mississippi there was the least discontinuance of the manufacturing of textiles within the family. Out of a total of 262 counties in 1840 there were 159 with a per capita value of $2.00 or more. This number had decreased to but 125 in 1860, there being an actual per capita increase between these dates in North Carolina, and a decrease of but 7 cents in Mississippi, 62 cents in Tennessee, 91 in Alabama, and a per capita value of more than $2.00 in each of them in 1860. (4) The system never assumed the importance in Louisiana, Florida, Texas, Iowa, California, Minnesota, Oregon, and the remaining sections of the country settled between 1840 and 1860 that it did in all the foregoing regions, the per capita value in 1840 in Louisiana being but 18 cents; in Florida but 37; Iowa, 60; and in 1860 but 97 cents in Texas, 8 in California, 5 in Minnesota, and 88 in Oregon. Table XIX brings out the truth of this generalization more adequately than the foregoing figures by uncovering the fact that 46 of the 91 counties represented therein had in 1860 a per capita value of less than 26 cents. An additional fact is also established by this table, when it is considered in conjunction with Table XVIII, that, in 1860, recency of establishing a given community bore little or no relation to the amount of manufacturing done in the home, the relatively high per capita values in certain counties in Georgia, Tennessee, Kentucky, and North Carolina and the very low ones in most of those in Minnesota, Oregon, and Kansas proving this.

Various factors must be considered in interpreting and accounting for the foregoing general conclusions and certain other facts exhibited by the tables. The one big factor in all this change was the era of unprecedented prosperity and industrial expansion that the country enjoyed during the two decades after 1840. A series of good crops, prodigious commercial activity, an improved financial system, a large intersectional trade, the firm establishment of the factory system, the enormous increase in inland transportation facilities through the building of canals and railroads, the rise in the price of farm produce and a corresponding fall in the price of factory-made goods, the manufacture and introduction of modern farm implements, all working conjointly, made it possible for the people in all sections of the country where these factors operated to put aside their primitive implements, costumes, and food for mill- and factory-made goods of all descriptions. Western farmers became well-to-do, replacing their log cabins with frame houses and their homespun with the finer goods of the East; the once surplus supply of labor in the urban homes secured employment in the mills and factories, and the southern plantation-owners found it more profitable to engage their slaves in the fields than in plantation manufacturing, since there was such an increased demand for their staple products.[1]

It would lead this discussion too far afield to give details regarding the foregoing factors which were responsible for the passing of the family system of manufacturing. In fact, details seem quite unnecessary, for when one considers the facts that the value of manufactures in the United States increased nearly tenfold during the five decades just prior to 1860, while the population increased but four and one-half fold;[2] that the price of wheat increased from 56 cents a bushel (wholesale at Cincinnati) in 1830 to $1.03 in 1858, and corn from 20 to 70 cents a bushel during the same time;[3] that the railroad mileage increased from 8,589.79 miles in 1850 to 31,196.25 miles in 1860; that there were 5,428.05 miles of canal and river improvements in the country in 1860;[4] that ready-made clothing and improved farm machinery were in the reach of the majority, and a number of other industrial changes equally as far-reaching, the reasons for what happened to the family factory during these decades become evident and need no exposition.

[1] For an excellent discussion of this era of prosperity, see Dodd, *Expansion and Conflict*, chap. x.

[2] *Eighth Census of the U.S.*, "Manufactures," Preliminary View, p. v.

[3] Gephart, *Transportation and Internal Development in the Middle West*, p. 264.

[4] *Eighth Census of the U.S.*, "Mortality and Miscellaneous Statistics," pp. 331, 335 f.

The close relation between the operation of the foregoing factors in any given section of the country and the discontinuance or maintenance of the family factory accounts for the four general conclusions listed above. In the states covered by the first generalization these factors were present in abundance, hence an all but discontinuance of family manufacturing by 1860; while in states where they were not present to any considerable extent, like Tennessee, North Carolina, Arkansas, Alabama, and Mississippi, there was on the whole little or no diminution in the amount of household manufacturing between 1840 and 1860.[1]

The influence that some or all of the foregoing factors had in diminishing the amount of goods made in the home is as evident in a single state as in a larger area. A study of the location of the counties in Virginia, South Carolina, Georgia, Kentucky, and Tennessee with respect to transportation facilities alone and of their corresponding per capita values of household manufactures in 1860 reveals this fact. As a general rule, all the counties with a high per capita value in these states were those unfavorably located with reference to rivers, canals, and railroads, and counties with a low per capita, those favorably located in this respect. For example, in North Carolina, Macon County had a per capita value of $8.64 in 1860; Yancey,

[1] For the number of manufacturing establishments in each state in the Union in 1860, as well as the products made and their value, the number of miles of railroads and canals, see *Eighth Census of the U.S.*, "Manufactures," and "Mortality and Miscellaneous Statistics"; also Gephart, *op. cit.;* Tanner, *Canals and Railroads of the U.S.* (1840); and Dunbar, *Hist. of Travel in Am.*, IV, Apps. A and B.

$5.00; and Ashe, $5.00. In Tennessee, at the same date, Roane County had a per capita value of $11.46; Wilson, $8.52; Cannon, $7.20; Dekalb, $8.73; and Henderson, $8.45—all being out-of-the-way counties which things modern had not yet reached. The converse of this situation was found in counties like Berkeley, Clarke, Elizabeth City, and Westmoreland in Virginia; Hyde, Carteret, Martin, and Mecklenburg in North Carolina; Shelby, Davidson, and Montgomery in Tennessee; and Campbell, Jefferson, and McCracken in Kentucky—all favorably located with reference to trade and transportation facilities. While there was occasionally an exception to the general rule, yet on the whole there was a direct relation between the discontinuance or maintenance of the family system of manufacturing within a given county and its location with respect to the factors which made possible the great era of prosperity that the country of 1850–60 enjoyed.[1]

To account for the last general conclusion based on the foregoing tables, namely, that in 1860 the recency of establishing a given community bore little or no relation to the amount of manufacturing done in the home, is not difficult. The situation as it existed in new settlements between 1850 and 1860 was quite the reverse of what it was in, say, 1810, when the settlements were made first and a demand for things modern was created by them; while after 1850, or even before in certain sections, the

[1] For the location of counties in 1850, see Colton's *General Atlas* (1857). In Clark's *Hist. of Manufactures in the U.S.* there is a table showing relation of population and railway mileage to the value of manufactures produced in shops and factories and in households in 1840, 1850, 1860. For this table see Appendix XII.

settlements were preceded and induced by modern improvements, for which reason it was not necessary for them to pass through the primitive pioneer stage as those made earlier in the century were forced to do. Coming as they did in such large numbers after 1820 was also economically advantageous to the western emigrants, for the demand for factory-made goods made it profitable to provide ways and means to secure them. These were found either in increased transportation facilities or in the setting up of manufacturing establishments in the several localities.

Such in brief is an explanation of the low per capita values in the western states and territories in 1860, which in turn signaled the final passing of the family system of manufacturing, for when the system ceased to move westward with the new settlements and at the same time was being crowded out of many sections of the country east of the Mississippi it ceased to exist except locally. The foregoing three tables show that by 1860 the system had either entirely disappeared or was rapidly disappearing; hence the reason for closing the discussion here. While it is true that it lingered locally for years after 1860, and was quite generally revived in the South during the Civil War, yet as a factor in the economic life and prosperity of the country as a whole it was practically nil at the end of the sixth decade of the nineteenth century.

BIBLIOGRAPHY

Because of the space which they would have consumed out of all proportion to their value, many items have been omitted from this bibliography. Particularly is this true of the section on local histories, where less than one-tenth of the volumes carefully examined and used to some extent appear. In fact, a very small percentage of the volumes examined are listed in any section, for the character of the material in them made a careful selection necessary to avoid unnecessary duplications. Where practically the same data were found in several accounts, which was often the case in town and county histories, only the best ones have been included. The list presented below aims to contain ample authority for all the facts, opinions, and conclusions found in the entire discussion.

A. PRIMARY SOURCES

I. COLONIAL, STATE AND NATIONAL LAWS, RECORDS, ARCHIVES, AND DOCUMENTS

Anjou, Gustave. *Ulster County, New York, Probate Records*, "Wills." Vol. II. New York, 1906.

Connecticut: *Public Records of the Colony of Connecticut* (1636–1776). Compiled by J. H. Trumbull and C. J. Hoadly. 15 vols. Hartford, 1850–90. Two additional volumes of *State Records* (1776–80). Hartford, 1894–95.

Coxe, Tench. "Digest of Manufactures," in *American State Papers*, "Finance," II, 666 ff.; exists also in a separate volume. Philadelphia, 1814.

Delaware: *Laws of the State of Delaware.* Printed by M. Bradford and R. Porter. Vol. IV. Wilmington, 1816. *Journal of the House of Representatives*, 1808.

Gallatin, Albert. "Report on Manufactures, Communicated to the House of Representatives, April 19, 1810," in *American State Papers*, "Finance," II, 425 ff.

Georgia: *Colonial Records of the State of Georgia* (1732–74). Edited by A. D. Candler. 17 vols. Atlanta, 1904–6.

Hamilton, Alexander. "Report on Manufactures, Communicated to the House of Representatives, December 5, 1791," in *American State Papers*, "Finance," I, 123 ff.

Hamilton Papers for 1790–91 (MSS). Manuscript Division of the Library of Congress. Among these papers are found the original reports on which Hamilton based his famous general account of 1791. Many of the individuals who were asked to report went into considerable detail concerning household manufactures in their respective communities.

Maine: *Documentary History of the State of Maine.* Maine Historical Society Collections, 2d series. 16 vols. Portland, 1869–1910.

Maryland: *Archives of Maryland.* Edited by W. H. Browne and Clayton Colman. 34 vols. Baltimore. 1883–1914.

Laws of Maryland (1704–1809). Edited by Virgil Maxcy. 3 vols. Baltimore, 1811.

Massachusetts: *Records of the Governor and Company of the Massachusetts Bay in New England* (1628–86). Edited by N. B. Shurtleff. 5 vols. Boston, 1853–54.

Acts and Resolves, Public and Private, of the Province of Massachusetts Bay (1692–1780). 17 vols. Boston, 1869–1910.

Acts and Laws of the Commonwealth of Massachusetts (1780–81 and 1784–85). Boston, 1781 and 1784. Reprinted, 1890.

New Hampshire: *Documents and Records Relating to the Province, Town, and State of New Hampshire* (1623–1800). Edited by N. Bouton and others. 31 vols. Concord, etc., 1867–1907.

Laws of New Hampshire (1697–1745). Edited by A. S. Batchellor. 2 vols. Manchester and Concord, 1904 and 1913.

New Jersey: *Archives of the State of New Jersey.* Edited by W. A. Whitehead and others. 1st series, *Documents Relating to the Colonial History* (1631–1800). 27 vols.; 2d series, *Documents Relating to the Revolutionary History* (1776-80). 4 vols. Newark, Paterson, and Trenton, 1880–1914.

New York: *Documents Relative to the Colonial History of New York.* Edited by E. B. O'Callaghan and B. Fernow. 15 vols. Albany, 1856–87.

Laws of New York. 31st, 33d, 35th, 40th, 42d, and 43d sessions of the Assembly in the years 1808, 1810, 1812, 1816, 1819, and 1820.

Documentary History of the State of New York. E. B. O'Callaghan. 4 vols. Albany, 1849–51.

Censuses of the State of New York for the Years 1821 and 1825, in *Journal of the Assembly of New York,* 45th Session. Albany, 1822, Appendix A; and *New York Senate Journal,* 49th Session. Albany, 1826, Appendix A.

Censuses of the State of New York for the Years 1835, 1845, 1855. Albany, 1826, 1836, 1857.

North Carolina: *Colonial Records of North Carolina* (1662–1776). Edited by W. L. Saunders. 10 vols. Raleigh, 1886–90.

State Records of North Carolina (1776–90). Edited by Walter Clark. Vols. XI–XXVI. Winston and Goldsboro, 1895–1906.

Pennsylvania: *Colonial Records* (1683–1790). Published by the State. Philadelphia and Harrisburg, 1851–53.

Archives. 4th series. Edited by G. E. Reed. Vol. III. Harrisburg, 1900.

Statutes at Large. Vol. III, 1712–24. Compiled by J. T. Mitchell and Henry Flanders. Harrisburg, 1896.

Pickering, Danby. *Statutes at Large, from Magna Charta to . . . . 1761.* Continued by Pickering and others to 1807. 46 vols. Cambridge, 1762–1807. Much use made of Vols. X, XI, XIII, XIV, XX, XXX, XXXIII, XXXIV.

Providence: *Early Records of the Town of Providence, R.I.* Vols. I–XX. Providence, 1892–1909.

Plymouth: *Records of the Colony of New Plymouth in New England* (1620–92). Edited by N. B. Shurtleff and others. 12 vols. Boston, 1855–61.

Rhode Island: *Records of the Colony of Rhode Island and Providence Plantation in New England* (1636–1792). Compiled by J. R. Bartlett. 10 vols. Providence, 1856–65.

South Carolina: *Statutes at Large.* Edited by T. Cooper and D. J. McCord. 10 vols. Columbia, 1836–41.

United States: *The Public Statutes at Large of the United States of America.* Edited by Richard Peters. Vols. I, II, and III. Boston, 1854–61.

Annals of Congress, 1789–91, Vol. I. Compiled by Joseph Gales. Washington, 1834; also 16th Congress, 1st Session. Vol. II, column 2041.

Journal of the Continental Congress (1774–82). Library of Congress edition. Edited by W. C. Ford. 23 vols. Washington, 1904–14.

Executive Documents. 1st Session, 22d Congress, 1831–32.

Documents Relative to the Manufactures in the United States. Collected and transmitted to the House of Representatives, in compliance with a resolution of January 19, 1832, by the Secretary of the Treasury. 2 vols. Washington, 1833.

Eighth Census of the United States (1860). "Manufactures," "Mortality and Miscellaneous Statistics," "Agriculture," and "Population."

Compendium of the Enumeration of the Inhabitants of the United States, etc., from the returns of the *Sixth Census* (1840). Washington, 1841.

The Seventh Census of the United States (1850). Washington, 1853.

Vermont: *Records of the Council of Safety and Council of the State of Vermont.* Edited by E. P. Walton. 8 vols. Montpelier, 1873–80.

Virginia: Hening, W. H., *The Statutes-at-Large, being a Collection of all the Laws of Virginia* (1619–1792). 13 vols. Various editions. Much use made of Vols. I, II (New York, 1823), and III (Philadelphia, 1823).

II. CONTEMPORARY ACCOUNTS

American Husbandry. Containing an account of the soil, climate, productions, and agriculture of the British colonies in North America and the West Indies. By an American. 2 vols. London, 1775.

Acrelius, Israel. *A History of New Sweden; or The Settlements on the Delaware River.* Stockholme, 1758. Translated from the Swedish by W. M. Reynolds. Philadelphia, 1874.

Anburey, Thomas. *Travels through the Interior Parts of America in a Series of Letters.* 2 vols. London, 1791.

Anonymous. "The Present State of the Colony of West Jersey, in America, September, Anno Dom. 1681," in *Pennsylvania Magazine of History and Biography.* Vol. XVIII. Philadelphia, 1894.

Ashe, Thomas. *Travels in America Performed in 1806.* London, 1808.

Baily, Francis. *Journal of a Tour, 1796 & 1797.* London, 1866.

Bassett, J. S. (editor). *The Writings of Colonel William Byrd.* New York, 1901.

"Belknap Papers," Part II, in *Massachusetts Historical Society Collections.* 5th series, Vol. III. Boston, 1877.

Beverly, R. *The History and Present State of Virginia.* London, 1705.

Brock, R. A. (editor). "The Official Letters of Alexander Spotswood," in *Collections of the Virginia Historical Society.* New Series, Vols. I and II. Richmond, 1882.

Budd, Thomas. *Good Order Established in Pennsylvania and New Jersey in America.* Printed in 1685. A reprint from the original, edited by J. F. Shepard. Cleveland, Ohio, 1902.

Burnaby, Andrew. *Travels through the Middle Settlements in North America, in the Years 1759 and 1760. With Observations upon the State of the Colonies.* Second edition, London, 1775.

Burke, Edmund. *An Account of the European Settlements in America.* 2 vols. in one. London, 1757.

Crèvecœur, St. John de. *Letters from an American Farmer, Describing Certain Provincial Situations, Manners, and Customs, and*

Conveying Some Idea of the State of the People of North America. Written to a Friend in England by J. Hector St. John, a farmer of Pennsylvania. Philadelphia, 1793.

Cummings, F. *Sketch of a Tour to the Western Country, 1808, 1809,* in Thwaites, *Early Western Travels.* Vol. IV. Cleveland, Ohio, 1904.

Denton, Daniel. *A Brief Description of New York Formerly Called New Netherlands.* A reprint from the original edition of 1670 by Burrows Brothers Company. Cleveland, Ohio, 1902.

Doddridge, Joseph. *Notes on the Settlements and Indian Wars of the Western Parts of Virginia and Pennsylvania from 1763 to 1783, Inclusive, Together with a Review of the State of Society and Manners of the First Settlers of the Western Country.* Pittsburgh, Pa., 1912. First edition was in 1824.

Drake, Daniel. *Pioneer Life in Kentucky.* A series of reminiscential letters from Daniel Drake to his children. Edited by his son, C. D. Drake. Cincinnati, 1870.

Drayton, John. *A View of South Carolina.* Charleston, 1802.

Duncan, R. B. "Old Settlers Papers," in *Indiana Historical Society Publications.* Vol. II, No. 10. Indianapolis, 1895. Duncan came to Indiana in 1820. The foregoing papers were written for the *Indianapolis Herald* and appeared in the issues of January 11, 18, 25, and February 1, 1879.

Dwight, Timothy. *Travels in New England and New York.* Vol. II. New Haven, Conn., 1821.

Ellicott, Andrew. *The Journal.* Philadelphia, 1814. Ellicott was commissioned by the government to run the boundary between the southern part of the United States and Spain. He worked at this during the years 1797, 1798, 1799, and 1800. The *Journal* was kept during these years.

Finch, J. G. "Settlement of Noblesville, Hamilton County, Indiana," in *Indiana Quarterly Magazine of History.* Vol. VI. Indianapolis, 1910. Finch was nine years old when his father came to Indiana in 1819. In 1893 he wrote the account of the founding of the settlement.

Ford, Thomas. *A History of Illinois from Its Commencement as a State in 1814 to 1847.* Chicago, 1854. A contemporary account by a rather important citizen of Illinois during the years covered by his history.

A Description of South Carolina. London, 1761. Authorship attributed to Governor James Glen.

Goodrich, S. G. *Recollections of a Life Time or Men and Things I Have Seen.* 2 vols. New York, 1856. An account of New England life during the first quarter of the nineteenth century.

Harris, T. M. *The Journal of a Tour into the Territory Northwest of the Alleghany Mountains.* Boston, 1805.

"Diary of John Harrower, 1773–76," in *American Historical Review.* Vol. VI. New York, 1901.

Hodgson, Adam. *Letters from North America Written during a Tour in the United States and Canada.* 2 vols. London, 1824. Much of this material is also in *Remarks during a Journey through North America in the Years 1819, 1820, and 1821.* By the same author. New York, 1823.

Holmes, Isaac. *An Account of the United States of America,* derived from actual observations during a residence of four years in that republic. London, 1823.

Hoppin, Ruth. "Personal Recollections of Pioneer Days," in *Michigan Pioneer and Historical Collections.* Vol. XXXVIII. Lansing, 1912. Miss Hoppin was three years old when her father moved to Michigan in 1836. The foregoing was written in 1893.

Howells, W. C. *Recollections of Life in Ohio, from 1813 to 1840.* Cincinnati, 1895. Written between 1880 and 1894. Revised and published by W. D. Howells, his son, after the father's death.

Imlay, Gilbert. *A Topographical Description of the Western Territory of North America.* An account of population, agriculture, manners, and customs. Third edition. London, 1797.

Jameson, J. F. (editor). "Letters of Phineas Bond," in *Reports of the American Historical Association.* 1896, Vol. I, and 1897. The letters cover the years 1787–94.

Jefferson, Thomas. *Notes on the State of Virginia.* London, 1787. Contains a brief account of manufactures in 1781.

———. *Works.* Federal edition. Edited by P. L. Ford. 12 vols. New York, 1904–5.

Johnson, Edward. *Wonder-Working Providence, 1628–1651.* Edited by J. F. Jameson. Original Narrative of Early American History Series. New York, 1910.

Jones, Hugh. *The Present State of Virginia.* London, 1824. (Sabin's reprints, No. 5. New York, 1865.)

Kalm, Peter. *Travels into North America* (1748–49). Translated into English by J. R. Forster. Second edition. 2 vols. London, 1772.

Lawson, John. *The History of North Carolina, Containing the Exact Description and Natural History of That Country.* London, 1714.

Martzolff, C. L. (editor). "Reminiscences of a Pioneer," in *The Ohio State Archaeological and Historical Society Publications.* Vol. XIX. Columbus, 1910. The pioneer was Thomas Rogers, who moved from Virginia to Kentucky in 1795.

Melish, John. *Travels in the United States of America in 1806, 1807, 1809, 1810 and 1811.* 2 vols. London, 1818.

Michaux, F. A. *Travels to the West of the Alleghany Mountains in the Year 1802,* in Thwaites, *Early Western Travels.* Vol. III. Cleveland, Ohio, 1904.

"New England's First Fruits" (London, 1643), in *Massachusetts Historical Society Collections.* 1st series, Vol. I. Boston, 1806. A reprint of the edition of 1792.

Olmsted, F. L. *A Journey in the Back Country.* New York, 1860.

"A Relation or Journal of a Plantation Settled at Plymouth in New England and Proceedings Thereof." First printed in 1622. Original probably written by one of the Company. Reprint from Purchas' *Pilgrims,* Book X, chapter iv, in *Massachusetts Historical Society Collections,* 1st series, Vol. VIII. Boston, 1810. A reprint of the edition of 1794.

"Representation of the Board of Trade to the House of Lords, etc., January 1733–34," in *Connecticut Historical Society Collections.* Vol. V, 445 ff. Hartford, 1896.

Reynolds, John. *My Own Times: Embracing Also The History of My Life.* Chicago, 1879.

Weld, Isaac. *Travels through the States of North America and the Province of Upper and Lower Canada during the Years 1795, 1796, and 1797.* Fourth edition. London, 1800.

Welsh, Mary J. "Recollections of Pioneer Life in Mississippi," in *Mississippi Historical Society Publications.* Vol. IV. Oxford, 1901.

"The Case of Good Intent," Annapolis, 1770. Authorship attributed to Stephen West. Reprint from a transcript of the original in *Maryland Historical Magazine.* Vol. III. Baltimore, 1908.

Wilkeson, Samuel, "Recollections of the West," in *Publications of the Buffalo Historical Society.* Vol. V. Buffalo, 1902.

Winthrop, John. *History of New England.* Edited by J. K. Hosmer. Original Narrative of Early American History Series. 2 vols. New York, 1908.

III. PRIMARY SOURCES OF A GENERAL NATURE

American Museum. Mathew Carey, Printer and Editor. 13 vols. The first twelve extend from January, 1787, to December, 1792. The thirteenth was published in 1798.

American Pioneer. 2 vols. 1842 and 1843. Edited and published by John S. Williams. Cincinnati, Ohio.

Board of Trade Papers, Proprieties. Transcripts in Pennsylvania Historical Society, Philadelphia, Pennsylvania.

Commons, J. R., and others. *Documentary History of American Industrial Society.* Vols. I and II. Cleveland, Ohio, 1910–11.

De Bow, J. D. B. *Industrial Resources of the South and West.* 3 vols. New Orleans, 1852–53.

Force, Peter. *Collection of Tracts and Other Papers.* 4 vols. Washington, 1838.

Hazard, Samuel. *Register of Pennsylvania.* Vol. II. Philadelphia, 1828.

Macpherson, David. *Annals of Commerce, Manufactures, Fisheries, and Navigation.* 4 vols. London, 1805. Much use made of Vols. II, III, and IV.

Niles' Weekly Register. 75 vols. Baltimore, 1811–49. Much use made of Vols. I, VI, VII, IX, X, XI, XII, XVII, XX, XXI, XXII, XXIII, XXIV, and XXXIX.

Pitkin, Timothy. *A Statistical View of the Commerce of the United States in Connection with Agriculture and Manufactures.* Hartford, Conn., 1816.

———. *A Statistical View of the Commerce of the United States of America, Including an Account of Banks, Manufactures, and Internal Trade and Improvements.* New Haven, Conn., 1835.

Reichel, W. C. *Memorials of the Moravian Church.* Vol. I. Philadelphia, 1870.

Saxby, Henry. *The British Customs; containing an historical and practical account of each branch of that revenue; the rates of merchandise, as settled by the 12th of Car. II, cap. 4, and 11 Geo. I, cap. 7.* London, 1757.

Seybert, Adam. *Statistical Annals.* Philadelphia, 1818.

Transactions of the Albany Institute. Vol. IV. Albany, 1858–64. Contains an account of the premiums awarded by law in New York for the encouragement of household manufacture of woolen cloth.

Transactions of the Society for the Promotion of Useful Arts. New York State. Vol. III. Albany, 1814. This society and the Albany Lyceum of Natural History were united in 1824 to form the Albany Institute.

Whitworth, Sir Charles. *State of the Trade of Great Britain in Its Imports and Exports, 1697–1773.* London, 1776.

B. SECONDARY AUTHORITIES

I. GENERAL SECONDARY WORKS

Bagnall, W. R. *The Textile Industries of the United States.* Vol. I, 1639–1810. Cambridge, Mass., 1893.

Bishop, J. L. *A History of American Manufactures from 1608 to 1860.* 3 vols. Philadelphia, 1861–68.

Bolles, A. S. *Industrial History of the United States.* Third edition. Norwich, Conn., 1881.

Brown, J. H. (editor-in-chief). *Textile Industries of the United States.* Vol. I. Boston, 1911.

Callender, G. S. *Selections from the Economic History of the United States, 1765-1860.* New York, 1909.

Clark, V. S. *History of Manufactures in the United States, 1607–1860.* Washington, D. C., 1916.

Colton, G. W. *General Atlas.* New York, 1857.

Coman, Katharine. *Industrial History of the United States.* New York, 1907.

Coxe, Tench. *A View of the United States of America.* Philadelphia, 1794. Contains a series of papers written at various times between 1787 and 1794; also some documents. Coxe was for a time Assistant Secretary of the Treasury.

Dodd, W. E. *Expansion and Conflict.* New York, 1915.

Douglas, William. *A Summary Historical and Political of the First Planting, Progressive Improvements, and Present State of the British Settlements in North America.* 2 vols. London, 1765.

Dunbar, Seymour. *A History of Travel in America.* Vol. IV, Appendixes A and B. Indianapolis, Ind., 1915.

Earle, Alice Morse. *Home Life in Colonial Days.* New York, 1906.

Faust, A. B. *The German Element in the United States.* 2 vols. Boston, 1909.

Fessenden, T. G. *Register of Arts.* Philadelphia, 1808.

Hall, James. *Romance of Western History.* Cincinnati, 1885.

Hanna, C. A. *The Scotch-Irish, or the Scotch in North Britain, North Ireland, and North America.* 2 vols. New York, 1902.

Hildreth, S. P. *Pioneer History: Being an Account of the First Examination of the Ohio Valley and the Early Settlement of the North West Territory.* Cincinnati, 1848.

Holmes, Abiel. *American Annals, or a Chronological History of America.* 2 vols. Cambridge, Mass., 1805.

Howard, G. E. *Preliminaries of the Revolution,* in American Nation Series. New York, 1905.

Hubbard, William. *A General History of New England from the Discovery to MDCLXXX;* second edition collated with original manuscript; in *Massachusetts Historical Society Collections.* 2d series, Vols. V–VI. Boston, 1848. The first edition was printed in 1815 by the same society.

Kittredge, G. L. *The Old Farmer and His Almanac. Being Some Observations on Life and Manners in New England a Hundred Years Ago, Suggested by Reading the Early Number of Mr. Robert B. Thomas's Farmer's Almanac.* Boston, 1904.

Rogers, J. E. T. *History of Agriculture and Prices in England, 1259–1793.* 7 vols. Oxford, England, 1866–1902.

Roosevelt, Theodore. *Winning of the West.* 4 vols. New York, 1889–96.

Smith, H. E. *Colonial Days and Ways.* New York, 1900.

Strickland, W. P. *Autobiography of Rev. James B. Finley, or Pioneer Life in the West.* Cincinnati, 1854.

Swank, J. M. *History of the Manufacture of Iron in All Ages.* Second edition. Philadelphia, 1892.

Tanner, H. S. *A Description of the Canals and Railroads in the United States.* New York, 1840.

Weeden, W. B. *Economic and Social History of New England, 1620–1789.* 2 vols. Boston, 1890.

Winterbotham, W. *An Historical, Geographical, Commercial, and Philosophical View of the United States of America and of the European Settlements in America and the West Indies.* 4 vols. New York, 1796.

II. MONOGRAPHS AND ARTICLES

Abbott, Edith. *Women in Industry.* New York, 1910.

Beer, G. L. *The Commercial Policy of England toward the American Colonies*, in "Columbia University Studies in History, Economics and Public Law." Vol. III, No. 2. New York, 1893.

Clark, Victor, "Colonial Manufactures," in *The South in the Building of the Nation.* Vol. V. J. C. Ballagh (editor). Richmond, 1909.

Dexter, F. B. "Estimates of Population in American Colonies," in *Proceedings of American Antiquarian Society.* New Series, Vol. V. Worcester, Mass., 1889.

Duffield, G. C. "Pioneer Mills in Iowa," in *Annals of Iowa.* 3d series, Vol. VI. Des Moines, 1903–5.

Durrett, R. T. "The State of Kentucky; Its Discovery, Settlement, and Progress for a Hundred Years," in *Filson Club Publications*, No. 7. Louisville, 1892.

———. "The First Act in the Siege of Bryant's Station," in *Filson Club Publications*, No. 12. Louisville, 1897.

Gephart, W. F. *Transportation and Industrial Development in the Middle West.* New York, 1909.

Giesecke, A. A. *American Commercial Legislation before 1789.* University of Pennsylvania, Publications in Political Economy and Public Law. New York, 1910.

Goodwin, F. P. "Rise of Manufactures in Miami County, Ohio," in *American Historical Review.* Vol. XII, No. 4, 1907.

Haines, James. "Social Life and Scenes in the Early Settlement of Southern Illinois," in *Transactions of the Illinois State Historical Society*, No. 10. Springfield, 1906.

Hall, G. S. "Boy Life in a Massachusetts Town Thirty Years Ago," in *Proceedings of the American Antiquarian Society.* Vol. VII. Worcester, Mass., 1892.

Heatwole, Cornelius. "Hand-Weaving in Rockingham County, Virginia," in Wayland, *History of Rockingham County.* Dayton, Va., 1912. An excellent account of the process of weaving on the handloom.

Hubbard, L. M. "Manufacturing Interests of Wallingford," in *New England States.* Vol. II. Boston, 1897.

Hunter, W. H. "The Pathfinders of Jefferson County," in *Ohio State Archaeological and Historical Society Publications.* Vol. VI. Columbus, Ohio, 1898.

Lippincott, Isaac. *A History of Manufactures in the Ohio Valley to the Year 1860.* New York, 1914.

———. "Pioneer Industry in the West," in *Journal of Political Economy.* Vol. XVIII. Chicago, 1910.

Lord, E. L. *Industrial Experiments in the British Colonies of North America,* in "Johns Hopkins University Studies." Extra Vol. XVII. Baltimore, 1898.

McMath, J. M. "The Willow Run Settlement," in *Michigan Pioneer and Historical Society Collections.* Vol. XIV. Lansing, 1890.

Morriss, M. S. *Colonial Trade of Maryland, 1689–1715,* in "Johns Hopkins University Studies." Vol. XXXII, No. 3. Baltimore, 1914.

North, S. N. D. "New England Wool Manufactures," in *The New England States.* Vol. I. Boston, 1897.

Parker, B. S. "Pioneer Life," in *Indiana Magazine of History.* Vol. III, No. 1. Indianapolis, 1907. Parker was an old resident of Henry County, Indiana. The articles were intended to form parts of his history of Henry County. They date back into the twenties.

Patterson, R. W. "Early Society in Southern Illinois," in *Fergus Historical Series.* Vol. I, No. 14. Chicago, 1880.

Perley, Sidney. "The Manufacture of Nails in Essex County, Massachusetts," in *Essex Antiquarian.* Vol. II, No. 5. Salem, Mass., 1898.

———. "Shoemaking," in *Essex Antiquarian.* Vol. V, No. 4. Salem, Mass., 1901.

Philbrick, Eliza. "Spinning in the Olden Time," in *Essex Antiquarian.* Vol. I, No. 6. Salem, Mass., 1897.

Rabbeno, Ugo. *The American Commercial Policy.* Second edition (translation). London, 1895.

Rush, Benjamin. *Essays, Literary, Moral and Philosophical.* Philadelphia, 1794.

———. *An Account of the Manners of the German Inhabitants of Pennsylvania Written in 1789.* Notes added by I. D. Rupp in 1875. Reprint of the original in *Pennsylvania German Society Proceedings and Addresses.* Vol. XIX. Lancaster, Pa., 1908.

Schultz, T. *First Settlement of Germans in Maryland.* Frederick, 1896. A paper read before the Frederick County Historical Society, January 17, 1896.

Swank, J. M. "The Manufacture of Iron in New England," in *The New England States.* Vol. I. Boston, 1897.

Tyson, M. E. "A Brief Account of the Settlement of Ellicott's Mills," in *Maryland Historical Society Publications.* Vols. I–VI, No. 4. Baltimore, 1865.

Vogel, William. "Home Life in Early Indiana," in *Indiana Magazine of History.* Vol. X, Nos. 2 and 3. Bloomington, Ind., 1914.

Welker, Martin. "Farm Life in Central Ohio Sixty Years Ago," in *Western Reserve Historical Society Tracts.* Vol. IV, Tract No. 86. Cleveland, Ohio, 1895.

Wheeler, Cyrenus. "Inventors and Inventions of Cayuga County, New York," in *Cayuga County Historical Society Collections,* No. 2, 1882.

Williams, M. C. "The Homespun Age," in *Magazine of American History with Notes and Queries.* Vol. XXV. New York, 1891.

Woodward, Henry. "Manufacturing Interests of Hartford," in *New England States.* Vol. II. Boston, 1897.

Wright, C. D. "The Factory System of the United States," in *Tenth Census of the United States* (1880), "Report on Manufactures," pp. 533–611.

III. STATE AND LOCAL HISTORIES

Anderson, P. W. *Counties of Warren, Benton, Jasper, and Newton, Indiana.* Chicago, 1883.

Arnold, S. G. *History of Rhode Island and Providence Plantation, 1636–1790.* 2 vols. New York, 1860.

Atkinson, G. W. *History of Kanawha County, from Its Organization in 1789 until the Present Time, Embracing the Accounts of Early Settlements, and Thrilling Adventures with the Indians.* Charleston, W. Va., 1876.

Baird, C. W. *History of Rye, Westchester County, New York, 1660–1870.* New York, 1871. A chapter on manners and customs in 1680.

Bigelow, E. V. *Narrative History of the Town of Cohasset, Massachusetts.* Published by the Town, 1898. Good discussion of "Industries and Firesides."

Blood, H. A. *History of Temple, New Hampshire.* Boston, 1860.

Booth, M. L. *History of the City of New York from Its Earliest Settlement to the Present Time.* New York, 1863.

Bourne, E. E. *The History of Wells and Kennebunk, Maine, from Earliest Settlement to 1820.* Portland, Me., 1875.

Bouton, Nathaniel. *History of Concord, New Hampshire.* Concord, 1856.

Brown, Warren. *History of the Town of Hampton Falls, New Hampshire, 1640 to 1900.* Manchester, 1900.

Bruce, P. A. *Economic History of Virginia in the Seventeenth Century.* 2 vols. New York, 1896. A chapter in Vol. II on "Manufactured Supplies—Domestic."

Callahan, J. M. *History of West Virginia.* Published by the Semi-Centennial Commission of West Virginia, 1913. Contains an excellent chapter on "Industrial and Social Expansion."

Cartmell, T. K. *Shenandoah Valley Pioneers and Their Descendants.—A History of Frederick County, Virginia, 1738–1908.* Winchester, 1908. A chapter on "Mills and Other Developments."

Chase, Benj. *History of Old Chester, New Hampshire, from 1719 to 1869.* Auburn, 1869. A fine chapter on the industrial history of the town.

Child, W. H. *History of the Town of Cornish, New Hampshire, 1763–1910.* 2 vols. Concord, 1911.

Claiborne, J. F. H. *Mississippi as a Province, Territory, and State.* Jackson, 1880.

Clute, J. J. *Annals of Staten Island, from the Discovery to the Present Time.* New York, 1877. Contains an account of domestic life in olden times.

Cochrane, W. R., and Wood, G. K. *History of Franceston, New Hampshire, 1758–1891.* Nashua, 1895.

Coffin, Joshua. *A Sketch of the History of Newbury, Newburyport, and West Newbury, 1635–1845.* Boston, 1845.

Cogswell, L. N. *History of the Town of Henniker, Merrimac County, New Hampshire, 1735 to 1880.* Concord, 1880.

Cravens, C. E. *A History of Mattituck, Long Island, New York.* Privately published, 1906. Good chapter on "Life in Mattituck in 1700."

Donovan, D., and Woodward, J. A. *The History of the Town of Lynderborough, New Hampshire, 1735–1905.* Lynderboro, 1906. Good chapter on "The Olden Times."

Drake, S. G. *The History and Antiquities of Boston, from 1630 to 1770.* Boston, 1856.

Emery, Edwin. *History of Sanford, Maine, 1661–1900.* Fall River, Mass., 1901. Compiled, edited, and arranged by his son, W. M. Emery.

Esarey, Logan. *A History of Indiana from Its Exploration to 1850.* Indianapolis, Ind., 1915.

Felt, J. B. *History of Ipswich, Essex, and Hamilton.* Cambridge, 1834.

Ford, A. E. *History of the Origin of the Town of Clinton, Massachusetts, 1653–1865.* Clinton, Mass., 1896.

Griffin, S. G. *A History of the Town of Keene, New Hampshire.* Keene, 1904. Contains some excellent material on "Pioneer Life in Keene."

Hatch, W. C. *History of Industry, Franklin County, Maine, from Its Earliest Settlement in 1787 Down to the Present Time.* Farmington, 1893.

Hayes, L. S. *History of the Town of Rockingham, Vermont.* Bellows Falls, 1907.

Jackson, J. R. (editor). *History of Littleton, New Hampshire.* 3 vols. Littleton, 1905. Some excellent material in Vol. I.

Johnson, Amandus. *The Swedish Settlements on the Delaware.* 2 vols. University of Pennsylvania, 1911. Some excellent chapters on social and economic life.

Jones, C. C. *The History of Georgia.* 2 vols. Boston, 1833.

Judd, Sylvester. *History of Hadley, Massachusetts.* Northampton, 1863.

Kercheval, Samuel. *A History of the Valley of Virginia.* Winchester, Va., 1833.

King, Rufus. *Ohio, First Fruits of the Ordinance of 1787.* New York, 1888. Good chapter on "The Pioneer."

Kingman, Bradford. *History of North Bridgewater, Plymouth County, Massachusetts, from Its First Settlement to the Present Time with Family Registers.* Boston, 1866.

———. *History of Brockton, Massachusetts.* Syracuse, New York, 1895. Contains good accounts of early habits and customs, raising and manufacturing flax, and the drink of the colonies.

Lapham, W. B. *History of Bethel, Formerly Sudbury, Canada, Oxford County, Maine, 1768–1890.* Augusta, 1891.

Lee, Frances Bazley. *New Jersey as a Colony and as a State.* 3 vols. New York, 1903.

Little, William. *History of Weare, New Hampshire, 1735–1888.* Lowell, Mass., 1888.

Levering, J. H. *Historic Indiana.* New York, 1909.

McDuffee, Franklin. *History of the Town of Rochester, New Hampshire, from 1722 to 1890.* 2 vols. Manchester, 1892.

McLellan, H. D. *History of Gorham, Maine.* Compiled and edited by his daughter, Katharine B. Lewis. Portland, 1903.

Macy, Obed. *The History of Nantucket, Being a Compendious Account of the First Settlement of the Island by the English.* Boston, 1835.

Martin, F. X. *History of Louisiana.* New Orleans, 1882. A reprint of the two-volume edition of 1827, continued to 1861 by J. F. Condon.

Moore, J. B. *History of the Town of Candia, Rockingham County, New Hampshire.* Manchester, 1893.

Mordecai, Samuel. *Virginia, Especially Richmond in Bygone Days.* Richmond, 1860.

Musgrove, R. W. *History of the Town of Bristol, Grafton County, New Hampshire.* 2 vols. Bristol, 1904.

Norton, J. F. *The History of Fitzwilliam, 1752–1887.* New York, 1888.

Nourse, H. S. *History of the Town of Harvard, Massachusetts, 1732–1893.* Harvard, 1894.

Parker, W. F. *History of Wolfeborough, New Hampshire.* Cambridge, Mass., 1901.

Peterson, Edward. *History of Rhode Island.* New York, 1853.

Phelan, James. *History of Tennessee.* New York, 1889. A chapter on "Manners, Customs, and Mode of Life."

Putnam, A. W. *History of Middle Tennessee.* Nashville, 1859.

Ramsay, David. *The History of South Carolina from Its First Settlement in 1670 to the Year 1808.* 2 vols. Charleston, 1809.

Raum, J. O. *The History of New Jersey from the Earliest Settlement to the Present Time.* 2 vols. Philadelphia, 1877.

Scharf, J. T., and Westcott, Thompson. *History of Philadelphia, 1609–1884.* 3 vols. Philadelphia, 1884.

Scott, W. W. *History of Orange County, Virginia, 1734–1870.* Richmond, 1907.

Sheldon, George. *A History of Deerfield, Massachusetts.* 2 vols. Deerfield, Mass., 1895–96.

Sibley, J. L. *History of the Town of Union, in the County of Lincoln, Maine, to the Middle of the Nineteenth Century.* Boston, 1851.

Simms, J. R. *History of Schoharie County and Border Wars of New York.* Albany, 1845.

Smith, Albert. *History of the Town of Peterborough, Hillsborough County, New Hampshire.* Boston, 1876. A good chapter on "Home Life" and one on "Home Manufactures."

Smith, Frank. *Narrative History of Dover, Massachusetts.* Dover, 1897.

Smith, J. E. A. *The History of Pittsfield (Berkshire County), Massachusetts, from the Year 1800 to the Year 1876.* Springfield, 1876.

Somers, A. N. *History of Lancaster, New Hampshire.* Concord, 1899.

Stoddard, Amos. *Sketches Historical and Descriptive of Louisiana.* Philadelphia, 1812. An excellent chapter on "Commerce and Manufactures."

Street, G. E. *Mount Desert, Maine, A History.* Edited by S. A. Eliot. Boston, 1905.

Taylor, C. J. *History of Great Barrington, Berkshire County, Massachusetts.* Great Barrington, 1882.

Temple, J. H. *History of the Town of Whately, Massachusetts, 1660–1781.* Boston, 1872.

———. *History of North Brookfield, Massachusetts.* Published by the Town, 1887.

Thompson, D. P. *History of the Town of Montpelier, from the time it was first chartered in 1781 to the year 1860.* Montpelier, 1860. Good chapter on "Life in the Early Days of Montpelier."

Tucker, W. H. *History of Hartford, Vermont, July 4, 1761—April 4, 1889.* Burlington, 1889. Some material on customs of "Ye Olden Times."

Walker, C. M. *History of Athens County, Ohio.* Cincinnati, 1869. One of the good county histories. Each township is treated separately.

Wayland, J. W. *A History of Rockingham County, Virginia.* Dayton, Va., 1912.

———, *The German Element of the Shenandoah Valley of Virginia.* Charlottesville, Va., 1907. A good chapter on "Home Life and Industrial Habits."

Weeden, W. B. *Early Rhode Island. A Social Study of the People.* New York, 1910.

Weise, A. J. *The History of the City of Albany, New York, from the Discovery of the Great River in 1524, by Verazzano, to the Present Time.* Albany, 1884.

Wells, D. W. and R. F. *A History of Hatfield, Massachusetts, 1660–1910.* Springfield, 1910. Contains considerable material on the social and industrial development of the town.

Weston, Thomas. *History of the Town of Middleboro, Massachusetts.* New York, 1906. A chapter on "Social Custom of the 18th Century."

Whittlesey, Charles. *Early History of Cleveland, Ohio, Including Original Papers and Other Matter Relating to the Adjacent Country.* Cleveland, 1867.

Williams, Samuel. *Natural and Civil History of Vermont.* Walpole, N. H., 1794. Good account of manufactures in Vermont about 1790.

Williams, W. W. *History of the Fire Lands, Comprising Huron and Erie Counties, Ohio.* Cleveland, 1879.

Winsor, Justin (editor). *Memorial History of Boston, 1630–1880.* 4 vols. Boston, 1880–81.

Wise, J. C. *Ye Kingdome of Accawmacke or the Eastern Shore of Virginia in the Seventeenth Century.* Richmond, 1911.

Worthen, Mrs. Augusta Harvey, comp. *The History of Sutton, New Hampshire.* 2 vols. Concord, 1890.

INDEX

INDEX

Spotted something that isn't quite right?

Let us know and we'll fix it for future reprints. And as a thank you for your diligence, we'll send you a free Sothis book of your choice.

publisher@sothis.press

This page intentionally left blank

Made in United States
Orlando, FL
04 November 2026

90207243R00249